THE GOVERNANCE OF FRIENDSHIP

THE GOVERNANCE OF FRIENDSHIP

Law and Gender in the *Decameron*

Michael Sherberg

THE OHIO STATE UNIVERSITY PRESS · COLUMBUS

Copyright © 2011 by The Ohio State University.

Library of Congress Cataloging-in-Publication Data

Sherberg, Michael.
The governance of friendship : law and gender in the Decameron / Michael Sherberg.
    p. cm.
Includes bibliographical references and index.
ISBN 978-0-8142-1155-7 (cloth : alk. paper)—ISBN 978-0-8142-9253-2 (cd-rom)
1. Boccaccio, Giovanni, 1313–1375. Decamerone—Criticism and interpretation.
2. Friendship in literature. 3. Man-woman relationships. I. Title.
PQ4293.F75S54 2011
853'.1—dc22

This book is available in the following editions:
Cloth (ISBN 978-0-8142-1155-7)
CD-ROM (ISBN 978-0-8142-9253-2)

Cover design by Laurence Nozik
Text design by Jennifer Shoffey Forsythe
Type set in Adobe Bembo
Printed by Thomson-Shore, Inc.

♾ The paper used in this publication meets the minimum requirements of the American
National Standard for Information Sciences—Permanence of Paper for Printed Library
Materials. ANSI Z39.48–1992.

9 8 7 6 5 4 3 2 1

CONTENTS

ACKNOWLEDGMENTS

WITH THIS book I repay a debt to the author who first inspired me to study Italian literature. I begin therefore by thanking several *galeotti* who arranged trysts with the *Decameron* over the course of my education. Elissa Weaver set my future course when she assigned the tale of Madonna Oretta in my first-year Italian course. In my struggles to understand the *novella*, I received generous assistance one night from Margery Schneider, then a graduate student at the University of Chicago; her patient instruction in Boccaccio's syntax awakened a pleasure in me I had not before known. One tale led to the entire book, first with Elissa and then with Marga Cottino-Jones, with whom I studied Boccaccio at UCLA, and whose socially grounded readings continue to inform much of my thinking about the text. Finally, the late Fredi Chiappelli could have had no idea that a single lesson on the forensic nature of Boccaccio's text would be so inspiring, or so fondly remembered.

At Washington University and beyond I have also enjoyed the *piacevoli ragionamenti d'alcuno amico.* Stanley Paulson unintentionally abetted my interest in constitutionalism when he introduced me to the work of Hans Kelsen. Eric Brown, Cathleen Fleck, and Julie Singer supplied some missing links on other topics. Harriet Stone read two of the chapters in draft form and helped me remember what good style is all about, and my undergraduate research assistant, Andrew Hiltzik, did a great deal of proofreading. Lynne Tatlock listened as I talked through my ideas, and Joe Loewenstein cheered from the sidelines. Across the country Ted Cachey, Victoria

Kirkham, Dennis Looney, Christian Moevs, Lucia Re, and Jon Snyder have all been fast friends. In Italy, Roberto Fedi and Sergio Zatti have also shown unfailing generosity.

I could not have completed this project without a senior fellowship from the National Endowment for the Humanities. My chair in Romance Languages, Elzbieta Sklodowska, kindly supported my research leave for the grant year, as did the dean of Arts and Sciences at Washington University, now provost, Ed Macias.

My editor at The Ohio State University Press, Malcolm Litchfield, read my prospectus and contacted me in what had to be record time, and throughout this process he has been peerless in his support and good humor. He also secured readings from Albert Ascoli at Berkeley and Teodolinda Barolini at Columbia. One could not ask for better readers, who gently but firmly exposed weaknesses in my argument. I consider myself fortunate to have had their input, and I can only hope to have equaled the challenge they set for me.

The present study finds its origins in some earlier published work of mine: first, an essay I published in *Romance Quarterly* in 1991, "The Patriarch's Pleasure and the Frametale Crisis: *Decameron* IV–V." The arguments I first advanced there find themselves, significantly revised, in chapter III. Another essay, "The Sodomitic Center of the *Decameron*," which appeared in *Essays in Honor of Marga Cottino-Jones*, formed the basis for some of my arguments about the *novella* of Pietro di Vinciolo, in chapter III as well.

Finally, my three wonderful boys, Adam, Eric, and Eli, don't entirely understand why I have spent so much time staring at a computer screen, but for the most part they have let me. Through it all I have enjoyed the extraordinary patience and support of my beloved Simeon, a true friend in every way. In the end this book can only be for him.

The Governance
of Friendship

THIS STUDY takes its title from two observations about the *Decameron:* first, that it traces its origins to a gesture of friendship, and second, that its initial focus on friendship opens onto a wide-ranging exploration of the relationship between friendship and governance, both in the household and in the state. Boccaccio's first mention of friendship seems almost incidental to the broader thrust of the Proem, subsumed as it is by the structuring metaphors of suffering and relief (Hollander, "The *Decameron* Proem"): "Nella qual noia [his unrequited love] tanto rifrigerio già mi porsero i piacevoli ragionamenti d'alcuno amico e le sue laudevoli consolazioni, che io porto fermissima opinion per quelle essere avenuto che io non sia morto" (Proem.4). Of course, as readers of the *Decameron* know all too well, his friends' ministrations do not just save the author, they also inspire him to return the favor—though, as I shall discuss later, in a decidedly asymmetrical way, not by a direct reimbursement of those same friends, but by a gesture of friendship toward women in love. The gesture takes the form of the *Decameron* itself.

That friendship is not the isolated qualifier of nonfamilial, nonsexual (and, depending on one's definition, some sexual) relationships of caring that we see it as today is something Boccaccio would have known well, thanks to his own familiarity with Aristotle's *Ethics* and Thomas Aquinas's Commentary on same. Back in 1968 Anna Maria Cesari identified codex A 204 inf. of the Biblioteca Ambrosiana in Milan, a copy of the *Ethics* in William of Moerbeke's Latin translation along with Aquinas's Commentary, as an autograph by Boccaccio himself. Since then one critic, Francesco Bausi, has studied the influence of Aristotle and Thomas on the *Decameron*, specifically in the tenth day, and others, including Victoria Kirkham and Giuseppe Mazzotta, have found Thomistic echoes in the text. However, no one has yet undertaken to elucidate how the Aristotelian theory of friendship informs the *Decameron* at all levels: in the interventions of the authorial voice (Proem, Introduction to Day IV, Conclusion), in the *cornice*, and in the stories themselves. Likewise absent from Boccaccio criticism has been a systematic look at how Boccaccio might have applied his knowledge of law and legal theory, acquired over six apparently unpleasant years of study that he laments in the *Genealogie*, in the *Decameron*.[1] This book undertakes to fill both lacunae, linking the two.

For the sake of readers who are not readily familiar with Books VIII and IX of the *Ethics*, in which Aristotle elaborates his theory of friendship, herewith I offer a summary. Aristotle defines three kinds of friendship, each a feeling of affection directed at a human object. The first is based on utility: we care for another because the other can do something for us. The second is grounded in pleasure: we care for another because the other makes us feel good. The third type lies in goodness: one is a friend of the other for the other's sake and not for one's own. The first two motives, Aristotle explains, generate transitory friendships and are often associated with less mature phases of life, while the third offers the possibility of a more enduring friendship.

While these initial definitions presuppose friendship between equals, Aristotle then complicates matters by examining the possibility of friendship between unequals. Here the concept of friendship broadens to include parents and children, husbands and wives, and siblings. Such relationships qualify as friendships because they offer a means to compensate for their inherent inequity: the inferior party shows greater affection for the superior one than vice versa. Aristotle's analysis of unequal relations also enables him to introduce the concept of justice to his discussion of friendship. Unequal friendships achieve justice thanks to the greater affection that the inferior shows for the superior, thus compensating for his or her subordinate status and achieving a parity that is not readily apparent in the social standing of the two parties.

All of the above serves as a basis for the second half of Aristotle's argument, which addresses the relationship between friendship and political communities. The political models he discusses—monarchy, aristocracy,

---

1. Fredi Chiappelli proposed such a study, advancing a suggestive theory of the influence of Boccaccio's legal studies on his masterpiece; see "Discorso o progetto per uno studio sul *Decameron*."

and timocracy and their negatives, tyranny, oligarchy, and democracy—actually mimic, to his mind, the relationships, functional and dysfunctional respectively, found in families. Parenting assumes the form of monarchy or tyranny; marriage can take the form of an aristocracy or an oligarchy; and sibling relations are either timocratic or democratic. In their positive forms each model enacts justice as well by establishing some form of parity, whereas in their negative forms there is no friendship, and therefore also no justice.

Underlying Aristotle's theory are two important concepts. First, he believes that the dynamic of friendship involves both reciprocity and goodwill. The former seems self-evident; according to the latter the friend "wishes and does what is good, or appears good, for the sake of the other" (1166a1²). He does so because he wants for his friend what he wants for himself, because he is a good friend to himself; according to this equation the friend becomes "another self" (1166a31).³ Today we might call such an impulse altruism, and it finds immediate expression in Boccaccio's opening aphorism: "Umana cosa è aver compassione degli afflitti" (Proem.1). The same notion that friendship consists in wanting what is best for the other, for the sake of the other, braces the narrative that follows, in which *alcuno amico* saved him from amorous perdition through, and this is especially important, *piacevoli ragionamenti*: those friends, already good friends to themselves, wanted what was best for Boccaccio, that he should end his suffering. Even the notion of *piacevoli ragionamenti*, which McWilliam has translated as "agreeable conversation" (45), may carry an Aristotelian nuance, as Aristotle dedicates a significant portion of Book VII of the *Ethics* to the notion of pleasure, which he defines as an unimpeded activity (1153a14). Boccaccio will return the favor, as we know, by attending to the *piaceri* of ladies in love, imagining for them the unimpeded activity of reading.⁴

---

2. In citing Aristotle, I refer to the standard numbering, so that readers can consult any translation they wish. Throughout, unless otherwise specified, I am using Rowe's translation. I find it to be the clearest and most thorough of the many translations available, and readers will appreciate Broadie's thorough commentary as well.

3. William of Moerbeke gives the Aristotelian passage as follows: "Est enim amicus alius ipse." Moerbeke's translation appears in Aquinas, *In decem libros Ethicorum;* see 475.

4. The gesture also presupposes female literacy, though the text itself also makes the point that women need not be literate to "read" the *Decameron*. The arrangement of telling stories out loud adumbrates a setting in which a literate woman might read the book aloud to others. Whether what Boccaccio dreams for women comes to pass in his own time remains unclear. Victoria Kirkham notes (*The Sign of Reason* 118) that Florentine mercantile families numbered among the many early owners of copies of the book, and she cites a 1373 letter from Boccaccio to Maghinardo Cavalcanti, in which the author discourages his interlocutor from allowing women to read the book, as proof that it may have found its way into women's hands. I

Such gestures are possible thanks to the notion of the friend as "another self," as Aristotle explains in a key passage: "if being alive is desirable, and especially so for the good, because for them existing is good, and pleasant (for concurrent perception of what is in itself good, in themselves, gives them pleasure); and if, as the good person is to himself, so he is to his friend (since the friend is another self): then just as for each his own existence is desirable, so his friend's is too, or to a similar degree" (1170b2–b8; Rowe trans. 238). This concept, that being alive is desirable, lurks behind Pampinea's early claim that "Natural ragione è, di ciascuno che ci nasce, la sua vita quanto può aiutare e conservare e difendere" (I.Intro.53). Her speech, in which she undertakes to convince the other six young women that they should escape Florence, exemplifies the principle that Aristotle is enunciating here: that if you want what is good for yourself, then so too will you want what is good for your friend.

Aristotle's own concept of like-mindedness, implied here and made explicit shortly thereafter, leads not only to personal friendships but to political ones as well. He distinguishes between two forms of like-mindedness, the first suggested in the quotation above: a shared belief that to exist is good and pleasant, which leads each friend to want for the other what is good. Beyond that, there is another, more impersonal form, which allows Aristotle to make the transition from personal friendships to what he calls friendship between citizens. In this latter case, "a city is said to be like-minded when its citizens share judgements about what is advantageous, reach the same decisions, and do what has seemed to them jointly to be best" (1167a27; Rowe trans. 232). The basis for such like-mindedness is a generalized form of goodwill. Aristotle posits two different types of goodwill. The first is personal, based on "excellence, or a kind of decency, where one person appears to another a fine character, or courageous, or something like that" (1167a19–20). In its second, generalized form, goodwill allows people to enter into relationships even though they do not know one another personally: "good will occurs even in relation to people one does not know, and without their being aware of it" (1166b31). In this latter sense it is important to recall that while the members of the *brigata* already share links before they meet in Santa Maria Novella, friendship is not their

---

should add in passing that I disagree with Marilyn Migiel's inference, based on a reading of the same letter, that "Boccaccio might not have meant women to read his book at all" (4). Boccaccio clearly distinguishes his feelings now about dissemination of the text among women and its effect not only on them but on his own reputation, from what he wanted when he wrote the book, when he was younger and implicitly under Cupid's control. In other words, the letter assumes the character of a late expression of regret about a youthful indiscretion, though we can only speculate on the sincerity of the gesture.

only connection: "si ritrovarono sette giovani donne tutte l'una all'altra o per amistà o per vicinanza o per parentado congiunte" (I.Intro.49); and the men "andavan cercando . . . di vedere le lor donne, le quali per ventura tutte e tre erano tralle predette sette, come che dell'altre alcune ne fossero congiunte parenti d'alcuni di loro" (I.Intro.79). In other words, the mix of relationships that one finds among the members of the *brigata* mirrors the mix of relationships that one would expect to find among a single class in a city:[5] some are friends—including erotic relationships—while others are relatives or simply neighbors. They therefore do not constitute a preexisting unit, either political or personal, prior to their departure for the countryside, and the goodwill they feel for one another falls more into the broader category of friendship between citizens than into the specific category of personal friendships.

One final point in Aristotle's theory of friendship may be the most important of all, for the present purposes: that friendship consists in spending time together in conversation. Friends seek friends, he argues, because one seeks in his other self "to observe decent actions that bear the stamp of his own" (1170a3; Rowe trans. 237). That perception results from time spent together: "this will come about in their living together, conversing, and sharing their talk and thoughts; for this is what would seem to be meant by 'living together' where human beings are concerned, not feeding in the same location as with grazing animals" (1170b12–14; Rowe trans. 238). This idea, that friendship consists of spending time together in conversation—Aquinas's "convivendo sibi secundum communicationem sermonum et considerationem mentis" (1910),[6] resonates throughout the *Decam-*

---

5. The ladies are of "sangue nobile" (I.Intro.49), and by extension one may assume the same about the men as well.

6. I cite using the standard numbering for Aquinas's commentary; Litzinger translates this passage as "constant association and the exchange of ideas and reflection." Aristotle's distinction between the living together of humans and the living together of animals may find resonance in the description of the plague. Aquinas comments: "Hoc enim modo homines dicuntur proprie sibi convivere, secundum scilicet vitam quae esta homini propria, non autem secundum hoc quod simul pascantur, sicut contingit in pecoribus" (1910), picking up on the Latin "non quemadmodum in pecoribus in eodem pasci" of William of Moerbeke's translation. Now, in the Introduction to Day I Boccaccio recounts that as the plague ravaged the city, so too did it strike the countryside: "per le sparte ville e per li campi i lavoratori miseri e poveri e le loro famiglie, senza alcuna fatica di medico o aiuto di servidore, per le vie e per li loro colti e per le case, di dì e di notte indifferentemente, non come uomini ma quasi come bestie morieno" (I.Intro.43). As a consequence, Boccaccio continues, "adivenne i buoi, gli asini, le pecore, le capre, i porci, i polli e i cani medesimi fedelissimi agli uomini fuori delle proprie case cacciati, per li campi, dove ancora le biade abbandonate erano, senza essere non che raccolte ma pur segate, come meglio piaceva loro se n'andavano, e molti, quasi come razionali, poi che pasciuti erano bene il giorno, la notte alle lor case senza alcuno correggimento di pastore si tornavano satolli" (I.Intro.45–46). The passage appears to reverse the very distinctions on which Aristo-

eron. The author himself benefited from the *piacevoli ragionamenti* of his friends, and he attempts to return the favor through an indirect form of companionship, the book, offered "in soccorso e rifugio" of women in love (Proem.13).[7] Moreover, time spent together in conversation is the activity that Boccaccio represents—almost to the exclusion of every other—in the ten young people. While initially their friendship is arguably more political than personal, it quickly assumes the trappings of genuine friendship, even if through the rather artificial means of storytelling.

Aristotle's logic, which leads from friendship to community and from household to state, offers an exceptionally plastic means of drawing together concerns that would otherwise seem to be quite disparate. While today we still resort to metaphors that suggest analogies, such as that of the tyrannical father, or of George Washington as the father of our country, less often do we consciously associate the way we run our families with the way we run our country. And yet—my second point—it is the comprehensive nature of Aristotle's vision that allows Boccaccio to play with the themes of friendship and the structuring of relationships, whether domestic or political, in the *Decameron.*[8] At times he appears overtly to apply Aristotle's analogous reasoning—the *novella* of Tancredi and Ghismonda (IV.1) springs to mind—while elsewhere he applies lighter tracings. Still there can be little doubt that the idea of friendship, first introduced in the Proem, moves steadily through the text, binding together the textual levels—author's statements, frame tale, and stories—in suggestive ways. The concept of friendship first introduced in the Proem carries over into the frame tale and from there into the stories. Whereas in the Proem Boccaccio does not develop his definitions or his taxonomies with particular attention, the Aristotelian details come into play in the frame tale and the stories, which reflect back and forth upon one another in an ongoing investigation of the forms and implications of friendship. As friendship unites the ten young people as they plan their escape from a stricken Florence, so too does it yield a political community, as the group decides on the rules

---

tle's argument rests, as Boccaccio recounts that grazing animals began to behave *quasi come razionali*, while humans died like beasts, and it is a clear example of engaging in unimpeded activity—"come meglio piaceva loro"—that is Aristotle's definition of pleasure.

7. This idea of the book as indirect or substitute companion would appear also to inform Boccaccio's choice of a subtitle for the *Decameron, prencipe Galeotto.* In invoking Dante's great go-between for Paolo and Francesca, he reminds his reader of the power of texts to touch us, to reach intimate recesses of our lives, even if not with the positive results that Aristotle attributes to friendship.

8. Boccaccio surely was familiar with other theories of friendship, such as Cicero's as set forth in the *De amicitia.* However, Cicero limits his definition of friendship to relations between excellent men; his theory thus does not provide the sort of extensive architecture that characterizes Aristotle's.

by which they will live during their self-imposed exile. Moreover, as I shall argue, each of the three young men in the group conceives of his role as king in unique terms, according to Aristotle's definitions of friendship and types of government. Finally, the smooth elision between domestic and state governance enacted by Aristotle finds its way into many of the stories told, mirroring, almost as "another self," the ten narrators.

From its grounding in Aristotle's theory of friendship grow other important considerations. Not least among these is the role that gender plays in relations within the *brigata*. Not for nothing does the *brigata* come together in two separate moments, first as a group composed exclusively of women, and second as a group of women integrated with men. Significantly, Boccaccio never focuses on the men as a group; all we know of them when they first appear is that they are searching for their *donne*. They have missed mass, and if there is a leader among them, we are not privy to any conversations that would expose him. The admixture of men, who bring with them conceptions of male leadership that will charge the *Decameron*, will have critical implications for the way in which the *brigata* works and works together.

A fuller understanding of the group's function, and the ideologies and theologies that inform it, comes with the assistance of another important theorist, the great Austrian legal philosopher Hans Kelsen. Dubbed the best lawyer of the twentieth century by Bernhard Schlink in the *New York Times*, Kelsen was the author of countless books and articles, which have in turn generated a raft of critical studies. His first book was a study of Dante's *Monarchia*, *Die Staatslehre des Dante Alighieri*, published in 1905 and translated into Italian as *La teoria dello stato in Dante*. He is perhaps best known today for the *Reine Rechtslehre*, the first edition of which (1934) appears in English as *Introduction to the Problems of Legal Theory*, while the 1960 second edition is available under the title *Pure Theory of Law*. Another important work, *General Theory of Law and State*, was translated from a manuscript and never published in the original German.[9]

A legal positivist, Kelsen offered, in answer to natural law theory, the theory that the law is a coercive order that monopolizes the use of force. For him law is "the social technique which consists in bringing about the desired social conduct of men through threat of coercion for contrary conduct" ("The Law as Specific Social Technique" 236). Kelsen recognizes the paradox that the coercive element of law is the same type of act that law attempts to repress in individuals, but distinguishes state-sanctioned coer-

---

9. There is also an excellent critical anthology on Kelsen, *Normativity and Norms*, which contains 30 articles by legal scholars around the globe.

cion because it seeks to promote peace, whereas the use of force by individuals subverts peace: "Law is an order according to which the use of force is forbidden only as a delict, that is, as a condition, but is allowed as a sanction, that is, as a consequence" (238). The goal of law is not therefore justice, in the ethical sense that we attach to the word, but rather the maintenance of order, even at the cost of acts—think of Lincoln's suspension of *habeas corpus* during the Civil War—that some may subjectively consider to be unjust.[10] Boccaccio addresses this very problem in the famous *novella* of Madonna Filippa (VI.7), which I shall discuss later. I shall also have occasion later to comment on this distinction with regard to private acts of force undertaken by characters in the *Decameron*.

Kelsen's critique of natural law theory comes very close to Boccaccio's position on the question, at least as I infer it from the *Decameron*. Kelsen labels natural law theory an ideology:

> The need for rational justification of our emotional acts is so great that we seek to satisfy it even at the risk of self-deception. And the rational justification of a postulate based on a subjective judgment of value, that is, on a wish, as for instance that all men should be free, or that all men should be treated equally, is self-deception or—what amounts to about the same thing—it is an ideology. Typical ideologies of this sort are the assertions that some sort of ultimate end, and hence some sort of definite regulation of human behavior, proceeds from "nature," that is, from the nature of things or the nature of man, from human reason or the will of God. In such an assumption lies the essence of the doctrine of so-called natural law. This doctrine maintains that there is an ordering of human relations different from positive law, higher and absolutely valid and just, because emanating from nature, from human reason, or from the will of God. . . . When the norms claimed to be the "law of nature" or justice have a definite content, they appear as more or less generalized principles of a definite positive law, principles that, without sufficient reason, are put forth as absolutely valid by being declared as natural or just law. (*General Theory of Law and State* 8–10)

---

10. Kelsen's analysis of Aristotle's concept of justice as equity supports his theory: "The substitution of the logical value of noncontraction for the moral value of justice, inherent in the definition of justice as equality before the law, is the result of the attempt to rationalize the idea of justice as the idea of an objective value. Although this substitution is no solution, but an elimination of the problem of justice, it seems that the attempt will never be abandoned—perhaps, because of its important political implications. This type of rationalistic philosophy, pretending to answer the question what is just, and hence claiming authority to prescribe to the established power how to legislate, ultimately legitimizes the established power by defining justice as equality before the law and thus declaring the positive law to be just" ("Aristotle's Doctrine of Justice" 134).

The language of Kelsen's analysis—that natural law is an ideology that asserts certain assumptions, and that the claim of natural law is used to defend the validity of principles of positive law—leads to an inevitable conclusion. Natural law theory, particularly as expressed in language, is a rhetoric, a rhetoric employed by those in power to maintain their power by asserting the transcendent basis of a law that favors them and their ordering of society.

This analysis is crucial to any reading of the *Decameron*. As readers well know, the *brigata* as a group of seven women and three men reaches its final form thanks to a claim made by Elissa: "Veramente gli uomini sono delle femine capo e senza l'ordine loro rade volte riesce alcuna nostra opera a laudevole fine" (I.Intro.76). She is of course citing a phrase found in Paul's letter to the Ephesians, "vir caput est mulieris" (Eph. 5.23), though to understand the full import of Elissa's assertion one needs to return the phrase to its original context. In the latter, Paul exhorts the Ephesians to abandon paganism. His argument includes a series of norms for the Ephesians to follow. The Ephesians, he explains, should try "to imitate God, as children of his that he loves, and follow Christ by loving as he loved you, giving himself up in our place as a fragrant offering and a sacrifice to God" (Eph. 5.1–3). In the sentence containing the citation from Elissa he narrows his focus to apply the imitation of Christ to the structuring of the home: "Wives should regard their husbands as they regard the Lord, since as Christ is head of the Church and saves the whole body, so is a husband the head of his wife; and as the Church submits to Christ, so should wives to their husbands, in everything" (Eph. 5.22–24). Paul thus derives a norm for domestic behavior, "so should wives to their husbands, in everything," from the hierarchical ordering of Christianity: as the Church submits to Christ as its authority, so too should wives submit to their husbands. Christ thus indirectly authorizes the norms of domestic life, if one assumes—at some risk, as I shall discuss later—that men correctly understand Christ's law. Paul's argument is consistent with natural law theory, inasmuch as it relies, as Alf Ross puts it, on "principles that have not been created by man but are discovered, *true* principles binding on everyone, including those who are unable or unwilling to recognize their existence" (151).[11] Among

---

11. I shall have occasion to discuss the specifics of medieval natural law theory in the course of my argument. For now I cite the following general definition, coined by Ross, which includes the phrase I have given in the text: "Despite manifold divergencies, there is one idea common to all natural law schools of thought: The belief that there exist universally valid principles governing the life of man in society, principles that have not been created by man but are discovered, *true* principles, binding on everyone, including those who are unable or unwilling to recognize their existence. The truth of these laws cannot be established by the methods of empirical science, but presupposes a metaphysical interpretation of the nature of

the latter we may count the non-Christian Ephesians. That the exercise is essentially rhetorical is manifest in Paul's own use of a standard rhetorical device, argument by analogy: a husband's relationship to his wife is as Christ's relationship to the Church. As Boccaccio will make clear, the only real basis for Paul's claim is his belief that Christ is the son of God; the fact of competing religions, each of which claims legitimacy over the other two, undermines Paul's claim.

As an alternative to natural law theory Kelsen proposed the much-discussed Pure Theory of Law, which relies on the concept of the basic norm.[12] He makes the following distinction: "the norms of natural law, like those of morality, are deduced from a basic norm that by virtue of its content—as emanation of divine will, of nature, or of pure reason—is held to be directly evident. The basic norm of a positive legal system, however, is simply the basic rule according to which the norms of the legal system are created; it is simply the setting into place of the basic material fact of law creation. . . . Tracing the various norms of a legal system back to a basic norm is a matter of showing that a particular norm was created in accordance with the basic norm" (*Introduction to the Problems of Legal Theory* 56–57). Kelsen then offers the example of how one rationalizes incarceration. He shows how the judge's act of incarceration relies on the criminal code, which was formulated by authorities instituted by the state constitution, whose validity may be retraced to the "the first constitution, historically speaking, established by a single usurper or a council, however assembled. What is to be valid as norm is whatever the framers of the first constitution have expressed as their will—this is the basic presupposition of all cognition of the legal system resting on this constitution" (*Introduction to the Problems of Legal Theory* 57).

Identifying the basic norm of a legal order turns out to be rather more challenging. To the extent that it reflects the will of the framers, it requires a certain reading between the lines of whatever documentary evidence

---

man. For this reason, the *validity* of these laws and the *obligations* deriving from them do not imply anything observable. The validity of the laws stemming from natural law has nothing to do with their acceptance or recognition in the minds of men, and the obligations they create have nothing to do with any sense of being duty-bound, any sanction of conscience, or any other experience. The unconditional validity of the laws, and the non-psychological character of the obligations, are simple consequences of the point of departure, namely, that these laws are discovered, objectively given, a reality, although not the reality of sensory observation. . . . 'natural law' is considered to be the part of general ethics that deals with the principles governing the life of man in organized society with his fellows, making it possible for him to attain his moral destiny" (151–52). Boccaccio's own insistence upon subjective, as opposed to objective, reality, makes natural law theory difficult to sustain.

12. For a comprehensive introduction to this notion, see Raz, "Kelsen's Theory of the Basic Norm."

remains. A statement of the basic norm of the Constitution of the United States is not necessarily to be found *in* the words of the Constitution, because the Constitution is the expression of the framers' will, which necessarily antedates the document. The norms of a positive legal system thus trace their origins to an event whose content must be inferred, just as the norms of natural law or morality trace their origins to an equally elusive figure, God. The virtue of Kelsen's theory, however, lies in the fact that it traces law to human will rather than divine. Given the immanent nature of human beings and human will, the law thus finds a firmer basis than it does when traced to God, whose existence remains an inference at best.

As I shall argue in the pages that follow, both of these key elements of Kelsen's legal theory—the concept of the coercive nature of the legal order and the notion of the basic norm—find residence in the *Decameron*. Boccaccio was not reading Kelsen, obviously, but he was reading natural law theory, such as that offered by Aquinas, and, I believe, he was gifted with an intellectual detachment that facilitated a critique of it. If his medieval predecessors had often sought to codify received wisdom, Boccaccio addresses it more questioningly. Years ago—in 1964, to be exact—Carlo Dionisotti observed that Boccaccio did not enjoy the sort of intellectual respect accorded the other two crowns, Dante and Petrarch.[13] The seriousness with which Boccaccio studies has progressed since Dionisotti first published his *j'accuse* would tend to put the lie to that claim today, and I offer the present study in a line of engagement with Boccaccio as a serious and committed intellectual.

Once the *Decameron* deals away the claims of Christian natural law—and it does so in its first three stories, as I shall demonstrate—it has to offer another basis for the law that undergirds so much of it. I believe that Boccaccio understood, some six hundred years before Kelsen, that the law—particularly the same domestic law that Paul addresses in Ephesians—founds its authorization in the coercive power of men over women, which in turn

---

13. "Qui, con Dante non si scherza. Le più assurde ipotesi sono state e sono, come s'è visto, lecite, ma non se tocchino il religioso culto della *Commedia*. Pertanto l'idea che possano esserci stati cantari dugenteschi in terza rima ai quali Dante si sia ispirato, non è mai stata presa, grazie a Dio, in seria considerazione. Anche non è lecito scherzare col Petrarca. Questo culto è stato nel secolo scorso e nel nostro molto più tepido e controverso. Ma vivo e morto il Petrarca ha sempre imposto una salutare soggezione. Anche quelli che si tengono a distanza e ne parlano a denti stretti, non possono sottrarsi al fascino. Col Boccaccio il rapporto sempre è stato ed è diverso. Necessariamente, né mette conto spiegare perché. Ma a guardar bene, si ha l'impressione che fin dal Trecento le debolezze scoperte dell'uomo e dell'artista, la sua stessa generosa umiltà e devozione di discepolo dei due maggiori che lo avevano immediatamente preceduto, si siano prestate a una famigliarità eccessiva e ingiustificata e un po' anche alla rivalsa dei minori e minimi, con lui e più di lui, seppure meno generosamente e intelligentemente, soggetti all'imperio dei due maggiori" (127–28).

derives from two sources: first, the rhetoric of natural law theory itself, and second and more important, the superior physical strength of men, which enables them to institute a coercive domestic legal order. Like Elissa, women may subscribe to the rhetorical claims of natural law theory, but in the end they must subscribe to the everyday threat of violence that men incarnate. No man, however, wants to say that he controls women because he can—and sometimes does—beat them up. Such a statement might work for a Machiavelli,[14] but of course he is not talking about himself when he says it, and he couches the claim in metaphor. The more circumspect man says that he controls women because God authorizes him to.

The question of men's power over women, first expressed by Elissa, plays itself out at all levels of the *Decameron*. Boccaccio first refers to it in the Proem when he talks about how women suffer isolation at the hands of men, then returns to it in the dynamic of male–female relations among the members of the *brigata*. While readers of the *Decameron* have focused, for multiple reasons, on the question of which boy loves which girl, or on the moments in the frame tale that bring erotic questions to the fore—Tindaro and Licisca, or the Valle delle Donne—far less attention has gone to the way in which the men and women negotiate issues of governance, and how the tensions among them play out in the stories they tell, particularly in the third, seventh, and tenth days, all ruled by men. In the chapters that follow, I examine these questions. In chapter I, "The Order of Outsiders," I propose that the *Decameron* rhetorically marginalizes men only to enact their return, vehemently and at times vindictively, to the textual space. In this chapter I focus in particular on the three important authorial interventions, the Proem, the Introduction to Day IV, and the Author's Conclusion, as well as on the organization of the *brigata* in the Introduction to Day I. In chapter II, "Lessons in Legal Theory," I undertake to expose in a more systematic fashion Boccaccio's deconstruction of the claims of natural law theory, with particular attention to the first three stories of Day I and the last two of Day VI. These two chapters function as a diptych that prepares for the three that follow, in which I look at what happens to the *brigata*—both among the ten and in their storytelling—when men take control. Chapter III, "Strategies of Coercion: Filostrato," examines the deployment of male power by the king in Day IV and Fiammetta's attempt to provide a remedy in Day V.

---

14. In *De principatibus* 25: "la fortuna è donna, ed è necessario, volendola tenere sotto, batterla e urtarla. E si vede che la si lascia più vincere da questi, che da quelli che freddamente procedano; e però sempre, come donna, è amica de' giovani, perché sono meno rispettivi, più feroci, e con più audacia la comandano." Even Machiavelli, however, must temper his claim about male power over women by asserting that it is okay to beat up on women because they like it.

Chapter IV, "Dioneo and the Politics of Marriage," focuses on Day VII and Dioneo's governance of it, particularly the paradox of his position as an outsider who becomes an insider and the sincerity of his rhetoric of support for women. Finally, chapter V, "The Rule of Panfilo: Fables of Reconciliation," looks at Day X with particular concern for how women fit into the idealized world of male friendship represented in that day's stories.

Throughout the book I undertake to bind concepts of legal theory to notions of friendship. The *brigata*, as I have already stated, enacts various forms of friendship, but always under the umbrella of the governance of the tiny state the group has founded. The domestic world of the *Decameron* stories relies on a legal principle, enunciated by Elissa, while at the same time addressing the various sorts of friendship models—both between peers and among family members—that Aristotle discusses. The governance of friendship thus involves both the rules that govern friendship and the way in which friendship creates rules that govern us.

My aim here, in sum, is to introduce a new paradigm for reading the *Decameron*, one that looks closely at how issues of law and gender combine to create a dense interplay between various textual levels. Given the amount of textual space they occupy and their sheer number, it is really no surprise that *Decameron* criticism has often focused on the tales at the expense of the frame, as the former can easily be extracted from the work and read as autonomous units. This critical practice has in fact led in my scholarly lifetime to a series of excellent English-language studies, beginning with Guido Almansi's *The Writer as Liar* (1975) and continuing with Millicent Marcus's *An Allegory of Form* (1979), Giuseppe Mazzotta's *The World at Play in Boccaccio's* Decameron (1986), Pier Massimo Forni's *Adventures in Speech* (1996), Robert Hollander's *Boccaccio's Dante and the Shaping Force of Satire* (1997), and most recently Marilyn Migiel's *A Rhetoric of the* Decameron (2003). Other critics, such as Joy Hambuechen Potter in *Five Frames for the* Decameron (1982), and Marga Cottino-Jones in *Order from Chaos* (1982), have undertaken to read the *Decameron* more organically, with an eye to the relation between textual levels (Potter) or as a text that moves purposefully from a beginning point to an endpoint (Cottino-Jones). The present study borrows from both critical trends, highlighting individual tales to advance an argument about gender relations and law, and outlining a programmatic approach to the question of gender relations that originates in the frame—both the author's statements and the narrative of the *brigata*—and plays out in the stories.

Looking back over the critical tradition as it has evolved in the last few decades affords telling insights into where we were and where we have come. In the introduction to *An Allegory of Form* Marcus unwittingly echoes

Dionisotti's earlier lament that the critical tradition has not taken Boccaccio seriously: "Although Boccaccio chose and perfected a genre utterly alien to his two predecessors, although he took his literary inheritance in a direction distinct from theirs, critics persist in reading him as a 'fallen' Dante, as a Petrarch wanting in refinement and conscience, as an apostate from the world of serious moral concerns" (1). It seems hard to believe today that as recently as 1979 someone writing about the *Decameron* would feel the need to rise to its defense, especially given the accelerated attention the work has enjoyed since then. Nor does it seem plausible any longer to think of Boccaccio as shying away from serious moral concerns. One of those concerns, which the *Decameron* addresses but for which it has only recently begun to receive its due, regards the status of women. Important voices foregrounding gender in the *Decameron* include the aforementioned Migiel and, before her, Teodolinda Barolini, whose 1993 essay *"Le parole son femmine e i fatti sono maschi:* Toward a Sexual Poetics of the *Decameron"* is perhaps the first to signal how gender-based readings can expose previously invisible features of the text. I offer but one small example to demonstrate not merely the shift but how dramatically it has altered our understanding of the work. Forni comments on Dioneo's privilege almost in passing: "The only narrator not bound by the rule of topic is Dioneo, who is granted this privilege by Filomena at the end of Day I" (*Adventures in Speech* 7). Migiel, on the other hand, sees the question of the privilege as a significant site of gender tension in the group, upending the received notion that Pampinea is the group's natural leader: "But the fact remains that Dioneo has served as Pampinea's guide by shaping the possibilities for the groups' future discussions" (27–28). It is precisely the feminist critical framework that enabled Migiel to recognize a dynamic that others had overlooked.

The present book also owes a strong debt to gender studies, acknowledging the significance of Boccaccio's protofeminism along the lines enunciated by Barolini: "the *Decameron* can be inscribed within a specific tradition, which, if not in itself feminist, is arguably the tradition in which feminism could later take root" ("Notes toward a Gendered History of Italian Literature" 376). At the same time, my perspective differs from that of other feminist readings of the text, such as Migiel's. Migiel's book, as the title suggests, continues the rhetorical/narratological tradition of *Decameron* studies. "Our task," she states, "is to examine the very structure of the questions that the *Decameron* poses about reading and sexual difference. Only then will we be able to grasp the intellectual and political investments that contemporary readers have in trying to understand—or to ignore—these issues" (15). The second sentence is key to understanding her intentions:

her book seeks to expose what contemporary readings of the *Decameron* say about both the text and its readers. My own study takes questions of gender in a different direction, turning the mirror of the *Decameron* back not on the reader but on the intellectual and ideological backdrop of its age. In my readings I am guided by Cesare Segre's claim that "[o]gni testo è la voce di un mondo lontano che noi cerchiamo di ricostruire" (*Semiotica filologica* 7). Segre continues: "Chiunque componga un testo opera una sintesi di elementi analitici della sua esperienza. Sintesi discorsiva (linguistica) di elementi culturali. A sua volta il lettore—il filologo, nel nostro caso—analizza la sintesi attuata dallo scrittore, e ne ricostruisce gli elementi in una sintesi interpretativa. Questo ciclo analisi-sintesi-analisi-sintesi costituisce un'attività eminentemente semiotica, dato che sono in gioco, in ogni fase del ciclo, dei significati, e che la comprensibilità è comprensibilità di significati." Following these principles, I have attempted to reconstruct (some of) the cultural elements that are comprised in the *Decameron*, particularly with regard to the status of women. I find that status to be rooted in a notion of social order that is finally juridical, inasmuch as the family models that cast women in certain roles (wife, daughter, sister) are replicated in governmental institutions.

Boccaccio would have learned of these relations through Aristotle, as mediated by Aquinas, and he also would have understood the application of the moniker of friendship to this discourse. It bears remembering that for a Boccaccio reading Aquinas, Aristotle's philosophy remains compelling. Still, Boccaccio appears to receive philosophic wisdom less as dogma than as discourse to be held at a critical arm's length.[15] At the same time, however, I would argue that Boccaccio does not excuse himself from the traditional duty of the intellectual to formulate a comprehensive vision of the universe, even if that vision highlights the universe's many contradictions. Despite its fractious nature the *Decameron* also subscribes to an order, as demonstrated by the careful organization of the *brigata* and the naming of themes for the eight of the ten days of storytelling. My reading, which privileges the organization of the *brigata* as a conditioning force of their narrative and not simply as a pretext for storytelling, attempts to identify a comprehensive notion of how the world of the *Decameron*, both the artificial world of the *brigata* and the world reflected in the stories, functions.

As readers know, the *Decameron* never exhausts its lessons, nor does it make them easy to grasp. The steady pace of new studies of Boccaccio's masterpiece over the last 35 years is testimony to both its vitality and its

15. Indeed, Aristotle's status would soon come under fire by none other than Petrarch, who questioned it in the *De sui ipsius et multorum ignorantia*. On the medieval origins of anti-Aristotelianism and its humanist evolution, see Bianchi.

ingenious hermeneutic resistance. Like a many-faceted jewel, it continues to expose new surfaces to the light while hiding still others from view. It is my hope that this study will illuminate one of those facets, and in so doing enhance the overall beauty of the invaluable stone that is the object of so much scrutiny.

CHAPTER I

The Order of
Outsiders

I N DEDICATING the *Decameron* to women in love, Boccaccio executes a seemingly innocuous first step in orienting his text toward women. That decision does not lack for ramifications, however, for just as the *Decameron* puts women and their experiences at its center, so too does it relegate men to its sidelines, only to represent them as angling to reassert their authority. They do so as critics of the author, as kings whose choices challenge the ladies in their company, or as characters in the stories who overpower women in multiple ways. In this sense the book offers a variant of what Francesco Orlando has called the return of the repressed, specifically as the "ritorno del represso come presenza di contenuti censurati da una repressione ideologico-politica" (27), the repression here being specifically that of masculinist claims to control. The *Decameron* thus enacts a version of the model of revenge literature that Richard Posner discusses in *Law and Literature*. While in the first two instances the repressed returns in fairly harmless ways—Boccaccio deftly defends himself against the critics' barbs, and the three kings do not finally derail the women's survival project—the stories themselves either enact or envision more extreme practices of revenge that make clear what is at stake, particularly for women. Moreover, both the frame narrative and the stories involve variants of the essential means of revenge, which according to Posner are tantamount to "taking the law into your own hands" (32), with consequences for women that depend entirely on the extent to which men reassert their power.

The impulse to vengeance, as Posner argues, "depends on a cluster of emotions, such as wrath and touchiness and unforgivingness, and, above all, refusing to behave 'rationally' in the face of slights . . ." (30). Any argument therefore that posits a revenge system at work in the *Decameron* must first identify those offenses that would provoke a desire for retributive justice. At all three textual levels the slights take the form of gestures of exclusion, rhetorical or real, of men, as either readers of the *Decameron* or participants in the creation of the law that will govern the *onesta brigata,* or finally as authorities in the lives of female characters who assert their own agency despite men's rules. In this chapter I shall detail how each of these gestures is enacted. I shall also discuss forms of retaliation as narrated in the author's statements and in some of the stories, leaving the question of the responses of the three kings, both in their leadership and in the types of stories they engender, to the succeeding chapters. I shall conclude this chapter with a reading of a single tale, the story of the scholar and the widow, which falls outside of the three days led by men but best reflects the revenge motive that to my mind is a principal structure of the *Decameron.*

Be Nice to Your Friends

In his essay "Semiotica e filologia," Cesare Segre elaborates on a theory of culture first introduced by Juri Lotman to explicate the position of the writer with respect to the world he describes. The writer, explains Lotman, divides the world in two according to an inside/outside paradigm, locating himself in one of these two spaces. The consequent "us vs. them" model implies the writer's identification with a group that in turn stands in opposition—or at the very least in juxtaposition—to all other groups. Applying this concept to medieval Christian models, Segre details a "Christian vs. infidel," "order vs. chaos" dynamic, with Christianity and order inside, the infidel and disorder outside. One may readily intuit in Lotman's model, and in Segre's expansion on it, the rudiments of contemporary theories of alterity. In its simplicity, however, this model offers an important reminder: that the discourse of alterity, with its emphasis on the Other, can overlook the identity of the agent *perceiving* the other, and in particular that agent's own identity with a group.[1]

---

1. Lotman's model rather complicates the theory of alterity. In subsuming the individual agent within a group Lotman unwittingly creates a model that subdivides repeatedly: the group labeled "us" can easily divide into two, subgroups "us" and "them," with each of these subgroups dividing as well. For example, the self-identified white Christian heterosexual male may see himself in opposition to nonwhite, non-Christian, nonheterosexual women, but just as easily in opposition to white, Christian, nonheterosexual males, and so forth. In identifying

The question of one's identity within a group leads us to the authorial voice, more or less identified with Boccaccio, of the *Decameron* Proem.[2] Boccaccio's own double and paradoxical identity, disclosed in the Proem, gives entry to the patriarchal discourse that informs and troubles the book.[3] He in fact identifies sequentially with two different groups in the Proem, first that of spurned (male) lovers, and second that of women suffering in love. He unites the two groups through the key word *afflitti*, which famously appears in the *Decameron*'s opening aphorism: "Umana cosa è aver compassione degli afflitti" (Proem.2). As proof of his assertion he offers the example of his own experience when, thanks to the "piacevoli ragionamenti d'alcuno amico e le sue laudevoli consolazioni" (Proem.4), he survived the torments of unrequited love, which eventually diminished. Unlike the Dante of the *Vita nuova*—who will emerge as an important figure here—Boccaccio conquers his love not by sublimating erotic desire in a theology of eros, but by letting nature take its course, so to speak. He does so, moreover, not with the assistance of women endowed with a Dantean *intelletto d'amore*, but with the help of men who undertake to distract him.

The *Decameron* here takes its first noteworthy turn. Explaining that while the suffering has diminished, the memory of the consolation rendered has not, Boccaccio feels obligated to return the favor: "ho meco stesso proposto di volere, in quel poco che per me si può, in cambio di ciò che io ricevetti, ora che libero dir mi posso, e se non a coloro che me atarono, *alli quali* per avventura per lo lor senno o per la loro buona ventura non abisogna, a *quegli* almeno a' quali fa luogo, alcuno alleggiamento prestare. E quantunque il mio sostentamento, o conforto che vogliam dire, possa essere e sia a' *bisognosi* assai poco, nondimeno parmi quello doversi più tosto porgere dove il bisogno apparisce maggiore, sì perché più utilità vi farà e sì

---

with other Christians, however, he may see himself as a Catholic in opposition to Presbyterians, Anglicans, and so forth. Identity and difference end up overlapping.

2. I use the name "Boccaccio" here while fully cognizant that this narrative voice, like all those in the *Decameron*, is a construct. Wayne Booth's distinction between real author and implied author remains wholly valid for the *Decameron*. Booth writes, and it is well to remember, that "The 'implied author' chooses, consciously or unconsciously, what we read; we infer him as an ideal, literary, created version of the real man; he is the sum of his own choices" (74–75). Janet Smarr has demonstrated the indebtedness of this voice to Ovid; see *Boccaccio and Fiammetta* 166 and "Ovid and Boccaccio: A Note on Self-Defense."

3. I use the term "patriarchy" in the sense given by Gayle Rubin, though I disagree with her limitation of it to Old Testament characters: "Patriarchy is a specific form of male dominance, and the use of the term ought to be confined to the Old Testament–type pastoral nomads from whom the term comes, or groups like them. Abraham was a Patriarch—one old man whose absolute power over wives, children, herds, and dependents was an aspect of the institution of fatherhood, as defined in the social group in which he lived" (168). Boccaccio affirms the absolute power of the father in his Proem and in many of the stories the *brigata* tells.

ancora perché più vi fia caro avuto" (Proem.7–8; italics mine). Through his gendering of nouns and pronouns Boccaccio suggests that he will return the favor whence it came, continuing a cycle of male camaraderie and exchange. Quite unexpectedly then he announces that he will lend his assistance, as consolation and entertainment, to another group, ladies in love: "E chi negherà questo, quantunque egli si sia, non molto più alle vaghe donne che agli uomini convenirsi donare?" (Proem.9). This is a strange comment coming from a man whose very life was saved by the *piacevoli ragionamenti* of generous male friends. Indeed, he now speaks of men in the third person, distancing himself from them rhetorically: "Essi [the *innamorati uomini*], se alcuna malinconia o gravezza di pensieri gli *affligge,* hanno molti modi da alleggiare o da passar quello . . ." (Proem.12; italics mine). If Boccaccio himself had tried these remedies, they apparently did not work, for language cured him, not sport.

This passage also marks Boccaccio's shift from identification with love-lorn men and subscription to the norms of male friendship, which involved personal gestures of goodwill, to identification with lovelorn women and subscription to a depersonalized code of goodwill. Boccaccio's gesture toward the women is not one of friendship *per se,* for as Aristotle points out, people can feel goodwill even toward others whom they do not know. Rather, Boccaccio's goodwill toward women represents an Aristotelian "starting point of friendship, just as the pleasure gained through sight is of being in love" (1167a3–4; Rowe trans. 232). The analogy says much about the novelty of Boccaccio's move here, for in attempting to establish a nonerotic relationship with his female audience—he undertakes to please them, though without any expectation that they will reciprocate sexually—he appears to work outside of the traditional courtly dynamic as it had applied to literature. Rather than send a single woman a poem in which he entreats her to reciprocate his love, he sends an entire group of women a far weightier text, while asking nothing from them in return but the goodwill he feels toward them. Indeed, nothing more can develop because author and audience will never know one another personally.

So while recognizing men's affliction, and even associating their suffering with his own etymologically, Boccaccio neither caters to them nor repays any debt to them. He minimizes men's suffering in comparison to that of women, who require his own *piacevoli ragionamenti* much more acutely: "delle quali [novelle] le già dette donne, che queste leggeranno, parimenti diletto delle sollazzevoli cose in quelle mostrate e utile consiglio potranno pigliare, in quanto potranno cognoscere quello che sia da fuggire e che sia similmente da seguitare: le quali cose senza passamento di noia non credo che possano intervenire. Il che se avviene, che voglia Idio che così sia, a Amore ne rendano grazie, il quale liberandomi da' suoi legami m'ha conceduto il potere attendere a' lor *piaceri*" (Proem.14–15; italics mine). The debt to men may not be so great after all, for it was Amore himself, and not the chatty companions, who really made the difference. The distance between the philogynist voice of the *Decameron*'s author and the later misogynist voice of the *Corbaccio*'s narrator finds its full realization here, where a Boccaccio who has loved fruitlessly rededicates himself to pleasing women, rather than to execrating them. And yet his final claim is not so clear-cut. The noun *piaceri* logically refers to "le già dette donne," but its grammatical referent is another, "[i] suoi legami," the pleasures of love's ties. The oxymoron finds its rationale in the very gesture of writing for ladies in love, of Boccaccio's decision to revisit his own amorous experience by undertaking a lengthy exercise whose origin he locates in his own past pain. Boccaccio creates a chiasmus of identity: he identifies with the lovesick ladies, and he identifies the pain of love with pleasure.

By speaking of men in the third person, Boccaccio thus signals their removal from the communicative system of the *Decameron*, marking their presence as an intrusion into his direct relationship with the ladies to whom he dedicates the book.[4] Indeed, in his description of the plight of ladies in love, he labels men, and more generally the patriarchal order, as the source of much of women's suffering: "ristrette da' voleri, da' piaceri, da' comandamenti de' padri, delle madri, de' fratelli e de' mariti, il più del tempo nel piccolo circuito delle loro camere racchiuse dimorano e quasi oziose sedendosi, volendo e non volendo in una medesima ora, seco rivolgendo diversi pensieri, li quali non è possibile che sempre sieno allegri" (Proem.10). The world of women in love is one of conflicting desires and pleasures. On the one hand there are the *voleri* and *piaceri* of the men who control women's lives, and of those women, specifically the mothers, who likewise subscribe to the patriarchal order. On the other there is the "volendo e non volendo" of the ladies themselves, specifically their desire for pleasure and their resistance to it. For the erotic pleasure denied them Boccaccio offers a substitute: the pleasure of literature.[5] The *Decameron* thus immediately construes itself as

4. At all levels of the semiotic model of communication, the figure that Seymour Chatman calls "the transmitting source" (147)—be it narrator, implied author, ideal author, or author—establishes a second-person relationship with its audience. While Boccaccio no doubt wrote the *Decameron* expecting men to read it, rhetorically he distances them from the text. The historical record bears out the validity of the "return of the repressed." According to Victoria Kirkham, "the *Decameron*'s most avid early readers belonged to the very group whom he is least concerned about reaching: powerful men of business" (118). Kirkham names the Buondelmonti, Acciaiuoli, Bonaccorsi, Cavalcanti, and Verazzano among the early owners of manuscripts of the book.

5. For Luciano Rossi the offer to please the ladies must be understood "anche nell'accezione

a subversion of the patriarchal order, and indeed many of the stories, all of which instruct ladies in "quello che sia da fuggire e che sia similmente da seguitare," offer models of how women can and must protect themselves from men, and how best to avoid trouble with men when circumventing male authority.

Boccaccio solidifies his rhetorical exclusion of men in the first sentence of the Introduction to Day I, where the narrator now addresses the *grazio-sissime donne* to whom he has dedicated the book. From now on, any male who reads the *Decameron* does so as an interloper, eavesdropping on a private conversation between Boccaccio and his female readers. It comes as no surprise, then, given the degree of control that Boccaccio attributes to men when it comes to women's lives, that by the beginning of Day IV he is reporting that very sort of intrusiveness and more, for men have not only been reading his book but talking about it, and not saying nice things. Thus he rises to his own defense. Underscoring his exclusive relationship with women, he replies to his male critics through a conversation with the [c]*arissime donne* and *discrete donne* who are his intended readers. While the ostensible subject of the Day IV introduction is envy, here viewed ironically since Boccaccio claims to see no good reason for men to receive his work with hostility, in fact the first paragraph contains gender markers that suggest a more pointed retort. According to the author, the "'mpetuoso vento e ardente della 'nvidia" would normally "percuotere . . . l'alte torri o le più levate cime degli alberi" (IV.Intro.2);[6] therefore he cannot understand why his own work would be an object of envy, because "non solamente pe' piani ma ancora per le profondissime valli mi sono ingegnato d'andare" (IV. Intro.3). In other words, he has done nothing worthy of envy. Glossing this remark, Boccaccio equates the *alte torri* to the high style of Latin writing, and his frequenting of the valleys as the use of Florentine vernacular to write in *istilo umilissimo*, not just a humble style, but the abjectly humble style of the *profondissime valli*, a remark that in combination evokes the low style of Dante's *Inferno*. The metaphors certainly work as Boccaccio explains them, but his gloss also draws attention away from the gendered

---

sessuale" (41). Such a strategy would be consonant with the choice of the book's *cognomen*, *prencipe Galeotto*, inasmuch as the book would serve as a go-between between its author and his future lovers. The whole introduction would thus assume the form of an elaborate seduction: having failed in love in the past, Boccaccio here tries a different strategy.

6. The metaphors come from *Paradiso* XVII.133–35: "Questo tuo grido farà come vento, / che le piú alte cime piú percuote; e ciò non fa d'onor poco argomento." That Cacciaguida then notes that Dante has traversed the *monte* (of Purgatory), and the *valle dolorosa* (of Hell) further associates Boccaccio's own remark about the *profondissime valli* with Hell. On the various Dantean intertexts of the Day IV self-defense see chapter 2 of Marchesi, who argues for a triangular relationship between Boccaccio, Dante, and the Horace of the *Satires*.

nature of the metaphors themselves. One need only recall the many towers that populate the *Decameron* with phallic connotations, or the Valle delle Donne to which the seven ladies repair at the end of Day VI, to understand the sexualized nature of the imagery Boccaccio here adopts.[7] Claiming that he has avoided the high towers for the deep valleys, Boccaccio actually reasserts a central point of the *Decameron*, first made in the Proem: that he has written the book for women, not men. The remark thus represents a first—and in truth definitive—defense against the salvos leveled against him: men have no business criticizing his stories because they should not be reading them in the first place.[8]

Boccaccio then goes on to describe himself as attacked for five reasons, the first three of which concern the appropriateness of his relationship with his female readers. The attacks are carefully worded as concerns for Boccaccio himself: "onesta cosa non è che io tanto diletto prenda di piacervi e di consolarvi e . . . di commendarvi, come io fo"; "alla mia età non sta bene . . . a ragionar di donne o a compiacer loro"; "dicono che io farei più saviamente a starmi con le Muse in Parnaso che con queste ciance mescolarmi tra voi" (IV.Proem.5–6). Moreover, these detractors are clearly male; Boccaccio labels them *alcuni*, [*a*]*ltri, molti, quegli*. Boccaccio thus figures his

---

7. I believe one may similarly gender the imagery with which Boccaccio describes the unpleasant reading of the plague story and what follows: "Questo orrido cominciamento vi fia non altramenti che a'camminanti una montagna aspra e erta, presso alla quale un bellissimo piano e dilettevole sia reposto" (I.Intro. 4). For Branca this passage evokes the dark wood and the mountain that Dante attempts to climb in *Inferno* I (*Boccaccio medievale* 34 ff.), but the analogy is imperfect. The *montagna* may in fact recall Dante's *colle* (*Inferno* I.13), but there is no geographic equivalent in Dante to the "bellissimo piano e dilettevole" that lies nearby, to which one arrives after climbing and descending the mountain. It is explicitly not therefore the Earthly Paradise, which lies atop Mount Purgatory. Rather, it is a flat counterpart to the rise of the mountain, arguably the female space of the *Decameron* stories, which stand in juxtaposition to the tale of the Plague, here gendered as masculine. For more on the gendering of space in the *Decameron* see Psaki.

8. Whether Boccaccio's first thirty stories did in fact circulate, drawing the criticism he reports, remains an open question. Scaglione asserts it as fact (102), without offering any substantial evidence; he cites a late remark by Petrarch (1373) about attacks on the book, though these could easily have come after the entire text issued, and not as a reaction to early circulation of the first three days. On the other hand Padoan ("Sulla genesi del *Decameron*") furnishes compelling textual evidence in support of the early-circulation thesis, which one should not ignore. Still, Boccaccio's defense, coming when it does and in the overall context of the rhetorical strategies Boccaccio is deploying, has a contrived quality that mitigates against Padoan's argument (on the rhetorical and thematic value of the placement of the author's self-defense see Fedi, "Il 'regno' di Filostrato"). Moreover, the idea relies on the assumption that Boccaccio wrote the *Decameron* in the order in which we read it. There is no proof for this assumption, and indeed it would appear to fly in the face of both modern and medieval practices (for the latter see, for example, the history of Petrarch's composition of the *Canzoniere* as summarized in Fedi, *Francesco Petrarca* 61–67).

male detractors as expressing a concern for his well-being—for the fourth complaint he lists a concern that he would do "più discretamente a pensare donde io dovessi aver del pane" (IV.Proem.7)—that masks their true misogyny, though he takes care to expose the latter.

Boccaccio frames the list with hyberbolic rhetoric that does not appear to match the nature of the criticisms themselves. After listing his detractors' objections, he returns to the metaphor of strong winds, though the word he now uses, *soffiamenti*, aligns those winds more closely with gossip through the allusion to a puff of breath.[9] The *soffiamenti*, however, are then subsumed into a double *gradatio* that extends the attacks far beyond mere chatter: "da così fatti soffiamenti, da così atroci denti, da così aguti, valorose donne, mentre io ne' vostri servigi milito, sono sospinto, molestato, e infino nel vivo trafitto" (IV.Intro.9).[10] The general situation he describes, along with the noun *servigi* and the verb *militare*, combine to conjure the image of Boccaccio as knight-errant, here heroically wounded in a duel with a male rival: friendship has ceded to something else entirely. The reference to his woundedness, "sono . . . infino nel vivo trafitto," suggests the risk he is willing to take on behalf of women while also figuring himself through the imagery of penetration as subject to the same sort of attack from men as women are. Boccaccio now has renewed reason to identity with women: he can share with them the feeling of being the object of male hostility.

In both the Proem and the Introduction to Day IV, therefore, Boccaccio speaks not only on his own behalf but for the ladies with whom he now identifies. In his Day IV answer he avers that he will not waste much time on these objections, though he does offer a carefully crafted two-part defense, first, the half-tale of Filippo Balducci and his son, and second, a series of answers to the specific objections.[11] Significantly, the two parts have different addressees. Boccaccio directs the Filippo Balducci tale "a' miei assalitori" (IV.Intro.11), but after suspending the narrative, he carefully

---

9. Just a few pages from now Ghismonda will be telling Guiscardo, as she hands him her fatal love letter wrapped in a reed, "Fara'ne questa sera un soffione alla tua servente, col quale ella raccenda il fuoco" (IV.1.7).

10. There have been various efforts to specify the identity of these critics. For Marga Cottino-Jones the group is composed of "extreme moralists," "middle aged 'wise men,'" "would-be *litterateurs*," materialists, and realists (*Order from Chaos* 6). I find less convincing Gregory Stone's claim that "These detractors . . . are clearly recognizable as protohumanists, those who dictate that the writer should compose in the paternal rather than the maternal tongue, in Latin rather than in Italian" (67). It is frankly easy to identify these critics as protohumanists, knowing of the advent of humanism, of which Boccaccio would have been unaware. Moreover, the debate over Latin versus vernacular does not arise with humanism but informs the work of such rigorously late-medieval authors as Dante. For the present purposes I limit myself to the observation that Boccaccio insists that all his critics are men.

11. The self-defense belongs to the genre of epideictic rhetoric, as Tronci details (94–102).

redirects himself to the ladies: "Ma avere infino a qui detto della presente novella voglio che mi basti e a coloro rivolgermi alli quali l'ho raccontata. Dicono adunque alquanti de' miei riprensori che io fo male, o giovani donne . . ." (IV.Intro.30). Claiming that he will now *rivolger[si]* at the tale's addressees, he in fact does not, carefully speaking instead to the ladies in the second person and referring to the men always in the third person. Men who read these defenses once again read as outsiders. Moreover, by alternating the addressees—first women, then men, then women again—Boccaccio highlights the extraordinary nature of the Filippo Balducci tale, which joins the Proem as the only two parts of the *Decameron* not specifically written to women. The Day IV introduction thus actually collapses the discourse of the Proem, aimed at a broader audience including men, and the Introduction to Day I, in which the author first speaks directly to women.

The two extraordinary aspects of the Filippo Balducci tale—its unique set of addressees and its claimed suspension—may in fact be linked. The story's willful brevity may reflect, through aposiopesis or interruption,[12] a growing irritation on Boccaccio's part with his cranky detractors.[13] He seems not to want to provide the same narrative satisfaction to his male reader that he does to his legitimate female audience, so he offers a story about which he suggests there is more that he is withholding. If, as Rossi suggests, the gratification he seeks to provide to women extends to the sexual, then Boccaccio seems to want to consign men to the same narrative/sexual frustration that he experienced during his period of unrequited passion.[14] The tale's significance for men extends further, however. The principal analysis of the *novella* has converged on the idea that it demonstrates the power of nature. Giuseppe Mazzotta's reading typifies this line; for him the tale asserts the principle of "the failure of the artifice to contain within its bounds Nature's wondrous powers, as well as the failure of that educa-

---

12. "Stopping suddenly in midcourse—leaving a statement unfinished" (Lanham 15).

13. There are two lines of argument about the story, first that its unfinished nature represents false modesty on the part of its author, and second that by remaining unfinished the story assumes the status of *exemplum*. Branca advocates the former ("egli finge forse di considerarla monca e non rifinita per modestia," 1199), while Giovanni Getto (30) and Raffaello Ramat propose the latter. Antonio D'Andrea rejects both readings in favor of a third, that the unfinished quality of the story serves to highlight its standing as a somewhat risqué apology for Boccaccio's love for women: "l'apologo diventa un pretesto di malizioso divertimento alle loro [his critics'] spalle, nella complicità, nella tacita intesa fra l'autore e il suo uditorio femminile" (127). Federico Sanguineti offers yet another solution: "espressione di una passione che è del Boccaccio stesso, la novella resta interrotta perché l'autore può portarla a termine solo realizzando fino in fondo la propria vocazione poetica con l'intero *Decameron*" (144).

14. Rossi, "Il paratesto" 41. On a similar technique, though with a different purpose, see Daniel Javitch's classic essay on the *Orlando furioso*.

tion, imparted by the father, which attempts to repress the natural compulsions of sexuality" (133).[15] True enough, though such a reading does not complete the message delivered to the male readers. The latter concerns not simply the power of nature but the power of art as well. The father has not really failed in educating his son; rather, he has inadvertently succeeded.

The tale itself, a parody of the medieval eremitic tradition (Delcorno, "Modelli agiografici" 350–45), offers a sort of *reductio ad absurdum* of male aversion to women, in that the protagonist, despite having had a rewarding marriage, upon his wife's death spurns all future intercourse, sexual or otherwise, with the opposite sex, and attempts to instill an aversion to women in his son. The story rests on a series of dichotomies: life with women versus life without women; the lay life versus the monastic life; culture versus nature; as well as a contrast between Filippo's choice of an all-male community and the ladies' decision to integrate their community with men. His wife dead, he follows her into a sort of living death, devoting himself to God and to his son in a rustic monastic existence outside of the city: "rimaso solo, del tutto si dispose di non volere più essere al mondo ma di darsi al servigio di Dio e il simigliante fare del suo piccol figliuolo" (IV.Intro.15). The ambiguous syntax admits two possible readings of "il simigliante fare": Filippo does the same either by compelling his son to live in the service of God or by giving himself over to his son. Both possibilities play out in the story itself, where the father undertakes to educate the boy in religion, thus promoting his own dedication to God while serving his son's needs.

Upon returning to Florence one day with his young son in tow, the father learns an unexpected lesson in the power of nature: "sentì incontanente più aver di forza la natura che il suo ingegno" (IV.Intro.29). The phrase underscores not the nature/culture dichotomy, which will appear elsewhere, but a new opposition between the power of nature and the rage to order, here identified with the father's *ingegno*.[16] At this point the tale finds its common ground with the *Decameron* Proem, which similarly highlights the patriarchal desire for control. As a response to Boccaccio's *assalitori*, however, the tale extends the critique of the will to control to the censorious efforts of the (male) critics who wish to control him. Filippo impersonates those critical male readers who are eager to isolate themselves from the reality of desire and its attendant consequences. In the young boy,

15. See also Scaglione 101–13, which details the tale's many sources; Sanguineti; D'Andrea; Fedi, "Il 'regno' di Filostrato"; and Virgulti. Best takes the tale in a different direction.

16. For Marchesi *ingegno* is synonymous not with *cultura* in opposition to *natura*, but rather with *industria*, and in this case the father's pedagogical efforts. For his reading of the *novella*, which similarly focuses on the problem of the father's pedagogy, see *Stratigrafie decameroniane* 51–56.

on the other hand, one may identify Boccaccio himself, who must endure the misogynist critiques of powerful men but who is finally too captivated by women's beauty to resist them or to succumb to the misogynist norms that would hogtie him.[17] The tale itself, as Mazzotta argues (133), demonstrates the futility of such repressive efforts.

While narratively incomplete—we never learn what Filippo Balducci does next—the story remains a central philosophical statement of the *Decameron*, specifically as a parody of medieval nominalism. Filippo Balducci exposes what Mazzotta calls his "naïve nominalism" when he refuses to use the word *femina* to identify the women his son is seeing: "Il padre, per non destare nel concupiscibile appetito del giovane alcuno inchinevole disiderio men che utile, non le volle nominare per lo proprio nome, cioè femine, ma disse: 'Elle si chiamano papere'" (IV.Intro.23). Unike Dante, who claims that "Nomina sunt consequentia rerum" (*Vita nuova* xiii.4), Filippo thinks that "Res sunt consequentia nominum," in other words, that the word *femine* itself carries an erotic power independent of the object to which it refers, so that by dislodging the object from its name one can effectively remove the object from the erotic sphere.[18] The story, however, suggests that eroticism inheres in the object and not in language, as the boy's reaction proves: "Maravigliosa cosa a udire! Colui che mai più alcuna veduta non avea, non curatosi de' palagi, non del bue, non del cavallo, non dell'asino, non de' denari né d'altra cosa che veduta avesse, subitamente disse: 'Padre mio, io vi priego che voi facciate che io abbia una di quelle papere'" (IV.Intro.24). So the story remarks on the futility of censorship. Filippo thinks he can stem his son's desire by playing with language, but he fails.[19]

If, as I have suggested, Filippo represents Boccaccio's critics and the boy Boccaccio himself, then the story demonstrates the foolishness of the

---

17. Federico Sanguineti likewise links the Balducci boy to Boccaccio, principally through autobiographical material found in the *Genealogia deorum gentilium*.

18. For Marcus, in fact, the tale "is less about a boy's sexual awakening than his father's lesson in fiction-making" (*An Allegory of Form* 51). Best argues that "The father changes the name of the women to *papere* in order to shield his son not merely from desiring the women, but from the danger of female sexuality." She also points out that Filippo's choice of *papera*, which refers metaphorically to "'a stupid, awkward woman,' reinforces the feminine presence in the text with comic effect. Filippo's particular choice of name in this instance demonstrates the ineffectiveness of discursive repression, and specifically repression of 'dangerous' material" (158–59).

19. As Tronci puts it, "Filippo Balducci è . . . convinto che i nomi siano *substantia rerum* e siano dotati di caratteri universali e astratti; il sano empirismo del figlio, che collega il nome all'esperienza e lo priva, perciò, di valore conoscitivo universale, smentirà le convinzioni del padre" (98).

book's critics in thinking that their own censorship would work.[20] Herein then lies Boccaccio's paradoxical rationale for writing the *Decameron:* in a sense, it has already been written. He affirms as much in the Introduction to Day I, where he figures himself as a mere transcriptionist: "sì come io poi da persona degna di fede sentii" (I.Intro.49). The book does not claim to set forth an ideology; rather, it simply records empirical reality, the same reality that Boccaccio records in the exchange between Tindaro and Licisca at the beginning of the sixth day. That some might find that reality to be too erotically charged is finally their problem, for as Boccaccio reminds his female readers in the Conclusion, "Niuna corrotta mente intese mai sanamente parola" (Conc.11): the subjectivity of reading trumps any claims a book might make.

I argued above that Dante would be a key player here, and he is, not simply in Boccaccio's parody of his nominalism but also in the comprehensive parody of the *Vita nuova* that subtends the Filippo Balducci tale. The son's discovery of women in fact conflates two encounter scenes featuring Dante and Beatrice. The first takes place when Dante, by now almost 18, meets Beatrice as she strolls along a Florentine street with two female friends. Dante summons the courage to look at her, and she responds with her famous greeting. The later meeting, in chapter XIV, occurs after Beatrice has withdrawn her *saluto* out of pique with Dante, and it involves a chance encounter at a wedding celebration. Near collapse after sensing her presence, Dante pretends to study a fresco that decorates the walls of the house he is visiting. Elements from both scenes appear in the son's discovery of women. He first sees them on the street in a group of "belle giovani donne e ornate, che da un paio di nozze veniano" (IV.Intro.20). Moreover, as Dante had sought refuge in a fresco, so too does Filippo's son make recourse to art as a means to express his wonder at what he has just seen: "Elle son più belle che gli agnoli dipinti che voi m'avete più volte mostrati. Deh! Se vi cal di me, fate che noi ce ne meniamo una colà sù di queste papere, e io le darò beccare" (IV.Intro.20, 28). As the punch line makes clear, any attempt to read this encounter in the lofty key of the *Vita nuova* will not stand up: attempts to sublimate desire in intellection run up hard against an erotic impulse having its roots in nature, not culture.[21]

---

20. Curiously, the question of censorship enters into only one of the five accusations against him that Boccaccio details: "Altri, più maturamente mostrando di voler dire, hanno detto che alla mia età non sta bene l'andare dietro a queste cose, cioè *a ragionar di donne* o a compiacer loro" (IV.Intro.6; italics mine). As the tale demonstrates, however, Boccaccio perceives his critics' overall thrust as aimed at getting him to change the subject.

21. Michelangelo Picone sums it up: "In effetti, alla donna-demonio deprecata dal modello orientale, e alla donna-angelo esaltata da Dante, l'autore del Centonovelle sostituisce la donna-donna, nella sua identità sociale e psicologoica, ma anche nella sua diversità affettiva e

That is not the only point, however, and by no means does culture lie outside the mix. Filippo's isolation, which sequesters him from literature's function as mediator of erotic desire that is foundational both to the *Decameron* and to the story told in the *Vita nuova*,[22] is not complete: for he has been studying art. The object of his study, the *agnoli dipinti*, is what Maria Corti calls an *ipersegno* or hypersign.[23] It is an especially complex type of hypersign because its referents lie both within and beyond Filippo's discourse. In the ongoing context of the story the son's invocation of painted angels suggests the inevitability of culture, even in the most isolated settings; most significantly, it denotes how culture mediates even our relationship with God. In this context the father's efforts to educate his son have inadvertently succeeded, for without realizing it he has taught the boy an appreciation of aesthetics. The son has focused on the paintings less for what they signify, angels, than as aesthetic objects: in effect, their transcendental signification is irrelevant, as he uses them as a basis of comparison with the beauty of women. His father had insisted on an education in divinity: ". . . sommamente si guardava di non ragionare, là dove egli fosse, d'alcuna temporal cosa né di lasciarnegli alcuna vedere, acciò che esse da così fatto servigio nol traessero, ma sempre della gloria di vita eterna e di Dio e de' santi gli ragionava, nulla altro che sante orazioni insegnandogli" (IV.Intro.15). In showing his son the *agnoli dipinti* Filippo would have insisted on their divinity; they were not a *temporal cosa*. But the son clearly understood them, as paintings, to be a *temporal cosa*, artifacts rather than true angels, signifying the world of man-made things.

Outside the story, the affiliation of angels with women necessarily recalls the notion of the *donna-angelo*, which Louise George Clubb has defined as "the most foreign to Boccaccio's thinking" of the many Stilnovist

---

sessuale" ("Il macrotesto" 25). Delcorno observes: "L'*amérimnia*, la deliberata rimozione del passato, e soprattutto dei legami affettivi, si tramuta nel divieto di ogni cognizione della società; la 'vita angelica,' che si raggiunge con una dolorosa lotta contro le tentazioni del demonio, si riduce ad un insipido baloccarsi con gli 'agnoli dipinti' nella cella" ("Modelli agiografici" 353–54).

22. Here I would distinguish the *Vita nuova* qua text from the story it tells. Literature functions to mediate erotic desire in the experience of the young Dante in that he writes poetry as his story unfolds. Only *ex post facto*, and specifically in the encounter of the pilgrim Dante with Paolo and Francesca in *Inferno* V, does he realize that the book itself, the *Vita nuova* in its combination of prose narrative and poetry, could function to mediate someone else's erotic desire.

23. "La denominazione di ipersegno, che qui si assume per l'opera d'arte in prospettiva semiologica, nasce dal fatto che l'opera può produrre un grado altissimo di informazione proprio in quanto in essa si potenzia il complesso, come tale, dei segni che la costituiscono . . ." (*Principi* 121).

concepts he had inherited.[24] If the *Vita nuova*, and the Stil novo more generally, attempted to rationalize love for women by identifying them as the embodiment of angels, this story makes a joke of such an association by flipping it. No longer is the angelic the standard for female beauty, for female beauty transcends the angelic, at least as far as Filippo's son can imagine thanks to his study of paintings. These metaliterary considerations, which simultaneously locate art as a mediator for our understanding of the divine and as inadequate in the face of nature, collide in the highly combustible space of the unfinished tale. The contradictions resolve themselves in their affirmation of the centrality of art, a point that paradoxically completes the argument that the tale celebrates the power of nature. The tale establishes art as the touchstone, the point of reference, for our understanding both of God and of nature. We do not understand art through God or nature; rather we understand God and nature through art. This anthropocentric view of the universe finds resonance elsewhere in the *Decameron*, as I shall detail later.

In addressing the specific objections leveled against him, Boccaccio recurs not to the lessons of the Filippo Balducci tale, which he leaves to his readers to divine, but rather to metaphors of wind, which he uses to suggest both the vacuousness of the critiques and the way they inadvertently give him greater credibility with women. So completely in fact does he discount his male readers that in his final authorial statement, the "Conclusione dell'autore," he addresses himself to *female* readers who might voice objections. Having recommitted himself to the ladies at the end of the Day IV introduction ("E se mai con tutta la mia forza a dovervi in cosa alcuna compiacere mi disposi, ora più che mai mi vi disporrò," IV.Intro.41), he now worries that he may not entirely have succeeded. Using the same rhetorical strategy undertaken in the Introduction to Day IV, he first speaks to the ladies in the second person, "Nobilissime giovani" (Conc.1), then reverts to the third person when anticipating objections from his female readers: "Saranno per avventura alcune di voi che diranno" (Conc.3); "Saranno similmente di quelle che diranno qui" (Conc.16), and so forth. Unlike the testy male readers, however, these women, even if not entirely happy with the product, are entitled to read the *Decameron*. They thus receive a more respectful hearing: there is no gesture of exclusion, but rather serious engagement with his interlocutors.

A comparison of the objections raised by the two groups exposes telling differences. In the Introduction to Day IV Boccaccio cites five objec-

---

24. See Clubb (191), who locates Boccaccio's parody of the courtly love tradition and *stilnovismo* in the tale of Frate Alberto and Lisetta (IV.2) . See also Marcus, "The Sweet New Style Reconsidered," for a treatment of this problem in the *Decameron*.

tions from the men: first, that he likes the ladies too much, and that taking so much pleasure in pleasing, consoling, and worse, commending ladies is indecent ("onesta cosa non è," IV.Intro.5); second, that he is not acting his age; third, that the Muses on Parnassus would make wiser company than the ladies whom he chooses to frequent; fourth, that he would do well to think about how to earn some money rather than pursue idle chatter; and finally, that the stories as he tells them are factually inaccurate. The female readers, on the other hand, might object first that he has been too licentious in writing the stories; second, that some of the tales could easily have been left out; third, that some of the stories are too long; fourth, that the tales are sometimes too frivolous for a writer of Boccaccio's merit; and finally, that Boccaccio has spoken with a poisoned tongue by telling the truth about friars. Of these, only the fourth approaches any of the objections raised by the men, specifically that he is not acting his age. Overall, the male readers are represented as engaging in *ad hominem* attacks against Boccaccio, often with an indirect assault on women, while the female readers emerge as much more interested in a conversation about the nature and content of the tales themselves, regardless of their factual accuracy.

With regard to the question of his seriousness, after first thanking the ladies for their concern about his reputation, Boccaccio offers his final and enduring self-image: "Io confesso d'esser pesato e molte volte de' miei dì essere stato; e per ciò, parlando a quelle che pesato non m'hanno, affermo che io non son grave, anzi son io sì lieve, che sto a galla nell'acqua . . ." (Conc.23). The statement puns on the projected objection that the light-hearted nature of the tales "non convenirsi a un uomo pesato e grave" (Conc.22). It also recalls the earlier metaphor Boccaccio had used to characterize himself, that of dust, and the two function in similar ways. The comparison to dust is paradoxically a metaphor of triumph: sometimes it remains obstinately on the ground, despite the wind; at other times it rises above the heads of men and the symbols of their power, and if it drops it can drop only as far as its place of departure, the ground itself. In other words, Boccaccio can only rise or remain essentially in place on the wind of his critics; he can never suffer true abasement.

These three components—the Proem, the Introduction to Day IV, and the Author's Conclusion—together enact the first level of exclusion/inclusion interplay in the *Decameron*. They project a fantasy of safety and security, where men can suffer disappointment in love but reward women rather than abjure them; where an author can insulate himself from his male critics; and where women read, and read critically, challenging their author and earning a respectful reply. At the same time, however, Boccaccio exposes the negative consequences of the same safety to which men may claim recourse when they lock women in their rooms: boredom, loneliness, a sense of suffocation. Yet these women risk further suffering by somehow procuring reading material to which their jailers, the record shows, would object. In this way the author creates another frame beyond the so-called frame tale of plague and flight. It intersects with the latter in two significant ways: first, by asserting that women can actively participate in the literary conversation, and second, by projecting the risks that women might run by venturing to chat, thus reciprocating his gesture of friendship. While the frame tale itself will show women reconstructing the world to suit their interests and concerns, they cannot avoid all dangers.

The Organization of the *Brigata*

Proof of the omnipresence of danger comes in a form that adds another layer of irony to the *Decameron:* mankind's betrayal by nature, the same element that Boccaccio had so extolled in his author's statements. The plague that afflicts Florence in 1348 wields its destructive force not only against humans (and animals), but also by extension against human institutions, whose collapse Boccaccio details in the Introduction to Day I. In the face of a double peril, disease and social disarray, the ten young people who will recount the book's 100 tales flee the sick city, but always keep an eye on it.[25] Glancing over their collective shoulder, they organize themselves in a way that reflects and comments on the world they have left, and that appears to offer new possibilities for those very women whose status Boccaccio so laments in the Proem. Boccaccio himself notes that "in tanta afflizione e miseria della nostra città era la reverenda auttorità delle leggi, così divine come umane" (I.Intro.23), so it is not surprising that as one of its first tasks the *brigata* restores some sense of legal order.

The group's effort at restoration reflects both the generalized disorder of Florentine society and their own disordered initial structure. The seven women come together, as Stillinger underscores, in an "initial chance meeting" ("Place of the Title" 31), with only tangential common traits: beyond displaying the religious devotion that leads them to the church, they are "savia ciascuna e di sangue nobile e bella di forma e ornate di costume e di

---

25. Pier Massimo Forni offers a brilliant intuition about the relationship between the plague and storytelling, casting the former in a therapeutic context: "By killing fathers, mothers, brothers, and husbands [the oppressors of women Boccaccio names in the Proem], the plague occasions the idyllic retreat of the *brigata*, allowing the female readers to imagine an alternative world unencumbered by relentless figures of authority" ("Therapy and Prophylaxis in Boccaccio's *Decameron*" 161).

leggiadra onestà." Each of these is, however, an individual quality, not a unifying one, and the ties that do bind them are various, suggesting that they
do not already constitute a formal group of any sort: "tutte l'una all'altra
o per amistà o per vicinanza o per parentado congiunte" (I.Intro.49). Their
group identity will eventually emerge in two phases, first when Pampinea
furnishes the rationale that unites them—the need to survive—and later,
when Dioneo presses for the elucidation of principles that will inform both
their governance and their storytelling. In these two phases they person-
ify two of Aristotle's three types of friendship. By recognizing a practical motive for staying together, they establish a utilitarian friendship, and
later, when affirming that the purpose of their sojourn is to live together
festevolmente, they form a friendship based on pleasure. Both types are,
by Aristotle's analysis, imperfect, in contrast with friendship that is based
in the good. Both are also common among adolescents and the young, and
markedly transitory: ". . . these friendships are friendships incidentally; for
the one loved is not loved by reference to the person he is but to the fact
that in the one case he provides some good and in the other some pleasure.
Such friendships, then, are easily dissolved, if the parties become different . . ." (1156a15; Rowe trans. 211).

Indeed, the *Decameron* offers no evidence that the group's friendship
progresses beyond these limits to something more enduring. In the last
sentence of the *brigata* narrative, the group returns to Florence and dissolves into its old life, coming apart in the reverse order of its formation:
". . . .i tre giovani, lasciate le sette donne in Santa Maria Novella, donde con
loro partiti s'erano, da esse accommiatatosi, a' loro altri piaceri attesero, e
esse, quando tempo lor parve, se ne tornarono alle lor case" (X.Conc.16).
Having returned to the scene of death and disease, the ten young people
appear to pick up where they left off.[26] The three young men attend to their
altri piaceri, suggesting retroactively the role that pleasure has played in
structuring their experience, while the young women return home, a place
marked most recently by death, abandonment, and abject loneliness. While
we often note the fiabesque quality of the Day X stories we perhaps overlook that the entire book has a fablelike quality, that the harmony conjured
among its ten protagonists, so rooted in history, is also wholly removed
from it, and that the book's insistent marking of time serves as a mask for
the almost complete ablation of real time.

In its fade to black the *Decameron* thus reminds its readers of the group's
wholly incidental nature, its initial formlessness. That formlessness also

---

26. For Joseph Gibaldi the return to the church completes "the cyclical movement of the
archetypal adventure: separation-initiation-return" (354).

offers unanticipated advantages, as the group coalesces with no prior sense of identity and therefore no preconceived notion of governance. While the group surely borrows from extant models, there is no one governmental model to which it refers, either civic or religious. Thus the women in particular pay lip service to entrenched ideologies, most notably regarding the need for male leadership, while simultaneously flouting them.

Their first decision, to flee and reorganize themselves elsewhere, recalls a solution already practiced within the confines of Florence, that of segregation, voluntary confinement, and moderate living. While frightened Florentines shut themselves in their homes, however, in the countryside the ten live principally in the open air, as if in silent defiance of the urban conventions they have come to see as unhealthy. Moreover, unlike those who remain in Florence, who either delude themselves into thinking that they still have a functioning government or do not care, the ten young people intuit the need to codify their relationship with both a new constitution and a series of statutes. Distancing themselves from the city, they appear to recognize that they no longer live under Florentine law, and their social organization reflects more than simply the survival instinct that drove their Florentine counterparts to seclude themselves and to live in moderation.

Arriving at the first villa, the *brigata* formulates its constitution, what Joseph Gibaldi has called a "democratic autocracy" (352), complete with a Kelsenian basic norm. Dioneo unintentionally gives voice to the basic norm when he tells the ladies that "o voi a sollazzare e a ridere e a cantare con meco insieme vi disponete (tanto, dico, quanto alla vostra dignità s'appartiene), o voi mi licenziate che io per li miei pensier mi ritorni e steami nella città tribolata" (I.Intro.93). The sentence itself discloses a concept of male–female relations that was not entirely clear when the group first gathered in Santa Maria Novella. Dioneo acknowledges the ladies' authority over him, because they can grant him license to leave, if not physically then mentally,[27] but he also implies that by agreeing to their plan he is indebted them to him: they must join him in merrymaking.[28] This conception of dual roles is consistent with Pampinea's statement, appar-

---

27. The exact nature of Dioneo's threat is unclear. While some have translated this passage to indicate his intention physically to return to Florence, it is equally possible that he means to say that unless they endeavor to entertain him he will have no choice but to brood about Florence. If this interpretation is correct, then the storytelling itself enacts yet another irony, as many of the stories do in fact return the *brigata* metaphorically to Florence.

28. As Alessandro Duranti points out, Dioneo's request is typical of his status as an outsider within the group: "Fino dal suo esordio è chiaro che Dioneo pensa alla brigata non nell'ordine della decina, ma come a un composto, provvisorio e di non facile mantenimento, di nove più uno" (6). While Duranti does not pause to consider the implications of Dioneo's arithmetic, they are nonetheless evident.

ently out of earshot of the men, that "la fortuna . . . hacci davanti posti discreti giovani e valorosi, li quali volentieri e guida e servidor ne saranno" (I.Intro.80), though her remark hardly has the binding quality implied in Dioneo's.[29] Pampinea borrows from the courtly love lexicon (*servidor*) to suggest that the men will have the same sort of status as the courtly lover,[30] being both the servant who submits to the lady's will and the guide, as all men ultimately have authority over women. The actual invitation she extends to the men is less explicit: "pregogli per parte di tutte che con puro e fratellevole animo a tener lor compagnia si dovessero disporre" (I.Intro.87). Whereas her earlier position had been wholly hierarchical, now Pampinea could not be more ideologically egalitarian. She appeals to the men's pure and brotherly disposition or affection, to keep the ladies company, literally to break bread with them.[31] The shift from a vertical to a horizontal rhetoric would appear to be politically motivated: Pampinea neither wants to offend the men by suggesting that the ladies will govern nor wants the men to think that they will rule over the ladies. She also appears to want to clarify the exact nature of the company they will share: it will be fraternal, and therefore not erotic.

Upon hearing Dioneo's ultimatum, Pampinea converts it into the basic norm on which the constitution will rest: "Dioneo, ottimamente parli: festevolmente viver si vuole, né altra cagione dalle tristizie ci ha fatte fuggire. Ma per ciò che le cose che sono senza modo non possono lungamente durare, io, che cominciatrice fui de' ragionamenti da' quali questa così bella compagnia è stata fatta, pensando al continuar della nostra letizia, estimo che di necessità sia convenire esser tra noi" (I.Intro.94–95). Pampinea demonstrates here again her extraordinary political skills. The narrator describes her as "non d'altra maniera che se similmente tutti i suoi [pensieri] avesse da sé cacciati" (I.Intro.94): she appears to abandon all thoughts of her own in order to affirm Dioneo's. She then concurs with him, that they fled Florence in order to live *festevolmente:* before he had arrived in the church she had in fact argued that by fleeing to the country they could find "quella festa, quella allegrezza, quello piacere . . . senza trapassare in alcuno atto il segno della ragione" (I.Intro.65).[32] At the same time, however, she makes

---

29. Dioneo himself in fact reverses Pampinea's claim that men will act as *guida* when he tells the ladies that "il vostro senno più che il nostro avvedimento ci ha qui *guidati*" (I.Intro.92; italics mine).

30. Each in fact is linked amorously to one of the three ladies (I.Intro.78).

31. According to Zingarelli the noun *compagno* comes from the medieval Latin *companion*, a compound of *cum*, with, and *panis*, bread.

32. On this crucial sentence see Kirkham 7–12. Mazzotta interprets "ragione" here as "restraint, rather than as an abstract rationality which would conform either to the order of nature, which in reality is sheer chaos, or to the order of the garden to which they move, for

a subtle and curious distinction: "né altra cagione dalle tristizie ci ha *fatte fuggire.*" She speaks only for the ladies, not for the men. She may technically be correct, since all we know from the narrative is that she "loro [to the men] la lor [the ladies'] disposizione fé manifesta" (I.Intro.87). In other words, Pampinea may have told the men of the ladies' plan to leave the city, neglecting to mention their resolve to have fun at their destination, in which case she cannot fairly speak for any festive intentions on the part of the men in coming to the place. Supporting such an interpretation is Dioneo's remark that "io non so quello che de' vostri pensieri voi v'intendete di fare" (I.Intro 93). In any event, the exchange, while enacting the sort of compact that appears to satisfy the desires of both parties, in fact installs a certain gender-based tension: Dioneo demands compensatory pleasure for his companionship, whereas Pampinea tries to return to the question of the ladies' pleasure.

Rather than dwell on any potential disharmony between her and Dioneo, Pampinea continues seamlessly along the rhetorical path she has laid out. She emphasizes the egalitarian notion of *compagnia* that had informed the original invitation, while simultaneously reverting to a hierarchical sense of order. The group needs *modo,* which Branca glosses as "ordine e misura" (999), in order to endure, and Pampinea claims the right to establish that *modo* by virtue of the fact that she had first opened the discussion that led to the present moment. Her assertion of authority here is significant: after all, she could just as easily defer to Dioneo, asking him how he would propose to organize the group and its time. She appears finally to be only secondarily interested in the pleasure or the authority of the men. Despite her earlier notion that the men could be the ladies' *guida,* in fact she has no real intention to defer to them.

Pampinea's concept of governance does however enable a compromise between her egalitarian and hierarchical impulses. On the one hand she acknowledges the need for a "principale, il quale noi e onoriamo e ubidiamo come maggiore," charged to arrange things so that all can *lietamente vivere* (I.Intro.96). On the other she proposes the sharing of this duty, so that each day at vespers the monarch will appoint a successor who "secondo il suo arbitrio, del tempo che la sua signoria dee bastare, del luogo e del modo nel quale a vivere abbiamo ordini e disponga" (I.Intro.96). Thus she again balances notions of pleasure and discipline along with egalitarian and hierarchical impulses. Having concurred with Dioneo about happy living, she also argues that the group's happiness can endure only within a framework

---

the garden is an artifice of nature" (42). He then continues by making a link between Pampinea's phrase and a Dantean tercet (*Par.* XXVI.115–17).

of governance. While she acknowledges that there is pleasure in ruling, she also sees how the burdens of office can finally dilute one's pleasure, hence the rotation. Finally, she assumes that the rulers will be both men and women, as indicated by a somewhat belabored insistence on *colui* and *colei*, him and her, when discussing the question of succession.

Pampinea's constitution wins quick and unanimous consent, as does her election as queen. There follow in quick order several provisions that emanate from the constitutional principles. Filomena weaves a laurel crown that will endure as the symbol of authority, passed from ruler to ruler. Pampinea then issues a series of statutes pertaining to the group's daily life. In a continuation of the *pas de deux* that has been her interaction with Dioneo up until now, she first appoints Parmeno, Dioneo's manservant, as her steward.[33] Her language throughout remains consistent: she refers to "la nostra compagnia" and invokes the values of *ordine* and *piacere*, as well as the need to live "senza vergogna" (I.Intro.98). Elsewhere her lexicon borders on the legalistic: she uses the verb *constituire* in her appointment of Parmeno, and she names Chimera and Stratilia "al governo delle camere delle donne" (I.Intro.101). She concludes with a statute intended to put in force the basic norm: "E ciascun generalmente, per quanto egli avrà cara la nostra grazia, vogliamo e comandiamo che si guardi, dove che egli vada, onde che egli torni, che che egli oda o vegga, niuna novella altra che lieta ci rechi di fuori" (I.Intro.101). The sentence has unforeseen consequences, as we shall see in the fourth day, because it apparently conflicts with Pampinea's earlier constitutional provision that each ruler will have the power ("il suo arbitrio") to determine "del luogo e del modo del quale a vivere abbiamo ordini e disponga" (I.Intro.96). To the extent that this norm extends from the basic norm "festevolmente viver si vuole," it would appear that the *arbitrio* to which Pampinea refers is circumscribed by the normative notion that life be festive. Her second statute, cited above, may in fact extend only to the length of her rule: just as each new ruler will determine a new theme for the next day's narration, so too is it not clear that the other provisions made by previous rulers carry over into future days. This ambiguity in Pampinea's legal order, the only apparent one, will provoke the constitutional crisis of Day IV.

---

33. While Dioneo has traditionally been coupled amorously with Fiammetta (*Decameron* ed. Branca 997), I would not overlook the tension between Dioneo and Pampinea as suggesting a possible relationship between them. Kirkham prefers to see Panfilo as Pampinea's allegorical complement (Prudence and Reason) and even goes so far as to suggest that they may be two of the relatives among the group to which the narrator alludes (166), but a triangulation of Pampinea's prudence with Panfilo's reason and Dioneo's concupiscence nuances Pampinea's character in intriguing ways.

Superficially, then, the new constitution bears all the marks of positive law, and its elaboration by a woman would appear to detach it from any natural law moorings. However, while emphasizing women's pleasure, using her rhetorical skills to consolidate her own leadership, and proposing a constitution that will empower women, Pampinea in fact cleverly engages natural law principles. Elissa's remark that "Veramente gli uomini sono delle femine capo e senza l'ordine loro rade volte riesce alcuna nostra opera a laudevole fine" (I.Intro 76), with its Pauline echoes, repeats a basic corollary of natural law theory that genders the order of the universe as male. Natural law theorists such as Aquinas and Dante repeatedly affirm the patrilinear order of the universe. In *On Kingship* I.1, Aquinas writes: "And so we refer to those who rule perfect communities, that is, cities or provinces, as kings in the fullest sense. And we call those who rule households fathers of families, not kings, although fathers are analogous to kings, and we for that reason sometimes call kings fathers of their peoples" (*On Law, Morality, and Politics* 207). Dante elaborates a similar hierarchy in *Monarchy*: "Again, every son is in a good (indeed, ideal) state when he follows in the footsteps of a perfect father, insofar as his own nature allows. Mankind is the son of heaven, which is quite perfect in all its working; for man and the sun generate man, as we read in the second book of the *Physics*. Therefore mankind is in its ideal state when it follows the footsteps of heaven, insofar as its nature allows" (13).[34] Both authors predicate their argument on the assumption that God is male, no doubt encouraged by the statement in Genesis 1:27 that "God created man in His own image."[35] In asserting her own leadership and in seizing authority Pampinea therefore appears to challenge basic assumptions about the ordering of the universe, as well as to endanger the status of her little monarchy. To read such a move simply as consistent with the "world turned upside down" theme of the *Decameron* skirts some of the richer implications of Pampinea's effort.

Indeed, Pampinea shows herself to be quite a creative reader of natural law theory. In the *Summa*, Question 91, Aquinas discusses the relationship between three types of law, eternal, natural, and human. Natural law is

---

34. "Item, bene et optime se habet omnis filius cum vestigial perfectis patris, in quantum propria natura mermictis, ymitatur. Humanum genus filius est celi, quod est perfectissimum in omni opera suo: generat enim homo hominem et sol, iuxta secundum *De natura auditu*. Ergo optime se habet humanum genus cum vestigia celi, in quantum propria natura permictis, ymitatur" (I.ix). The Latin noun *genus* is neutral, so the masculine attribution, *filius*, is deliberate.

35. Alter translates the entire verse as follows: "And God created the human in his image, / in the image of God He created him, / male and female He created them." He further points out that "In the middle clause of this verse, 'him,' as in the Hebrew, is grammatically but not anatomically masculine" (19n.). It seems unlikely that medieval commentators would have perceived this subtle distinction.

for Aquinas human participation in eternal law: "Among them [all things] intelligent creatures are ranked under divine Providence the more nobly because they take part in Providence by their own providing for themselves and others. Thus they join in and make their own the Eternal Reason through which they have their natural aptitutdes for their due activity and purpose. Now this sharing in the Eternal Law by intelligent creatures is what we call 'natural law'" (*ST* 1a2æ. 91, 2). Natural law, Aquinas continues, is the reflected light of eternal law, literally imprinted on men. God's law is thus made visible in a way that allows rational creatures to perceive it: one can almost discern Plato's allegory of the cave behind Aquinas's discourse. For Pampinea to know natural law, in other words, for her to share in the eternal law, would appear therefore to depend on whether one can count her among rational creatures. Filomena would appear not to, for she argues that "non ce n'ha niuna sì fanciulla, che non possa ben conoscere come le femine sien ragionate insieme e senza la provedenza d'alcuno uomo si sappiano regolare" (I.Intro.74). She also describes women in terms that make them antithetical to reason: "Noi siamo mobili, riottose, sospettose, pusillanime e paurose" (I.Intro.75). And yet her very logic furnishes its own loophole in her insistence on the "provedenza d'alcuno uomo." Seeing women as fundamentally irrational, Filomena insists that they need men, the rational creatures, to lead them, thus furthering the hierarchical order imposed from above. Her language would appear to make that claim, but the noun *provedenza* has divine associations, as Aquinas suggests above.[36] One wonders therefore whether Filomena's remark about the need for "la provedenza d'alcuno uomo" cannot be satisfied by following divine providence, God being after all male and Christ himself having been a man, as long as one can prove that women are capable of being rational creatures.

Boccaccio seems to think so, for the logic of Pampinea's arguments, and her ability to elaborate the group's constitution, suggests that she is sublimely rational. At the beginning of her speech to the assembled women in Santa Maria Novella, she recalls the oft-repeated assertion that "a niuna persona fa ingiuria chi onestamente usa la sua ragione," and she continues by arguing that "Natural ragione è, di ciascuno che ci nasce, la sua vita quanto può aiutare e conservare e difendere" (I.Intro.53). As an example of that point she cites killing in self-defense, and she casts her own proposal for the group's survival against this extreme: "E se questo concedono le leggi, nelle sollecitudini delle quali è il ben vivere d'ogni mortale, quanto maggiormente, senza offesa d'alcuno, è a noi e a qualunque altro onesto

---

36. See for example *Paradiso* XI.28–30: "La provedenza, che govern ail mondo / con quel consiglio nel quale ogni aspetto / creato è vinto pria che vada al fondo. . . ."

alla conservazione della nostra vita prendere quegli rimedii che noi possiamo?" (I.Intro.54). Her argument thus rests on an understanding of the
general purpose of a legal order as set forth, for example, by Aquinas in the
Summa: "the chief and main concern of law properly so called is the plan
for the common good" (*ST* 1a2æ. 90, 3).[37] As well, her insistence that the
group's activities in the country not "trapassare in alcuno atto il segno della
ragione" (I.Intro.65) marks her as someone for whom engagement with
reason is tantamount.[38]

Moreover, Pampinea engages with a specific type of reason, practical
reason, an extension of natural law that for Aquinas gives rise to human
law: ". . . law is a dictate of the practical reason. Now the processes of the
theoretic and practical reasons are parallel; both, we have held, start from
certain principles and come to certain conclusions. . . . also from natural law
precepts as from common and indemonstrable principles the human reason comes down to making more specific arrangements. . . . called 'human
laws.' . . . The practical reason is concerned with things to be done, which
are individual and contingent, not with the necessary things that are the
concern of the theoretic reason" (*ST* 1a2æ. 91, 3).[39] There is no question
but that Pampinea concerns herself with practical matters: her speech in
Santa Maria Novella, her outline of the constitution, and her first statutes all share a practical, contingent orientation. Now, one may argue that
her reason in fact diverges from natural law because she does not follow
"general and indemonstrable principles" in insisting on *festevolmente viver.*
However, her claim that survival is paramount certainly follows such a first
principle, and in general her proposals conform to Aquinas's own definition of law as oriented to the common good. The sequence of events, in
which Pampinea first proposes escape from the ruined city as clearly to the
common good—both to avoid its dangers and corruption and to enjoy the
pleasure the women deserve—and then carefully articulates the principle
of *festevolmente viver* as serving the purposes of the whole group, reflects
her intention, as a lawgiver, to act in the best interests of all, as natural law
dictates.

Pampinea thus reveals herself to be well versed in natural law theory;

---

37. Aquinas derives his argument from Aristotle, citing *Ethics* V.1: "we call just the things
that create and preserve happiness and its parts for the citizen community" (1129b18–19;
Rowe trans. 159).

38. Kirkham traces the origins and implications of this statement through Dante and
Aquinas, the latter of whom is foundational for much of my argument—while identifying
Pampinea as the personification of Prudence (*The Sign of Reason* 7–12).

39. Pampinea's ability to deploy practical reason is consistent with her figuration as
Prudence, whose purpose, as Kirkham summarizes it from Aquinas, "is to perfect the rational
power of the soul" (*The Sign of Reason* 150).

her own ideas extend from and capitalize on it as she envisions a new society for her friends. In assigning this role to a woman, Boccaccio executes a careful coup. The world of the *brigata* does not reject the predicates of the world of men; rather it affirms them. It is in her understanding of law and of the theory that subtends it that Pampinea realizes the full force of her leadership and becomes such a compelling figure. She does not lead the group outside of male structures; rather, she shows how they can now deploy previously established structures and principles to their own profit. Her legerdemain does not come free of charge, however, for her rhetoric of inclusion and practical marginalization of men will lead to various efforts by Filostrato, Dioneo, and Panfilo to right the balance when they assume power.

Enter the Eavesdropper

Cognizant that the rhetorical exclusion of men from the world of the book does not equate to the exclusion of men from the world, Boccaccio assigns a specific place to men, at all three textual levels: they are eavesdroppers. Boccaccio's male critics, consigned to a state of unrequited desire because he never concludes the story of Filippo Balducci, and who must listen in as a third party as Boccaccio answers them through the ladies, are forced to eavesdrop. So, too, in a sense, are the three young men who accompany the seven ladies outside of town. Invited because the women doubt their ability to survive without men, as an audience to the storytelling they remain at the margins. Boccaccio makes this clear by having every narrator, in introducing his or her story, specifically address the women: the men are present and listen, but they remain secondary. Perhaps their own sense of living at the edges of this narrative world will inform the sorts of reactions we witness when they are finally in charge.

Complementary to the role of the three *brigata* males listening at the sidelines is the figure of the eavesdropper that Boccaccio inserts into his tales at critical moments. The first eavesdroppers of the hundred stories are the little-noted pair of Florentine brothers who offer housing to Ser Ciappelletto, and the Pratese Ciappelletto himself. The latter is in fact, among other things, the first affirmed eavesdropper of the *Decameron*, overhearing the two brothers' worried conversation as he languishes on his deathbed: "Ser Ciappelletto, il quale, come dicemmo, presso giacea là dove costoro così ragionavano, avendo l'udire sottile, sì come le più volte veggiamo aver gl'infermi, udì ciò che costoro di lui dicevano . . ." (I.1.27). In addition, therefore, to being a great raconteur and liar, Ciappelletto is a gifted listener, though this particular endowment carries an extraordinary price tag: terminal illness. He can also muster the sort of generosity—offering to commit yet another sin against God ("Io ho, vivendo, tante ingiurie fatte a Domenedio, che, per farnegli io una ora in su la mia morte, né più né meno ne farà," I.1.28) in order to spare his hosts any difficulty at his death—that nuances his character in suggestive and comic ways.[40] The healthy Florentine brothers listen more intentionally: "Li due fratelli, li quali dubitavan forte non ser Ciappelletto gl'inganasse, s'eran posti appresso a un tavolato, il quale la camera dove ser Ciappelletto giaceva dividea da un'altra, e ascoltando leggiermente udivano e intendevano ciò che ser Ciappelletto al frate diceva; e aveano alcuna volta sì gran voglia di ridere, udendo le cose le quali egli confessava d'aver fatte, che quasi scoppiavano" (I.1.78). In the notes to his edition Branca glosses the adverb *leggiermente* as *facilmente* or *comodamente* (1013n.9): the brothers strive to hear well because they distrust their houseguest. They quickly discover that they have nothing to fear and indeed marvel at his shamelessness in the face of death. While the *tavolato* or partition behind which they hide functions within the economy of the narrative to further their purpose of spying, it also marks their exclusion from the narrative proper, their status as audience rather than participant.

In his essay on the tale of Bergamino (I.7), Michelangelo Picone notes that "the curtain of the *Decameron* rises on Paris" ("The Tale of Bergamino" 164). In Ciappelletto as "a Tuscan transplanted to Paris" and Abraham the Jew who goes from Paris to Rome, Picone intuits "a passage, a real *translatio studii*, of the art of the tale from its land of origin, France, to its new home, Italy" (165). I would supplement this observation with another one: that Boccaccio asserts, through the figures of Ciappelletto and the two Florentine brothers, that the best listeners, and by extension the best reception of the narrative tradition, are Tuscan. One cannot help therefore but see behind the *tavolato* of this narrative an allusion to Boccaccio himself, as one supremely gifted not only to hear but to transform narrative models and narrative content into the tales of the *Decameron*. Beyond that, however, his Tuscan trio serves to establish the theme of overhearing and eavesdropping that will recur elsewhere in the book. As well, they associate these activities with men.

---

40. While Boccaccio thus assigns to Ciappelletto a multitude of sins, he explicitly denies that he is a traitor to benefactors, the very worst kind of sinner according to Dante. Panfilo's claim that he was "il piggiore uomo forse che mai nascesse" (I.1.15) appears therefore to be somewhat hyperbolic, and the *forse* an important qualifier. It is convenient for Branca to read Cepparello as a Judas figure, as it squares with his thesis of the overall direction of the *Decameron* (*Boccaccio medievale* 18), but his analysis fails to take note of these significant qualifiers. For another critique of Branca's claim, see Almansi, *The Writer as Liar* 37–38.

Indeed, the second great eavesdropper of the *Decameron*, one who embodies not just the relegation of the male to the borders of women's lives but also the power of men to chasten autonomous women, is Tancredi, prince of Salerno. It is no coincidence that the tale of Tancredi, who eavesdrops so transparently (to us) and sinisterly, enters the narrative scene immediately after Boccaccio answers his male critics: the prince's blatant eavesdropping serves to signal us about a broader male activity spread across the pages of the book. Boccaccio's critics share, after all, the same misogynist ideology used to rationalize the forced enclosure of women. While Tancredi's daughter Ghismonda may enjoy the right to come and go as she pleases, or at the very least has discovered the means to escape her own enclosure, by entering her room at will Tancredi shows how misogynist ideology denies women not only their freedom but also their privacy.

In one of the *Decameron*'s most unsettling scenes, Tancredi enters Ghismonda's bedroom, an activity that is in itself not unusual: "Era usato Tancredi di venirsene alcuna volta tutto solo nella camera della figliuola e quivi con lei dimorare e ragionare alquanto e poi partirsi" (IV.1.16).[41] Unbeknownst to Tancredi, the bedroom itself has just acquired new meaning as Ghismonda's private space. The paragraph in which he enters the room follows quickly upon the lengthy exposition of how Guiscardo gains access to the *grotta* where Ghismonda meets him in order to steal into her room, where they have sex. The father's customary visits, *tutto solo*, thus assume a new, disturbing quality, as Tancredi enters not merely his daughter's bedroom but the space that she has assigned for her sexual activity.[42] Not finding her there, he resolves to remain: "Il quale un giorno dietro mangiare là giù venutone, essendo la donna, la quale Ghismonda aveva nome, in un suo giardino con tutte le sue damigelle, in quella senza essere stato da alcuno

---

41. This scene, along with other elements of the story, has contributed to a critical tradition that focuses on Tancredi's incestuous desire for his daughter. Alberto Moravia suggests as much, as does Mario Baratto (*Realtà e stile* 185). Almansi developed the notion into a full essay in *The Writer as Liar* (133–57), and Marcus takes it up in her essay on the story, which appears in *An Allegory of Form*. Mazzotta casts the tale, along with that of Filippo Balducci and his son, under the umbrella of "the relationship between the laws of passion and the power of political authority" (136), while Picone at once accepts the incest theme and dismisses it, arguing that "non arriva a spiegarci il perché della ripresa del registro tragico—invece di quello comico—nella trattazione della tematica della *fol'amor* romanza" ("L'amoroso sangue'" 121), a question that his analysis seeks to answer. Finally, one should not ignore Jordan's essay on this story, which refreshingly refuses to heroicize Ghismonda. It is Jordan's quite brilliant intuition that "Ghismonda, true to the incest motif which lies at the heart of the tale, makes her father the agent of her own seduction" by blaming Tancredi's esteem for Guiscardo for her own love for the valet (106).

42. It bears insistence here that Ghismonda could, after all, have had sex with Guiscardo in the *grotta* where they meet. The *Decameron* does not lack for scenes of sexual activity in unusual or uncomfortable places.

veduto o sentito entratosene, non volendo lei torre dal suo diletto, trovando le finestre della camera chiuse e le cortine del letto abbattute, a piè di quello in un canto sopra un carello si pose a sedere; e appoggiato il capo al letto e tirata sopra sé la cortina, quasi come se studiosamente si fosse nascoso, quivi s'adormentò" (IV.1.17). Here we have another one of the great *Decameron* sentences whose narrative illogic demands careful parsing. Tancredi appears to know that Ghismonda will not be in her room when he enters it, or at the very least he learns where she is while in the room, observing her in the garden with her ladies. If he knew before entering, then his decision to come there at this time becomes highly suspect; if he learns it while there, then one may at most charitably attribute his decision to stay to the fact that the room, all closed up, invited a nap. Clearly he does not interpret all the signs of closure—the windows and the curtains—as indications that he should leave. Either way, he opts not to interrupt her fun in the garden, but he likewise does not opt to return later. Moreover, his unobserved entry has a suspicious air, one that the narrator, Fiammetta, will reinforce with her remark "quasi come se studiosamente si fosse nascoso," which itself creates a curious distance between narrator and subject: who better than Fiammetta would know Tancredi's motives? The curtain behind which he hides here replaces the *tavolato* used by the Florentine brothers, again separating the observer from the action he will witness. Unlike the brothers, however, Tancredi does not understand that by wrapping himself in the curtain he is excluding himself from the ensuing action. He does not perceive what we recognize to be his own marginalization.

Tancredi awakens to find Ghismonda and Guiscardo in the bed, having sex: "Tancredi si svegliò e sentì e vide ciò che Guiscardo e la figliuola facevano" (IV.1.18). What he hears and sees is indeed the story itself, as it unfolds; the tale thus effects a sort of surreal redoubling in which a character *in* the story is also a reader *of* the story.[43] Rather than reveal his presence, he opts to stay hidden: "prima gli volle sgridare, poi prese partito di tacersi e di starsi nascoso, s'egli potesse, per potere più cautamente fare e con minor sua vergogna quello che già gli era caduto nell'animo di dover fare" (IV.1.19). He begins at once to plan, developing a counternarrative to the one he has just witnessed and reasserting the link between listening and emplotment that Boccaccio had already suggested when Ciappelletto overheard the Florentine brothers' fretting and hatched a plan to rescue them.

---

43. Mazzotta makes a very good point: "More substantively, as Tancredi sees unseen the two lovers playing and cavorting together, there is both an assertion and an ironic reversal of the omniscient perspective he enjoys in the court. His present viewpoint gives him a knowledge that effectively sanctions his power; it also reveals to him the existence of an unsuspected world, the world of a passion he represses" (140).

Tancredi also significantly advances the role and the power of the eavesdropper beyond the limits first assigned to it. Ciappelletto's eavesdropping leads to a successful offer of assistance to his hapless Florentine hosts, sparing them the scandal of having a man die in their home outside of the orders of the Church. Their eavesdropping results simply in their wonder at Ciappelletto's fearlessness and ability to fabricate lies. Tancredi, however, has absolute power over his daughter and her lover, as he quickly demonstrates by having Guiscardo imprisoned and murdered, and by confronting Ghismonda about his perceived betrayal by her. The very embodiment of law, Tancredi demonstrates through his actions the power of law to discipline activities that it deems transgressive, though Boccaccio significantly complicates matters by locating the transgression somewhere between sex outside of marriage and the betrayal of incestuous desire. Positioned right after Boccaccio's self-defense in the Introduction to Day IV, the tale reasserts the tension between the marginalization of men in the world of the *Decameron* and the fact that men, when marginalized, will react to reassert their power.

A variant of the eavesdropper, the spy, marks the pages of Days IV and V. Like Tancredi, Lisabetta's brother in IV.5 inadvertently witnesses her sexual congress, and likewise resolves to take action at a later moment: "E in questo continuando e avendo insieme assai di buon tempo e di piacere, non seppero sì segretamente fare, che una notte, andando Lisabetta là dove Lorenzo dormiva, che il maggior de' fratelli, senza accorgersene ella, non se ne accorgesse. Il quale, per ciò che savio giovane era, quantunque molto noioso gli fosse a ciò sapere, pur mosso da più onesto consiglio, senza far motto o dir cosa alcuna, varie cose fra se rivolgendo intorno a questo fatto, infino alla mattina seguente trapassò" (IV.5.6). Significantly, the oldest of the brothers discovers the tryst: as natural leader of the family, he will then guide the discussion of possible remedies. Likewise significant is Boccaccio's use of the verb *trapassare*, which here, according to Branca (1232n8), stands simply as a synonym for *passare*, but with a prefix that associates the verb with sinful trespass (Kirkham, *The Sign of Reason* 8), nuancing the brother's overnight deliberations negatively. The tale's denouement, which sees the brothers fleeing Messina, confirms that they have overstepped.

Espionage in Day V leads instead beyond the crisis to a resolution satisfactory to all. In V.4, Caterina's father discovers that she has spent the night with her boyfriend, Ricciardo, on the balcony of their home: "E andato oltre pianamente levò alto la sargia della quale il letto era fasciato, e Ricciardo e lei vide ignudi e iscoperti dormire abbracciati nella guisa di sopra mostrata . . ." (V.4.32). The scene establishes this father, messer Lizio, as a foil to Tancredi: both violate the sanctity of their daughter's sexual space, in both cases marked by drapery, but messer Lizio responds to his discovery with the sort of calm deliberation that facilitates a happy ending. It helps of course that Ricciardo is, as Lizio says, "gentile uomo e ricco giovane," whereas Guiscardo, Ghismonda's lover, was Tancredi's page and therefore socially inappropriate for his daughter. So too does the father's emotional investment in his daughter differ in each case, and Lizio's is clearly not pathological. In V.7, Messer Amerigo makes a similar inadvertent discovery, when he chances upon his daughter's childbirth scene, evidence of prior sexually activity. The girl's mother had deliberately concealed her daughter, "per celare il difetto della figluola a una lor possessione ne la mandò" (V.7.23), but the father's unexpected arrival underscores the ineluctable nature of male authority. The girl and her child survive only because the boyfriend turns out to be the son of a nobleman, and therefore of marriageable stock.

One final case of eavesdropping resembles that of Tancredi in that the eavesdropper involuntarily witnesses the events. In the final story of Day V, that of Pietro di Vinciolo, the protagonist returns home early from dinner at his friend Ercolano's house, upsetting his wife's plan to dine with and enjoy the company of her new lover. She has hidden him, much as Ghismonda had hidden her relationship with Guiscardo: "non avendo accorgimento di mandarlo o di farlo nascondere in altra parte, essendo una sua loggetta vicina alla camera nella quale cenavano, sotto una cesta da polli che v'era il fece ricoverare e gittovvi suso un pannaccio d'un saccone che fatto aveva il dì votare . . ." (V.10.28). The young man can thus listen in on the conversation between Pietro and his wife. He is not however the most important eavesdropper in the tale, as Boccaccio's source, Apuleius, makes clear.[44] In Apuleius the ass, Lucius, tells the story, boasting of his position as eavesdropper: "I was congratulating myself less on being freed from my labors than on the fact that, my eyes being now uncovered, I had an uninterrupted view of all this woman's carryings-on" (159). He also prides himself in furthering the action, specifically in order to avenge the wife's infidelity: "As I was going by I saw the man's fingers sticking out from under the edge of the trough, which was rather too narrow for him; and treading sideways on them as hard as I could I ground them to a pulp" (162). In Boccaccio's reworking of the tale the ass does not narrate, so we cannot know his opinion of the goings-on with Pietro's wife; nor does his

---

44. For a thorough review of Boccaccio's reworking of the source material in Apuleius, see Sanguineti White, *Boccaccio e Apuleio*. A number of other critics have addressed this tale; see my own discussion in chapter III for a thorough review.

trampling of the lover's fingers appear to be deliberate: "tanto fu la sua ventura, o sciagura che vogliam dire, che questo asino ve gli pose sù piede, laonde egli, grandissimo dolor sentendo, mise un grande strido" (V.10.49). Here the two narratives diverge significantly, for while the miller in Apuleius punishes the lover with rape and flogging, and his wife with divorce, Pietro seizes on an opportunity, motivated by his own homoerotic desire, to effect a reconciliation between the three parties.

In the *ménage à trois* solution described in the story's final paragraph, Pietro gets to realize the very transgressive desire—here sodomitic rather than incestuous—whose fulfillment was denied to Tancredi. Men who respect women's desire rather than suppress it, who are willing to accommodate it, to integrate it into the legal order, earn unique rewards. Unlike the Florentine brothers and Tancredi, Pietro explicitly uncovers the lover in hiding, breaking down the artificial wall that divides the eavesdropping audience from the action and bringing the eavesdropper into the action: "Pietro, non men lieto d'averlo trovato che la sua donna dolente, presolo per mano con seco nel menò nella camera nella quale la donna con la maggior paura del mondo l'aspettava" (V.10.53).

The story thus replicates the order of events in the tale of Tancredi and Ghismonda: the eavesdropper happens upon an ongoing narrative and decides to enter into it. The antenarrative, that of Ercolano and his wife, somewhat obscures the resemblance, but it also facilitates Pietro's own recognition of what is happening when he finds the proverbial fox in the henhouse. Another important commonplace, one that serves to point both stories beyond themselves, is the verbosity of the female characters. Ghismonda; Pietro's wife; and the old woman who assists the wife in finding a lover all deliver lengthy defenses of the sexual freedom of women, whose directness contrasts with the rather more circumspect voices of the *Decameron*'s female narrators. And in presenting male protagonists who stumble upon narrative and enter it—as the ass Lucius had done in Apuleius—the stories allude to the status of the three men who have accompanied the ladies, themselves stumbling upon an ongoing narrative, the ladies' decision making, and, once invited, entering it. However, while the *brigata*'s constitution puts something of a rein on the men, the men in the stories suffer no such limits and are free to act as they please. Tancredi chooses to act against women, while Pietro discovers a way to accommodate his wife.

More broadly, these stories call attention to how the *Decameron* works, to the way in which characters can stand both outside and inside of narrative at the same time. This positioning reflects the status of the ten young people, themselves characters in a story who in turn recount stories, just as

Pietro does when he comes home and tells his wife what happened at Ercolano's. Pietro's story also gives comic closure to the troubling narrative arc that opens with the tale of Tancredi and reaches over both Days IV and V,[45] as well as to the figuration of eavesdropping as elaborated in the book's first half. Like Boccaccio's male critics, the eavesdropper reserves the right not only to witness narrative but to mix into it, crossing the barrier figured by the screen, the wall, the curtain. In crossing over, presumably to safeguard his own interests against the transgressors of his norms, the eavesdropper thus becomes himself a transgressor, violating the space reserved to women that the *Decameron* delimits.

One final story from the first half of the book, that of Nastagio degli Onesti, fully plumbs this dynamic. Indeed, if there were any doubt that Boccaccio wants to explore the issue of men as narrative audience, this tale allays it. The scene that Nastagio witnesses, calqued from Dante, has a transparently metanarrative aspect, replicating the infernal hunt scene in Dante's wood of the suicides. It also establishes a different sort of relationship between audience and narrative than the one first installed with Tancredi. In this case Nastagio does not have a prior history with the characters in the scene he witnesses, and his position as outsider becomes patent when he attempts to intervene to help the victimized girl: "Ma il cavaliere che questo vide gli gridò di lontano: 'Nastagio, non t'impacciare, lascia fare a' cani e a me quello che questa malvagia femina ha meritato'" (V.8.19). Unaware that Nastagio feels "ultimamente compassione della sventurata donna" (V.8.17), the knight comically misinterprets his motives, thinking that the young man intends to join the punitive pursuit. The misunderstanding underscores Nastagio's distance from the narrative—he does not read it properly, seeing the girl as victim rather than as sinner—as does the narrator's remark that the knight calls out to Nastagio "da lontano." The scene evidences none of the proximity or intimacy of the other scenes in which we find witnesses or eavesdroppers, but there is one important common aspect: Nastagio reads the scene self-interestedly. Though denied the right to intervene in the infernal hunt, he trespasses nonetheless, turning something that is expressly none of his business into his business.

In each of the tales over Days IV and V, exposure has implications for one or another female character, and the degree of danger depends uniquely on the power and the anger of the male witness. In the case of Nastagio and the girl who will become his wife, the nature of her fate is ambiguous. On the one hand, she avoids the torments to which the girl in the infernal scene is subject, which is good, while on the other she finds herself marrying a

---

45. See my essay "The Patriarch's Pleasure and the Frametale Crisis: *Decameron* IV–V."

man in whom she had had little interest: "Le quali [opere], quantunque grandissime, belle e laudevoli fossero, non solamente non gli giovavano, anzi pareva che gli nocessero, tanto cruda e dura e salvatica gli si mostrava la giovinetta amata, forse per la sua singular bellezza o per la sua nobiltà sì altiera e disdegnosa divenuta, che né egli né cosa che gli piacesse le piaceva" (V.8.6). One wonders what he sees in her, so fully do their desires not correspond. Undaunted, however, Nastagio presses his case and wins the girl, not by inspiring her affection but by shocking her with fear: "E tanta fu la paura che di questo le nacque, che, acciò che questo a lei non avvenisse, prima tempo non si vide, il quale quella medesima sera prestato le fu, che ella, avendo l'odio in amor tramutato, una sua fida cameriera segretamente a Nastagio mandò, la quale da parte di lei il pregò che gli dovesse piacere d'andare a lei, per ciò che ella era presta di far tutto ciò che fosse piacer di lui" (V.8.41). Such a conversion to reciprocity may reasonably happen in a tale where characters witness a scene from Hell, but it does not ring with verisimilitude. Relying on her survival instinct, the girl finds the correct rhetorical approach to Nastagio, which suffices for him. The narrator, Filomena, is perhaps less willing to swallow all of this, commenting that once the two were married "con lei più tempo [Nastagio] lietamente visse" (V.8.44). Branca's claim that by using a hendecasyllable here Boccaccio "fa svanire il bagliore sinistro della caccia infernale e lo trasfigura in una rosea luce di fiaba" (1304) overlooks a bigger point, that Nastagio has exploited narrative to achieve his purpose.

Filomena's role in making such a point should not in the end surprise us. She is, after all, the perfect echo of Pampinea herself, repeating in the introduction to another important story about the reading experience, VI.1, the very words Pampinea had used in her introduction to I.10.[46] It makes sense that such a statement about men as readers should come from someone other than Pampinea, for she is clearly far too diplomatic in her relations with men to broach the question. The Nastagio story thus stands as a thematically important tale, a meta-*novella*, though it does not appear in a particularly marked place as do the others. Boccaccio locates it as close to the end of Day V as possible, but he must still accommodate Fiammetta's story, with the ninth slot by now regularly going to the ruler, and of course Dioneo's. Along with Boccaccio himself, Filomena asks whether men can be trusted as readers, whether they can be sympathetic enough to women to be fair in their appraisal of women's texts. The answer here is equivocal, since Nastagio does not transfer his sympathy for the woman in the infernal

---

46. Stewart's essay "La novella di Madonna Oretta e le due parti del *Decameron*"is particularly good on the relationship between these two stories and how they unlock some of the *Decameron*'s organizing principles.

hunt to the woman he is hunting in a different sort of infernal way. In the end only Pietro di Vinciolo emerges as one whose sympathy for women's suffering we may analogize to Boccaccio's own.

The theme of eavesdropping will return in the second half of the *Decameron*, most notably in the episode of the Valle delle Donne and in some stories of the tenth day. In general eavesdropping is a man's job, and it alludes to the ubiquity of the threat of punishment, which will be applied against transgressors of norms. In the end safety is contingent not upon secrecy, but rather upon the benevolence or vengefulness of those who are authorized to apply the sanction.

The Widow and the Scholar

I now turn to one final story, significant to the present discussion because it combines revenge narrative with issues of male power over women. The *Decameron*'s longest tale, the tale of the widow and the scholar, stands out also for its overt misogyny; as Millicent Marcus points out, it "sounds a dischordant note" when measured against the book's philogyny ("Misogyny as Misreading" 23).[47] Startling too is Boccaccio's choice of a narrator: Pampinea, who better than anyone has given the lie to misogynist commonplaces through her words and actions.[48] And yet the choice of Pampinea ties this *novella* to the larger issues of revenge that lurk within the pages of the *Decameron*. She herself distinguishes the tale from those that precede it, pointing out that "Noi abbiamo per più novellette dette riso molto delle beffe state fatte, delle quali niuna vendetta esserne stata fatta s'è raccontato" (VIII.7.3). The sentence announces both the length of the story she is about to tell—the others are *novellette*, after all, not just smaller but somehow pettier—as well as a thematic shift away from derisive laughter at what she calls *l'arte* of the practical joke and onto the more serious terri-

---

47. Genre questions trail this story. For Almansi it "almost amounts to a short novel, with a proportional enrichment in the psychology of the characters" (*The Writer as Liar* 92). Picone, on the other hand, calls it "una Erziehungsnovelle, una novella di formazione, o meglio di riformazione, nel corso della quale il protagonista recupera, per non più perderlo, il tesoro conoscitivo che possedeva all'inizio" ("L'arte della beffa" 221). The story has two principal critical traditions, sometimes intertwined: the first posits an autobiographical origin and links the story to the *Corbaccio*; the second examines it in the broader context of medieval misogynistic literature. See Branca's footnote to the story for a bibliography of both (1430), updated by Picone ("L'arte della beffa" 220n.).

48. Durling argues that Boccaccio gives this *novella* to Pampinea as part of a generalized argument about the passage of time: Pampinea, the oldest of the group, tells the *Decameron*'s longest story, whose primary action takes place over two long nights ("A Long Day in the Sun" 269).

tory of the *vendetta*. Pampinea also avers an explicitly practical purpose for her story: "E questo udire non sarà senza utilità di voi, per ciò che meglio di beffare altrui vi guarderete, e farete gran senno" (VIII.7.3). In other words, laughter comes easily in the world of the *beffa*, which is the world of *arte*, but in the world of the *brigata* danger attends the *beffa*, and the ladies would do well to remember that. The message would appear to be a corrective not just to the tales of the eighth day but also to those of the seventh, whose intelligent female protagonists successfully play practical jokes on their easily duped husbands.[49] It thus also serves as a caution that one must judge carefully when choosing the object of a *beffa*, because an alert male may choose to wreak his revenge. As well, in urging the women here to learn how to distinguish themselves from other women, Pampinea echoes a remark she made in introducing her very first story, that the ladies learn how "per voi non si possa quello proverbio intendere che comunemente si dice per tutto, cioè che le femine in ogni cosa sempre pigliano il peggio." She wants them specifically to show themselves to be "per eccellenza di costume separate dall'altre" (I.10.8). Her concern that women not validate misogynist discourse by their actions may inform her choice of the story of the widow, who does just that.

Various elements in the story serve to increase its resonance both with the female members of the *brigata* and with the readers of the *Decameron*. Pampinea locates the story in a Florence of "non sono ancora molti anni passati" (VIII.7.4), and she describes her protagonist, Madonna Elena, as young, of good birth, and widowed. The six other young women can readily identify with these qualities, since they are similarly young, of good birth, and have suffered recent losses if not outright widowhood. In a nod to the extradiegetic audience she evokes the narrative vector to which the *Decameron* had first alluded by having the young scholar, Rinieri, return

---

49. Picone in fact casts the seventh-day *beffe* in a different tradition from this one: the former are *engaños* in the tradition of the *Libro dei sette savi*, while the latter is rather an example of *chastoiement*, "avvertimento" or "istruzione," found in Pietro Alfono's *Disciplina clericalis* ("L'arte della beffa" 223). He points out that the scholar denies that his *beffa* is a *vendetta*, calling it instead "gastigamento, in quanto la vendetta dee trapassare l'offesa, e questo non v'agiugnerà" (VIII.7.87). The argument opens up the difficult problem of authorial intentions. Rinieri may deny that his *beffa* is a vendetta, but given the rhetorical aspects of his denial, one wonders whether he is being sincere with either himself or his audience. Moreover, Pampinea, who reads the tale as a woman, repeatedly labels his actions a *vendetta*, as does Rinieri himself. One would suspect that Elena, who clearly lacks access to the philosophical substrate on which Rinieri presumably draws, would agree. While I do not deny Picone's point, I would simply argue that the tale itself suggests other interpretations of what Rinieri does, and that a full reading of the tale would undertake to accommodate both of them. Cottino-Jones, for example, makes such an effort, and convincingly (*Order from Chaos* 147–53), as does Durling ("A Long Day in the Sun").

to Florence from Paris. This time, however, Rinieri appears to bring back from Paris not a narrative corpus but a certain philosophical training, and above all expectations conditioned by the theory of courtly love.[50] Elena in fact has her maid communicate secretly to Rinieri that "io amo molto più lui che egli non ama me, ma che a me si convien di guardar l'onestà mia, sì che io con l'altre donne possa andare a fronte scoperta: di che egli se così savio è come si dice, mi dee molto più cara avere" (VIII.7.12). Her rationale is consistent with the courtly love code, and her appeal to him, "se così savio è come si dice," attaches his understanding of her position to the knowledge he has presumably acquired in Paris while engaging the same sort of rhetorical sleight-of-hand that Pampinea had used in managing Dioneo. He signals his understanding of her message by passively accepting her explanation and continuing to play the courtly love game, sending her letters and gifts, while she holds him off.[51]

When Elena undertakes to complete her self-appointed mission, to "[prendere] un apolin per lo naso," she does so by clearly relegating Rinieri to the outside, making a gesture of exclusion that he will finally understand to be just that. In doing so she shows herself to be far less adept at managing men than, say, Pampinea herself. On the night she finally invites him to join her, she confines Rinieri to a freezing courtyard—specifically a *corte*, which allusively mocks his courtly love values—all the while pleading, in a claim consistent with her stated desire to protect her *onestà*, that she cannot let him in because her brother has dropped by and will not leave. His marginalization is so complete that, like many of the men of the seventh day, he is within range to eavesdrop on his beloved's lovemaking but never sees or hears anything that would clue him in. By daybreak Rinieri has seen through her rhetoric: "accorgendosi d'esser beffato" (VIII.7.39) he ruminates over how to avenge himself: "seco gran cose e varie volgendo a trovar modo alla vendetta, la quale ora molto più desiderava che prima d'esser con la donna non avea disiato" (VIII.7.40). The extent of his vendetta, which will unfold in the following pages, confirms Pampinea's own lament that Elena "non sapeva ben . . . che cosa è mettere in aia con gli scolari" (VIII.7.13). Even more ominous is the fact that no amount of erst-

---

50. For Marcus "the allusion to Paris . . . has a meta-literary meaning. . . . Thus, by giving Rinieri an education in Paris, and not in Bologna or Padua, Boccaccio immediately brings to mind the French cult of courtly love which was so important a part of his own aesthetic formation" ("Misogyny as Misreading" 28). France assumes metaliterary status elsewhere in the *Decameron* as well, as detailed above.

51. Mazzotta identifies Elena as a strumpet: "a figure who at first disrupts the game of courtly love; who later is an emblem of free play, never allowing herself to be won, offering and denying herself, perverse and gullible, always herself by feigning, and whom the scholar fails to possess but succeeds in punishing" (44).

while attraction to the lady can deter Rinieri from his newly appointed task of avenging himself. In other words, the ladies err if they assume that men will refrain from harming them simply because they see women as objects of desire.

The threat posed by Rinieri redoubles because, "sì come savio," as Pampinea describes him, "sapeva niuna altra cosa le minacce essere che arme del minacciato" (VIII.7.42). In other words, Rinieri understands that to disclose his anger will simply give Elena an opportunity to guard against it, and so he holds his tongue. In this way he turns out to be a much more clever adversary than Elena had expected, and in her naïveté she demonstrates why women should avoid provoking men as she does. By the second half of the story, in fact, Pampinea is calling Elena "la donna poco savia" (VIII.7.48), in direct contrast to the *savio* Rinieri.[52] When the two meet to discuss Elena's new predicament, that her lover has abandoned her and she needs Rinieri's necromantic assistance to win him back, at first she strangely does not even recall her nasty history with him: "non ricordandosi ella che lui quasi alla morte condotto avesse" (VIII.7.51). Now he appears to be the more astute rhetorician, assuring her that he had learned necromancy in Paris, but that while he had forsworn it out of respect for God he would willingly practice it now out of love for her, even at the risk of eternal damnation. He thus positions himself as the patient lover that he had been before, ready to make the necessary sacrifices for his beloved, and given this consistency and her own forgetfulness she has no reason to disbelieve him. He then sets her up for her punishment by explaining that she will have to undertake the necromancy herself, with his training.

The features of Rinieri's revenge are well known, as is their eye-for-an-eye correspondence to what he suffered at her hands: he froze, she cooks; he was confined to a courtyard, stationed below her view, she is locked above him in a tower, a symbol of his power, and so forth.[53] When she begins to suspect Rinieri she continues vainly to condescend to him in her own mind:

---

52. For Picone Rinieri's newly acquired wisdom equates to a return to love of Philosophy, which excludes love for a mortal woman (222). For Marcus, on the other hand, Rinieri is anything but *savio*, as she argues that he misreads just about every text he has ever touched.

53. Almansi (*The Writer as Liar* 95–98) has written helpful pages on how the *contrappasso* functions in this tale. Marcus argues that Rinieri's subscription to "the equal-but-opposite school of punishment" violates the principles of the *contrappasso*: "The latter, which involves a literalization of the metaphors associated with the sins themselves . . . betokens a serious meditation on the nature of sinful acts and renders those lessons accessible to human cognition through the concrete language of poetry. Rinieri's justice, on the other hand, is no deep moral commentary on the nature of Elena's crime, but a superficial, intellectually elegant reversal of his own suffering at her hands" ("Misogyny as Misreading" 36–37). For Durling "the revenge is directed as much at the widow's mind as at her body: it is meant to be a lesson in the nature of time, as well as of life in the body, which is subject to time" ("A Long Day in the Sun" 270).

"Io temo che costui non m'abbia voluta dare una notte chente io diedi a lui; ma se per ciò questo m'ha fatto, mal s'è saputo vendicare, ché questa non è stata lunga per lo terzo che fu la sua . . ." (VIII.7.70). Then her concerns increase, going exactly to the question of her *onestà* that she had invoked as a false reason for not accommodating Rinieri in the first place. In other words, what she fears is the very sort of shameful marginalization to which, in her way, she subjected Rinieri, and to which in its own way the *Decameron* has subjected men. In her subsequent pleas to him she acknowledges that he has "ben di me vendicato," begging him to cease the "vendetta della ingiuria la quale io ti feci" (VIII.7.77–78) and not to steal her honor, which she could not reacquire. She concludes her plea: "Non voler le tue forze contro a una femina essercitare: niuna gloria è a una aquila l'aver vinta una colomba; dunque, per l'amor di Dio e per onor di te, t'incresca di me" (VIII.7.79). Apparently unwilling to admit that he has outsmarted her, she refers instead to his *forze*, describing Rinieri, the man, as the stronger, predatory bird. She thus affirms the physical inequities that govern relations between men and women, even though in this case they apply only indirectly. Rinieri has been wounded in his sense of gender superiority, so he must outmatch her to reestablish order.

At this point the tale takes a crucial turn, devolving into a series of exchanges between Rinieri and Elena. Pampinea takes care to point out that Rinieri has the choice to end Elena's suffering before it advances: "Lo scolare, con fiero animo seco la ricevuta ingiuria rivolgendo e veggendo piagnere e pregare, a un'ora aveva piacere e noia nell'animo: piacere della vendetta la quale più che altra cosa disiderata avea, e noia sentiva movendolo la umanità sua a compassion della misera; ma pur, non potendo la umanità vincere la fierezza dell'appetito, rispose . . ." (VIII.7.80). We all know that "Umana cosa è aver compassione degli afflitti"; in evoking his incipit to the *Decameron* Boccaccio sets a clear distance between himself and the protagonist of this tale. At the same time, however, he uses the tale, and Pampinea, to issue a stern reminder to women that not all men who get hurt in love can turn the other cheek or recover as Boccaccio did. At tale's end Elena, having recovered from her injuries, "da indi innanzi e di beffare e d'amare si guardò saviamente" (VIII.7.148): she appears to have acquired the wisdom she lacked early on. She also renounces love: the experience has changed her so profoundly that she will no longer participate in the dynamic of desire that led to this awful outcome. He, on the other hand, "parendogli avere assai intera vendetta, lieto senza altro dirne se ne passò" (VIII.7.148). He gains a happy outcome, and is apparently capable of moving forward into the future unencumbered by the sorrow and humiliation that her *beffa* provoked in him, because he had trumped her efforts.

Posner's analysis of revenge, and in particular of harm, is helpful for understanding the dynamic at work here:

> The problem [with retaliation] is that if you are "rational man," you will realize that the harm is a "sunk cost"—an irretrievable bygone. No matter how much harm you do to the aggressor, the harm you have suffered will not be undone. In fact whatever the dangers or other burdens you take on in order to retaliate will increase the cost to you of the initial aggression; they will be a secondary cost incurred in a futile effort to avoid the primary cost—which having already been incurred, can no longer be prevented. Knowing that you are "rational man," the aggressor will be all the more likely to attack you. He will realize that you may well decide not to retaliate, and this realization will lower his expected costs of aggression. (27)

If Elena undertook the sort of analysis that Posner describes, she likely concluded that Rinieri, thanks to his Paris education, was a "rational man," and would therefore, thanks to his own subscription to courtly love values, be unlikely to retaliate against her. She may also have felt insulated from danger, thanks to her wealth and position.[54] Of course she errs badly in assuming that Rinieri is a "rational man" just because he has studied in Paris—as Boccaccio has already demonstrated in the tale of Cimone (V.1), education and reason do not go hand in hand. Further proof that Rinieri is not rational comes in his satisfaction at the end of the tale. Despite his ability to undertake the cold, superficially rational calculations that lead to his successful revenge, he does not understand the concept of a sunk cost, and that what he has lost he will never retrieve. So while Boccaccio can describe men as capable of acts of revenge against women, by no means does he applaud their vengefulness.

Indeed, as Posner points out, the story conforms to a typical pattern of revenge literature in another way: the reader's initial great sympathy for the revenger cools as the vengeance happens (39). Two factors contribute here to this response. First, Rinieri's counter-*beffa* disproportionately exceeds its model, Elena's *beffa*. Her suffering lasts much longer than does Rinieri's and involves greater public humiliation, and a philogynist audi-

---

54. Posner posits self-protection as a means to avoid retaliation in the first place, noting however that "self-protection can be extremely costly—indeed, impossible for one who lacks the wealth necessary to surround himself with a wall and most, trusty guards, and so forth" (27).

ence cannot help but be disturbed by her victimization.[55] Moreover, the tale involves collateral damage, specifically in the person of Elena's maid, who suffers a broken thigh while trying to rescue her lady. The question of the maid's liability is not a frivolous one, because it demonstrates the contingencies of power that govern hierarchical systems of authority. One may deem the maid culpable because Rinieri had trusted her in revealing to her his love for Elena, and she had apparently agreed to help him out: "[Rinieri] s'accontò con la fante di lei e il suo amor le scoperse e la pregò che con la sua donna operasse sì, che la grazia di lei potesse avere. La fante promise largamente e alla sua donna il raccontò" (VIII.7.11–12). Rinieri errs, however, in assuming that the cause of love trumps the maid's primary duty to her employer, who concocts a lying response that the maid then reports to Rinieri: "La fante, trovatolo, fece quello che dalla donna sua le fu imposto" (VIII.7.13). Rinieri clearly never recognizes this relation, because at the tale's end, when he hears that the maid has suffered a broken thigh, "parendogli avere assai intera vendetta, lieto senza altro dirne se ne passò" (VIII.7.148). Clearly his desire for revenge extends to the maid, even though we as readers can see her as caught between these two protagonists and therefore not a fair object of cruelty.

Pampinea concludes the tale by warning her audience against undertaking *beffe:* "E per ciò guardatevi, donne, dal beffare, e gli scolari spezialmente" (VIII.7.149). Her tale thus seeks, like revenge itself, to restore order, specifically the threatened order of caution that should govern women's relations with men. As the personification of Prudence, she alerts the ladies not to "trapassare in alcuno atto il segno della ragione" in laughing about *beffe*, not to allow their own *Schadenfreude* at seeing men undone carry them too close to the *superbia* that would lead to their own fall, or that would make them somehow blind to men's capacity for vengefulness, as Elena had been.

The risk for women, the tale suggests, is in fact twofold: the clear danger of male retribution in the form of real physical harm, and the greater danger that women by their actions become fodder for the sort of misogynist literature that this story exemplifies. Rinieri himself makes that threat clear: "E dove tutti [i lacciuoli] mancati mi fossero, non mi fuggiva la penna, con la quale tante e sì fatte cose di te scritte avrei e in sì fatta maniera, che, avendole tu risapute, ché l'avresti, avresti il dì mille volte disiderato di mai

---

55. The ladies come to a remarkably fair judgment of the story: "Gravi e noiosi erano stati i casi d'Elena a ascoltare alle donne, ma per ciò che in parte giustamente avvenutigli gli estimavano, con più moderata compassione gli avean trapassati, quantunque rigido e constante fieramente, anzi crudele, reputassero lo scolare" (VIII.8.2). Their hearts do not go out to Elena quite as much as they otherwise might, especially given their judgment that Rinieri is cruel.

non esser nata. Le forze della penna son troppo maggiori che coloro non estimano che quelle con conoscimento provate non hanno" (VIII.7.99). His statement about the power of the pen anticipates the sort of logorrhea that characterizes the misogynist diatribes of the *Corbaccio*. It reads almost as a retort to Guiscardo's statement to Tancredi that "Amor può troppo più che né voi né io possiamo," but with none of its succinctness. In any event Rinieri proves prescient, for Elena becomes precisely what he threatens, a textual locus, as made explicit in Pampinea's description of her cooked flesh as burned parchment: "tutta la cotta pelle le s'aprisse e ischiantasse, come veggiamo avvenire d'una carta di pecora abrusciata se altri la tira" (VIII.7.114).[56] Indeed, by the end of her ordeal her body is so transformed that it resembles "non corpo umano ma più tosto un cepperello inarsicciato" (VIII.7.140). It is hard to see Boccaccio's choice of the noun *cepperello*, particularly in a story that links France and Tuscany, as anything but deliberate. The reference to Ser Ciappelletto through his given name, Cepparello, may be the final key to disentangling the tale's misogyny. Elena's body transcends itself, becoming thanks to Rinieri a site of misogynist inspiration and discourse.[57] And yet it is also marked, as a *cepperello/Cepparello*, as a site of fictions and lies. The prevarication is not limited to the lies she herself weaves in her false courtship of Rinieri; it extends as well to the lies about her that Rinieri purveys through his hyperbolic *vendetta*. The truth surely lies somewhere in between, just as the truth about women lies somewhere between their self-transcendence as a Stilnovist *donna-angelo* and as a misogynist *donna-diavolo*.

This tale thus demonstrates *in nuce* the connection between a man's sense of being slighted and his desire for revenge, a revenge that extends into literature. As I have suggested above, men repeatedly suffer slights in the pages of the *Decameron*. Boccaccio himself excludes them as readers and then mocks their criticism of what he has written. Pampinea invites men into the club she is forming, but then refuses to cede to them in formulating a plan for governance. Many of the tales' female characters undertake similar tactics of exclusion. At the same time, we see more or less overt forms of retaliation: the male readers of the *Decameron* lambaste Boccaccio

---

56. Migiel has discerned the same subtext in these statements, while taking them in a different direction, as part of a discourse about "how misogyny is fuelled by letters" (58), which she traces in a number of *Decameron* stories.

57. Durling's reminder that the etymon of Cepparello's name, *ceppo*, refers to "trunk, the old stock, the old Adam" ("Boccaccio on Interpretation" 287) further helps illuminate the remark here. Elena becomes, through her association with Adam, an exemplary fallen woman. If Rinieri's transgression consists in "raising himself up to be like God," as Durling argues ("A Long Day in the Sun" 274), then one may read the story in terms of Rinieri's perverse effort to redeem not just a fallen woman but fallen woman in general.

for what he has written, and male characters in the stories undertake to avenge the offenses they have suffered.

One remaining question concerns the extent to which the three male members of the *brigata* will seek to avenge any perceived slights. The principal insult, I would argue, lies in Pampinea's failure to put into action the superiority of men to which her female companions give voice. In other words, the ladies offend the men by not ceding full power to them, by insisting that women can share power within the *brigata* as equal partners. To the extent that revenge, whether subtle or overt, always seeks to restore order, the men will do so by using their rule to reclaim male power and consequence. The inversion of power that informs the *Decameron*'s order of outsiders rankles, and in showing how men attempt to reassert their authority Boccaccio gives us a clear and thorough picture of the order of the world.

CHAPTER II

Lessons in
Legal Theory

I N THE previous chapter I undertook to show how Boccaccio positions men at the outside at all three levels of his text—author's statements, frame tale, and stories—and how those gestures of exclusion inspire three parallel revenge narratives. Central to my argument there was the observation that, by dedicating the book to women, Boccaccio effectively turned his back on his (male) friends. This gesture in turn allowed him to describe a complementary scenario in which his choice fueled a polemic that his critics directed at him and which his characters directed at women. The present chapter constitutes something of a detour from the discourse of friendship, inasmuch as it looks at the rationale for men's claims for centrality in the first place, for an order that installs men as the dominant group while circumscribing female agency as a function of male privilege. Boccaccio locates the argument in natural law theory that, as I discussed earlier, grounds the patriarchal order. While Pampinea, who clearly understands natural law theory, also debunks it through her executive functions, her engagement with it remains rather more empirical than theoretical. The task of presenting a theoretical rebuttal remains under Boccaccio's purview, and he carves out space for this work in several key stories, all of which, not surprisingly, posit the world of men as the space within which to elaborate these issues.

In this chapter I study Boccaccio's engagement with legal theory as it develops in the first and sixth days. To the extent that, as Stewart and others have argued,[1] Day VI "restarts" the *Decameron*, it makes sense that questions of God and law first explored in Day I should reappear as the *Decameron* raises the curtain on its second half. Far from repeating points already made, however, Boccaccio elaborates further on the problem, creating as it were two halves of a whole. Together with the first three stories of Day I, the last two tales of Day VI raise the question of how we can know whether our notion of the legal order is correct. The answers reverberate with implications for a reading of the *Decameron*.

These five stories, which share a common discursive trajectory leading back to God, all locate that discourse in various aspects of the social world of men. Two of the Day I stories, the first and the third, cut across the grain of religion and money, while the second tale looks at religion and friendship, themes that will come to inform the third tale as well. In the sixth day the question of religion arises in the context of male fraternity, realized specifically as the tradition of Florentine eating clubs, while the last tale returns to the question of religion and money on a broader scale. Only that story, which stars Frate Cipolla, makes some allusion to women, in the form of a girlfriend of one of the secondary characters; its primary thrust lies in the tradition of the *beffa*, which later tales will represent as a form of male interaction. It is logical that Boccaccio would establish these overlapping contexts as the space in which to explore male claims to power. The world he describes in these stories is one in which men are in charge and assume it will be forever so. The theoretical discourse that emerges from these settings works a destabilizing effect on the legal predicates of the social world of men.

Lest the reader conclude from these theoretical ruminations that the world harbors promise for women, the *Decameron* takes care to suggest otherwise. This chapter concludes with an analysis of two stories that reassert the contingency of women's safety in the context of a male legal order. In the first tale, that of Madonna Filippa (VI.7), the protagonist avoids execution for adultery only because she successfully leads the way to a revision of the law of Prato by appealing to the interests of men. The second story, which features King Solomon (IX.9), links the state authority of the ruler to the domestic authority of the husband by having the king give oblique advice to the confused Giosefo about how best to handle his marital difficulties. The same story also features a parallel plot line that underscores how men can solidify the bonds of friendship outside of the context of women.

---

1. See Stewart, "La novella di Madonna Oretta"; and Neri, "Il disegno ideale," who argues that "Con la sesta giornata s'inizia un altro ordine di racconti: non più gli errori del caso, ma una scherma d'ingegno" (79).

My argument throughout rests in part on the taxonomy of law that Aquinas offers in the *Summa*. He lists and defines four different laws: eternal, divine, natural, and human. Eternal law, so called because it transcends time, is God's plan for the universe. Aquinas locates in it the source of all law: "Therefore the ruling idea of things which exists in God as the effective sovereign of them all has the nature of law" (*ST* 1a2æ. 91, 1). Natural law is man's perception of that plan: "Since all things are regulated and measured by Eternal Law . . . it is evident that all somehow share in it, in that their tendencies to their own proper acts and ends are from its impression. . . . Now this sharing in the Eternal Law by intelligent creatures is what we call 'natural law'" (*ST* 1a2æ. 91, 2). Human law in turn makes practical application of natural law to human behavior: ". . . from natural law precepts as from common and indemonstrable principles the human reason comes down to making more specific arrangements. Now these particular arrangements human reason arrives at are called 'human laws'" (*ST* 1a2æ. 91, 3). Divine law, on the other hand, consists of codes issued by God, in the forms of the "Old Law" and the "New Law," the Old and New Testaments respectively. While the first three types of law explain how the human legal order comes to reflect God's plan, the final type offers a specific complement to human law necessitated by the limitations of human reason.[2] The somewhat asymmetrical plan that Aquinas sketches posits both an abstract and a concrete relation between the human and the divine: abstract inasmuch as human law reflects the structure of eternal law through natural law, and concrete because in enacting their own laws humans must obey specific legal codes set forth by God.

Aquinas's taxonomy helps us see another of the many ways in which Boccaccio takes his leave from Dante: while the *Decameron* focuses principally on human law, the *Commedia* plumbs divine law.[3] Aquinas understands that these laws work in tandem: ". . . men can make laws on matters on which they are competent to judge. They cannot pronounce on inward motions which are hidden, but only on outward and observable behav-

2. Aquinas offers four reasons for Divine Law: first, to help direct men to their end of eternal happiness; second, to help men correct mistakes in judgment that result in different and contrary laws; third, as a law directed at interior acts, it complements human law, which is directed at exterior acts, the purview of human law; and fourth, to account for evil, which human law cannot do (*ST* 1a2æ. 91, 4).

3. On the question of the relationship between Boccaccio and Dante readers may consult a number of excellent studies, including Franco Fido, "Dante personaggio mancato del libro galeotto," *Il regime della simmetrie imperfette* 111–23; Giorgio Padoan, "Il Boccaccio 'fedele' di Dante," *Il Boccaccio, le Muse, il Parnaso e l'Arno* 229–446; Pier Massimo Forni, "Boccaccio's Answer to Dante"; Luciano Rossi, "Ironia e parodia nel *Decameron*"; and of course Robert Hollander's essays, now collected in *Boccaccio's Dante and the Shaping Force of Satire*.

iour. . . . Since human law is not enough, the complement of divine law is needed to check and guide what goes on within us" (*ST* 1a2æ. 91, 4). Dante's insistence, in *Purgatorio* XVII, on sin as an error of *amore d'animo*, voluntary love, shifts the focus away from sin as an external action, the delict in human law, and toward sin as a disposition of the soul punishable by God, the internal act that divine law addresses.[4] The Dantean theology of sin bears only elliptical interest for the Boccaccio of the *Decameron*, who instead prefers to describe human behavior empirically. More than disinterest or contrariness is afoot here, however. Boccaccio's empiricism reflects, I believe, a philosophical attitude of doubt about the nature of things unseen, about whether that which one can see—the matter of human law—accurately reflects that which lies beyond human sight. Aquinas himself fuels Boccaccio's fire with his remarks about "common and indemonstrable principles," that is, principles that defy logical proof and must instead be accepted as predicates for all that follows. Since natural law furnishes the link between the indemonstrable principles of the eternal and those of the human, it makes sense that the *Decameron* would look carefully at natural law in order to rationalize its empiricism.

Day I: Asking the Question

The question of the ontological status of natural law returns us almost perforce to the tale of Ser Ciappelletto. The notary's false confession and subsequent sanctification signal an interest in otherworldly matters that does not trouble the frame tale. While the ladies first meet in Santa Maria Novella, having gathered there to attend morning mass,[5] they clearly do not see the church as offering permanent refuge in the face of the disaster.[6] The

---

4. Dante presents his *amore d'animo* in contrast to *amore naturale*, innate love; for the distinction, he relies on the Scholastics, for example Aquinas, *ST* 1a2æ. 60, 1. Readers of the *Comedy* will recall that *amore d'animo* "puote errar per malo obietto / o per troppo o per poco di vigore" (*Purg.* XVII.95–96): by directing itself at an evil object, or toward earthly goods with too much desire or too little desire.

5. The three young men, it bears noting, arrive after the mass has ended, and show up only because they are looking for their friends. Santa Maria Novella is a Dominican church, and the Dominicans were among the first orders to make gestures of inclusion toward women. Boccaccio may be making a veiled reference to same in having the women alone attend the mass, or he may wish to suggest that the men have already given up hope of the church protecting them.

6. Potter observes: "The protagonists of the *cornice* meet in the church of Santa Maria Novella and return to it as their dispersal point. This implies a very basic change in role: from that of valid institution, in whose rules and customs one can dwell, to that of threshold, a place of transition through which one passes to a valid experience" (44).

complex itself is nearly as empty as their homes,[7] and they meet there only to decide to leave both church and city behind. While in abandoning Florence they take leave of the urban ruin that Pampinea details in her speech, their departure from Santa Maria Novella may also represent a willful distancing from ecclesiastical institutions, which likewise have crumbled.[8] Matters of religion do have some impact on how the group spends its time: the ladies habitually fast on Saturday, "a reverenza della Vergine madre del Figliuolo di Dio" (II.Conc.6), but otherwise their gestures of devotion appear to be limited.[9] They attend mass only on the second Sunday, and they give Friday over to orations instead of storytelling because Christ died on a Friday, but there is no mention of other religious activities such as daily prayer.[10] Their generalized secularism—Getto rightly observes that "il sentimento del sacro è assente da queste pagine" (28)—dovetails with the behavior of Florentines in the face of plague. Indeed, among the various defenses he describes, Boccaccio does not list surrender to the hands of God. Nobody apparently considers accepting death, and subsequently arriving in Paradise, as a positive solution to the plague. While the ten do leave Florence, they do not appear ready to leave the earth.

---

7. Pampinea points out that they come to the church "d'ascoltare se i frati di qua entro, de' quali il numero è quasi venuto al niente, alle debite ore cantino i loro ufici. . . . E se alle nostre case torniamo, non so se a voi così come a me adiviene: io, di molta famiglia, niuna altra persona in quella se non la mia fante trovando, impaurisco e quasi tutti i capelli adosso mi sento arricciare, e parmi, dovunque io vado o dimoro per quella, l'ombre di colore che sono trapassati vedere . . ." (I.Intro.56, 59).

8. Indeed, the social decay in Florence is so extensive that, as Pampinea notes, even the nuns have abandoned their vows: "e non che le solute persone, ma ancora le racchiuse ne' monisteri, faccendosi a credere che quello a lor si convenga e non si disdica che all'altre, rotte della obedienza le leggi, datesi a' diletti carnali, in tal guisa avvisando scampare, son divenute lascive e dissolute" (I.Intro.62).

9. Boccaccio may be referencing the historic intensification of the cult of the *Mater Dolorosa*, which accompanied the plague. This cult, as Warner points out, "stressed [Mary's] participation in mankind's ordinary, painful lot, and so although the repercussions of the Black Death restored a degree of majesty and terror to the personality of Christ the Judge, the Virgin herself retained the common touch" (216). The *Mater Dolorosa* enjoyed particular currency in Tuscany, and Warner offers the example of Pisa's Camposanto frescoes as evidence. Bynum's observation, that "Mary is not really as important as one might expect in women's spirituality" (269), bears note, however. While Bynum records a strong presence for the *imitatio Mariae* in southern European saints' lives, she also points out that "it is male biographers of women who stress the theme of women's imitation of Mary," whereas women's Marian devotion served principally as a prelude to devotion to Christ. In the present case Boccaccio may be following that male habit or, as I suspect, he may be wishing to configure the women's devotion in a specific manner in anticipation of Panfilo's countermove. For details on the *Mater Dolorosa* cult, which originated in the twelfth century, see Warner 210–16 and Pelikan 125–36.

10. The Saturday fast has a long history, dating to the fourth century, and it served to prepare the body for reception of the Sunday Eucharist. Fasting thus involves one's relationship to Christ and only indirectly to the Virgin, thus making the ladies' practice rather than exception than the rule. For an overview of Christian fasting see Bynum 31–69.

Panfilo's invocation of God at the beginning of I.1 thus suggests the return of the repressed, not merely of a God who has unleashed the plague upon Florence[11] but of a repressed male hierarchy as well: "Convenevole cosa è, carissime donne, che ciascheduna cosa la quale l'uomo fa, dallo ammirabile e santo nome di Colui, il quale di tutte fu facitore, le dea principio" (I.1.2). The sentence hints at condescension, though not without irony, coming as it does from one who had missed mass the day before. Addressed to the ladies, it rhetorically excludes them from its ambit, focusing instead on the works of man, *l'uomo*, and God, *Colui*. Moreover, it fails to acknowledge the ladies' own habit of praying to the Virgin, whose official status as *mediatrix* Panfilo appears to want to supplant with his story of Ciappelletto.[12] In recounting one of God's wonders, Panfilo hopes to renew "la nostra speranza in Lui, sì come in cosa impermutabile" (I.1.2), implying that indeed their hope had been shaken. While he arrived after Pampinea's speech in Santa Maria Novella, which made no mention of God, he appears nevertheless to worry about his and the ladies' current relationship with the divinity. Moreover, he quickly reminds his female audience that without "spezial grazia di Dio" there is no repair from "le cose temporali," which are "in sé e fuor di sé . . . piene di noia, d'angoscia e di fatica" (I.1.3). In other words, the ladies should thank God, not Mary or Pampinea, for their successful flight from Florence.

Panfilo's careful self-positioning with respect to his female audience raises the question of the possible models that inform his speaking. His expertise as a storyteller may well come from experiences with oral narrative outside of an ecclesiastical setting, but his invocation of God suggests other possible models, specifically the *ars praedicandi* that Panfilo would have seen practiced in Santa Maria Novella and elsewhere. As James Murphy details in his compendious account of medieval rhetorical theory and practice, the *ars praedicandi* would have furnished a number of principles to an aspiring preacher such as Panfilo. The importance of preaching was

---

11. Boccaccio describes the plague as "per operazione de' corpi superiori o per le nostre inique opere da giusta ira di Dio a nostra correzione mandata sopra i mortali" (I.Intro.8). It bears note that one of the alternatives, "per operazione de' corpi superiori," excludes any human culpability for the plague, turning it into an act of whimsy that defies all explanation.

12. Pelikan explains the significance of Mary as *mediatrix:* "The title was a means of summarizing what had come to be seen as her twofold function: she was 'the way by which the Savior came' to humanity in the incarnation and the redemption, and she was also the one 'through whom we ascend to him who descended through her to us . . . , through [whom] we have access to the Son . . . ; so that through [her] he who through [her] was given to us might take us up to himself'" (131). Boccaccio's own language, in which he identified Mary as "madre del Figliuolo di Dio," underscores her status as *mediatrix,* though of course she appears to take back seat to a more important *mediator,* Galeotto, the book itself.

indisputable; Alain de Lille, in his *De arte praedicatoria*, had identified it as "the highest of the seven steps to perfect manhood" (Murphy 306).[13] Medieval theorists also uniformly insisted that preaching was about reaching an audience and not about showing off. From early on, as Murphy explains (279), parables became a favored vehicle for preaching to an unlearned audience, following Christ's practice as described in Mark 4:33–34.[14] Alexander of Ashby, in his *De modo praedicandi*, likewise points out the utility of the *exemplum* for preaching to an unlearned audience, and he adds that preachers should conclude by exhorting their audience to "continued devotion to God" (Murphy 313). While Boccaccio would not necessarily have had direct access to these texts, together—and they are rather abundant in number—they describe a fairly consistent practice that he, or Panfilo in his imaginary world, would have witnessed in church. Boccaccio then has Panfilo turn his learning around for use with an audience whom he no doubt identifies as unlearned, his female companions. That he would make use of an exemplum, or *parabola* as Boccaccio would likely call it,[15] squares not only with theory and practice but also with the fact that, as Carlo Delcorno points out, Boccaccio no doubt had at his fingertips any number of collections of *exempla* published specifically for preachers.[16]

In other words, the significance of the Ciappelletto story lies not simply in its recourse to the *exemplum* tradition, as Delcorno demonstrates, but in

---

13. The other steps are "confession, prayer, the act of grace, study of Scripture, more serious study of Scripture should some doubt occur, exposition of Scripture" (Murphy 306).

14. Boccaccio himself acknowledges as much in his commentary on *Inferno* I in the *Esposizioni*, when defending the use of poetic fictions for theological ends: "E ultimamente, acciò che io lasci star gli altri, li quali io potrei inducere incontro a questi nemici del poetico nome, non esso medesimo Gesù Cristo, nostro salvadore e signore, nella evangelica dottrina parlò molte cose in parabole, le quali son conformi in parte allo stile comico?" (I.103; cited in Rossi, "La decima giornata" 272). Boccaccio's awareness of the relationship between theology and poetic fictions, as well as his claim that *parabole* use the comic style, may well have informed his writing of the Ciappelletto story.

15. I am thinking of course of Boccaccio's description of the hundred tales as "novelle, o favole o parabole o istorie che dire le vogliamo" (Proem.13), assiduously parsed by critics (Stewart, Haug, and Marchesi, to name a few). This parsing has created something of a distraction from the oral setting of narration that the *Decameron* records. In the sentence in which the author, with feigned indifference, names his genres, he uses the verb *raccontare* to denote both the written ("intendo di raccontare cento novelle") and the oral ("raccontate in diece giorni da una onesta brigata"). Because the stories themselves come to us in written form, however, one might easily overlook the oral dynamic, and the specifics of how the *Decameron*'s own internal audience might have received these stories in the context of their prior experience with oral narrative.

16. Delcorno, *Exemplum e letteratura* 268, wherein he also advances the fascinating hypothesis that much of the structure of the *Decameron* owes itself to these books. One highly proximate example of a collection of *exempla* is Jacopo Passavanti's *Specchio della vera penitenza*; Passavanti was a preacher active in Santa Maria Novella around 1349.

the fact that the *Decameron* opens by associating storytelling with preaching. The tale itself provides the key to this coupling, inasmuch as Panfilo tells the story of a man whose life becomes the subject of preaching after he dies. The subjugation of storytelling to a preaching function finds its rationale not just in the point, however confused, that Panfilo wants to make about faith, but in the *Decameron*'s more generalized concern with the restorative function of storytelling, here expressed as restoring a faith that the historical moment has taxed.

Continuing on his path, Panfilo next focuses on the process whereby our prayers reach God and find reply. The "spezial grazia di Dio . . . non è da credere che per alcun nostro merito discenda, ma dalla sua propria benignità mossa e da' prieghi di coloro impetrata che, sì come noi siamo, furon mortali, e bene i suoi piaceri mentre furono in vita seguendo ora con Lui eterni son divenuti e beati; alli quali noi medesimi, sì come a procuratori informati per esperienza della nostra fragilità, forse non audaci di porgere i prieghi nostri nel cospetto di tanto giudice, delle cose le quali a noi reputiamo oportune gli porgiamo" (I.1.4). Sanctification comes to those who follow God's *piaceri*, which Branca glosses as *volontà* (1004n6). The whole sentence, which initiates Panfilo's "forensic or legal analogy" (Fido, "Ser Ciappelletto" 66), emphasizes the place of saints as go-betweens for humans and God. While this stress on the role of the go-between should come as no surprise in a book subtitled *Prencipe Galeotto*, it nevertheless rewards careful attention here. Sandwiched between God and humans, saints occupy the same mediating role assigned to natural law, but with a reversal in direction: while natural law renders eternal law comprehensible to humans, saints, who once had a human form and followed God's will *bene*, represent human desires before God: they are in a sense man's best friends. Proof of their holiness lies entirely in their works, that is, in how they lived, as the story of Ciappelletto makes clear, or perhaps more accurately in our perception of how they lived. The question of perception draws the analogy even closer to natural law, which relies entirely on perception for its successful function.

In this context Panfilo's subsequent claim that the system sometimes breaks down assumes capital importance: "E ancor più in Lui, verso noi di pietosa liberalità pieno, discerniamo, che, non potendo l'acume dell'occhio mortale nel segreto della divina mente trapassare in alcun modo, avvien forse tal volta che, da oppinione ingannati, tale dinanzi alla sua maestà facciamo procuratore che da quella con eterno essilio è iscacciato: e nondimeno Esso, al quale niuna cosa è occulta, più alla purità del pregator riguardando che alla sua ignoranza o allo essilio del pregato, così come se quegli fosse nel suo cospetto beato, essaudisce coloro che 'l priegano" (I.1.5). The passage makes three points. First, it rationalizes the eavesdropping that litters the rest of the *Decameron,* including this story, by identifying the archeavesdropper: God himself, who can heed our mislaid prayers only if He is already tuned in to our conversations. After all, prayers to a damned *san* Ciappelletto will never pass from the saint to God: God himself must lend an ear, even though we do not address Him directly.[17] God's sympathetic ear is a necessary element because—this is Panfilo's second point—men have erred repeatedly in electing false saints: Ciappelletto's case is but one example of a phenomenon of some extension.

Third, and with broader ramifications, Panfilo's claim that the human eye cannot penetrate "nel segreto della divina mente" calls into question the theory of transcendental signification that goes all the way back to Augustine. Augustinian semiotics posits two types of signs, the natural and the conventional, offering human language as the most common example of the latter.[18] In *On Christian Doctrine* he identifies the challenge that conventional signs represent: "even the signs which have been given us of God, and which are contained in the Holy Scriptures, were made known to us through men—those, namely, who wrote the Scriptures" (II.2). While Augustine is quick to affirm the validity of figural allegory, his caveat about the human means for communicating knowledge of the transcendental leads logically to the sort of affirmation Panfilo offers about the impossibility of knowing God's thoughts. Boccaccio has Panfilo use the key verb *trapassare,* already inflected by Pampinea to suggest trespass, and which here may carry some of that weight while also suggesting an impossible metaphysical leap.[19] At the same time Panfilo attempts something of a rescue, claiming that an omniscient God ("al quale niuna cosa è occulta") can register the purity of our faith and answer our requests accordingly. By no means limited to the present example, Panfilo's claim about the limits of human knowledge of the divine has implications as well for the status

---

17. The gravity of the error of praying to the damned becomes clearer when one considers that the archetype of the damned, he who "con eterno essilio è iscacciato," is none other than Satan himself.

18. Natural signs, to which Augustine devotes little attention, work as conventional signs do in signifying something else, but they are not arbitrary; Augustine offers the example of smoke, which indicates fire.

19. Completing the semantic grid associated with *trapassare* is Pampinea's other use of the term in her Santa Maria Novella remarks, with specific reference to death: "E se alle nostre case torniamo, non so se a voi così come a me adiviene: io, di molta famiglia, niuna altra persona in quella se non la mia fante trovando, impaurisco e quasi tutti i capelli adosso mi sento arricciare, e parmi, dovunque io vado e dimoro per quella, l'ombre di coloro che sono trapassati vedere . . ." (I.Intro.59); Panfilo uses the word in the same sense when referring to Ciappelletto's death (I.1.83). The verb *trapassare* clearly has metaphysical nuances, the passing from one state to another; whether it be intellectual or physical.

of natural law, likewise the result of a process involving human, that is, imperfect, discernment.

As an antidote to the *occulto* Panfilo offers this story, which he claims will make everything plain to see, beginning with God's generosity in answering our misdirected prayers: "Il che manifestamente potrà apparire nella novella la quale di raccontare intendo: manifestamente, dico, non il giudicio di Dio ma quel degli uomini seguitando" (I.1.6). The emphasis on the adverb *manifestamente* recalls Panfilo's earlier statement that "Manifesta cosa è" that we require God's special assistance to confront life's tribulations: he wants to discuss things we can know for sure, once we have drawn a curtain around that which we cannot know. Of course nothing is clear here, as Millicent Marcus has argued, calling his use of the adverb "hopelessly ambiguous": "Panfilo completely undercuts his discourse by suggesting that all he has said represents the limited point of view of mankind which he has previously characterized as so precarious and flawed that the reader will have difficulty assigning it any authority at all" (*An Allegory of Form* 14). Still, Panfilo's remarks here offer a clue as to the story's true intentions. Rather than demonstrate God's generosity, the tale instead gives an example of the risks attendant to the use of conventional signs for transcendental signification. In applying the theory of the conventional sign to sainthood, Panfilo takes Augustine's caution about how we know what we know about God a step further, reducing our epistemology to a human artifact.

Conventional signs, as Augustine defines them, "are those which living beings mutually exchange for the purpose of showing, as well as they can, the feelings of their minds, or their perceptions, or their thoughts. Nor is there any reason for giving a sign except the desire of drawing forth and conveying into another's mind what the giver of the sign has in his own mind" (II.2). They are, in other words, exactly what they sound like: arbitrary agreements among people that further understanding. The tale capitalizes on the notion of the conventional sign not as a linguistic construct, Augustine's preferred example, but rather in its behavioral and later corporeal manifestations. In his sermon to the Burgundians, Ciappelletto's confessor reviews the false saint's life, offering it explicitly as an example of saintliness: "cominciò e della sua vita, de' suoi digiuni, della sua virginità, della sua simplicità e innocenzia e santità maravigliose cose a predicare" (I.1.85). The specifics of Ciappelletto's recounted behaviors work to convince the friar's audience of his subject's sainthood because they conventionally signal sainthood. Ciappelletto was himself likely aware of their signification, which is why he used them in confession. These behavioral signs quickly lead to the intended conclusion, and consequently Ciappelletto's body and clothing acquire transcendental signification: "poi che fornito fu l'uficio, con la maggior calca del mondo da tutti fu andato a basciargli i piedi e le mani, e tutti i panni gli furono indosso stracciati, tenendosi beato chi pure un poco di quegli potesse avere" (I.1.86). The crowd invests in Ciappelletto's corpse a new transcendental signification: it no longer signifies death, but rather resurrection.

Of course, as Panfilo hastens to point out, the problem with this process, by which the ordinary rises to the level of the extraordinary, is that it is based on a lie, a lie whose origin is itself that same set of conventional signs, language, by which knowledge of the transcendental first came to men. The narrator takes care to qualify what has happened:

> Così adunque visse e morì ser Cepparello da Prato e santo divenne come avete udito. Il quale negar non voglio esser possibile lui esser beato nella presenza di Dio, per ciò che, come che la sua vita fosse scellerata e malvagia, egli poté in su lo stremo aver sì fatta contrizione, che per avventura Idio ebbe misericordia di lui e nel suo regno il ricevette: ma per ciò che questo n'è occulto, secondo quello che ne può apparire ragiono, e dico costui più tosto dovere essere nelle mani del diavolo in perdizione che in Paradiso. E se così è, grandissima si può la benignità di Dio cognoscere verso noi, la quale non al nostro errore ma alla purità della fé riguardando, così faccendo noi nostro mezzano un suo nemico, amico credendolo, ci essaudisce, come se a uno veramente santo per mezzano della sua grazia ricorressimo. (I.1.89–90)

The paragraph relies on various forms of the verb *potere: possibile, poté, può* (twice). Even his affirmation that Ciappelletto lies in the hands of the devil carries an aura of doubt, with Panfilo's *dovere essere* preceded by *dico,* asserting not objective knowledge of Ciappelletto's situation but rather Panfilo's subjective judgment, which supplants the unknowable judgment of God. In substituting for the unknowable *occulto* that which can *apparire* before us, he decertifies the transcendental signification of the pseudo-saint's life and body in favor of an empirical analysis whose limits he must admit: no one knows the true disposition of Ciappelletto's soul at the moment of his death.

Panfilo's apparent inconsistencies thus suggest not so much failure on his part as a frank acknowledgment that Christian theology cannot lead where it claims to. His well-intentioned attempt at preaching falls short perhaps because he has not received the type of indoctrination that would make him a convincing messenger, or perhaps because he has heard the arguments but seen their flaws. His continued caution provokes ever more complications. While seeking to reaffirm his initial point about God's benevolence, Panfilo slips into subjectivity with a conditional clause: "E se così è." The predicate is precisely that Ciappelletto has landed in hell, an event no one can certify any more than one can know if he is in heaven. If on the other hand Ciappelletto did somehow escape damnation at the eleventh hour, then the story's point shifts. No longer a tale about God's benevolence toward us, it demonstrates instead God's benevolence toward Ciappelletto, recalling Dante's Buonconte da Montefeltro, whose dying invocation of the Virgin saved him from the devil's grasp (*Purg.* V.85–129). Moreover, if Ciappelletto were saved Panfilo's argument that God listens to our messages even when we turn to erroneous intercessors collapses, because Saint Ciappelletto truly could advocate for us before God, so we still have no way of knowing whether God listens when we pray to false saints. The tale offers no categorical proof that God is always listening, so we have no way of knowing whether God is the archeavesdropper that Panfilo claims him to be. The only sure eavesdroppers are those circling among us.

Panfilo concludes also by insisting that the figure of the *mezzano* is an artifact. He twice uses the word in this paragraph, both times describing the go-between as a role assigned by men and not by God. If the *mezzano*, whose role parallels that of natural law as go-between between eternal and human law, is but a construct, the problems magnify. For in refusing to acknowledge that God might have created the *mezzano*, no matter its form, Panfilo reduces all theology to an artifact, as one can never be certain that the human order of the world accurately reflects the divine order. To a Dante who asserts that we can know what we cannot see, Boccaccio replies through Panfilo that we cannot in fact know what we cannot see: those indemonstrable principles are precisely that, indemonstrable. True, Panfilo carefully avoids denying anything of what we believe about God's order; rather, he simply denies that we can be sure about it. His final plea, that his companions keep the faith, "sicurissimi d'essere uditi" (I.1.91), rings hollow against an *exemplum* that offers no such proof, though in a sense what he asks of his listeners, that they pursue their faith against all evidence, is the more compelling message. Augustine sums up the challenge in a sentence that weaves together two passages from Corinthians: "although the light may begin to appear clearer, and not only more tolerable, but even more delightful, still it is only through a glass darkly that we are said to see, because *we walk by faith, not by sight,* while we continue to wander as strangers in this world, even though our conversation be in heaven" (II.7; italics mine).

For all of its denials, the tale does offer one final certainty about how we construct belief systems. As an alternative to the blocked verticality of Augustinian semiotics, this story offers a horizontal circularity. Delcorno has called attention to the "voci di testimoni" (*Exemplum e letteratura* 266) that pop up in various stories of the *Decameron:* Marino Bolgaro, Coppo di Borghese Domenichi, and others, some unnamed. One voice missing from his list is that of Ciappelletto's confessor, whose dissemination of the sinner's story may arguably be taken, within Boccaccio's larger fiction, as a distant source of Panfilo's own narrative. True, Panfilo knows more about Ciappelletto than the preaching friar does, so his account appears to have a number of sources, including—directly or indirectly—the Florentine brothers. The tale's emphasis on sourcing—the explicit source that Ciappelletto makes of himself, and the implicit ones that inform Panfilo's discourse, locates religious knowledge firmly in the sublunar sphere, and in particular in the rhetoric of preaching, which emphasizes the accommodation of audience. As the later story of Frate Cipolla demonstrates, the preacher enjoys a certain authority by virtue of his office, but he maintains that authority only by addressing his audience in a convincing and comprehensible manner. Authority and persuasion thus become the *Decameron*'s true articles of faith. The fact that their means is nothing other than the conventions of human language exposes in turn the constructedness of theology. In the end, it is persuasion effected through human language that gives us the conviction of the existence of God and His attendant order: our "knowledge" of the *occulto* remains limited to a faith supported by social life.

Questions of faith and their relation to the social order return explicitly in stories 2 and 3, through in different guises.[20] In introducing her story, which follows hard upon Panfilo's, Neifile makes overt reference to Panfilo's argument: "Mostrato n'ha Panfilo nel suo novellare la benignità di Dio non guardare a' nostri errori quando da cosa che per noi veder non si possa procedano: e io nel mio intendo di dimostrare quanto questa medesima benignità, sostenendo pazientemente i difetti di coloro li quali d'essa ne deono dare e con l'opere e con le parole vera testimonianza, il contrario operando, di sé argomento d'infallibile verità ne dimostri, acciò che quello che noi crediamo con più fermezza d'animo seguitiamo" (I.2.3). Neifile, whose name bears an etymological relation to Panfilo's, revisits a problem he had already posed, that of the form in which God's benevolence appears to us. Whereas for Panfilo it transpired in God's "non al nostro errore ma alla purità della fé riguardando" (I.1.90), for Neifile it appears as God's "sostenendo pazientemente i difetti di coloro li quali d'essa ne deono dare e con l'opere e con le parole vera testimonianza, il contrario operando." Pan-

---

20. Stewart calls the first three tales "a triptych on the paramount value of our faith in God" ("The Three Rings" 98); I am not sure whether they so much treat faith in God specifically as faith in general.

filo thus offers a more panoramic vision of where the sign appears, while for Neifile it comes in the more specific terms of God's patience with clerics. The two suggestions share God's acceptance of human error, either the error of our misdirected prayers or that of clerical defects.

The story also reinforces Panfilo's earlier point about faith by playing on the theme of things unseen and things seen, and in particular on the relationship between appearance and truth. The sinner Ciappelletto appeared to be saintly; so too does the shoddy behavior of the pope and members of the Roman curia ironically prove the power of Christianity: "E per quello che io estimi, con ogni sollecitudine e con ogni ingegno e con ogni arte mi pare che il vostro pastore e per consequente tutti gli altri si procaccino di riducere a nulla e di cacciare del mondo la cristiana religione, là dove essi fondamento e sostegno esser dovrebber di quella. E per ciò che io veggio non quello avvenire che essi procacciano, ma continuamente la vostra religione aumentarsi e più lucida e più chiara divenire, meritamente mi par discerner lo Spirito santo esser d'essa, sì come di vera e di santa più che alcuna altra, fondamento e sostegno" (I.2.25–26). As Cottino-Jones has pointed out ("Abraham the Jew" 86), these sentences ring with subjective observations: "per quello che io estimi," "per ciò che io veggio," "mi pare," "mi par discerner." Abraam avers no rational basis for the growth of Christian faith; if anything that growth is wholly irrational, because it flies in the face of curial dissoluteness. When he says that "mi par discerner lo Spirito santo esser di essa," he has found no proof of the existence of the Holy Spirit; rather, he has chosen to interpret human actions—the spread of Christianity—as proof of the Holy Spirit. His perception of the Holy Spirit in behaviors that are wholly antithetical to it suggests yet again how the human pursuit of articles of faith involves a subjective reading of empirical reality. Moreover, his observation that Christianity is becoming ever more *lucida* and *chiara* suggests that by its superficial visual brilliance it provides insight by means of eyesight, an operation not unlike natural law itself. As Aquinas puts it, "the light of natural reason by which we discern what is good and what evil, is nothing but the impression of divine light on us" (*ST* 1a2æ. 91, 2).

Abraam thus interprets what he sees as a sign of the power of faith: Christianity endures, indeed grows, in spite of itself. He surprises even his friend Giannotto, "il quale aspettava dirittamente contraria conclusione a questa" (I.2.28), and the two proceed, not surprisingly given the ladies' collective devotion to the Virgin, to Notre Dame for Abraam's baptism. The tale ends somewhat ambiguously, however, as Neifile recounts that Abraam, now Giovanni, "fu poi buono e valente uomo e di santa vita." In the light of what he had seen in Rome one is left to wonder exactly what Giovanni understands a *santa vita* to be, though we also know that Giannotto "il fece compiutamente ammaestrare nella nostra fede" (I.2.29). Studying the cathechism, Giovanni would perforce learn that faith itself is an act of free will, precisely this tale's point.[21] Abraam, named for the first Jew, chooses to believe in Christ, taking the name Giovanni after Giannotto, he who pointed the way to Christ. The conversion offers no solid reassurance, however, because as Giannotto well knows, Abraam could have returned from Rome with the opposite conclusion about Christianity.

The theme of caution implied in these two stories finds explicit reference in the third tale, told by Filomena: "La novella da Neifile detta mi ritorna a memoria il dubbioso caso già avvenuto a un giudeo. Per ciò che già e di Dio e della verità della nostra fede è assai bene stato detto, il discendere oggimai agli avvenimenti e agli atti degli uomini non si dovrà disdire: a narrarvi quella verrò, la quale udita, forse più caute diverrete nelle risposte alle quistioni che fatte vi fossero" (I.3.3). Filomena aligns her story as the logical heir to the first two while creating a sort of revisionist trinity. As the first story concerns man's relationship with the Father, "Dio," and the second the Holy Spirit, explicitly named, one might expect the Son somehow to appear in the third story. It does of course in Melchisedech's narrative, which Filomena encloses in her story about Saladin, so that the discourse about offspring becomes both textually and thematically secondary to the more urgent question of female self-protection. Hers is in fact the first tale of the *Decameron* explicitly advertised as containing the sort of advice for women that Boccaccio had anticipated in the Proem. While Panfilo had set an initial course that focused on relations between men, and Neifile appeared to be willing to go along, "sì come colei che non meno era di cortesi costumi che di bellezze ornata" (I.2.2), Filomena subtly redirects the conversation, offering that the *avvenimenti* and *atti* of men can serve as useful models for women's behavior.

In her introduction Filomena claims—and somewhat disingenuously, since the question of the "verità della nostra fede" returns unannounced in this story—to abandon questions of religion and explore instead the world of men. While she describes this shift in terms of descent, *il discendere*, she complements that move with the story's narrative of ascent: "sì come la sciocchezza spesse volte trae altrui di felice stato e mette in grandissima miseria, così il senno di grandissimi pericoli trae il savio e ponlo in grande e in sicuro riposo" (I.3.4). In other words, the narratives of human lives often

---

21. Aquinas is explicit on this point: "The object of faith permits three perspectives; the reason is that, since, as shown, belief engages mind as it is moved to assent by will, the object of faith can be viewed in its reference to mind and in its reference to will as prompting the mind" (*ST* 2a2æ. 2, 2).

take shape as comedy or tragedy, with each outcome linked to a degree of human ability, a sort of Machiavellian *virtù ante litteram*. Filomena's words in fact recall definitions of the comic and the tragic as can be found, for example, in Dante's Cangrande letter, which makes the same distinction though strictly in the context of narrative, not human experience.[22] She thus invites her audience to read human events through the prism of literary theory: literature gives human experience an identifiable shape. The tale she then tells exemplifies the relationship between the tragic and the comic, inasmuch as Melchisedech manages to avoid a potential tragedy and find a comic ending to his own story.

While claiming that it is time to look at men and not at God, Filomena nevertheless makes recourse to the technical language that anticipates the serious engagement with theology that the story will come to exhibit. Her companions need to become more *caute* specifically when answering the *quistioni* put to them. The Italian word *questione* translates the Latin *quaestio*, found in such works as Aquinas's *Summa* and Dante's *Questio de aqua et terra*. The word also appears twice in Melchisedech's answer to Saladin: the Jew, himself a master of diplomatic equivocation, becomes a model for the ladies to emulate. The tale's ecumenism extends so far that the Jew teaches a lesson not only to the Muslim Saladin but to the Christian ladies in Filomena's audience.

The tale addresses the challenge of caution in a way that mimics the structure of the *Decameron* itself, with a story within the story. Melchisedech escapes the Muslim Saladin's trap by telling the hoary tale of the three rings.[23] The tale actually begins with just one ring, an object that, "bellissimo e prezioso" (I.3.14), bears some resemblance to the *lucida* and *chiara* Christian religion of the previous story. When the father in Melchisedech's tale commissions two perfect replicas of the original ring, one suddenly becomes three: "li quali [due] sì furono simiglianti al primiero, che esso medesimo che fatti gli aveva fare appena conosceva qual si fosse il vero" (I.3.14). The multiplication of the rings becomes a metaphor for Melchisedech's own equivocation: "E così vi dico," he explains, "signor mio, delle tre leggi alli tre popoli date da Dio padre, delle quali la quistion proponeste:

---

22. "Ed est comedia genus quoddam poetice narrationis ab omnibus aliis differens. Differt ergo a tragedia in material per hoc, quod tragedia in principio est admirabilis et quieta, in fine seu exitu est fetida et horribilis. . . . Comedia vero inchoat asperitate mali cuius rei, sed eius materia prospere terminatur . . ." (§10: Comedy is therefore a genre of poetic narration that differs from all the others. It differs in fact from tragedy, in its subject matter, because tragedy is at the beginning wondrous and peaceful, but at the end or conclusion fetid and horrible. . . . Comedy, instead, begins with a difficult situation, but its subject matter has a happy ending . . . [translation mine]).

23. On the literary antecedents for this tale see Stewart, "The Three Rings" 89–95.

ciascun la sua eredità, la sua vera legge e i suoi comandamenti dirittamente si crede avere e fare, ma chi se l'abbia, come degli anelli, ancora ne pende la quistione" (I.3.16). Melchisedech says nothing to contradict Filomena's conviction about the "verità della nostra legge"; rather, he suggests that more than one truth may be afoot.

The full import of Melchisedech's response to Saladin emerges against the backdrop of his name. The character's namesake, the Old Testament Melchisedek, was the king of Salem, a high priest who in Genesis 14 blessed Abram when he returned from recovering goods and people taken from Sodom and Gomorrah.[24] The Letter to the Hebrews in the New Testament offers a commentary on this Melchisedek, identifying him as "king of righteousness" on the basis of his name, and it also notes his lack of genealogy, analogizing him in this way to Christ himself: "he has no father, mother or ancestry, and his life has no beginning or ending; he is like the Son of God" (7.2–3). This aspect of lack of genealogy, and the concomitant association of Melchisedek with Christ, has important implications for Filomena's story, as Melchisedech's own story, and a comparison with its sources, will demonstrate.

In Boccaccio's version, the man who bears the name of an Old Testament king without a genealogy shows a strong interest in questions concerning generations. This is readily apparent in the story itself, which features a father who must decide how to distribute his wealth among three sons. Beyond that superficial evidence, however, lies a more curious discourse, which appears to be of Boccaccio's invention. Here is the *incipit* of the Jew's story from the *Novellino*, number 73 in Segre's edition: "Messere, egli fu un padre ch'avea tre figliuoli, e avea un suo anello con una pietra preziosa la migliore del mondo" (*Prosatori del Duecento* 125). Boccaccio's amplifies it:

> Se io non erro, io mi ricordo aver molte volte udito dire che un grande uomo e ricco fu già, il quale, intra l'altre gioie più care che nel suo Tesoro avesse, era uno anello bellissimo e prezioso; al quale per lo suo valore e per la sua bellezza volendo fare onore e in perpetuo lasciarlo ne' suoi discendenti, ordinò che colui de' suoi figliuoli appo il quale, sì come lasciatogli da lui, fosse questo anello trovato, che colui s'intendesse essere il suo erede e dovesse da tutti gli altri esser come maggiore onorato e riverito. E colui al

---

24. The name of the Hebrew patriarch has not yet been changed: God will rename him Abraham only in Genesis 17. The fact that he is Abram at this point lends further credence, I believe, to the association of this story with the Old Testament Melchisedek story, inasmuch as the name Abram is the same as that of the protagonist of Neifile's story, who will likewise undergo renaming.

quale da costui fu lasciato tenne simigliante ordine ne' suoi discendenti, e
così fece come fatto avea il suo predecessore; e in brieve andò questo anello
di mano in mano a molto successori, e ultimamente pervenne alle mani a
uno il quale aveva tre figliuoli belli e virtuosi e molto al padre loro obedienti,
per la qual cosa tutti e tre parimente gli amava. (I.3.11–12)

Most of this information is gratuitous, as the antecedents to Boccaccio's
version suggest: the tale stands on its own without the generational background Melchisedech offers.[25] These additions must therefore serve some
purpose that transcends the tale itself, as indeed they do. First, by saying "io
mi ricordo aver molte volte udito dire" Melchisedech establishes for Boccaccio that the tale itself has a genealogy: like the ring, it has passed from
person to person. Not only that, but the ring too comes to embody genealogy, having passed from father to son across generations, though it does
not have an origin. The first father named had it in his treasury, though
Melchisedech is unclear about whether he was its first owner. Beyond that,
however, this introduction allows Melchisedech's allegoresis to open the
door to a far more disturbing suggestion. By analogizing the father in the
tale to God the Father ("E così vi dico, signor mio, delle tre leggi alli tre
popoli date da Dio padre," I.3.16), he suggests that God the Father is also
a son, the latest in a line of Gods, each of whom, until the present time,
had preferred one (presumably pre-Hebraic) religion over another.[26] In
other words, the man whose namesake is associated with the immortality
of Christ turns around and implies not only that God is mortal but that
religions are too. They pass from generation to generation, changing along
the way, while nevertheless sharing an incorruptible, unchangeable quality
embodied in the original ring. That quality may be inferred from the language used by both Saladin and Melchisedech to talk about religion: *legge*,
understood not as the specific rules that govern human behavior but rather
as an abstract organizing principle that each religion embodies.

It is difficult in the end to argue with Melchisedech, however heretical
his claims may superficially appear to be. Other gods, and other religions,

---

25. These details also do not appear in the versions of the tale found in Gaston Paris's
study. This story is subject to considerable censorious attention in the sixteenth century,
though none of the manipulations appears to recognize anything scandalous per se about this
incipit. The details remain in the pre–Counter Reformation 1527 *Decameron* and as well in the
Deputati edition of 1573, though the latter manipulates the tale's conclusion in such a way as
to make it less even-handed. Salviati's "corrected" edition of 1582 suppresses Melchisedech's
story entirely. Finally, Groto's 1588 *riforma* of the *Decameron* includes these details but in the
context of an entirely new story. See Chiecchi and Troisio 121–31 for side-by-side versions.

26. Boccaccio will in fact make clear in his later *Genealogie deorum gentilium* that the gods
have family trees.

did in fact predate Judaism, Christianity, and Islam, and others may indeed follow, though all will aim as a *legge* to organize humanity by establishing some sort of connection between the human and the divine. Nevertheless, by implying that the gods are mortal, by tying them to temporality, Melchisedech effectively liquidates religion of any claim to transcendence. Religion becomes an artifact.

Filomena's suggestion that the time has come for the group to turn "agli avvenimenti e agli atti degli uomini" thus finds its full realization in a tidily enclosed discourse according to which the "verità della nostra fede" lies in a misunderstanding about what is transcendent and what is transitory. The *avvenimenti* and *atti* of men involve not just the joust between Saladin and Melchisedech but also the ways in which men put religion to their own use. That element emerges in the duel between the *novella*'s two named principals, one of whom, the Muslim, attempts to trip up the other, the Jew, on a religious question in order to extract money from him. Melchisedech's agility in avoiding the trap laid for him by Saladin is the aspect of the tale that Boccaccio's rubric features: "Melchisedech giudeo con una novella di tre anella cessa un gran pericolo dal Saladino apparecchiatogli" (I.3.1). The rubric also ignores the story's denouement, which rewrites the dead-end outcome of its earlier versions. Beyond that, however, the tale makes a point about how men can become friends, namely by being honest with one another about their motives. Once Saladin tells Melchisedech the truth, the latter seizes the opportunity to demonstrate that he transcends his reputation as *avaro* and to emulate the generosity for which his namesake is known. The tale thus opens the door to a discourse about male friendship that will find its apotheosis in another tale about Saladin, the ninth story of the tenth day, like this one featuring the Saracen leader as finding friendship with a man of another religion, the Christian Torello. That Saladin succeeds in establishing real friendships, grounded in a concern for the other's well-being, with two men of other faiths again suggests that, like the rings themselves, what matters are not so much the differences as the commonalities.

Despite Filomena's reconfiguration of the religious discourse of the previous two tales, the story she tells shares with both a significant interest in questions of evidence. All three tales have forensic elements: Ciappelletto as proof, curial misbehavior as proof, the rings as proof. Each in its own way asserts that we base our conclusions on matters of transcendence on the evidence of the material world. Each may also be construed as a parodic exposure of the bad faith of Dante's *Commedia*. Dante lays out his poem's central rhetorical claim in its second and third tercets, which insist on the relationship between seeing and telling: "ma per trattar del ben ch'io vi trovai, / dirò dell'altre cose ch'i' v'ho scorte" (*Inf.* I.8–9). He declares his poem to be one of witness; by reporting on what he saw he hopes to renew his readers' faith, which he will define in *Paradiso* XXIV as "sustanza di cose sperate / ed argomento delle non parventi" (1. 64–65).[27] By substituting the discourse of things seen for faith in things unseen, the poem appears to question the sustainability of blind faith, or whether the earthly evidence of transcendence—miracles and the like—can suffice. Faith comes to rest on believing not in God but in Dante, who emerges from this system as yet another Galeotto, a pander of faith. Readers who are not disposed to believe him either come away empty or return to their place of departure, left to believe simply because they choose to.

Boccaccio answers Dante's bad faith with a faith of his own, one that, precisely because it destabilizes the forensic authority of material evidence, is both stronger and more fragile than Dante's.[28] Relocating everything that Dante exposed to human perception back behind the screen of mystery, Boccaccio compels his protagonists, and Panfilo as well, to choose to believe: faith becomes an act of will unmoored from empirical testing. While error abounds—the friar, Abraam, and the sons in Melchisedech's parable all reach conclusions that fly in the face of the evidence—faith becomes stronger, because it loses its contingency on human discourse or behavior or the material artifact. Thus, while both the *Commedia* and the *Decameron* are cast against a moment of crisis—for Dante, the spiritual decline of his era and his personal fall into error, and for Boccaccio, the plague—the argument in response to the crisis differs. While Dante tries to dazzle his audience into faith, Boccaccio, by systematically undermining the authority of evidence in the propagation of the faith, requires his readers to hitch their faith to a far more tenuous hook.

Day VI: All Is Rhetoric

If the trinity of tales in Day I concluded with the status of Christianity left hanging, the Day VI tales concerning religion, the ninth and tenth stories of the day, serve to raise more urgent doubts, this time with specific com-

---

27. Dante takes the definition from Hebrews 11.1: "Only faith can guarantee the blessings that we hope for, or prove the existence of the realities that at present remain unseen."

28. Hollander makes a similar point in the context of I.1, specifically Boccaccio's use of the word *cappello*, or garland, which appears as a *hapax* in *Purg.* XXV.9: "[Dante]'s insistence on the veracity of his *Commedia* is thus to be considered as being nonetheless proximate to Cepparello's totally false confessional autobiography, one which similarly asks to be taken as gospel truth" (31).

mentaries on the relationship between religion and language. The story of Guido Cavalcanti occupies the important ninth slot of the day. Numerologically and narratologically the ninth story, over eight of the ten days, is associated with perfection.[29] Nine is for Dante the sign of "un miracolo, la cui radice, cioè del miracolo, è solamente la mirabile Trinitade" (*Vita nuova* XXIX.3). Thus the trinity of theological tales of Day I, multiplied by itself, points to the ninth tale of the restarted book, which hinges on a central unanswered question about the existence of God. In narratological terms, that story is perfect because its teller is the day's monarch, in this case Elissa, and thus one may infer that it most closely reflects what the monarch had in mind when issuing the day's theme.[30]

Like V.8 before it, this tale returns us to Dantean terrain. Guido Cavalcanti, exiled from the *Commedia*, here assumes a starring role in a context that cannot help but recall his mention during the *viator* Dante's encounter with Cavalcante de' Cavalcanti, Guido's father.[31] The father famously arises from a burning tomb in a graveyard populated by heretics. Dante calls the place the Città di Dite, and in its general configuration, surrounded by walls which Dante penetrates thanks only to the intervention of a celestial messenger, it recalls a medieval Italian city, thereby associating urban life with heretical thinking. Boccaccio suggests an analogy between the City of Dis and Guido Cavalcanti's Florence. He locates his own narrative in a specifically delineated downtown area ranging between the Orsanmichele, Corso degli Adimari, the Baptistry, and Santa Reparata, at the center of which, just as in the City of Dis, lies a graveyard. As if to affirm the analogy, Elissa, the narrator, makes explicit mention of Guido's presumed Epicureanism, which may have led to his estrangement from Dante.[32] The story also relies

29. Getto calls it "il vertice della giornata sesta, non foss'altro che per la presenza in essa, straordinariamente ricca di determinazioni, del motivo ideale che raccoglie quella giornata in evidente ed interiore unità" (156).

30. Typical of Boccaccio's gamesmanship, only eight stories appear in this privileged position. Exceptional are Day I, in which Pampinea speaks last, and Day VII, in which Dioneo, the king, occupies his normal position, tenth. In that day the ninth story goes significantly to Panfilo, another man; I shall have more to say on this later.

31. Michelangelo Picone sees Cavalcanti as Dante's substitute: "Non volendo introdurre nel suo capolavoro la massima gloria della poesia fiorentina, Dante Alighieri, Boccaccio fa spazio al poeta che, a suo vedere, occupava il posto più vicino all'autore della *Commedia*: Guido Cavalcanti. Così facendo egli riesce a rettificare la severa condanna comminata in contumacia al poeta fiorentino nel X canto dell'*Inferno*" ("Leggiadri motti" 182).

32. Interestingly, Boccaccio does not read Dante's "Forse cui Guido vostro ebbe a disdegno" (*Inf.* X.63) as associating Guido with Epicureanism; rather, he reads it as referring to Guido's rejection of Virgil: "Guido Cavalcanti, uomo costumatissimo e ricco e d'alto ingegno . . . seppe molte leggiadre cose fare meglio che alcun altro nostro cittadino: e, oltre a ciò, fu nel suo tempo reputato ottimo loico e buon filosofo, e fu singularissimo amico dell'autore, sì come esso medesimo mostra nella sua *Vita nuova*, e fu buon dicitore in rima; ma, per ciò che la

for background on the Florentine tradition of organized *brigate,* basically eating clubs formed by "gentili uomini delle contrade" (VI.9.5), whose members would share expenses by rotating the responsibility for paying for everyone's dinner.[33] They would also participate in popular festivals at regular intervals during the year.

In Boccaccio's story, Guido Cavalcanti becomes the object of a membership campaign by one of these clubs, led by Betto Brunelleschi. Elissa's description of Guido makes him not simply an unwilling candidate but an imperfect one as well. She explains that Guido "fu un de' miglior loici che avesse il mondo e ottimo filosofo naturale (delle quali cose poco la brigata curava)," so it does not appear that they would have much to say to one another. On the other hand, they know him to be "leggiadrissimo e costumato e parlante uom molto e ogni cosa che far volle e a gentile uom pertenente seppe meglio che altro uom fare" (VI.9.8)—in other words, a good conversationalist. They attribute his reluctance to join their group to the fact that "Guido alcuna volta speculando molto abstratto dagli uomini divenìa": he tends to drift off. Moreover, common knowledge holds that he "alquanto tenea della oppinione degli epicuri," with the inference that his speculations "erano solo in cercare se trovar si potesse che Iddio non fosse" (VI.9.9). They thus attribute to him efforts to undermine previously advanced ontological arguments for the existence of God, such as Anselm's simple proof or Aquinas's *Quinquae viae,* his five-part proof contained in the *Summa.*[34] The *brigata*'s question suggests that for them at least such a proof would lead to nothing, as it would have no practical impact: the

---

filosofia gli pareva, sì come ella è, da molto più che la poesia, ebbe a sdegno Virgilio e gli altri poeti" (*Esposizioni sopra la* Comedia 526). The description of Guido here recalls Elissa's own presentation of him, which Boccaccio would have written earlier, with the exception that there is no mention in the *Esposizioni* of Guido's reputation as an Epicurean. For a singular analysis of the *novella* see Barański, who points out that the Guido of the *Esposizioni* "is a cultural cliché—in this instance, an amalgam of some of the widely circulating stock notions which, at the end of the Duecento, had collected around his name" (283).

33. This is one of many traditions whose passing Elissa laments: "furono nella nostra città assai belle e laudevoli usanze, delle quali oggi niuna ve n'è rimasa" (VI.9.4). The ninth tale thus repeats the nostalgic reverie for lost traditions that Filomena had initiated in the first story. While it may have disappeared by the mid-fourteenth century, the tradition does reappear later, being featured for example in the *Novella del Grasso legnaiuolo.*

34. Anselm advances his proof in his *Proslogion,* in which he concludes the existence of a being of whom none greater can be conceived to exist, in other words, God. Aquinas introduces the *Quinquae viae* in *ST* 1a. 2, 3. The five arguments are as follows: *ex motu* or the unmoved mover (God is the unmoved mover from whom all motion proceeds), *ex causa* or the first cause (God is the uncaused cause of all things), *ex contingentia* or contingency (God is the being whose existence does not depend upon other beings), *ex gradu* or degree (God is the perfection that is the source of all perfections), *ex fine* or design (God is the intelligent being that guides all other beings to their ends).

world would continue as before. Despite the risks attendant in any association with him—though one may assume that, being in their own way
Epicureans, they have their own heretical leanings—the group still wants
him. Guido's own resistance makes him irresistible. It is perhaps the tale's
central irony that a character commonly believed to deny the existence of
God should himself be an object of veneration.[35]

The story hinges on both the question asked of Guido and his non-
answer to it. Meeting up with him among the tombstones adjacent to the
Baptistry—a setting that implies the entire life cycle, not simply its earthly
conclusion—the members of the *brigata* tease him about where his speculations will lead: "Guido, tu rifiuti d'esser di nostra brigata; ma ecco, quando tu
avrai trovato che Idio non sia, che avrai fatto?" (VI.9.11). Their verbal attack
constitutes, in Elissa's words, an oxymoronic *assalto sollazzevole* (VI.9.10);
he parries with words and a *salto* over one of the gravestones: "Signori, voi
mi potete dire a casa vostra ciò che vi piace" (VI.9.12).[36] Guido's refusal to
answer, coupled with his invitation that they continue to speculate about
him, exposes the real topic of this tale: it is about gossip. The members of
the *brigata*, among others, theorize about what Guido is thinking; in his
reply he acknowledges his status as an object of interest to them but refuses
to satisfy their curiosity, marshaling instead a rejoinder that effectively cuts
off the cycle of chatter that he finds odious.

At first the group puzzles over the remark and deems Guido a *smemorato* or ignoramus; they particularly do not understand it because they
see this place not as uniquely theirs but as belonging to all Florentines,
including Guido. Betto then glosses the remark: "queste arche sono le case
de' morti, per ciò che in esse si pongono e dimorano i morti; le quali egli
dice che son nostra casa, a dimostrarci che noi e gli altri uomini idioti e
non letterati siamo, a comparazion di lui e degli altri uomini scienziati,

---

35. Marcus makes an acute point in this regard: "[T]he very gifts which would most adorn
[Guido] in polite company—eloquence and gentle manners—are precisely those which elevate
him beyond the pale of normal social activity." With regard to his Epicureanism she notes:
"His Epicurean rejection of the soul's immortality would necessarily distance him from the
society whose entire moral system depends on an afterlife of reward and punishment" (*An
Allegory of Form* 67). Robert Durling, in his fascinating study of the *novella*, describes the activities of the *brigata* in comparison to Guido's speculations as "the familiar antithesis between
the active and the contemplative life. . . . [t]he fact that it has apparently not occurred to the
brigata to honor Guido by feasting him, according to their custom, is part of the suggestion of
their lack of discernment" ("Boccaccio on Interpretation" 275).

36. As Durling points out ("Boccaccio on Interpretation" 282–83), the leap over the
gravestones, which connotes resurrection and salvation, suggests that Guido is anything but a
heretic: "The suggestion is very strong that if anyone in the *novella* is an Epicurean—*porcus
de grege Epicuri*—it is the *brigata* that lives mainly for dressing up, parading, and eating."
Barański, reaches similar conclusions on both of these points.

peggio che uomini morti, e per ciò, qui essendo, noi siamo a casa nostra" (VI.9.14). It turns out that Betto is not such a bad logician either, though as Robert Durling points out, Betto takes only a first step in his interpretation and fails to make the second, which would involve becoming a follower of Guido ("Boccaccio on Interpretation" 291). Indeed, the most significant result of the encounter, besides the group's decision to leave Guido alone, is that his companions gain renewed respect for Betto, whom they deem a "sottile e intendente cavaliere" (VI.9.15). The tale thus casts reflected light on Betto, who positions himself as yet another Galeotto, a go-between between Guido and the other members of the *brigata*.[37]

While Guido enjoys a triumphant moment in which he secures his freedom from gossip, with its insistence on the uselessness of the *brigata*'s speculation the story offers a rather more guarded conclusion about the value of inquiry. Betto and his friends never get the answer to their question because their interlocutor refuses to answer it: Guido remains impenetrable. Betto himself, while admitting to being an *idiota* and *non letterato*, ends up making a point that Guido himself affirms: speculation succeeds only if the object of speculation is willing to cooperate, and Guido proves to be no more cooperative than God himself. His inscrutability, his rejection of transparency, would appear to be of a piece with his Christological nature (Barański, 321), an affirmation of his duty, as part of a greater mystery, to remain one. In like manner, one may infer that since Guido is a human, his speculative efforts about God would meet with similar resistance.

The story thus removes the question of what would happen if God turned out not to exist at all from the realm of theology, relocating it within the realm of language: it is finally but one of many questions for which there are no clear answers. Reducing ontological inquiry to the equivalent of gossip, inasmuch as both are functions of language, it relocates the former firmly within the range of human activity, whether solitary or in conversation with others. The members of the *brigata* finally resolve their frustration only by solving the linguistic riddle that Guido offers as a substitute for the more substantive answers they have sought from him. The riddle itself turns out to be a masterful pun on the verb *speculare:* seeing themselves reflected in the tombstones, Betto and his friends find the sort of concrete satisfaction, consistent with their own materialistic Epicureanism (Barański, 307–8), that enables them to move on. The story comes to rest in the solidity of the tombstones, which stand in opposition to the eva-

---

37. Getto, who sees in the tale's denouement the establishment of "un rapporto gerarchico fra una nobile forma di vita e una altra forma più nobile e alta, tra un tono raffinato e un più raffinato tono di civiltà," describes Betto as "come il mediatore tra Guido e la brigata," though without connecting his role to the subtitle of the *Decameron* and its implications (159).

nescence of Guido's alleged Epicurean speculation. By denoting birth and death through solid structures, San Giovanni and the tombstones respectively, the tale marks the limits of human knowledge about life: in the end we can be sure only that once born, we will die, and the rest remains hidden. Coming as it does during a day that focuses on the transformative power of language,[38] the tale also assigns limits to it, which correspond to limits on the human ability to know.

Dioneo's tale follows logically from this conclusion, inasmuch as it demonstrates the extent to which religion remains a human construct. The story has generated a variety of readings, ranging from Mario Baratto's focus on the representation of the Florentine countryside, to Millicent Marcus's analysis of its metaliterary aspects, to Joy Potter's emphasis on its critique of ecclesiastical institutions.[39] Being an exceptionally busy story, it tends to resist global interpretations; it appears to touch on too many themes—the nature of relics, the operations of con men, clerical failings, storytelling, language and seduction, style versus substance, and so forth— to fuse into a coherent whole. That said, I would first hazard two points absent from previous readings, and which will inform my own claims about the tale's messages. First, this is a story about marketing, specifically about the marketing of God. Readings that touch on its ecclesiastical themes insist that the story limits itself to critiquing Church institutions; Potter, for example, notes "a careful separation of God and Church" consistent with the frame tale and the Ciappelletto story (67). These claims seem to me to participate in a misplaced Boccaccio apologetics. To defend Boccaccio properly, one would apparently need to deny that he would ever want to put God into play, as if to do so would constitute an insurmountable attack on his character. Whether Boccaccio believed in God or not remains at best a matter of speculation. Regardless of that, he does not shy away from the same ontological questions he had Guido Cavalcanti asking, nor should we fear to acknowledge same.

Second, the story's metaliterary considerations are neither exclusively theoretical—the art of storytelling, understood abstractly—nor directed uniquely at other texts, such as the *Commedia*. The tale also self-consciously

---

38. Elissa's theme explicitly relates language to change: "chi, con alcun leggiadro motto tentato, si riscotesse, o con pronta risposta o avvedimento fuggì perdita o pericolo o scorno" (V.Conc.3).

39. See Baratto, *Realtà e stile* 379–82; Marcus, *An Allegory of Form* 64–78; Potter 62–67. Other readings include Getto 160–64, who sees the *novella* as celebrating the "arte del vivere" (160), and who offers incisive comparisons between Frate Cipolla and Guido Cavalcanti; Mazzotta 63–67; Picone, "Leggiadri motti" 183–85; and Bruni 87–92. The tale has also been the object of detailed examination of its Dantean intertext; see Hollander, *Boccaccio's Dante* 41–52, and Usher.

reproduces in microcosm the storytelling arrangement of the *Decameron* as a whole. It bears note, as Jonathan Usher has already pointed out,[40] that while Frate Cipolla delivers his fraudulent address to the people of Certaldo, listening in the wings are the two thieves, Giovanni del Bragoniera and Biagio Pizzini, who took his feather in the first place and know full well that his claims about relics are wholly false: "Li quali stati alla sua predica e avendo udito il nuovo riparo preso da lui e quanto da lungi fatto si fosse e con che parole, avevan tanto riso, che eran creduti smascellare" (VI.10.55).[41] Cipolla thus confronts two distinct audiences, the people of Certaldo, ignorant of his fraud, and the two men, aware of it. The arrangement mirrors a number of audience arrangements: that of Ciappelletto's confession, made before a gullible priest and the two knowing Florentine brothers; Dioneo's primary intended audience of the seven ladies and secondary audience of the two other men; and the book's primary audience of women in love and the secondary audience of male readers. Consistent with Boccaccio's awareness of his multiple audiences, Frate Cipolla appears to have a message for both: "per presto accorgimento fece coloro rimanere scherniti, che lui, togliendogli la penna, avevan creduto schernire" (VI.10.55). This *mise en abyme* effect, combined with the tale's theme of marketing, necessarily creates an ontological slippery slope, the result of which is to call into question the existence of God.

In introducing his protagonist, Dioneo makes clear that Frate Cipolla is not only a professional marketer but a snake oil salesman as well. He has a regular circuit: "usò un lungo tempo d'andare ogni anno una volta a ricoglier le limosine fatte loro dagli sciocchi un de' frati di santo Antonio" (VI.10.6). The description of his donors as *sciocchi* marks Cipolla's activity as a con game, which his audience of the faithful naïvely or stupidly fails to recognize. When Cipolla first addresses the people of Certaldo, he reminds them about the customary nature of his visits. He first recalls their annual gifts, "del vostro grano e delle vostre biade, chi poco e chi assai, secondo il podere e la divozion sua" (VI.10.9). In exchange, he explains, St. Anthony protects their livestock. There is also a special *debito* paid by, though not limited to, members of the confraternity of St. Anthony. These remarks explicitly link faith and capital. The people of Certaldo demonstrate their

---

40. Usher takes the distinction in a different direction from the one I do, referring to "two very different kinds of listener: on the one hand the rustic Certaldesi unversed in either doctrine or doubletalk, on the other the two sophisticates, Giovanni della [*sic*] Bragoniera and Biagio Pizzini, who can appreciate the friar's discourse at a far higher level of complexity and allusion" (22).

41. Their response is strikingly reminiscent of that of the two Florentine brothers in the Ciappelletto tale: "ascoltando leggiermente udivano e intendevano ciò che ser Ciappelletto al frate diceva; e aveano alcuna volta sì gran voglia di ridere, che quasi scoppiavano" (I.1.78).

faith through their gifts of agricultural products, and in exchange the saint protects their animal capital; the remark about the extra fee turns membership in the confraternity into something more than particular devotion to the saint.

Frate Cipolla continues by explaining that he will collect all these gifts, "dopo nona, quando udirete sonare le campanelle," thus linking his own accumulation of capital to the liturgical hours. He links the collection to yet another custom as well, his performance: "*io al modo usato* vi farò la predicazione, e bascerete la croce; e oltre a ciò, per ciò che divotissimi tutti vi conosco del barone messer santo Antonio, di spezial grazia vi mostrerò una santissima e bella reliquia, la quale io medesimo già recai dalle sante terre d'oltremare . . ." (VI.10.10–11). Display of the relic does not appear to be unique to this year's visit, for as Dioneo points out, Frate Cipolla ends up saving the promised relic, a feather from the archangel Gabriel, for next year. For their sacrifices, the people of Certaldo thus receive a long-term benefit, the saint's protection of their animals, and a short-term benefit, the religious experience that, through the display of the cross and the relic, increases their proximity to God. Frate Cipolla strikes a deal with them, and his acquisition of their goods depends in no small part on delivery of his own. The exchange must happen.

The tale's central scene finds Frate Cipolla without the "relic" he had promised to show his audience. Dioneo recounts the events leading up to the display in a way that suggests that the exhibition of the feather will be the climax of the friar's performance. He has already delivered his *predica*, which he tailors "in acconcio dei fatti suoi" (VI.10.33), in other words, to suit his own purposes. There follows the confession, made *con gran solennità*, then the lighting of two large candles, and finally the almost painfully slow unwrapping of the box containing the feather: "soavemente sviluppando il zendado, avendosi prima tratto il cappuccino, fuori la cassetta ne trasse" (VI.10.34). The sequence reads as a tease, which continues with the friar's bout of logorrhea as he undertakes to explain how he wound up with a box of coals instead of a feather. Having promised the latter he must now sell the former, which will be the only relic he shows among the many he names.

The friar avoids calamity thanks only in part to his verbal dexterity. The other component, essential to the success of his con game, is the clerical authority that he carries with him from place to place, an authority that derives in part from his association with the order of St. Anthony[42]

---

42. Cipolla's association with St. Anthony in no way alters the fact that he is an ordained friar. Dante has Beatrice rail against the Friars of St. Anthony for employing the *modus operandi* that Boccaccio attributes to Cipolla, that of preaching *ciance*, but he does not deny the le-

and in part from his ability to speak convincingly about God.[43] His speech serves as an example of how he accomplishes the latter task: not through the argumentative logic of an Anselm or an Aquinas, but rather by judging the overall intelligence of his audience and speaking above it. His rhetorical sleight of hand thus becomes for his audience, which does not fully grasp what he is saying, a sign of knowledge. The speech itself functions as a preamble to the display of the relic and as a means of validating his claim about its authenticity. However, just as Cipolla's speech lacks any authenticity, so too does the relic. The means of his promotion of coals to sacred object, absent any objective proof, thus offers a lesson in the semiotics of relics. Their transcendental signification paradoxically relies on an immanent coefficient, human speech, making them something of a rhetorical *adynaton*, a figure of impossibility. The story thus serves to demonstrate how religion functions within the human sphere. Even more significantly, it shows how religion expands its claims and its influence thanks to human activity. The sphere of God originates in man, not in the heavens.

Cipolla's marketing of God thus has an entirely human purpose, though it carries an important side effect. For all his fraudulence the friar does succeed in reinforcing the faith of the people of Certaldo: "li quali [carboni] poi che alquanto la stolta moltitudine ebbe con ammirazione reverentemente guardati, con grandissima calca tutti s'appressarono a frate Cipolla e migliori offerte dando che usati non erano, che con essi gli dovesse toccare il pregava ciascuno" (VI.10.53). The economics of the friar's con equates conviction with contribution, the increased gifts reflecting the success of his enterprise. While the people of Certaldo may come away a bit poorer, they also leave richer in faith, a faith that seems unlikely to be compromised by a later discovery of the fraud. Thus we arrive at the tale's central irony: faith does not require the existence of God. Dioneo replies to Panfilo's earlier effort to keep God in the circuitry by all but eliminating Him. The faith of the people of Certaldo relies not upon any sure proof of God's existence,

---

gitimacy of Anthony's order. See *Paradiso* XXIX.109 ff. for the comments about St. Anthony's followers.

43. Proof of Cipolla's preparation emerges in a speech that reveals his ability to think in threes, as if he had somehow so integrated the concept of the trinity that it became part of his mind-set: "Di cui [Guccio] spesse volte frate Cipolla era usato di motteggiare con la sua brigata e di dire: 'Il fante mio ha in sé nove cose tali che, se qualunque è l'una di quelle fosse in Salamone o in Aristotile o in Seneca, avrebbe forza di guastare ogni lor vertù, ogni lor senno, ogni lor santità. Pensata adunque che uom dee essere egli, nel quale né vertù né senno né santità alcuna è, avendone nove!'; e essendo alcuna volta domandato quali fossero queste nove cose e egli, avendole in rima messe, rispondeva: 'Dirolvi: egli è tardo, sugliardo e bugiardo; negligente, disubidente e maladicente; trascutato, smemorato e scostumato; senza che egli ha alcune altre teccherelle con queste, che si taccion per lo migliore . . .'" (VI.10.16–18). This same verbal mannerism will inform his speech before the assembled throng.

but rather on the material coefficients presented by a clever charlatan. The relics claim to make the unseen visible, but in fact they only expose the workings of faith: that it comes from within, not without, and functions as an act of will and not as a response to a demand.

Complicating matters further, in his account of the various relics he has seen Cipolla focuses on objects that are at once material and immaterial: the finger of the Holy Spirit, rays of light that appeared to the three Magi, bell sounds from Solomon's temple. He invites his audience to imagine each of these items encased in a reliquary, when in fact none could be. Each thus assumes the status of an image, as if Boccaccio were shoveling into this sermon a lesson on how metaphors function. Indeed, one of the relics he sees, the "vestimenti della santa Fé catolica," holds the key to Cipolla's own success. While Branca explains this item as part of a female personification of the faith (1352n.13), the object also makes literal reference to the clothing worn by the faith, its rhetorical dress, which Frate Cipolla deftly exploits. The metaphor itself emphasizes the visual aspect of the faith along with the reference to the "Verbum-caro-fatti-alle-finestre," which distorts the Latin "Verbum caro factum est" of John 1.14, reducing the central miracle of Christian faith, the incarnation, in which God became visible to mankind, to a Florentine street scene not unreminiscent of those later evoked in *canti carnascialeschi.* That his nonsense language thoroughly convinces his audience suggests the power of language to create its own reality, in essence to construct faith, and in so doing trumping the knowledge that allows the spectator to distinguish between the real and the false sign.

Dioneo invites us to laugh at the people of Certaldo, to condescend to them because they are *stolti,* but in truth stupidity is a relative, not an absolute, category. As Dante makes clear when referring disparagingly to the friars of St. Anthony, the world teems with preachers who speak "con motti e con iscede" (*Par.* XXIX.115), with so many false promises in indulgences that "tanta *stoltezza* in terra crebbe, / che, sanza prova d'alcun testimonio, / ad ogni promission si correrebbe" (11. 121–23; italics mine). In the context of Dante's earlier diatribe about St. Anthony, Boccaccio's use of the adjective *stolta* cannot be a coincidence, and its echo of a more universal foolishness in matters of faith raises the question of just where to draw the line. Dante insists on the need for a "prova d'alcun testimonio," approval by competent ecclesiastical authorities, but such a condition only raises the question of how one defines competency. The tale alludes to a problem of no small import. Cipolla is a fraud, but he is a fraud who thanks to his ordination enjoys public authority, and who, because he intimately understands the rhetoric of Christianity and the power of its reliquary traditions, makes a convincing case. It is by no means clear what certifies other preachers, who enjoy the same authority and use the same means, as less fraudulent. In this sense Boccaccio's central metaphor of the onion conjures another meaning beyond the linguistic one suggested by Marcus.[44] Cipolla is but one layer in a multilayered Christian hierarchy. Readers of the *Decameron* are smart enough to understand that Cipolla is a fraud, but perhaps not smart enough to perceive the bigger frauds purveyed higher up the ladder. After all, every layer of an onion resembles the one above it; if the innermost layer, represented by the Cipollas and the Ciappellettos of the world, is rotten, then the other layers could be rotten too.

In remarking about "il dito dello Spirito Santo così intero e saldo come fu mai," Boccaccio has Frate Cipolla identify a nexus between the spiritual and the material that lies at the core of all five of these stories. The people of Burgundy believe Ser Ciappelletto to be a saint and rend his garments in their desire for relics. Abraam converts to Christianity because what he sees in Rome unexpectedly convinces him of the truth of the faith. Melchisedech gives Saladin a lesson in faith by analogizing it to material objects, the three rings. Guido Cavalcanti's alleged Epicureanism questions what becomes of the immaterial soul after the death of the material body. And Frate Cipolla offers proof of Christian faith by holding up coals that hours before had littered the floor of his room.

The Rhetoric of Natural Law

In the *Summa* Aquinas offers the following definition of natural law:

> Law is a rule and measure, as we have said, and therefore can exist in two manners, first as in the thing which is the rule and measure, second as in the thing which is ruled and measured, and the closer the second to the first the more regular and measured it will be. Since all things are regulated and measured by Eternal Law, as we have seen, it is evident that all somehow share in it, in that their tendencies to their own proper acts and ends are from its impression.
>
> Among them intelligent creatures are ranked under divine Providence the more nobly because they take part in Providence by their own providing for themselves and others. Thus they join in and make their own the Eternal Reason through which they have their nature aptitudes for their

---

44. "Thus Cipolla's name becomes an elaborate literary joke, serving as an organic metaphor for the very linguistic relativity which governs his discourse. Like the onion with its manifold skins and seedless center, Cipolla's rhetoric contains layer upon layer of identical signs which harbor no underlying truth" (*An Allegory of Form* 76).

due activity and purpose. Now this sharing in the Eternal Law by intelligent creatures is what we call "natural law."

That is why the Psalmist after bidding us, *Offer the sacrifice of justice,* and, as though anticipating those who ask what are the works of justice, and adding, *There be many who say, Who will us any good?* makes reply, *The light of thy countenance, O Lord, is signed upon us,* implying that the light of natural reason by which we discern what is good and what evil, is nothing but the impression of divine light on us.

Accordingly, it is clear that natural law is nothing other than the sharing in the Eternal Law by intelligent creatures. (*ST* 1a2æ. 91, 2)

Aquinas here specifically relates natural law to eternal law. He will later define the latter: "the Eternal Law is nothing other than the exemplar of divine wisdom as directing the motions and acts of everything" (*ST* 1a2æ. 93, 1). That plan of divine wisdom, Aquinas explains, has the nature of law, because all law is ordered to an end, which is the common good, and the eternal law specifically moves "all things to their due ends." In other words, God's plan for the universe is a legal order. When the rational creature provides for itself and others, it imitates the divine plan. It can do so because it has received the imprint of God's light as the imprint of natural reason, a reason that allows rational creatures to discern good from evil.

In order for Aquinas's system to work, that which is received must somehow correspond to that which is sent. Aquinas neatly skirts the principal danger of his argument, which modern semiotic theory has addressed, specifically the problem of the encoding and decoding of a text. The text of eternal law, itself quite complex, undergoes encoding by God when it is transformed into something deceptively simple, the light of natural reason. It then falls upon humans who perceive this light to decode it, restoring complexity where they view simplicity, and to apply the law they have decoded to human law. This process corresponds to what Wolfgang Iser has called "the intersubjective structure of the process through which a text is transferred and translated" (108), and specifically how meaning is generated: "meaning must clearly be the product of an interaction between the textual signals and the reader's act of comprehension. And, equally clearly, the reader cannot detach himself from such an interaction; on the contrary, the activity stimulated in him will link him to the text and induce him to create the conditions necessary for the effectiveness of that text. As text and reader thus merge into a single situation, the division between subject and object no longer applies, and it therefore follows that meaning is no longer an object to be defined, but is an effect to be experienced" (9–10). In other words, the process by which a reader perceives a text, regardless of its original form, ablates the distinction between subject and object; the text itself finally becomes nothing more than the reader's experience of it. Under such conditions natural law ceases to be an object received by the human subject, and becomes instead, inevitably, an invention of the human subject, in the double sense of discovery and fabrication. The extent to which this process transforms the object, making it human, cannot be measured, because it lies outside of human capacity to perceive objectively, to "see" it as God made it. Moreover, as a function of individual experience, natural law differs with each human subject. Its authority finally rests on a consensus that coalesces around an authority such as Aquinas who grounds his argumentation in the prior authority of sacred texts. Such a consensus does not however preclude the possibility of dissent.

Boccaccio quite presciently understands this dilemma, and he elucidates it in these stories, in which nominally rational creatures neither always perceive correctly nor always perform rationally.[45] Beginning with the tale of Ciappelletto and moving through the series, Boccaccio argues that what we think we know about God we cannot finally be sure to know. In casting doubt on the epistemological basis of natural law theory, Boccaccio effectively releases it from its moorings. Aquinas insists on the notion of the rational creature in part to distinguish us from animals, but also because he is trying to avoid the problem of intersubjectivity by suggesting that humans, thanks to natural reason, can be objective. As the *Decameron* details, however, humans make mistakes. Moreover, rational creatures face limits in what they can perceive.

This argument gains particular resonance in the story of the three rings. Kelsen points out in a sentence that resonates with this story: "there are, as a matter of fact, very different systems of morality and very different systems of law, whereas there is only one system of nature" ("Natural-Law Doctrine" 141). In other words, the existence of different religions is testimony to the fact that men can "read" the same information received from nature in different ways. Melchisedech's tale underscores that all three reli-

---

45. Aquinas's own reluctance to confront the weaknesses of his argument emerges in another discussion of natural law: "Now, a truth is self-evident at two stages, one, in itself, two, in our minds. A proposition is self-evident in itself when the Predicate is of the essence of the Subject. At the same time the proposition may not be self-evident to a man who does not know the definition of the Subject. For instance, 'Man is a rational animal,' is a self-evident proposition of its nature, since to say 'man' is to say 'rational.' Yet to somebody who does not grasp what man really is, the proposition is not self-evident" (*ST* 1a2æ. 94, 2). The proposition is not self-evident, as arguing the contrary readily demonstrates. If men are self-evidently rational, then men who are not rational are no longer men. Dante and Boccaccio will both cite instances of irrational human behavior—the term *matta bestialità* springs to mind—but in neither case does the association with animals deny the humanness of the subjects in question.

gions have the same God, not that each has its own. They must all therefore retrace themselves to the same source, with their discrepancies reflecting differences in reception.

More is at stake here than Boccaccio's entry into a heady theological debate. The predication of human law upon natural law has wide-reaching implications for the world of the *Decameron*. Aquinas explicitly links human law to natural law: "Augustine observes that *there never seems to have been a law that was not just:* hence a command has the force of law to the extent that it is just. In human matters, we call something 'just' from its being right according to the rule of reason. The first rule of reason is natural law, as appears from what has been stated. Hence insofar as it derives from this, every law laid down by men has the force of law in that it flows from natural law. If on any head it is at variance with natural law, it will not be law, but spoilt law" (*ST* 1a2æ. 95, 2). The final sentence here topples the entire structure. If the light of natural reason enables men to make human law in imitation of eternal law, there should be no divergence between the product, human law, and its source, eternal law; indeed, there should be only one human law. At the same time, however, Aquinas suggests that human error can lead to "spoilt" law, and that error could easily result from a misguided sense that one has correctly perceived natural law. He appears to be saying that "spoilt" law, in contrast to just law, would not have the force of law. Nevertheless, it remains law, and even if logically unenforceable, under some circumstances it can still be enforced.

To the extent that one cannot accurately assess the extent to which human law reflects natural law, or indeed whether humans perceive the divine light correctly, natural law becomes little more than a rhetorical prop designed to authorize human law. Aquinas gives this away when making his own recourse to metaphor to describe the transfer: "the light of natural reason." Kelsen makes this point repeatedly in his legal writings; I offer here but one example: "The dualism of natural law theory has been shown to consist in the assumption that, above the state system of positive law, there is a legal system that is superior, divine, based on reason or natural law. And—a point that cannot be over-emphasized—the function of this higher system, at least according to the classical representatives of seventeenth- and eighteenth-century natural law theory, was essentially that of conservative legitimization" (*Problems* 36). Elsewhere Kelsen argues that "The norms allegedly deduced from nature are—in truth—tacitly presupposed, and are based on subjective values, which are presented as the intentions of nature as a legislator" ("Natural-Law Doctrine" 141). This statement affirms the rhetorical basis of natural law theory. Kelsen's remark about "conservative legitimization," how the system perpetuates itself, laying claim to authority by invoking the divine order, translates in this latter statement to his remark about "the intentions of nature as a legislator." The true legislator is in fact the human one, who attributes his legislation not to himself but to God as a means of reinforcing his claim to power.

If natural law theory is finally rhetorical, one is left to wonder why the rhetoric is necessary, what it dresses. Kelsen furnishes an answer to that question in his positive legal theory, which locates authority not in natural law but in the coercive power of the state. While Kelsen's theory addresses natural law primarily as conceptualized from the seventeenth century onward, and thus focuses on the state, his theory applies as well to conditions of the medieval world and specifically to family and governmental structures as first outlined by Aristotle and adapted, again, by Aquinas. While the elaborate mechanism of the modern state develops after the Middle Ages, comparable institutions, such as monarchy and its domestic equivalent, the patriarchal family, display a similar interest in perpetuating their own authority. In the latter case, as Boccaccio will amply demonstrate, the patriarch claims particular authority over women.

In its own dissection of natural law theory, both in the frame tale and in the stories themselves, the *Decameron* calls patriarchal claims into question. Like Kelsen, Boccaccio intuits the true source of male claims to authority in the domestic sphere: their coercive power based on their superior physical strength. The stories themselves provide examples of same, most notably in Cimone (V.1), as well as others in which men coerce women through more indirect means. The fact that men can hurt women, that contemporary laws recognized a husband's *ius corrigendi*, no matter its theoretical bases, suggests a different source for legal authority than the one claimed by theologians.[46]

Women and Law: Two Cases in Point

While throughout the *Decameron* women must confront ways in which the law restricts them, two stories appearing in the second half specifically address theoretical issues involving the law and women. The first, the famous tale of Madonna Filippa (VI.7), addresses two legal questions

---

46. Guerra Medici traces the husband's authority to the principle *rex in regno suo est imperator*, which for Aquinas applies in both the public and the private sphere: "as a prince is governor of the State so a head of the family is governor of the household" (*ST* 1a2æ. 90, 3). On the various laws that either affirmed or defined marital authority (including limits on how a man could beat his wife), see Guerra Medici 62–65.

discussed by Aquinas in the *Summa:* first, the notion of equity, which he borrows from Aristotle, and second, the question of when and to what purpose human law may be revised. The second, Emilia's tale of King Solomon's advice about wives and friendship, exposes the hierarchical system whereby law arrives in the household. If on the one hand Madonna Filippa offers women some hope that even in the direst of circumstances they can save themselves and improve their lot, Solomon serves to remind women readers just how much they live in a man's world.

Located in Prato, the tale of Madonna Filippa centers on "uno statuto, nel vero non men biasimevole che aspro, il quale senza alcuna distinzion far comandava che così fosse arsa quella donna che dal marito fosse con alcun suo amante trovata in adulterio, come quella che per denari con qualunque altro uomo stata trovata fosse" (VI.7.4).[47] In his phrasing Filostrato insists on the categorical nature of this law, "senza alcuna distinzion," a key problem that Aristotle's theory of equity[48] undertakes to address. As Aristotle explains, a law can be good or correct (Lat. *recta*), but because it seeks to address a universal question it can sometimes overlook contingencies: "... all law is universal, and yet there are some things about which it is not possible to make correct universal pronouncements. . . . So whenever the law makes a universal pronouncement, but things turn out in a particular case contrary to the 'universal' rule, on these occasions it is correct, where there is an omission by the lawgiver, and he has gone wrong by having made an unqualified pronouncement, to rectify the deficiency by reference to what the lawgiver himself would have said if he had been there and, if he had known about the case, would have laid down in law" (1137b14–b24; Rowe trans. 174). Equity is the process of making these adjustments. Aquinas characterizes it as a function of reason: "reason rightly dictates,"—*ratio recte se habet*—"that a person should correct what is deficient in the law" (*Commentary* 468). I insist here on Aquinas's use of the word *ratio* for two reasons. First, Aristotle's theory of equity will find something of an equiva-

---

47. This introductory sentence, and indeed general plot lines of the tale, may have come from a *controversia* in the *Gesta romanorum*, as Cherchi points out ("From *controversia* to *novella*" 127).

48. I use the term "equity" here even though translations of the *Ethics* contain different English equivalents for the Greek *epieikeia*. While "equity" predominates, Rowe uses "reasonableness" in his translation. To be sure, the Greek resists translation; William of Moerbeke did not even try, settling for *epiichia* in his thirteenth-century Latin translation, and Aquinas apes him in his commentary. In the *Summa* 1a2æ. 120, 1, Aquinas offers a Latin translation for the term: "epicheia quae apud nos dicitur aequitas." I thank my friend and colleague Eric Brown for the following note: "What is EIKOS is reasonable, probable, and (most often in Attic) likely, and so the condition of being EPI TO EIKOS (= EPIEIKEIA) is usually a very general sort of reasonableness."

lent in Aquinas's own musings about law in the *Summa*, when he discusses revisions to human law. He gives two reasons why human laws may be revised: "because of the workings of reason and because of the human lives which are regulated by law" (*ST* 1a2æ. 97, 1). It is the nature of human reason, he explains, to advance from imperfection toward perfection, so as reason becomes more perfect—presumably as the perception of natural law becomes clearer—laws may be revised accordingly.[49] In the course of this argument he describes a situation that sounds remarkably like the one Aristotle had envisioned: "So also in practical questions; those who first attempted to draw up useful regulations for the human community were of themselves unable to take everything into consideration; they set up certain institutions which were lacking in many respects, yet which served for their successors to work on and make alterations, so that they might in fewer respects prove defective for the common benefit" (*ST* 1a2æ. 97, 2). In other words, lawgivers cannot account for all contingencies when making a law; as new cases arise and reason undergoes refinement, laws change.

My second purpose in insisting on the language of reason has to do with the story itself. After listening to Madonna Filippa's argument, the people of Prato "quasi a una voce tutti gridarono la donna aver *ragione* e dir bene" (VI.7.18). The remark not only identifies a woman as a unique arbiter and purveyor of *ragione;* it also demonstrates, in the story's key parodic stroke, the very contingency of that which should be categorical: right and wrong. The reason of a higher order that the people of Prato wish to locate in Madonna Filippa really is nothing other than an alternate logic, rooted in a different set of values.

The law itself, it must be said, offers anything but a model of good phrasing, at least in Filostrato's paraphrase: "uno statuto . . . il quale senza alcuna distinzion far comandava che così fosse arsa quella donna che dal marito fosse con alcun suo amante trovata in adulterio, come quella che per denari con qualunque altro uomo stata trovata fosse." Unclear here is the antecedent of the pronoun *quella*. Translators have read it in two ways, as referring simply to *donna*—that is, any woman, married or not—or to the entire clause beginning with *quella donna*—specifically married women who prostitute themselves.[50] The ensuing changes in the law, which elimi-

---

49. Aquinas suggests as much: "The natural law is a participation of the eternal law, as stated above, and therefore endures without change, owing to the unchangeableness and perfection of the Divine Reason, the Author of nature. But the reason of man is changeable and imperfect: wherefore his law is subject to change" (*ST* 1a12æ. 97, 1).

50. McWilliam reads the phrase as "a statute . . . which without exception required that every woman taken in adultery by her husband should be burned alive, whether she was with a lover or simply doing it for money" (498). Musa and Bondanella translate it instead as: "a statute . . . which, without any extenuating circumstances whatsoever, required that any

nate the crime of uxorial infidelity while retaining that of uxorial prostitution, would appear clearly to validate the latter reading. In its original form, however, the law would punish two delicts equally, even though one, adultery for purposes of prostitution, is arguably more egregious than the other.[51]

The logic behind the law would appear to cast both delicts under the umbrella of a derailed female sexuality. Medieval marriage was conceived as providing a sanctioned zone in which a woman could practice her sexuality—leading to procreation—while furnishing the economic security that would obviate the need for her to seek support elsewhere. An adulterous woman, or one who prostituted herself to boot, would thus demonstrate by her actions her own moral failings as well as the failure of marriage institutionally to fulfill its promise. Moreover, by risking pregnancy by a man not her husband, she would threaten the patrilinear social order that had evolved in the later Middle Ages (Herlihy 79–88). As Guerra Medici points out, the restructuring of the medieval family that took place in the twelfth and thirteenth centuries "doveva rispondere alle finalità politiche ed economiche dei gruppi dominanti nell'ambito del comune" (47)—in other words, of men. The legal lexicon itself suggests commonality between the two crimes. Canonists used the term *meretrix* interchangeably for a commercial prostitute or a loose woman, so the word could refer to both an adulterous wife and one who prostituted herself (Karras 244).

The discovery of Filippa's adultery allows Filostrato, the tale's narrator, to introduce an observation about justice in Prato. Filippa's husband, Rinaldo de' Pugliesi, first wants to kill her himself, but then refrains because "di se medesimo dubitava" (VI.7.6): he appears to worry about the legal consequences for himself. He turns instead to the law, which conveniently will accomplish the task for him: "non si poté temperare da voler quello dello statuto pratese che a lui non era licito di fare, cioè la morte della sua donna" (VI.7.7). Prato's criminal statutes, here invested in the figure of the *podestà*, have assumed the power of vendetta, thus eliminating the

---

woman caught by her husband committing adultery with a lover should be burned alive, just the way a woman who goes with a man for money would be" (396). Branca does not parse the phrase.

51. One need but think of the order of sin in Dante's Hell to see the difference. Adultery, *lussuria*, is punished early as one of a number of sins of incontinence. Sins involving money—simony, barratry, usury—are punished lower down, in the Malebolge. The history of prostitution in the Middle Ages, and specifically in Italy, is one of regulation of a necessary evil, rather than of efforts to eliminate it entirely, and scholars have relayed no evidence of the application of capital punishment for simple prostitution. This fact as well encourages the theory that the specific crime foreseen by Prato's law involves uxorial prostitution as something measurably worse than simple prostitution.

primitive and potentially chaotic tradition of self-help.[52] The statute accommodates the primitive impulse toward vengeance by instituting the same punishment that Rinaldo would have undertaken by himself.[53] No longer a private function, uxoricide now belongs to the commune.[54]

Filostrato describes two options for Filippa, either to flee or to face the tribunal of justice. She rejects the former because in doing so she would "negarsi degna di così fatto amante come colui era nelle cui braccia era stata la notte passata," opting instead for the latter, because "di gran cuore era, sì come generalmente esser soglion quelle che innamorate son da dovero" (VI.7.9). At this point the story begins to open up. Filippa subscribes to a different ethical and legal code than do the lawmakers of Prato; her thinking finds its roots in the courtly love tradition, specifically inasmuch as it idealizes adulterous love.[55] It is perhaps her very idealism that draws Filostrato to her. The story in fact reveals its narrator's heretofore unseen admiration for women who are truly in love, *da dovero*, suggesting that his own amorous disappointment may have something to do with the limitations on reciprocity established by the courtly code.[56] He seems to long

---

52. Kelsen explains, "The social technique that we call 'law' consists in inducing the individual, by a specific means, to refrain from forcible interference in the spheres of interests of others: in case of such interference, the legal community itself reacts with a like interference in the spheres of interests of the individual responsible for the previous interference. Forcible interference in the spheres of interests of another, the measure of coercion functions as delict and also as sanction. Law is an order according to which the use of force is forbidden only as a delict, that is, as a condition, but is allowed as a sanction, that is, as a consequence" ("The Law as a Specific Social Technique" 238). For Madonna Filippa's husband this means that he must rely on the law to represent his interests rather than take matters into his own hands, lest he incur sanctions against himself.

53. Though likely not by the same means: the law specifically envisions burning at the stake for the crimes of female adultery and prostitution. This may be an allusion to the punishment of Sodom and Gomorrah; see Jordan 31–32.

54. The prohibition on uxoricide had a basis in canon law. Brundage explains: "Canonical authorities, like their Roman predecessors, forbade the betrayed husband to slay his guilty wife, although the courts were notably reluctant to punish the husband who killed his wife's lover" ("Sex and Canon Law" 42). Roman law allowed the cuckolded husband to kill the adulterer, and the *Lex Julia de adulteriis* specifically invested in the father, not the husband, the right to kill his adulterous daughter (Brundage, "Adultery and Fornication" 132).

55. As Power explains, "Courtly love . . . was held to be impossible between husband and wife. 'Marriage is no excuse for not loving' is the first of the rules of love. It was based on the conviction that affection binding married persons—though real and valuable—had nothing in common with the sentiment of love, which might, and indeed must, therefore, be sought outside marriage" (15–16). So too De Rougement: "[C]ourtly love established a *fealty* that was independent of legal marriage and of which the sole basis was love. It was even contended—for example, in the famous judgement delivered by a court of love in the house of the Countess of Champagne—that love and marriage were incompatible" (34). One finds a narrative application of these notions in Francesca's courtly love rationalizations of her adultery in *Inferno* V.

56. Filostrato's use of the phrase *da dovero* underscores his indebtedness to a courtly love

for a woman such as Filippa who risks everything for amorous principle. Whereas he once figured himself as the unrequited courtly lover, here he undertakes to construct a rationale whereby the beloved can fully satisfy her lover's desire. In this sense it is significant that he implies that Filippa has found true love with Lazzarino de' Guazzagliotri, "oltre a ogni altra innamorata" (VI.7.5), while making no statement about her affection for her husband. Indeed, when she later defends herself she describes herself as passive to her husband's needs, "egli ha sempre di me preso quello che gli è bisognato e piaciuto" (VI.7.17), though active to her lover's, describing her sexual gifts to her lover in terms of service.

Arriving before the court, Filippa reveals herself to be an excellent advocate, not just because she makes a good speech but because she has the mannerisms of a fine rhetorician, "bellissima e di maniere laudevoli molto e, secondo che le sue parole testimoniavano, di grande animo" (VI.7.11). She appears to have studied rhetoric, for she carefully deploys the three different types of voice outlined in the *Ad Herennium*. In first addressing the judge, she assumes the dignified conversational tone, which requires "the full throat but the calmest and most subdued voice possible,"[57] corresponding to what Filostrato terms her *salda voce* (VI.7.11). As she begins her defense, she shifts to the narrative conversational tone, which enables the speaker to "seem to recount everything just as it took place."[58] This voice allows a variety of delivery tones corresponding to content, thus Filippa's "voce assai piacevole" (VI.7.13), which belies no regret on her part—indeed, she speaks "senza sbigottire punto"—and seems intended to charm the judge. Both the dignified voice and the narrative voice require that the speaker's facial expression correspond "to the sentiments of the subject—gaiety or sadness or an emotion intermediate;"[59] thus her *fermo viso* (VI.7.11), which suggests both her resolve and the seriousness of her discourse. Later, as she draws her famous conclusion, she resorts to what the *Ad Herennium* calls the facetious conversational tone: "with a gentle quiver in the voice, and a slight suggestion of a smile, but without any trace of immoderate laughter, one ought to shift one's utterance smoothly from

---

ideology. Translated by McWilliam as "genuinely" and by Musa and Bondanella as "truly," the phrase bears a punning relation to the verb *dovere,* suggesting that Filippa's love lies somewhere at the crossroads of genuine and dutiful. The latter notion evokes a fundamental theorem of courtly love, that of reciprocity, immortalized by Francesca da Rimini: "Amor, ch'a nullo amato amar perdona" (*Inf.* V.103).

57. III.xiv.24: "plenis faucibus quam sedatissima et depressissima voce."

58. III.xiv.24: "ut in ipsa pronuntiatione eas res quas demonstrabium inserrer atqe insecare videamur in animis auditorium."

59. III.xv.26: "hilaritate, tristitia, mediocritate vultus ad sermonis sententias adcommodata."

the Serious Conversational tone to the tone of gentlemanly jest."[60] Filostrato suggests this shift when remarking on her smooth transition after her husband's reply to her question, "seguì prestamente la donna," and by stating that she had made a "piacevol domanda" (VI.7.17, 18). Moreover, the crowd's *molte risa* (VI.7.18) correspond to the purpose of the facetious conversational tone: "The Facetious can on the basis of some circumstance elicit a laugh which is modest and refined."[61] One almost senses that Filippa insists on going to trial because it represents the opportunity to unfurl her forensic talent.

In her defense strategy Filippa undertakes to expose the contingency for which the law, in its universal orientation, had not accounted. She first questions the law's very constitutionality. Readily admitting to her husband's accusation, she argues that "le leggi deono esser comuni e fatte con consentimento di coloro a cui toccano" (VI.7.13).[62] In her assertion that laws must be *comuni*, here understood as applying equally to men and women, she critiques the law not for being too universal but for not being universal enough. Moreover, she takes pains to point out that "niuna [donna] ce ne fu mai chiamata" (VI.7.14) to consent to the law, and therefore it cannot be valid. Her argument here relies on the notion, advanced for example by Marsilius of Padua in the *Defensor pacis*, that the legislator "is the people or the whole body of citizens," in other words, that the validity of law depends upon the consent of the governed.[63] To be sure, Marsilius explicitly excludes women from the body of citizens whose consent validates law, but Madonna Filippa solves this problem by convincing *tutti i pratesi*, a group that includes those citizens authorized to make or change law, to effect the change she wants.

As she concludes her defense, Filippa finds her most powerful point, specifically entailing the theory of equity. She first asks the judge to interrogate her husband as to whether she has ever denied him sex. When the husband replies that in fact she has not, she concludes her argument: "domando io voi, messer podestà, se egli ha sempre di me preso quello che

---

60. III.xiv.25: "liviter tremebunda voce, cum parva significatione risus, since ulla suspicione nimiae cachinnationis leniter opportebit ab sermone serios torquere verba ad liberalem iocum."

61. III.xiii.23: "Iocatio est oratio quae ex aliqua re risum pudentem et liberalem potest comparare."

62. This argument demonstrates clear knowledge of the history of adultery laws. As Brundage points out, "Although theologians maintained that extramarital sex was as sinful for a man as for a woman, canon law treated adultery primarily as a female offense and only occasionally punished men for violations of their marriage vows" (42).

63. *Defensor pacis* 45. Marsilius derives the argument from Aristotle's argument in the *Politics* that "the mass of the people ought to be sovereign" (1281a39).

gli è bisognato e piaciuto, io che doveva fare o debbo di quel che gli avanza? debbolo io gittare a' cani? non è egli molto meglio servirne un gentile uomo che più che sé m'ama, che lasciarlo perdere o guastare?" (VI.7.17). These words locate the contingency for which the theory of equity attempts to provide accommodation. The fact that Filippa's adultery comes not at the expense of her husband's sexual gratification mitigates it: it would be one thing to deny sex to her husband while sleeping with another man, but it is quite another to serve her husband's needs as well as someone else's. Indeed, the courtly love notion of service, here expressed in the phrasing *servire un gentile uomo*,[64] clearly subtends her argument. The service she has rendered to a lover evokes the desired end of the courtly love game, with the implication here that he deserves her service because he loves her: "più che sé m'ama." And anyway, her husband has suffered no real harm.

While the story thus demonstrates the theory of equity put into practice, it also enacts a parody of Aquinas's rationale for making changes in human law as a consequence of human reason becoming more perfect. When discussing changes in human law—"may a human law be altered in some way?"—Aquinas takes on the following objection: "Furthermore, it has always been said that it is a quality of law to be just and right. But once right always right. Accordingly once law always law." Aquinas replies: "When you say that a physical thing is 'right' you are speaking less relatively than when you apply the term to a law. For a physical thing is looked at just as it stands, and in this sense it is always right. A law, however, is right by reference to the common good, and one and the same thing does not stand always in a fixed proportion to it. Hence, as we have argued, legal rightness can vary" (*ST* 1a2æ. 97, 2). Aquinas distinguishes here between what we may empirically affirm about the physical world and the contingency of law, which projects how we would like the world to be. His notion that laws relate to the common good introduces a new factor into his legal theory that opens the door to Boccaccio's story. One may argue that in his intention Aquinas defines the common good as broadly congruent with God's plan for the universe, the eternal law. As the tale demonstrates, however, the definitions of the common good may come from above, but they may just as easily come from below, that is, from the human sphere. Here the common good privileges a system that maximizes the sexual satisfaction of men over any moral code that might condemn adultery. In the story's final irony, the "reason" that triumphs is paradoxically the reason of desire. Filippa may have superior intellectual gifts, but she applies them

---

64. Branca informs us that the Pugliesi family was one of the most famous in Prato, and that several members of the family served as *gonfalonieri* of the city (1337), so Filippa's lover is *gentile* both in the courtly sense of *gentilezza* and in the class sense of being one of the *gens*.

to lead the way for greater happiness in Prato at the expense of presumably immutable norms.

In counterpoint to this story, which posits that a clever woman can save herself by intimating advantages for men, Boccaccio introduces a far more troubling story, the ninth of the ninth day. This tale, told by Emilia, is the last one told by a queen, and it enjoys particular pride of place thanks to the reduplication of the number nine, associated with perfection. As the last tale told by a female monarch, it may be read as offering its own *summa* of women's experience in the *Decameron*. Notwithstanding the tale of Dioneo that follows it, Emilia's story also serves as a sobering anticipation of the content of Day X, whose theme, as yet unannounced, will bring other kings and potentates back into the pages of the *Decameron* in celebration of what David Herlihy has called the "fellowship of males." This story too celebrates such fellowship, at the expense of women.

The tale begins with an extended introduction by Emilia that addresses the place of women in the universe: "Amabili donne, se con sana mente sarà riguardato l'ordine delle cose, assai leggermente si conoscerà tutta la universal moltitudine delle femine dalla natura e da' costumi e dalle leggi essere agli uomini sottomessa e secondo la discrezione di quegli convenirsi reggere e governare, e però, a ciascuna che quiete, consolazione e riposo vuole con quegli uomini avere a' quali s'appartiene, dee essere umile, paziente e ubidente oltre all'essere onesta, il che è sommo e spezial tesoro di ciascuna savia" (IX.9.3). Emilia echoes the location of her story by insisting on trinities in this sentence and the following one. Women are subordinate to men according to nature, custom, and law; in order to live in quiet, consolation, and repose with those same men, women should be humble, patient, and obedient, beyond being *oneste*, which she identifies as a woman's "sommo e spezial tesoro." Arguing in inverse order, she then elaborates on how each of the three elements she has mentioned, *le leggi, il costume,* and *la natura,* have determined the position of women. Laws, she says, "il ben comune riguardano in tutte le cose," while custom's "forze son grandissime e reverende" (IX.9.4), and nature has made women physically, psychologically, and mentally weaker than men. These distinctions allow us to see how Emilia configures her argument about female subordination. If laws subordinate women, they do so for the common good, including that of women; if custom does so, we must revere its judgment. And even if one were to doubt the authority of law and custom—"E quando a questo le leggi . . . non ci ammaestrassono, e l'usanza, o costume," she argues in a careful hypothetical—nature offers the proof, in making women in all aspects weaker than men. Such demonstrable weakness, Emilia explains, translates into a need to be governed: "E chi ha bisogno d'essere aiutato e governato, ogni ragion vuol lui dovere essere obediente e subgetto e reverente al governator suo: e cui abbiam noi governatori e aiutatori se non gli uomini?" (IX.9.5). The logic of her argument points inexorably to the rule of men.

Emilia does not speak in a vacuum. Rather, her theory of the relationship between law, custom, and nature has a significant philosophical genealogy, leading back to Cicero through Aquinas. Aquinas cites an important passage from the *De inventione* to explain how human law is grounded in nature and custom: "Hence Cicero says that *justice took its start from nature, and then certain things became custom by reason of their usefulness; thereafter the things put forward by nature and approved by custom were sanctioned by fear and reverence for the law*" (*ST* 1a2æ. 91, 3). His citation emends Cicero's statement: "Justice is a habit of mind which gives every man his desert while preserving the common advantage. Its first principles proceed from nature, then certain rules of conduct became customary by reason of their advantage; later still both the principles that proceeded from nature and those that had been approved by custom received the support of religion and the fear of the law" (*De inventione* II.liii.160).[65]

Cicero's explanation clarifies Emilia's, which presents the argument in reverse order. The ultimate source of law is nature, and it encodes practices that have become customary, arising out of nature. Nor does Emilia's erudition end there. Her further remark that "le leggi . . . il ben comune riguardano in tutte le cose" (IX.9.3) finds echo in Cicero's remark that justice preserves the common advantage, "communi utilitate conservata," as well as in Aquinas's statement in the *Summa* that "every law is ordained to the common good" (*ST* 1a2æ. 90, 3: "ad bonum commune ordinatur"). While Emilia may believe that women are by nature inferior to men, she might well deny that they are intellectually inferior. Indeed, if anything she affirms the intellectual equality of women when referring to *ciascuna savia*.

Moreover, it is difficult to determine the inflection she gives her rhetorical question, "e cui abbiam noi governatori e aiutatori se non gli uomini?" Certainly everything that has happened over the previous twelve days gives the lie to this claim, and her facial expression, *lieta*, further undermines it. As I detailed above, of the three declamatory tones discussed in the *Ad Herennium*, the first two, the narrative conversational tone and the serious conversational tone, require that facial expression match content. The third type, the facetious conversation tone, is the tone of irony, and it allows for a disconnect between facial expression and content. Emilia's happiness, her

---

65. "Iustitia est habitus animi communi utilitate conservata suam cuique tribunes dignitatem. Eius initium est ab nature profectum; deinde quaedam in consuetudinem ex utilitatis ratione venerunt; postea res et ab nature profectas et ab consuetudine probatas legum metus et religio sanxit."

condition of being *lieta*, seems out of place in a discourse on how women must act to accommodate male authority. In fact, her advice to women has a political air to it: "Dunque agli uomini dobbiamo, sommamente onorandogli, soggiacere" (IX.9.5). A woman, after all, *appartiene* to men, the verb suggesting both kinship and ownership, so she faces the challenge of finding a way to live in peace. In her earlier reference to *onestà* as the gift of *ciascuna savia*, Emilia had suggested the wise conservation of a woman's *onestà* as a means of survival. Her argument about women's submission to men has a similar survivalist subtext, for these are relations determined by power, and power implies the right to punish transgression. Her argument is not exclusively moral, if indeed at all: rather, it is fundamentally practical.

Emilia offers such advice because, as she well knows, women live surrounded by violence. As a reader of the *De inventione* Emilia would have been aware of Cicero's myth of the foundation of civilization, how a *sapiens* used his eloquence to induce men to give up violence and work toward the common good, *communis commodi*: "Certainly only a speech at the same time powerful and entrancing could have induced one who had great physical strength to himself be put on a par with those among whom he could excel, and abandoned voluntarily a most agreeable custom, especially since this custom had already acquired through lapse of time the force of a natural right" (*De inventione* I.ii.3).[66] Prior to that time, Cicero explains, men had allowed brute force to rule them: "And so through their ignorance and error blind and unreasoning passion satisfied itself by misuse of bodily strength, which is a very dangerous servant" (*De inventione* I.ii.2). Emilia no doubt understands that law does not prevent all violence; rather, it sanctions some forms of violence as punishment for a delict. Such forms of sanctioned violence may be public or domestic, for as Aquinas points out, "the ruler of a family can issue precepts and standing orders," even if they do not apply outside the home: "these are not such as to possess the nature of law properly so called" (*ST* 1a2æ. 90, 3). Violence does not disappear from the human landscape; rather, it morphs into a tool for the preservation of the social order.

The constant threat of violence emerges also in the positioning of Emilia's tale with respect to several others, which together constitute a brief cycle. Emilia suggests as much when introducing the story, referring to Pampinea's earlier tale of Talano d'Imola, whose dream that his unpleasant wife would be attacked by a wolf comes graphically true, leaving the wife

---

66. "Profecto nemo nisi gravi ac suavi commotus oratione, cum viribus plurimum posset, ad ius voluisset sine vi descendere, ut inter quo posset excellere, cum eis se pateretur adquari et sua voluntate a iucundissima consuetudine recederet quae praesertim iam naturae vim obtineret propter vetustatem."

to rue her refusal to heed her husband's warning. In the next story, which appears just before Emilia's, Lauretta tells of a *beffa* and counter-*beffa* in which Ciacco, tricked out of a nice meal of lampreys by Biondello, avenges himself by having Biondello beaten up. Lauretta herself introduces this story by referring to Pampinea's earlier one of the widow and the scholar, characterizing the scholar's actions specifically as a *vendetta*. She thus creates a sort of genealogy of violence that runs through the late days of the *Decameron*. The three tales each present a different scenario: the violence of nature, here specifically directed at a woman; the violence of men against men; and the violence of men against women. It comes as little wonder then that Emilia advises women to consider their options carefully.

Emilia offers her story as proof of the dictum "Buon cavallo e mal cavallo vuole sprone, e buona femina e mala femina vuol bastone" (IX.9.7). She avers that one may interpret the saying in two ways: *sollazzevolemente* or ironically, or *moralmente*, taking the statement seriously. She claims to do the latter, arguing that it accounts appropriately for female shortcomings: "Son naturalmente le femine tutte labili e inchinevoli, e per ciò a correggere la iniquità di quelle che troppo fuori de' termini posti loro si lasciano andare si conviene il baston che le punisca; e a sostentar la vertù dell'altre, ché trascorrer non si lascino, si conviene il bastone che le sostenga e che le spaventi" (IX.9.9). The sentence itself, which echoes the misogynistic discourse of Filomena and Elissa in the Introduction to Day I, also constitutes a perfect statement of the dual purpose of law: to coerce people to behave by threat of punishment, and to punish those who transgress.[67] The law thus covers both the *buona femina* and the *mala femina* by shaping the conduct of the former and correcting that of the latter. At the same time, however, there is something strangely incomplete about this introduction: it ignores fully half of the story. Emilia speaks of "un consiglio renduto da Salomone" (IX.9.7), even though the king ends up offering two pieces of advice. Nor does the second piece of advice exist in a vacuum; indeed, it serves as an important complement for the other, as I shall argue below.

---

67. In his early *Introduction to the Problems of Legal Theory*, Kelsen wrote: "The purpose of the legal system is to induce human beings—by means of the notion of this evil threatening them if they behave in a certain way, opposite what is desired—to behave in the desired way. In this motivation lies the efficacy aimed at by the legal system. With an eye to efficacy, the content of legal norms (like that of social norms generally) is limited to human behaviour, for only the human being, endowed with reason and will, can be motivated by the notion of a norm, motivated to behave in conformity with that norm" (29). Earlier he had explained that "the consequence attached in the reconstructed legal norm to a certain condition is the coercive act of the state—comprising punishment and the civil or administrative use of coercion—whereby only the conditioning material fact is qualified as an unlawful act, and only the conditioned material fact is qualified as the consequence of the unlawful act" (26).

Not surprisingly given all its triplication, the tale involves three men, who find themselves unexpectedly in a triangular relationship. Melisso meets Giosefo while heading toward Jerusalem to consult Solomon. He has spent a great deal of money without making any friends, and he wants to ask Solomon "come addivenir possa che io amato sia" (IX.9.13). Giosefo likewise seeks counsel, but in his case with regard to his wife, "più che altra femina ritrosa e perversa" (IX.9.12). They form something of a utilitarian friendship rooted in their common destination; Emilia describes them as *compagni* and Giosefo addresses Melisso as *compagno*, though late in the tale Melisso calls Giosefo *Amico*. The tale in no way suggests that the friendship endures beyond the trip; the two separate at Giosefo's house after a few days of company there.

In Jerusalem the two receive equally enigmatic advice from the king. Solomon tells Melisso, "Ama," and Giosefo, "Va al Ponte all'Oca." Having none of the intellectual skills that Emilia can boast, the two cannot understand Solomon's advice and depart feeling slighted. They chance what upon will turn out to be Ponte all'Oca, where a mule driver is attempting to coax his recalcitrant charge across the bridge. Melisso and Giosefo urge the gentler approach used with horses, but the mule driver suggests that they mind their own business, and by dint of repeated beatings, he finally convinces the animal to move. Upon learning the name of the bridge, Giosefo declares that he understands Solomon's advice: "assai manifestamente conosco che io non sapeva battere la donna mia: ma questo mulattiere m'ha mostrato quello che io abbia a fare" (IX.9.22). The mule driver thus functions as an extension of Solomon himself, who according to Emilia was a most generous *mostratore* of his wisdom. Returning home with Melisso in tow, he decides once and for all to discipline his wife, taking up a *bastone*—the same weapon that Cimone had brandished in the first story of Day V—and beating her nearly to death. At first the wife resists, but as her husband's intentions become clearer, she begs him that he not kill her, finally affirming "oltre a ciò di mai dal suo piacer non partirsi" (IX.9.29), seconding Emilia's argument that "agli uomini dobbiamo, sommamente onorandogli, soggiagere" (IX.9.5). Despite her pleas Giosefo continues to beat her until he tires himself out, breaking every bone in her body. With telling attention to grisly detail, Emilia then notes that he washes his hands and eats dinner with Melisso, while the wife can barely drag herself off the floor.

The tale thus affirms, in ways we have seen before in the *Decameron*, the ease with which men can make recourse to violence, not only against other men but against women as well. They do so by claiming sanction, even when none is readily apparent. Giosefo only believes that the scene he witnesses at the bridge fulfills Solomon's advice, though in fact he makes a subjective interpretation of language that remains enigmatic. Whether he has understood Solomon correctly is secondary to the fact that he seizes on the coincidence of Solomon's advice and the scene at the bridge to claim the authority to beat his wife. It is this aspect of the tale, combined with Emilia's attention to the bloody details of the beating, that suggests that her misogynistic language may be somewhat disingenuous. She may be interpreting the statement about wives and horses seriously, but she does so principally because she takes the question of domestic violence, and its basis in male claims to legal authority, seriously.

The Giosefo element of the story has something of a retrospective quality to it, completing as it does the *Decameron*'s cycle of violence. On the other hand, the advice given to Melisso, while something of an afterthought, will acquire a proleptic ring. Like Giosefo, Melisso does not understand Solomon's advice, so he presents it to a *savio* upon returning home. The man explains: "Tu sai che tu non ami persona, e gli onori e' servigi li quali tu fai, gli fai non per amore che tu a alcun porti ma per pompa. Ama adunque, come Salamon ti disse, e sarai amato" (IX.9.34). Melisso applies the advice, winning the love he had sought: Emilia ends the tale with the words "il giovane amando fu amato" (IX.9.35). She weaves the etymological figure *amore/Ama/amato/amando/amato* densely into her conclusion, with the key word *servigi* suggesting the philosophical basis for her theory of male friendship. In effect she reinvents courtly love for men. Men should deploy their courtesy not to enamor women but other men. Women leave the picture.

The tale thus offers three themes. The first two concern human relations: how women can get along with men and vice versa, and how men can get along with men—the former governed by law, the latter by the ethics of *communis commodi*. In addition, it thematizes interpretation in a way that recalls the story of Guido Cavalcanti, which as Durling has demonstrated treats questions of interpretation. Durling's observation that "one of the most important interpretive steps would seem to be that of considering how the text applies to [one]self" ("Boccaccio on Interpretation" 281) fully applies here. Solomon's advice remains opaque for both his visitors—themselves reminiscent of the *smemorati* of Betto Brunelleschi's *brigata*—until someone or something clarifies it. The tale's process of encoding and decoding of language is analogous to the encoding of eternal law into natural law, which men decode into human law. What remains unclear in the present case, however, is whether either of the two interpreters, Melisso or Giosefo, is *savio* enough to interpret Solomon's words correctly. The tale implies that they do, because they apply their interpretations in a manner that solves their initial problems. If that is indeed the case, then Solomon's advice reveals much about how the real world of men and women, not the idealized one of courtly love, functions. Men subordinate women using any means available while courting one another. Small wonder then that *onestà* is for Emilia the highest treasure of every *savia*. In the world of contingency and exclusion that she describes, women must hold themselves to their own high standards rather than rely on men to elevate them. A *savia* understands with Machiavelli that Fortune is a lady, and that she must develop strategies of accommodation to avoid the beating. As the *Decameron* offers no defense against a man's irrational rage, women must create a space within which they can maneuver and survive.

The comprehensive lesson in natural law that emerges from these pages is that it serves men well, because it gives them the rhetorical props they require to rationalize the violence—real and metaphorical—that they perpetrate against women. Women accrue far fewer advantages from natural law and must navigate the conjoint streams of rhetoric and coercion with tools that will keep them afloat. Unlike Madonna Filippa, most women cannot change their reality, but where they do enjoy agency, however limited, it comes from successfully addressing danger. Emilia's most important lesson, finally, is that women not be *oche*, because practical wisdom offers the only real chance for survival.

CHAPTER III

Strategies of Coercion

Filostrato

THE RESTORATION of men of the *brigata* from the margins of leadership to the center, their acquisition of the monarch's crown, occasions a change in the dynamic of the *brigata* and in the nature of the stories told. While the narrative shift comes most abruptly in the case of Filostrato, in fact all three kings posit themes that expand the range of narrative options applied to women. Filostrato's theme provokes some of his subjects to ponder what would happen if a woman were caught in a sexually compromising situation by a man who had the power and inclination to punish her transgression. Dioneo's theme causes his companions to conjure a narrative space where women manage to avoid the mortal danger of sexual compromise. Panfilo's theme leads his storytellers to consider the role of women in a world that privileges relationships between men. The unifying element, beyond the fact that each day has a king rather than a queen, is the predicate of male rule, either as paterfamilias or as political leader, as it extends to the stories.

The crowning of the king seems like the righting of an order that had gotten lost somewhere after Elissa had declared that "gli uomini sono delle femine capo" (I.Intro.76). The three young men had appeared immediately after she made this statement, but as events had evolved, they had not enjoyed the recognition as *capi* that Elissa's words should have entailed. Beyond the fact that Pampinea continues to wear the leadership mantle she had assumed when first addressing the other six women about their collective dilemma, the distribution of the men's narrative voices over the first day is even and underscores their membership in a group rather than their inheritance of a special gender-based privilege. Boccaccio does assign Panfilo the first story, but he then gives Dioneo the fourth and Filostrato the seventh. Surrounded by so many female voices, theirs seem smaller, domesticated. At the same time, the intervals anticipate a similar spacing of their rule over Days IV, VII, and X, moments at which the three emerge from the crowd to reorganize the narrative space.

While the monarch's authority comes to a man only at the end of the third day, two of them seek quickly to counteract the emerging trends of the first day. Panfilo opens the day by telling the story of Ser Ciappelletto, excluding women entirely from the picture and reminding them in a preacherly way of their debt to God. And as Day I winds down, Dioneo asks with legalistic formality to be excused from the rule of the theme: "Madonna, come tutti questi altri hanno detto, così dico io sommamente esser piacevole e commendabile l'ordine dato da voi. Ma di spezial grazia vi cheggio un dono, il quale voglio che mi sia confermato per infino a tanto che la nostra compagnia durerà, il quale è questo: che io a questa legge non sia costretto di dover dire novella secondo la proposta data, se io non vorrò, ma qual più di dire mi piacerà. E acciò che alcun non creda che io questa grazia voglia sì come uomo che delle novelle non abbia alle mani, infino da ora son contento d'esser sempre l'ultimo che ragioni" (I.Conc.12–13). Dioneo shows himself to be a clever rhetorician, careful to praise Fiammetta's theme, her *ordine,* before asking to be excused from it. The request recalls his earlier courteous and carefully defended demand that the ladies keep him entertained lest his thoughts return to Florence, though in the present case his logic falters. He offers a *quid pro quo,* implying that by speaking last he will face a greater challenge because others might already have told a story or two that he had in mind.[1] To the contrary, his options open up, because once he is free from the theme he can tell any story he pleases, retaining the choice to adhere or not to the stated theme. What remains is perhaps Dioneo's most honest statement of his motives, one that will characterize his choices throughout the *Decameron:* he wants to do what will give him the greatest pleasure, "qual più di dire mi piacerà." So while one may certainly read Dioneo's proposal functionally, as a means to introduce thematic variety and counterpoint to the themed days, the request that his difference be marked also functions within the economy of gender relations to connect being male with seeking pleasure.

Of the three men, only Filostrato does not disclose much about himself

---

1. This turns out to be the case in Dioneo's own day, the seventh, where he apologizes for not following his own theme by explaining that someone else had already told his story.

in the first day—or perhaps he reveals more than he wants to. Telling the tale of Bergamino and Can Grande della Scala, he shows an interest in both power relations and the transformative power of storytelling, but with a conclusion whose full import will emerge only against the light of the fourth day. Chastened by Bergamino's narrative of Primas and the Cluny abbot, Can Grande admits his own error: "Bergamino, assai acconciamente hai mostrati i danni tuoi, la tua virtù e la mia avarizia e quel che da me disideri: e veramente mai più che ora per te da avarizia assalito non fui, ma io la caccerò con quel bastone che tu medesimo hai divisato" (I.7.27). Can Grande's figurative language alludes to the primary means of enforcement of legal norms: the threat of coercion. As the lord of Ravenna Can Grande embodies the law, so he must punish his own transgressions, which he promises to do with the *bastone*, or club, of enlightening narrative that Bergamino provides. The association of storytelling with pain will become more marked in the fourth day, when several of Filostrato's subjects will protest the *fiera materia* he has assigned to them.

To differing degrees, then, each male member of the *brigata* adumbrates his future self, and his own rule, in the first day. Panfilo records a general disinterest in gender-related narrative. Dioneo marks his concern about issues of sex, and about how he may modify the ladies' order to suit his own needs. Filostrato signals his interest in the relationship between storytelling and suffering. Each of these tendencies will find full realization when the men come to rule. Filostrato's day will sever storytelling from pleasure. Dioneo will command a day of storytelling that involves sex. The stories told under Panfilo will include women, but only as they are incidental to the promotion of homosocial bonds. Two of these days, the fourth and the seventh, will evoke protests from the women. Only Panfilo's theme will raise no hackles, perhaps because he disguises his plan so well, or perhaps because the ladies understand, as they demonstrate in their storytelling, that the world to which they will soon return will focus on concerns that eclipse their own.

This chapter examines the first of the three days ruled by men, the fourth, in which we find the most vociferous objections from the ladies to the direction that male leadership takes them. In many ways the fourth day resembles the seventh, for in both cases the same dynamic links tensions within the *brigata* to storytelling. The political issues raised are constitutional in the case of Filostrato and related to decorum in the case of Dioneo, but they come down to the same questions: to what extent may the king force the ladies to tell stories against their will? To what extent may he coerce behavior from the ladies, and what means are at his disposal to enforce the coercion? The stories themselves explore these political tensions by transferring them into an exclusively domestic sphere, a household of fathers, brothers, and husbands who hold coercive power over their daughters, sisters, and wives. The choice of the home is dictated somewhat by the themes themselves, particularly in the case of Dioneo, who expressly requests stories about husbands and wives. At the same time, however, it reflects the double identity of the *brigata* itself, both as a political unit capable of drafting and modifying its own constitution and as an improvised family that substitutes for the lost real family of each member.

Much of the argument that follows here and in the succeeding chapters relies on Aristotle's analogies of state and household as presented in the *Ethics*. For Aristotle the household is a political microcosm. Paternal rule resembles a monarchy when executed well, a tyranny when exercised badly. The relationship between brothers looks like a timocracy or polity, because they are equal in all things except their age, with the elder sibling presumably having a leadership role. In a decayed form, the sibling relationship becomes a democracy "when the ruling figure is weak, and each part of the household has licence to do what he or she wants" (1161a9; Rowe trans. 220). Finally, spousal relations compare favorably to an aristocracy, inasmuch as the sharing of authority is based on merit, and unfavorably to an oligarchy when the wife rules because of superior wealth.[2] These three types of relations apply to the three kings in the way that they conceptualize their relationship to the women. Filostrato rules as a severe father, verging on the tyrannical. Dioneo's leadership resembles an aristocracy, not just because of his interest in marriage but also because aristocracy involves the sharing of resources, a theme that will emerge in the frame events surrounding Day VII. Finally, the timocratic nature of Panfilo's rule emerges in the lack of any objection to his theme, which suggests an unprecedented spirit of cooperation before a male ruler. The timocracy remains problematic, however, because the group's ostensible equality does not find expression in the stories themselves.

Filostrato and the Constitutional Crisis

The metaphors that accompany Filostrato's crowning as the first *re* of the group mark a gender tension that will spread throughout the day. As she crowns him Neifile observes, "Tosto ci avedremo se i' lupo saprà meglio gui-

---

2. As Blythe points out, several medieval theorists adapted Aristotle's arguments when elaborating their own theories about public and domestic rule, among others Aquinas, Giles of Rome, and William of Ockham. So these models, as applied by Boccaccio, would have been anything but unique to the Middle Ages.

dar le pecore che le pecore abbiano i lupi guidati" (III.Conc.1). The new king responds by playing on her language about wolves and sheep, repeating the obscene central metaphor of Dioneo's story about Alibech and Rustico, and lamenting the fact that the ladies are not interested in men's lessons about sex. Having recharged the analogy along explicitly sexual rather than gender-based lines, he concludes: "non ne chiamate lupi, dove voi state pecore non siete" (III.Conc.2). The women, in other words, are anything but sheep, that is, passive to sexually rapacious men, so there is no reason to assume that the men will be lupine. Neifile strikes back by accepting his recalibration of the metaphor in sexual terms and invoking another of the *Decameron*'s more pornographic tales: "Odi, Filostrato: voi avreste, volendo a noi insegnare, potuto apparar senno come apparò Masetto da Lamporecchio dalle monache e riaver la favella a tale ora che l'ossa senza maestro avrebbono apparato a sufolare" (III.Conc.3). The cascading obscene allusions here suggest not only how much Dioneo's story has stirred the group's collective libido, but also how readily one can slip from the discourse of power, the subject of Neifile's initial metaphor, into the discourse of sex. The verbal scuffle also comes at an intriguing moment, the first time in the *Decameron* that a male member of the *brigata* will enjoy political authority. Neifile's remarks in fact suggest concern about whether Filostrato can rule as well as the ladies have; about whether he is ready to rule; and above all about how male leadership, keyed here as predatory, will differ from that of women. In his reply he suggests that he will put sex on the table, particularly as it relates to power relations between men and women. In other words, the discourse of sex, here invoked through explicit reference to the pornographic first and last tales of Day III, will become the field of play for the debate over whether men can rule as well as women do.

The figurative language of this exchange also anticipates Filostrato's central move as king, to offer himself for figuration. His announcement of a theme stands out for its autobiographical grounding, a new element:

> Amorose donne, per la mia disaventura, poscia che io ben da mal conobbi, sempre per la bellezza d'alcuna di voi stato sono a Amor subgetto, né l'essere umile né l'essere ubidente né il seguirlo in ciò che per me s'è conosciuto alla seconda in tutti i suoi costumi m'è valuto che io prima per altro abandonato e poi non sia sempre di male in peggio andato; e così credo che io andrò di qui alla morte. E per ciò non d'altra materia domane mi piace che si ragioni se non di quello che a' miei fatti è più conforme, cioè di coloro li cui amori ebbero infelice fine, per ciò che io a lungo andar l'aspetto infelicissimo, né per altro il nome, per lo quale voi mi chiamate, da tale che seppe ben che si dire mi fu imposto. (III.Conc.5–6)

Filostrato offers solid logic for organizing his day in conformity with the principles of revenge narrative, detailing the slight—his rejection by one of those present—and the remedy he envisions. Recounting his own sad history of love in terms that hew closely to the courtly tradition (Fedi 43), he explains that it would please him if the next day's tales conformed to his own state; he thus invites his companions to allegorize his own experience in their storytelling. He is already a trope, and he knows it, referring vaguely to the *tale* who named him and who understood the name's meaning.[3] While Boccaccio himself lurks somewhere behind this statement, the text of the *Decameron* does not entirely allow a reading that equates that *tale* with Boccaccio. In the Day I introduction Boccaccio explains that he has renamed the ladies because "io non voglio che per le raccontate cose da loro, che seguono, e per l'ascoltate nel tempo avvenire alcuna di loro possa prender vergogna" (I.Intro.50); but he does not make the same claim about the three men. Instead, he simply states that each was called, *era chiamato* (I.Intro.78), Panfilo, Filostrato, and Dioneo: it is not altogether clear that the same shield that protects the ladies also covers the men. Here we learn that "Filostrato" is in fact likely a nickname that the character carries with him into the text, a reflection of his unhappy love history. Boccaccio enters the picture laterally, because in this complex fiction whoever gave Filostrato this name may have borrowed it from the title of Boccaccio's own *Filostrato*. The king's remark thus underscores his history of entanglement with literary texts, a history that he now wishes to advance by reversing the order of things. Rather than take his identity from a literary text, he now offers himself as a source for new literary identities.

The king's self-absorption is of a piece with the kind of degraded friend he is, or has become, toward the ladies. His motives in choosing the theme are essentially utilitarian, as he puts his companions to work making him feel better.[4] He shows no real concern for the *bene* of the ladies, as an ideal friend would by Aristotle's measure. This attitude also turns his monarchy

---

3. Fedi notes that Filostrato "squaderna al lettore, con una franchezza che sbalordisce, la sua totale letterarietà, il suo essere figura *ficta*, d'invenzione, in una parola la sua trasparente natura di pura 'funzione.' È la prima ed unica volta in cui Boccaccio svela al suo lettore la finzione strutturale della cornice, facendosi apertamente citare da un suo personaggio ('da tale che seppe ben che si dire mi fu imposto'), ed entrando così sulla scena dei narratori da uno dei quali è stato egli stesso personaggio fra i suoi personaggi, quasi un'altra figura letteraria" (43).

4. Aristotle explains utilitarian friendship in the following terms: "And indeed those who love because of the useful feel fondness because of what is good for themselves . . . they do not love by reference to the way the person loved is, but to his being useful" (1156a14–15; Rowe trans. 211). Utilitarian friendship, like friendship for pleasure, is essentially narcissistic: "for the one loved is not loved by reference to the person he is but to the fact that in the one case [utility] he provides some good and in the other some pleasure" (1156a18; Rowe trans. 211).

into a tyranny: "the tyrant considers what is of advantage to himself, while the king considers what is of advantage to those he rules" (1160b2–3; Rowe trans. 219). His self-centeredness in fact marks the difference between the Boccaccio of the Proem who, once healed, turned his unhappy love story into a gesture of boundless generosity toward women, and Filostrato who, not yet healed, not only cannot see beyond the implications of that unhappy love for himself but visits them upon the others. One wonders whether the *ragionamenti* of *alcuno amico* would have worked a curative effect on Filostrato as they did on Boccaccio. Or perhaps instead the day is meant to replicate Boccaccio's remedy, with the king hoping that by hearing stories of other unhappy loves he will actually manage to transcend his own misery. The text remains somewhat equivocal on this point, with Filostrato remaining distant through much of the day but apparently ready to move beyond the theme by day's end.

While his choice of theme provokes no immediate response, by the next day many of the ladies have aligned themselves against the king. Fiammetta opens the rebuttal in her introduction to the Ghismonda story: "Fiera materia di ragionare n'ha oggi il nostro re data, pensando che, dove per rallegrarci venuti siamo, ci convenga raccontar l'altrui lagrime, le quali dir non si possono che chi le dice e chi l'ode non abbia compassione. Forse per temperare alquanto la letizia avuta li giorni passati l'ha fatto: ma che che se l'abbia mosso, poi che a me non si conviene di mutare il suo piacere, un pietoso accidente, anzi sventurato e degno delle nostre lagrime, racconterò" (IV.1.2). Invoking the theme of compassion, Fiammetta appears to want to tell Filostrato, perhaps on behalf of the group, that she is of course sorry for his pain, as if by mollifying him in this way she might lead him to suspend the topic. She also reads a motive into Filostrato's choice: he wants to counterbalance the happiness of the previous days.[5] Whether she is jockeying or not, in the end she registers her resignation to his authority: "poi che a me non si conviene di mutare il suo piacere." The use of the noun *piacere* here must be read as ironic, because nobody will appear to have a very good time over the next ten stories, least of all Filostrato; and even when Pampinea tells her amusing tale, the king will crack nary a smile.

The constitutional issues here are actually less clear-cut than Fiammetta would have her friends believe. She accurately reminds Filostrato

---

5. Forni makes an important point about Fiammetta's protest. Acknowledging that she has "il diritto di protestare," he add that "il programma onestamente edonistico dei giovani deve, per così dire, fare i conti con quello dell'autore. . . . senza quegli aspri casi non potrebbe dirsi completo il programma di conforto e soccorso per le donne innamorate in cui il *Decameron* si trova ad essere iscritto" (*Forme complesse* 70). In this sense Filostrato becomes an agent of the author, who also records Fiammetta's protest while having it lead to nothing.

and the group of the basic norm of their constitution, "festevolmente viver si vuole" (I.Intro.94), when she compares their reason for convening, "dove per rallegrarci venuti siamo," to his insistence that they "raccontar l'altrui lagrime." Filostrato's command also abrogates the statute, issued by Pampinea, according to which "ciascun generalmente, per quanto egli avrà cara la nostra grazia . . . niuna novella altra che lieta ci rechi di fuori." (I.Intro.101). There should also be no doubt that her edict applied to the group's organized storytelling, for Dioneo had already interpreted it precisely in that key: "Amorose donne, se io ho bene la 'ntenzione di tutte compresa, noi siamo qui per dovere a noi medesimi novellando piacere; e per ciò, solamente che contro a questo non si faccia, estimo a ciascuno dovere esser licito (e così ne disse la nostra reina, poco avanti, che fosse) quella novella dire che più crede che possa dilettare" (I.4.3). To be sure, in this introduction to his first story Dioneo is interpreting Pampinea somewhat creatively. She had earlier argued that "novellando . . . può porgere, dicendo uno, a tutta la compagnia che ascolta diletto" (I.Intro.112), and upon hearing the group's assent calls on each of her companions "di quella materia ragionare che più gli sarà a grado" (I.Intro.114). Nowhere does she articulate the principle that Dioneo attributes to her; rather, he infers it from her suggestion that each tells the story that best suits him or her. Clearly sensing that his tale may raise hackles, Dioneo takes care to lay out the case for his right to tell it.[6] Nevertheless, his words imply a specific reading of Pampinea's intentions in establishing the rule of storytelling, namely that it aimed to provoke *piacere*, understood as synonymous with *diletto*. His reading goes unchallenged, suggesting that the group accepts its accuracy.

Arguably then, by issuing his command Filostrato shows that he does not hold *cara* the ladies' *grazia*, and that he has chosen willfully to ignore prior interpretations of Pampinea's intentions, particularly as articulated by Dioneo. By now, however, the precedent about statutes is clear: each ruler may issue new ones, and the group must abide by them. In this society, as in law in general, the rule *lex posterior derogat priori*, according to which statutes that are more recent supplant earlier ones, applies.[7] Still, given

6. Dioneo takes this argumentative risk in order to rationalize his choice of a *novella* with an explicitly sexual theme, the first such story in the *Decameron*. It bears note that the language of his rationale finds echo in his narrative, linking storytelling and sexual pleasure. His two key words *piacere* and *diletto* return as a metaphor for the monk's sexual activity: "Il Monaco, ancora che da grandissimo suo piacere e diletto fosse con questa giovane occupato, pur nondimeno tuttavia sospettava" (I.4.8).

7. "We must remember at this point that legal systems are not just sets of norms, but hierarchical structures. There are certain hierarchical relations among legal norms or, as we would say, between norm-contents belonging to a legal system. Such hierarchies may be established by the legislature (that is, by laws themselves) or determined by some general

Filostrato's apparent violation of the constitution, Fiammetta could plausibly refuse to obey his command. That she does not reflects two factors. First, a male member of the group, Dioneo, has already threatened to walk away, so Fiammetta may understand the consequences of direct defiance not just for the group's survival but for the integrity of the future queens' rule. Second, and more problematically, she concedes that it is not her place to "mutare il suo piacere": in other words, his rule is absolute. She is wrong: Dioneo had already endeavored to alter the monarch's *piacere* when he asked to be excused from the rule of themes. By acceding to Filostrato's demand Fiammetta suggests that the women will finally behave more submissively toward the men than vice versa: they are after all *pecore* to his *lupo*, the metaphor suggesting that nature has made women the meeker sex. While meeker, they may however also be more clever: already having intuited how the *lupo* will guide the *pecore*, and they may now be willing to let Filostrato show how poorly a wolf's teeth fit inside a man's mouth. In any event, metaphor distills here into a simple statement about why women obey men: because men are the physically stronger sex, and as such may coerce obedience. The implied acknowledgment of coercion roots the group's order firmly in the soil of positive law.[8]

---

criteria based on the date of promulgation (*lex posterior*), the competence of the promulgating authority (*lex superior*), or the degree of generality of norm-contents (*lex specialis*)" (Alchourrón and Bulygin 404). The present case is clearly one of *lex posterior*. There is no hierarchical difference between the two lawgivers, Pampinea and Filostrato, so the *lex superior* principle, according to which a law issued by a higher authority supersedes a law issued by a lower one, cannot apply. Nor is this a case of *lex specialis*, in which Filostrato would be carving out some sort of minor exception to the general rule of storytelling. His edict actually modifies the original rule by unlinking storytelling and pleasure, unless one wishes to argue, though the *brigata* does not, that storytelling is pleasureful no matter the content. An example of the *lex specialis* principle at work comes at the end of Day I, when Filomena sets the next day's theme: "È il vero che quello che Pampinea non poté fare, per lo esser tardi eletta sì al reggimento, io il voglio cominciare a fare: cioè a ristrignere dentro a alcun termine quello di che dobbiamo novellare e davanti mostrarlovi" (I.Conc.10). While she attributes Pampinea's failure to institute a theme as driven by time constraints, she nevertheless claims the right to do so: none of the norms already issued by Pampinea would prevent her from doing so, and her decision to impose a theme is not binding on the other monarchs (as Emilia demonstrates in Day IX). Finally, Filomena does not break the storytelling–pleasure link by instituting a theme.

8. Kelsen discusses the theoretical alternative of a community without force on pages 238–44 of his essay "The Law as a Specific Social Technique": "This is the doctrine of theoretical anarchism. It presupposes a social order immanent in nature, a kind of natural law, which differs from positive law by the fact that it requires no socially organized sanctions and therefore is no law in the sense we call 'law' the coercive orders to be found in historical reality. He who believes in the existence of such a natural social order believes in the existence of an order whose binding character results directly from its content; because this order regulates human behavior in a way that corresponds to the nature of men and to the nature of their relationships and is, therefore, a way satisfactory to all individuals whose conduct is regulated" (239–40). The *brigata*'s order does not fall into this category. While the group does flee to a

Less passive than Fiammetta, Pampinea will creatively challenge Filostrato's rule in telling the second story: "Pampinea, a sé sentendo il comandamento venuto, più per la sua affezione cognobbe l'animo delle compagne che quello del re per le sue parole: e per ciò, più disposta a dovere alquanto recrear loro che a dovere, fuori che del comandamento solo, il re contentare, a dire una novella, senza uscir del proposto, da ridere si dispose" (IV.2.4). Sisterhood is powerful, and Pampinea directs her *compassione* at the other women rather than the king, hoping "per alquanto gli animi vostri pieni di compassione per la morte di Ghismunda forse con risa e con piacer rilevare" (IV.2.7). Her story of Frate Alberto technically toes the line of "coloro li cui amori ebbero infelice fine," but its amusing plot does not feature female suffering; as Marcus notes, Pampinea "interprets for us 'l'animo delle compagne' as one hostile to tragedy" (*An Allegory of Form* 55).[9]

Pampinea makes her move in the wake of an important statement by Filostrato, his highly personal reaction to the Ghismonda story: "Poco prezzo mi parrebbe la vita mia a dover dare per la metà diletto di quello che con Guiscardo ebbe Ghismunda, né se ne dee di voi maravigliare alcuna, con ciò sia cosa che io, vivendo, ogni ora mille morti sento, né per tutte quelle una sola particella di diletto m'è data. Ma lasciando al presente li miei fatti ne' lor termini stare, voglio che ne' fieri ragionamenti, e a' miei accidenti in parte simili, Pampinea ragionando seguisca" (IV.2.2–3). His comment contains some interesting syntax. He does not express a longing to enjoy the same *diletto* that Guiscardo had known with Ghismonda, but rather the same *diletto* that Ghismonda had experienced with Guiscardo. In other words, by making her the grammatical subject of his relative clause he implicitly identifies with her, not him. He then explicitly avers that nobody should be surprised by what he said—"né se ne dee di voi maravigliare alcuna"—which actually calls even greater attention to the weirdness of the statement. While he then goes on to explain why he identifies with her ("ogni ora mille morti sento"—so really the pre-Guiscardo Ghismonda, not the sexually fulfilled one), one is left to wonder what precisely he means by *diletto*, a word he twice uses. He may plausibly be signaling his (correct) reading of the story, that she is the desiring subject, as he has been in his life, and Guiscardo the object of desire. Nevertheless, the fact that he limits

---

natural setting, they immediately set about organizing themselves with legal norms. The implied sanction for not obeying the norms is the collapse of the group and the attendant danger of death from the plague. For the women there is a second coercive threat in the traditional authority over them held by men.

9. For a suggestive reading of the story as a parody of the *donna angelicata* tradition, see Clubb. Auerbach's reading of the *novella* remains among the most important, but see as well Ascoli's essay, "Boccaccio's Auerbach."

his remarks about *diletto* to the contours of Ghismonda's relationship with Guiscardo, a relationship that we understand principally as the time they spend together in bed, one is left to wonder whether Filostrato might harbor some gender confusion. His final comment about "lasciando al presente li miei fatti ne' lor termini stare" is yet another metatextual statement that begs the question of what precisely those *termini* are, and why he does not want to interrogate them further. Yet in ordering Pampinea to speak "a' miei accidenti in parte simili," he appears to invite her to comment, albeit indirectly, on his situation, whatever it now is, which is by no means clear. It is little wonder then that she comments with a story that, to the extent that it reflects on Filostrato's *accidenti*, suggests that they are rightly *risibile*.

Her story in fact reveals a heretofore subversive impulse on Pampinea's part. She accepts Filostrato's suggestion that his own experience serve as a narrative model, but rather than allegorize his suffering in love she allegorizes his kingship. Like Filostrato himself, her male protagonist changes roles and exploits his newfound claims to authority, here spiritual rather than political, in order to gain pleasure at the expense of a woman, only to find himself honeyed and feathered in the end. Pampinea even creates an explicit metaphoric link between Frate Alberto and Filostrato, beyond the phonosymbolic resonance of the two names, when she says that the former "di lupo era divenuto pastore" (IV.2.11). Filostrato himself criticizes the tale for its imbalance: "Un poco di buono e che mi piacque fu nella fine della vostra novella; ma troppo più vi fu innanzi a quella da ridere, il che avrei voluto che stato non vi fosse" (IV.3.2). Indeed, the first two stories establish a pattern that will run throughout Day IV. Filostrato seeks characters with whom he can identify, and he judges the success of the story by the intensity of his identification. If the first tale is any measure, however, Filostrato defines narrative pleasure in the consummation of love. Perhaps his citation of Rustico and Alibech during his *battibecco* with Neifile was meant to signal that he wanted his day to contain stories with similar racy content, albeit ending much more badly. The subsequent stories will conform more to the model of the first tale than the second, though the narrative thread that generally emerges from the Ghismonda story, beyond the unhappy ending, is that of violent death, a pornography different from the one for which Filostrato may long.

Other speakers will follow Fiammetta's lead and comment on Filostrato's command, either by directly criticizing him or by markedly reacting to the stories themselves. The ladies repeatedly cry over the first story. In introducing the third tale, Lauretta tells the king, "Troppo siete contro agli amanti crudele, se pur malvagio fine disiderate di loro; e io, per ubidirvi, ne racconterò una di tre li quali igualmente mal capitarono, poco de' loro amori essendo goduti" (IV.3.3). Her story provokes scattered reactions of distress over the fate of the three pairs of lovers. When Filomena introduces the fifth story, she appears "tutta piena di compassione del misero Gerbino e della sua donna" (IV.5.2), whose story she had just heard. The ladies find her story of Lisabetta to be *carissima*. Neifile's account of Girolamo and Salvestra provokes "gran compassion . . . in tutte le sue compagne" (IV.9.2). Even Dioneo aligns himself with the ladies in introducing his story: "Le miserie degl'infelici amori raccontate, non che a voi, donne, ma a me hanno già contristati gli occhi e 'l petto, per che io sommamente disiderato ho che a capo se ne venisse. Ora, lodato sia Idio, che finite sono (salvo se io non volessi a questa malvagia derrata fare una mala giunta, di che Idio mi guardi), senza andar più dietro a così dolorosa materia, da alquanto più lieta e migliore incomincerò, forse buono indizio dando a ciò che nella seguente giornata si dee raccontare" (IV.10.3). In calling the theme a *malvagia derrata*, and in refusing to associate himself with it by continuing along the same path, Dioneo does what only he can do: put a stop to it, recognizing the need for some sort of repair.

These various expressions of discomfort contrast markedly with Filostrato's own withdrawn, severe posturing. He criticizes the first tale "con rigido viso" (IV.2.2); thinks at length before commenting on the second; appears to be "quasi da profondo pensier tolto" (IV.4.2) when intervening after the third; applauds the fourth *alquanto*; and expressly shows no compassion for Andreuola after the sixth. These comments record a marked shift from the pattern of the previous three days, where a singular reaction on the part of the queen is hardly ever recorded. The contrast between Filostrato's attitude and that of the women underscores their divergence of purpose and the discord that now informs their relations. Neifile had announced that a kingship would be something of an experiment, and readers are left at day's end to decide how successful it has been. Dioneo and the ladies clearly do not think all has gone well.

In announcing her theme for the next day, Fiammetta chides the king in a manner reminiscent of Dioneo's earlier objection: "Filostrato . . . acciò che meglio t'aveggi di quel che fatto hai, infino a ora voglio e commando che ciascun s'apparecchi di dover doman ragionare di ciò che a alcuno amante, dopo alcuni fieri o sventurati accidenti, felicemente avvenisse" (IV.Conc.5). Vengeance begets vengeance. Filostrato had sought to make the ladies suffer because he had suffered at a woman's hands, and now, having endured along with the other women, Fiammetta sets about to right things. Her theme wins universal acclaim: "a tutti piacque" (IV.Conc.6). The reaction echoes others. At the end of Day I, after Filomena announces her theme, we learn that "Le donne e gli uomini parimente tutti questo ordine [of a theme] commendarono e quello dissero da seguire" (I.Conc.12); even Dioneo approves, though he asks to be excused. At the end of Day II, after Neifile argues that the group should move and proposes her theme, "Ciascuno commendò il parlare e il diviso della reina, e così statuirono che fosse" (II. Conc.10). Boccaccio's silence about any initial reaction to Filostrato's theme is thus telling, as is the general enthusiasm about Fiammetta's. While it is difficult to imagine why Filostrato likes this new theme, the fact that he subscribes to it indicates that, as he is no longer king, he accepts the principle of the monarch's discretion, which he had earlier exploited.

The Day IV Stories and the Repressive Household

If Filostrato's storytellers both protest his theme and accept his rule, they also challenge him more subtly, by shifting the discussion of patriarchal rule onto the stories themselves. In this way they find a logical remedy for his command. After all, the king had initially demanded that the group tell stories of unhappy love to compensate for his own amorous misery; he thus made the first move of making the political personal. His subjects simply reply in kind, projecting their own distress onto the same narrative field. Both sides thus exploit narrative for a cathartic purpose, Filostrato by indulging his unhappiness, the women by critiquing the same patriarchal structures that currently vex them. Both thus see the Day IV narratives as providing a space for addressing a problem in the *brigata* itself. This dynamic replicates the use of themes in Days II and III, where questions of how one confronts adversity appear to shadow the plague. The issue now is arguably far more immediate, however. While the plague sits at a geographic remove, previously repressed patriarchal structures inhere suddenly to the group and trouble its function.

The topical unity that Filostrato's maneuver engenders, both in his declaration of a theme and in the group's reaction to it, casts the Day IV stories not just as single units but also as parts of a whole. That the *Decameron* here makes space for a formal investigation of a repressive male order becomes clearer when one considers the ordering of the nine stories told under the thematic umbrella. Three symmetrically arranged stories form the backbone of the day: the first, the fifth, and the ninth. In the first story a king and father, Tancredi, takes action against his servant and his daughter, Guiscardo and Ghismonda, for their amorous trangressions. In the fifth story three brothers act against their sister and their employee, Lisabetta and Lorenzo, for their amorous transgressions. In the ninth story, a husband, Guglielmo di Rossiglione, avenges the amorous transgressions of his wife and his best friend, Guglielmo Guardastagno. In each case of these "novelle tragiche per eccellenza" (Fedi 50), the relationship of the authoritarian male to the female transgressor varies: father, brother, husband. These different situations also replicate the three types of paterfamilias relations, namely father, brother, spouse, which Aristotle treats in Book VIII of the *Ethics*. The three stories thus share a subtle connection through Aristotle that creates a larger critical discourse.[10]

The first story offers an ideal bridge between the discourse of monarchy as a state institution and monarchy as a form of domestic patriarchal order. As Prince of Salerno and father to Ghismonda, Tancredi plays a dual role that confounds the crisis confronting him.[11] With Ghismonda, he is principally a domestic head of household, insisting that she has hurt him as a father, but his secretiveness in dealing with the two lovers suggests concern also about the political ramifications for him of a scandal.[12] With Guiscardo he is primarily the offended king, dwelling on the page's social inferiority: "E or volesse Idio che, poi che a tanta disonestà conducer ti dovevi, avessi preso uomo che alla tua nobiltà decevole fosse stato. . . ." In the same sentence, however, he implies that Guiscardo is almost a member of the family: "nella nostra corte quasi come per Dio da piccol fanciullo infino a questo dì allevato" (IV.1.27). The remark unwittingly betrays Tancredi's own sense of guilt, as he condemns the two lovers for a relationship that strikes him somehow as incestuous. But Guiscardo knows well that he is no son to Tancredi. He addresses his lord as *voi* in the one sentence he speaks in the story: "Amor può troppo più che né voi né io possiamo" (IV.1.23). Ghismonda, on the other hand, uses the familiar *tu* with her father, even as she distances herself from him by repeatedly calling him by name. In another sign that the broader domestic relationships of the king's court overlap with the more intimate relations of immediate family, Tancredi addresses both lovers using the *tu*.

The king himself describes conflicts over how to handle Ghismonda

---

10. Another significant factor in the arrangement of these three stories involves their narrator. Fiammetta tells the first story in anticipation of her becoming queen the following day; Filomena's putative love-relation with Filostrato likely determines her place in narrating the central story; and of course Filostrato tells the ninth story because as king he holds that place.

11. Marcus perceptively argues: "Sabotaged by his own system of repression and denial, the prince violates all the distinctions upon which the social order depends: those between parent and child, male and female, lord and subject, aristocrat and commoner, elder and youth" (*An Allegory of Form* 52).

12. Indeed, the sympathetic public reaction to Ghismonda and Guiscardo—their story provokes "general dolore di tutti i salernitani" (IV.1.62)—suggests that Tancredi's instincts were correct, that the public would be more sympathetic to the couple's love story than to their insult to his authority.

that suggest confusion about his own identity as king and father: "Dall'una parte mi trae l'amore il quale io t'ho sempre più portato che alcun padre portasse a figliuola, e d'altra mi trae giustissimo sdegno preso per la tua gran follia: quegli vuole che io ti perdoni e questi vuole che io contro a mia natura in te incrudelisca: ma prima che io partito prenda, disidero d'udire quello che tu a questo dei dire" (IV.1.29). The blurring of roles is essential to Tancredi's psychology, as the above sentence makes clear. He seeks Ghismonda's assistance in deciding what to do about her because he cannot decide whether to act as a father and spare her or as a king and have her executed. Unfortunately for him the two states are not mutually exclusive, so if he acts as a father he fails in his duty as king, and if he acts as a king he commits an unspeakable act, filicide. The fact that he consults her again reflects the inverted nature of their relationship, underscored by the tearful conclusion of his speech: "E questo detto bassò il viso, piagnendo sì forte come farebbe un fanciul ben battuto" (IV.1.29). The combination of submissiveness and assertiveness toward her, his own lack of clarity about their respective identities as relatives and members of a court, also enables her to summon the courage to speak forthrightly to him.[13]

Fiammetta's insistence on Tancredi's confusion may be read as well as an encoded critique of Filostrato, who seems likewise unable to distinguish between two identities, as lover and king. Guiscardo enunciates a theory of love that recalls the *stil novo* code, according to which the power of love is too great to resist. Filostrato would like this code to function in his own personal universe. Fiammetta offers an alternative in the form of Tancredi, according to which men vengefully subjugate women who do not reciprocate their love. Ghismonda clearly feels trapped: "E dimorando col tenero padre, sì come gran donna, in molte dilicatezze, e veggendo che il padre, per l'amor che le portava, poco cura si dava di più maritarla, né a lei onesta cosa pareva il richiedernelo, si pensò di volere avere, se esser potesse, occultamente un valoroso amante" (IV.1.5). Her recourse to secrecy represents the only solution to her dilemma: her father has not taken steps to find her another husband, and she does not feel right about asking him to do so. She intuits that Tancredi's motives involve the nature of his own love for her, a love that has interfered with the fulfillment of his paternal responsibilities. Tancredi and Filostrato begin to look a lot alike, at least in Fiammetta's construction. Both are lover-kings who abrogate their own duty—in Filos-

---

13. Mazzotta perceptively notes that this sentence echoes Dante's reaction to Beatrice's denial of his *saluto* in the *Vita nuova*, adding: "The use of the vocabulary from the *Vita nuova* discloses Boccaccio's strategy of suggesting how the prince's political discourse hides an erotic desire of which he is not aware" (145). On Tancredi see as well Forni's important pages, *Forme complesse* 121–46.

trato's case, to ensure that "niuna novella altra che lieta ci rechi di fuori"—because they cannot separate their emotions from their sense of duty.

The showdown between Tancredi and Ghismonda bears the markings of a trial, though tellingly Tancredi chooses to hold it not in his seat of power but in his daughter's bedroom, the locus of his scrambled desire. This is the first of many inversions that characterize the exchange between father and daughter, and which suggest that he is looking to her for a solution to his dilemma that obviates the need to punish her. Thus while the king appears as judge, guarantor of justice for the state, he remains the *tenero padre* who craves his daughter's acknowledgment. He levels two accusations, demanding a reply from the accused before passing sentence: first, that she has engaged in sexual relations outside of matrimony—he uses the telling phrase "sottoporti a alcuno uomo" (IV.1.26), graphically describing what he has witnessed and how it offends him—and second, that she has taken a lover beneath her station. In fact neither accusation may be contested, as Tancredi has witnessed her sexual activity with his own eyes and says as much, so clearly he is seeking something other from Ghismonda than a convincing counternarrative. She instead resists her initial impulse to behave stereotypically, summons her *animo altiero*, and prepares to self-immolate. She bases her decision on an awareness whose ambiguity commands attention: "Ghismunda, udendo il padre e conoscendo non solamente il suo segreto amore esser discoperto ma ancora preso Guiscardo, dolore inestimabile sentì" (IV.1.30). The possessive pronoun *suo* does not have a clear referent: it could be Ghismonda, but it could just as well be Tancredi. In other words, the daughter may have understood, through her father's speech, the precise terms of his affection for her, and she organizes her reply as a means to short-circuit the incestuous impulse that bears down upon her.

Ghismonda opens her reply with juridical argumentation, combining an absolute argument, that the act was in itself right, with an assumptive one, which shifts responsibility for her actions onto Tancredi himself: "Egli è il vero che io ho amato e amo Guiscardo, e quanto io viverò, che sarà poco, l'amerò, e se appresso la morte s'ama, non mi rimarrò d'amarlo: ma a questo non m'indusse tanto la mia feminile fragilità, quanto la tua poca sollecitudine del maritarmi e la virtù di lui" (IV.1.32). She will elaborate on the correctness of her act in the sentences that follow, insisting on her needs and the appropriateness of her choice of Guiscardo, despite his social standing, in no small part because Tancredi had repeatedly praised Guiscardo in the past.

Ghismonda peppers her discourse with references to law and sin, presenting a careful theory of both. Essentially, she denies Tancredi's authority by claiming to answer to a different set of laws that he does not embody.

She first refers to "le leggi della giovanezza" (IV.1.33), by which she apparently means laws that require young people to love, because the latter are filled with "concupiscibile disidero." Later she will refer to another law that distinguishes people by class, but she insists that "benché contraria usanza poi abbia questa legge nascosa, ella non è ancor tolta via né guasta dalla natura né da' buon costumi; e per ciò colui che virtuosamente adopera, apertamente sé mostra gentile, e chi altramenti il chiama, non colui che è chiamato ma colui che chiama commette difetto" (IV.1.40). Here she distinguishes between a "law" that affirms class differences—her father's law—and the custom that equates virtuous behavior with being called *gentile*.[14] Those who refuse to recognize that a person of lowly birth can belong to the *gens* in her mind commit a delict. Elsewhere she will cast her argument in terms of sin, referring to the *natural peccato* of sexual desire; later she again acknowledges "amorosamente aver peccato" (IV.1.38), but she will conclude by accusing her father of being "in prima cagion di questo peccato, se peccato è" (IV.1.44), which effectively walks back any acknowledgment of sin. In other words, Ghismonda describes a world of conflicting norms, the laws of nature and the laws of the father.[15] She claims to answer to the former, which contain neither social nor religious codes, and which allow what the paternal law would deny; one need only love sincerely. Arguing that desire is natural and not subject to social constructs, Ghismonda negates its sinfulness, and where there is no sin there can be no punishment. The irony of her speech is that it gives Tancredi precisely the counternarrative he needs to suspend punishment, but he cannot embrace it because to do so would mean to deny everything he understands himself to represent.

Through her reply Ghismonda also voices the response of a Fiammetta who objects to Filostrato's mixing of the personal and the political. With

---

14. Ghismonda's argument in fact echoes the one advanced by Dante in the *canzone* that opens the fourth treatise of the *Convivio:* "e dirò del valore, per lo qual veramente omo è gentile, / con rima aspr'e sottile; / riprovando 'l giudicio falso e vile / di quei che voglion che di gentilezza / sia principio richezza" (vv. 12–17). Boccaccio's alignment of her with Dante's thinking on the subject reinforces her position as exponent of an ideology that transcends the sclerotic notions of class represented by her father.

15. Michelangelo Picone casts the conflict in slightly different terms: "La novella quindi intende sceneggiare l'interazione fra due tipologie dell'amore: da una parte abbiamo la *storghe*, l'amore paterno e filiale che lega Tancredi e Ghismonda, e dall'altro troviamo l'*eros*, l'amore sensual che unisce Guiscardo e Ghismonda." He characterizes the two typologies as following "un pericoloso sentiero di collisione," leading to the "lotta fra Tancredi e Guiscardo per la conquista dell'Oggetto unico del loro desiderio, Ghismonda" ("Dalla lai alla novella" 329). While I agree for the most part with his fascinating reading of the story, I would only point out that the tale's outcome depends not entirely on the conflict between two typologies of love but also on the fact that the perverse code of love to which Tancredi subscribes is subsumed in his sense of legal authority over his household.

regard to Filostrato, the most important argument concerns Ghismonda's characterization of the laws of youth. Ghismonda does not represent herself as obligated to reciprocate the love of a man who chooses her; she defines herself not as desired object but as desiring subject. In mentioning the laws of youth, Ghismonda does not contest courtly love claims about love's reciprocity, but she does assert the right of women to choose for themselves. Fiammetta even offers a small linguistic hint to assert the connection. Having characterized Filostrato's theme as "fiera materia di ragionare," she describes Ghismonda's resolve in the face of her father's cruelty as a *fiero proponimento*. As Tancredi's harshness provokes Ghismonda's own harsh resolve, so too does Filostrato's provoke Fiammetta's assertion of the value women attach to their own amorous autonomy.

Significantly, the tale ends ambiguously, signaling that the conflicting sets of laws remain in conflict. Having administered private justice to Guiscardo and Ghismonda and "tardi pentuto della sua crudeltà," Tancredi has them buried together and in public: "con general dolore di tutti i salernetani, onorevolmente ammenduni in un medesimo sepolcro gli fé sepellire" (IV.1.62). It is by no means clear that the people of Salerno suffer *dolore* because of the lachrymose story of Guiscardo and Ghismonda or because Tancredi chose to bury them together.[16] This is a question of no small import, because it goes to whether Tancredi's final gesture in the matter satisfies a progressive populace or offends a conservative one. Finishing on this note, Fiammetta locates the story not on one side or the other of a cultural divide, but right on top of it. As an encoded statement about Filostrato's rule, it foregrounds the conflict that he has unleashed without predicting how the battle will end.

---

16. Critical reception of the story raises the question of whether this gesture is too little too late. Mazzotta, for example, points to Fiammetta's remark about Tancredi's having dirtied his hands in *amoroso sangue* (IV.1.3), arguing that it "hints at the conventional contrast (which Boccaccio, in the wake of St. Thomas Aquinas and John of Salisbury deploys in his commentary on *Inferno* XII) between the benign and temperate prince and the bloody tyrant. For Tancredi is a tyrant, who cannot rule over others any more than he can rule over himself, or, simply, he cannot rule over others *because* he cannot rule over himself, and who makes of the arbitrariness of his will the letter of the law" (141–42). Such a reading does not however account for how Tancredi summons self-control in the end, acceding to his daughter's wishes, though I agree with Mazzotta when he says that the joint burial "is both a simulacrum of the eternal love of Ghismunda and Guiscardo, and it is the emblem of the persistence of political authority, ready to change the death it inflicts into its own survival" (157). Still, inasmuch as for Aristotle the tyrant thinks only of his own interest, whereas the king considers that of his subjects, the tale's ending very much leaves the tyrant-versus-monarch question unanswered, because it is not clear whether Tancredi's final decision in the matter garners the sympathy of the people of Salerno or their hostility. For another reading of the tale's conclusion see Marcus, *An Allegory of Form* 61.

The monarchical model embodied in Tancredi will yield, in the fifth story, to the timocracy of Lisabetta's three brothers. The affiliation that Filomena describes in the story squares perfectly with Aristotle's description in the *Ethics:* "The community formed by brothers resembles a timocracy, since brothers are equals, except to the extent that their ages differ" (1161a4; Rowe trans. 220). Thus when the eldest of the three brothers discovers the relationship between his unmarried sister and his young employee, he brings the information to the others:

> per ciò che savio giovane era, quantunque molto noioso gli fosse a ciò sapere, pur mosso da più onesto consiglio senza far motto o dir cosa alcuna, varie cose fra sé rivolgendo intorno a questo fatto, infino alla mattina seguente trapassò. Poi, venuto il giorno, a' suoi fratelli ciò che veduto aveva la passata notte d'Elisabetta e di Lorenzo raccontò; e con loro insieme, dopo lungo consiglio, diliberò di questa cosa, acciò che né a loro né alla sirocchia alcuna infamia ne seguisse, di passarsene tacitamente e d'infignersi del tutto d'averne alcuna cosa veduta o saputa infino a tanto che tempo venisse nel quale essi, senza danno o sconcio di loro, questa vergogna, avanti che più andasse innanzi, si potessero torre dal viso. (IV.5.6–7)

The brother ponders his options but does not act because he is driven by "più onesto consiglio," which plays out as a sense of obligation not to his sister but to his brothers. The next sentence, in which the brothers reach a decision under his guidance, continues the choppy quality of the first. The almost breathless syntax reflects the distress they are feeling at the discovery of something revolting, a *vergogna* that they must remove from their *viso,* a punning anticipation of the return of Lorenzo's head—a literal return of the repressed—later in the story.[17]

---

17. The nature of the *vergogna* remains unclear. Fedi calls it the "effetto di una ossessionante e stravolta 'etica' mercantile e di un rapporto fraterno basato sulla sudditanza" (51). Mario Baratto had earlier offered a similar analysis, calling theirs "la logica dei mercanti fuori patria, esposti ai pericoli, danneggiati in ogni caso da scandali eventuali e quindi preoccupati del loro onore, abituati a una lunga ponderazione prima di decidere" ("Struttura narrativa" 41). I find Baratto's analysis particularly troubling, because in truth the story conveys no logic for the brothers' actions, and the only scandal that might accrue would come from their failure to act now to marry their sister: she and Lorenzo have acted discreetly, after all, and their affair comes to light only by chance discovery. Alessandro Serpieri in fact argues that "La scoperta dell'infrazione erotica li sconvolge in modo esorbitante, perché sentono la sessualità della sorella come una vergogna personale, una contaminazione che marchia i *loro* volti repressi" (65). While Fedi's and Baratto's analysis highlights the family's mercantile status and its attendant insecurities—which stands in contrast to the courtly world of the first tale and the chivalric world of the ninth—it does not account for the brothers' inexplicable reluctance to marry Lisabetta in the first place, an aspect of the tale that Serpieri points out. His interpretation draws a line from

As the story plays out, the brothers continue to act in unison. They go off together with Lorenzo, then ambush and kill him in a deserted place. Worried by his absence, Lisabetta inquires of all three as to his whereabouts, until one of them finally asks her, in feigned exasperation, why she cares. As Lisabetta's beauty fades while she mourns over Lorenzo's head, which she has disinterred and reburied in a pot of basil, the brothers worry together about her decline and eventually remove the pot. Their concern persists, for she continues to ask for the pot while lying on her deathbed, and together they discover the head hidden under the dirt. Paranoid about the implications for them should the head be discovered, they bury it and flee: "cautamente di Messina uscitisi e ordinato come di quindi si ritraessono, se n'andarono a Napoli" (IV.5.22), where presumably they will not have to explain their sister's absence but where they will also find no relief from their outsiders' paranoia. Their efficient timocracy remains intact; no dissent or conflicting purpose divides them. There is no decline from timocracy into its dangerous alternative, democracy.[18]

The story thus presents another strong object lesson for women who devise to be sexual agents. As Ghismonda did previously, Lisabetta here initiates the relation with Lorenzo, "il quale, essendo assai bello della persona e leggiadro molto, avendolo più volte Lisabetta guatato, avvenne che egli le incominciò stranamente a piacere" (IV.5.5). The brothers do not know this history, nor does it matter to them; what offends them is the relationship itself, which reminds them of their own shortcomings as collective head of household: "che che se ne fosse cagione, ancora maritata non aveano" (IV.5.4). Their dispatch in resolving the problem only makes them look worse. They show they can work together to solve domestic problems; they just never bothered to solve the problem of Lisabetta before she took matters into her own hands. At the same time, however, she does not escape blame: the brothers simply had not married her *yet*, and Filomena never suggests that they had no intention to marry her at all. Earlier Ghismonda had execrated her father for not attending to her needs, but the two cases are not exactly equivalent. Ghismonda reminds Tancredi that she had already been married, and her prior sexual experience had taught her "qual piacer

---

their failure to marry her to their revulsion at her behavior: and that line consists precisely in a discomfort with the notion of their sister as a sexual creature.

18. At the same time, however, this story, like the others, denies the full efficacy of the repressive actions that powerful men undertake. The brothers kill Lorenzo in secret and then quietly flee Messina, making every effort to hide their guilt. But never mind, for as the tale's conclusion makes clear, the story comes out anyway, in the form of the *canzone* whose first lines Filomena cites. On the history of the song and its place in the fourth day see Picone, "L''amoroso sangue'" 134–35. Poole has cleverly identified the source of the story for its eventual conversion into song in Lisabetta's *fante*.

sia a così fatto disidero dar compimento" (IV.1.34). Lisabetta has no prior sexual experience that we know of, only the same *concupiscibile disidero* that Ghismonda describes, and had she waited she might have entered the socially approved context, matrimony, in which to satisfy it.

The ninth story, told by Filostrato, examines male rule in marriage, the third Aristotelian category. Aristotle compares marriage to an aristocracy, because it relies on the sharing of resources and division of labor: "from the beginning their functions are differentiated, so that the man's are different from the woman's, and so they complement each other, making what belongs to each available to both in common" (1162a23–24; Rowe trans. 222). The aristocracy declines into oligarchy when "the man lords it over everything . . . for the distribution in that case takes no account of worth, or of where his superiority lies" (1160b35; Rowe trans. 220). In other words, the husband's natural superiority should put him in a position to share authority, not to function autocratically. Filostrato's story ironically reinvents this paradigm, focusing on the question of merit when addressing the wife's transgression.

The story begins as an investigation of the disruptive impact of women on homosocial bonds. Filostrato insists on the similarities that unite Guiglielmo Rossiglione and Guiglielmo Guardastagno, beginning with their common first name and extending to the fact that each is a feudal lord. He signals their closeness by pointing out that they often wore arms, and "in costume avean d'andar sempre a ogni torneamento o giostra o altro fatto d'arme insieme e vestiti d'una assisa" (IV.9.5). By wearing the same insignia, they make a public statement about their bond and their shared identity which, introduced first in the story, makes the fact that Rossiglione is married seem like a footnote. Indeed, if anything this choice of a story by Filostrato renews the question of whither his own desire, which first emerged when he disclosed his sense of identification with Ghismonda.

Given the closeness of the two knights, it comes as no surprise, as Mazzotta argues (152), that their friendship devolves into a love triangle, as Guardastagno falls in love with Rossiglione's beautiful wife.[19] This development may simply represent an extension of everything the two men share; their very identities are so linked that it makes sense that Guardastagno would fall in love with the same woman Rossiglione loves. Alternatively, and consistent with the theory of triangular desire elaborated by René Girard, the love can be seen as a transfer of Guardastagno's desire for Rossiglione onto his wife, and as a transfer of the wife's desire for her husband

---

19. Mazzotta, Almansi (The *Writer as Liar* 144–52), and Marcus (*An Allegory of Form* 48) all draw useful comparisons between these two tales.

onto the person he most loves. The wife reciprocates Guardastagno's feelings in no small part, it seems, because her husband by esteeming him has taught her to do the same. She knows him to be a *valorosissimo cavaliere* thanks to Rossiglione, who, in literally parading about dressed as his best friend, suggests that the two are perfect counterparts of one another and perhaps fuels some confusion in the wife about which one was her husband. It is noteworthy nevertheless that Filostrato chooses to criticize Guardastagno for violating the code of friendship between the two men, for falling in love "non obstante l'amistà e la compagnia che era tra loro" (IV.9.6). In other words, it is not the adultery per se that rankles, but rather the risk to which Guardastagno willingly puts the friendship.

Discovering the affair, Rossiglione puts an end to it, as readers know, by ambushing and killing Guardastagno, cutting out his heart, and serving it to his wife for dinner. The excision of the heart has particular resonance here, as it did in the first story, because the tale as much concerns Rossiglione's wounded love for Guardastagno—Filostrato tellingly calls it "il grande amore che al Guardastagno portava" (IV.9.8)—as it does Tancredi's for Ghismonda. Here Aristotle helpfully nuances things. Rossiglione has ironically failed to adhere to the principle of sharing that defines the aristocracy of marriage: jealous of his love for Guardastagno, he refuses to share him with her, and her with him. He cannot see the love between Guardastagno and his wife as contiguous with his own love for Guardastagno, a love that he can express only by dressing as his twin, whereas she can express it more intimately. One should also note, however, particularly given the story's Provençal context and its attendant amorous codes, that while the language alludes to a sexual relationship between Guardastagno and the wife, it does not explicitly confirm one.[20] The two behave indiscreetly, and Rossiglione soon becomes aware, *se n'accorse* (IV.9.8), that they are in love. There is no scene of discovery, as in the first and fifth stories, only rather a certain dawning in Rossiglione's mind.

Rossiglione defines their love as an act of disloyalty. As he ambushes Guardastagno he cries out, "Traditor, tu se' morto" (IV.9.11); later, when revealing to his wife that she has eaten her beloved's heart, he explains: "Quello che voi avete mangiato è stato veramente il cuore di messer Guiglielmo Guar-

---

20. Boccaccio seems to suggest that the two were indeed having sex, "insieme furono una volta e altra amandosi forte" (IV.9.7), though he may be interpolating from his Provençal source. Unfortunately, as John Matzke reports, we do not have Boccaccio's direct source, but in Matzke's reconstructed source there is no explicit reference to a sexual relationship, only to an intense love: "En Guill. De C. si amava la dompna per amor—et chantava de lieis, en fazia sas canzos. E la dompna q'era joves (e gaia) e gentils e bella, sill volia ben major che a ren de mon" (5). I thank my colleague Julie Singer for helping me with this passage.

dastagno, il qual voi come disleal femina tanto amavate" (IV.9.22). He senses, erroneously, that their love somehow excludes him, though it is really all about him, and he reacts by abrogating his friendship with both. His means with Guardastagno is straightforward, while his approach with his wife is somewhat more circuitous and vicious and denotes the decline from aristocracy into oligarchy. Rossiglione treats his wife imperiously, and in so doing he marks the difference between himself and Guardastagno—the capacity for cruelty—that helps explain the wife's suicide.

The wife disagrees with her husband's assessment of the situation: "Voi faceste quello che disleale e malvagio cavalier dee fare; ché se io, non isforzandomi egli, l'avea del mio amor fatto signore e voi in questo oltraggiato, non egli ma io ne doveva la pena portare" (IV.9.23). The crime, in other words, is hers, not Guardastagno's, because she willingly reciprocated his love. In punishing Guardastagno rather than his own wife, Rossiglione had been disloyal to his friend, because he has disobeyed the foundational principle of friendship, the giving of affection. A true friend, the wife seems to imply, would remain a friend to Guardastagno despite the perception of betrayal, particularly because in the end the punishable error lay with the wife, over whom Rossiglione has a domestic claim, and not the friend, on whom he can place no demands.

Like the other two, then, this story presents a tangle of problems. As in the first tale, much of the difficulty rests on the male protagonist's role confusion. Tancredi struggles to balance his dual roles as father and king, Rossiglione as husband and friend. Both define betrayal as a refusal to give them their due, though what they see as owed them varies according to the position of the debtor: daughter, servant, wife, friend. The common debt is loyalty, due principally by virtue of position and only once, in the case of Guardastagno, by virtue of action. The latter principle gives the Rossiglione–Guardastagno relationship a unique cast, providing perhaps a key to understanding the day. Filostrato is interested in tragic love, but he is also concerned with friendship. In the ninth story he defines friendship in terms of the Tenth Commandment: Thou shall not covet thy neighbor's wife. At the same time, it appears to offend him when something, namely a woman, interrupts the love that two men have for one another. In Filostrato's imagined world women understand their obligations and men can bond with men.

Gestures of Repair in Day V: Panfilo, Filostrato, Dioneo

The tension between Filostrato and Fiammetta takes a new turn when the king chooses a successor, Fiammetta herself. Filostrato identifies her as "colei la quale meglio dell'aspra giornata d'oggi, che alcuna altra, con quella di domane queste nostre compagne racconsolar saprai" (IV.Conc.3). While with this statement Filostrato implicitly acknowledges that some damage has been done, he also undertakes to restrict Fiammetta's choices.[21] Beneath his apparent altruism lies an attempt to extend his rule by influencing Fiammetta's own: she should structure her choices to furnish an antidote to the theme of unhappy love. She accepts his challenge, choosing her topic so that "meglio t'aveggi di quel che fatto hai" (IV.Conc.5), though her circumlocution leaves unanswered the question of what precisely he has done. Presumably, he, and we, will better understand the damage wrought by Day IV as the group moves into Day V.

Fiammetta's theme appears directly to answer Filostrato's: "ciò che a alcuno amante, dopo alcuni fieri o sventurati accidenti, felicemente avvenisse" (IV.Conc.5). As indicated by her use of the key adjective *fieri*, Fiammetta wants the group to follow the same narrative pattern established in Day IV, but to rewrite the ending: the characters will no longer die but instead will find remedy for their misfortune. She thus envisions the day as a palinode to the previous one, with the trajectories of the Day V characters tracking that of the *brigata:* both groups will experience happiness following despair. The plan goes somewhat awry, however, as the misery of Day IV, experienced both in the frame and in the *novelle,* tempers the much-longed-for happiness of Day V. In returning to Day IV paradigms, the next day takes shape more accurately as a palimpsest, under whose text lurks that of the previous day.

Indeed, in Day V issues raised in the previous day receive new consideration, with a narrowing of focus that helps retroactively to clarify some of the Day IV problems and strategies. The Day IV stories fall under a bigger umbrella than those of Day V: the issue of male repressiveness informs the most important stories, while the others describe other types of tragedy that can befall young lovers. Leaving aside the anomalous second story and the tenth, we have the third story, in which three sisters run away from home with their boyfriends only to face disaster; and the fourth, in which a man, Gerbino, defies the patriarch, his grandfather the king, and loses both his beloved and his own life.[22] The sixth, seventh, and eighth stories recount

---

21. Truth to tell, he is also not the first to do so. Dioneo, in introducing his story, had expressed the hope that it would give "forse buono indizio . . . a ciò che nella seguente giornata si dee raccontare" (IV.10.3). The remark puts indirect pressure on whoever will be the next monarch to find an antidote to what has transpired in the fourth day.

22. Unlike Tancredi this king, Guiglielmo, seems to have a clearer sense of priorities: "fece prendere il Gerbino: e egli medesimo, non essendo alcun de' baron suoi che con prieghi da ciò si sforzasse di rimuoverlo, il condannò nella testa e in sua presenza gliele fece tagliare, volendo avanti senza nepote rimanere che esser tenuto re senza fede" (IV.4.26). He also appears

sudden death, twice by natural causes and once by accidental poisoning. In Day V, on the other hand, the triangular model that informs stories 1, 5, and 9 of Day IV consistently repeats itself, as this day zeroes in on the function of male power in the household. While the broad question of male power concerns the storytellers, the narrower question of men's reactions to expressions of female agency constitutes their true focus. This issue, one of many in Day IV, coalesces from an impulse analogous to the one that drove it in Day IV, where the female storytellers insisted on their own agency in the face of patriarchal authority by highlighting active female protagonists. In both days, however, the success of women's agency remains contingent upon the benevolence of the man in charge.

The Day V stories focus on comic literary modalities through their emphasis on the happy ending of marriage. The triangular love relationships assume one of two forms. In most cases a male drawn into a female's sexual orbit threatens or obliterates the authority of the male head of household, who is, however, finally beneficent (stories 2 through 7). In an insidious revision of this dynamic, the lover either incorporates or is allied to institutional power in opposition to female will, and he resorts to coercion to reach his goal (tales 1, 8, and 9). Not all the happy endings are therefore alike, especially for the female characters. While one may argue that marriage in itself constitutes a happy ending for women for socioeconomic reasons, the stories suggest that happiness involves more than economic security and social standing. When the marriage results from a coercive act on the part of the lover, the outcome seems less positive for women, as for example in the story of Nastagio degli Onesti. Nor is marriage simply the new beginning that ends the story, for two stories also feature a marriage *in medias res*, furthering the exploration of marriage as aristocracy that Filostrato had initiated in Day IV.

In what follows I shall examine four of the ten Day V stories, the first, fourth, ninth, and tenth. These tales capture in different ways the problems I have described above: male domestic power, the happy ending, the representation of marriage in action. Three have male narrators. Panfilo tells the first story and Dioneo, of course, the last. Male voices thus bookend the day, with intriguing implications for the happy ending. Filostrato offers the fourth story as recompense for the harm he has done, returning to the problem of marriage as aristocracy. The stories told by the women, on the other hand, generally envision less problematic solutions to the knot the lovers create for themselves. Fiammetta's tale, however, perhaps

---

to understand the rhetorical importance of public executions, inasmuch as they reinforce the coercive power of the king. To his own detriment, Tancredi is too ashamed of his daughter and of his own feelings to execute anyone publicly.

best embodies the spirit of the day by exposing the problem implicit in the prescribed happy ending, how it finally limits women's choices.

Panfilo leads off, making no overt reference to the previous day but rather looking insistently forward: "Molte novelle, dilettose donne, a dover dar principio a così lieta giornata come questa sarà, per dovere essere da me raccontate mi si paran davanti: delle quali una più nell'animo me ne piace, per ciò che per quella potrete comprendere non solamente il felice fine per lo quale a ragionare incominciamo, ma quanto sian sante, quanto poderose e di quanto ben piene le forze d'Amore, le quali molti, senza saper che si dicano, dannano e vituperano a gran torto: il che, se io non erro, per ciò che innamorate credo che siate, molto vi dovrà esser caro" (V.1.2). Panfilo positions himself rhetorically in a manner analogous to that of Boccaccio in the Introduction to Day IV: he addresses the ladies directly while reducing critics of love, here presumably Filostrato, to third-person mention. He avers that he has chosen this story because it proves his thesis about the power of love, and he knows the ladies will like it because they are in love. He thus adopts the sort of big-topic rhetorical strategy that he had already practiced in the Ciappelletto story, which by his account evidenced the wealth of God's benevolence toward us. He shows that the power of love and the happiness of women do not always coincide, suggesting that women are inferior subjects in God's creation.

For all of his proleptic posturing, however, Panfilo constructs a story that is grounded in a number of earlier narratives, beginning with Filostrato's own autobiographical discourse at the end of Day III and the Filippo Balducci story. The king had declared that "sempre per la bellezza d'alcuna di voi stato sono a Amor subgetto" (III.Conc.5); Cimone likewise finds himself subject to Efigenia: "come che lo 'ndugio gli paresse troppo, pur, da non usato piacer preso, non si sapeva partire" (V.1.10). Filostrato laments that his service had gone unrecognized, "né l'essere umile né l'essere ubidente né il seguirlo in ciò che per me s'è conosciuto alla seconda in tutti i suoi costumi m'è valuto" (III.Conc.5). Cimone goes overboard in his attempts to win Efigenia, only to have her father remain steadfast in his promise to marry her to Pasimunda. Cimone's response to adversity is driven by the same sort of narcissism that characterizes Filostrato: "Io son per te divenuto uomo: e se io ti posso avere, io non dubito di non divenire più glorioso che alcuno idio: e per certo io t'avrò o io morrò" (V.1.25). He thus offers an alternate conclusion to Filostrato's own autobiography, one that is much more determined and dangerous. Moreover, as a sort of narrative extension of Filostrato, Cimone—whose name means *bestione* in his native Cypriot, but which in Italian sounds more like "big summit," perhaps a veiled reference to male rule—marks how much the shadow of Filostrato hangs over the new day.

Like the Filippo Balducci story, the Cimone story confirms the power of desire as catalyzed by a vision of womanhood.[23] As a *bestione,* Cimone is another *animale selvatico* (IV.Intro.32), the words used to characterize Filippo Balducci's boy. While for Filippo's son, however, the epiphany lies in the discovery of womanhood itself, Cimone awakens upon discovering a single beautiful woman, "colei che sola a me par donna," one is tempted to say.[24] The results are similar: "non altramenti che se mai più forma di femina veduta non avesse" (V.1.8). Both tales thus affirm women's inspirational power over men, with Cimone's story offering a variant ending to the Filippo Balducci tale. What exactly Efigenia inspires in Cimone remains unclear, however, for he retains his name and remains the *bestione.* The name points to his essence as a force, in accord with Panfilo's own, perhaps ironic, declaration of theme: "quanto sien sante, quanto poderose e di quanto ben piene le forze d'Amore."[25]

The phrase essentially rewrites an earlier one, suggesting another important link with Day IV: "Amor può troppo più che né voi né io possiamo" (IV.1.23). This point of contact with Guiscardo's famous words helps us understand the extent to which Panfilo's story rewrites Fiammetta's earlier one. The same conflict structures both tales: the law of nature on the one hand versus the legal order represented by paternal authority on the other. Panfilo alludes to the former in his reference to the *forze d'Amore.* The order that undertakes to tame our more dangerous impulses comes into play in the repeated interventions of Cimone's own father Aristippo who, after failing to discipline his oversized and handsome but *quasi matto* son, "mai né per fatica di maestro né per lusinga o battitura del padre o ingegno d'alcuno altro gli s'era potuto metter nel capo né lettera né costume alcuno" (V.1.4), sends him away from the city, locus of civilization, to the *villa.* Things go awry, however, when Aristippo, seeing Cimone's conversion into a *uomo* as a result of love, encourages him to pursue his desire:

---

23. Giovanni Getto inadvertently points to the seminal value of the Filippo Balducci story, not just for this tale but for many of the stories of Days IV and V, when he observes that it is "impostata . . . non tanto su un'azione quanto su una passione, che sorge improvvisa nonostante ogni cautela e su cui, anziché avere solo inizio, gravita e si conclude il racconto" (30). He finds Boccaccio's half-story to be unique to the *Decameron* in this regard, though given other more recent studies of the role that passion plays in these stories one is left to wonder whether Getto did not in fact overlook an important connection.

24. I cite from Petrarch's *Canzoniere,* 126, v. 3. Mazzotta sees the epiphany as leading to madness, with consequences for the *Decameron's* notion of order (200).

25. Cimone's names have been subject to interpretation elsewhere as well. Marcus notes the name's resemblance to *scimmione,* and she also sees Cimone as a figure of violence, through recourse to Dante ("The Sweet New Style Reconsidered"). Stavros Deligiorgis, on the other hand, provocatively notes the resemblance between Cimone's given name, Galeso, and Galeotto, the book's subtitle (110).

"in seguir ciò in tutti i suoi piaceri il confortava" (V.1.23), thereby unwittingly abetting the chaotic forces of love as they act against the civilizing power of law. In this sense the story constitutes a reconsideration of the tale of Ghismonda and Tancredi, imagining the implications for the social order had the king sanctioned his daughter's trespass.

The reimagining also substitutes the desiring female for a desiring male, with important implications. Perhaps more than any other in the *Decameron*, this story exemplifies the gendered basis of an order that privileges the satisfaction of male desire over women's autonomy. Panfilo may describe Cimone as passive to love's power, but the latter reverses that power onto his victim with a determination the begs the question of the sincerity of his conversion to courtliness. The narrative of that conversion recalls classical tales of the civilizing process offered by Cicero and Livy. At the beginning of *De inventione* Cicero explains the origin of eloquence in a need to persuade men to live according to reason:

> For there was a time when men wandered at large in the fields like animals and lived on wild fare; they did nothing by the guidance of reason, but relied chiefly on physical strength; there was as yet no ordered system of religious worship nor of social duties; no one had seen legitimate marriage nor had anyone looked upon children whom he knew to be his own; nor had they learned the advantages of an equitable code of law. And so through their ignorance and error blind and unreasoning passion satisfied itself by misuse of bodily strength, which is a very dangerous servant.
>
> At this juncture a man—great and wise I am sure—became aware of the power latent in man and the wide field offered by his mind for great achievements if one could develop this power and improve it by instruction. Men were scattered in the fields and hidden in sylvan retreats when he assembled and gathered them in accordance with a plan; he introduced them to every useful and honourable occupation, though they cried out against it at first because of its novelty, and then when through reason and eloquence they had listened with greater attention, he transformed them from wild savages into a kind and gentle folk.[26]

---

26. *De inventione* I.ii.1–2: "Nam fuit quoddam tempus cum in agris homines passim bestiarum modo vagabantur et sibi victu fero vitam propagabant, nec ratione animi quicquam, sed pleraque viribus corporis administrabant; nondum divinae religionis, non humani offici ratio colebatur, nemo nuptias viderat legitimas, non certos quisquam aspexerat liberos, non, ius aequabile quid utilitatis haberet, acceperat. Ita propter errorem atque inscientiam caeca ac temeraria dominatrix animi cupiditas ad se explendam viribus corporis abutebatur, perniciosissimis satellitibus. Quo tempore quidam magnus videlicet vir et sapiens cognovit quae materia esset et quanta ad maximas res opportunitas in animis inesset hominum, si quis eam posset elicere et praecipiendo meliorem reddere; qui dispersos homines in agros et in tectis silvestri-

Cicero's myth of how men came to accept law, transforming themselves from wild savages into gentle folk, helps clarify what is at work in Cimone. His education ultimately fails him because, paradoxically, it was not reason but passion that tamed him. Where rational argument from his teachers and his father had failed, desire had succeeded, but only to the extent that he assumed the trappings of a *homo rhetoricus,* more style than substance. He begins to wear elegant clothes, learns to converse with philosophers, changes his voice, studies music, horsemanship, and warfare.

Cimone becomes, in sum, a prototype for Castiglione's courtier, though with no commitment to the underlying principles of civilized life to which Cicero's early man had subscribed. Even after four years of education, Cimone still rejects his Christian name, Galeso, because in their first encounter Efigenia had addressed him by the nickname. He thus retains the verbal mark of the same bestial nature that he claims to renounce. Nor is the homophony between *Cimone* and *bestione* coincidental, for in fact words echoing this augmentative suffix create a semantic field of violence that permeates the story. When first traversing the woods Cimone carries a *bastone;* later Panfilo recounts that from a *montone* love had made him a man; when Cimone attacks Efigenia's boat he carries a "rampicone di ferro" and is "fiero come un leone"; upon their surrender his victims declare themselves *prigioni,* and he eventually ends up in *prigione.*

Cimone's reversion to his characteristic forceful nature, and specifically his kidnap of Efigenia as she travels from Cyprus to Rhodes, recalls another Roman narrative, the rape of the Sabine women. The question of rape, as both sexual violence and kidnap, arises repeatedly in the story, first when Efigenia fears for herself upon seeing Cimone looming above her: "cominciò a dubitare non quel suo guardar così fiso movesse la sua rusticità a alcuna cosa che vergogna le potesse tornare" (V.1.13). Later, when Cimone and Lisimaco have made off definitively with Efigenia and Cassandrea, Panfilo recounts that they "lieti della loro rapina goderono" (V.1.70). Beyond this act of carrying off the women, which recalls the Sabines, there is another common element: both the Romans and Cimone confront a ban on marriage. In Livy's narrative the Roman men had repeatedly asked to marry the women of neighboring cities, only to be rebuffed. In like manner Efigenia's father Cipseo refuses Cimone's request for her hand because he has already promised her to Pasimunda. Livy also singles out a "young woman of much greater beauty than the rest," (44) whom the Roman

---

bus abditos ratione quadam compulit unum in locum et congregavit et eos in unam quamque rem inducens utilem atque honestam primo propter insolentiam reclamantes, deinde propter rationem atque orationem studiosius audientes ex feris et immanibus mites reddidit et mansuetos." I am grateful to my colleague Wayne Fields for introducing me to this passage.

Thalassius had chosen for himself, and who was seized by a gang hired for that purpose. Cimone similarly identifies Efigenia as "la più bella cosa che già mai per alcun vivente veduta fosse" (V.1.8), and he hires a gang to help him kidnap her: "tacitamente alquanti nobili giovani richiesti che suoi amici erano" (V.1.26). After seizing her, he seeks to reassure her: "Nobile donna, non ti sconfortare; io sono il tuo Cimone, il quale per lungo amore t'ho molto meritata d'avere che Pasimunda per promessa fede" (V.1.33). In like manner the Romans attempted to calm the captured Sabine women: "The men, too, played their part: they spoke honeyed words and vowed that it was passionate love which had prompted their offense" (44). Both the Romans, who are lying, and Cimone rationalize their actions by claiming to answer to a higher power, which they claim supersedes the laws of men. Panfilo confirms as much when describing Cimone's first vision of the sleeping Efigenia: "dubitava non fosse alcuna dea; e pur tanto di sentimento avea, che egli giudicava le divine cose essere di più reverenza degne che le mondane" (V.1.10).

Like the Sabine women, whom Livy calls "the prize of whoever got hold of them first" (44), Efigenia and Cassandrea are finally property. Initially they passed from the control of their fathers to that of their husbands, Pasimunda and Ormisda, with whom their fathers had entered into a legitimate marriage contract. Having killed the two husbands, Cimone and Lisimaco assert their control over the two women by dint of the physical threat they represent to the women and the others. Never do the women enjoy any rights or privileges, particularly in the realm of sexual choice, as do the men. The fact that the men can finally keep their spoils affirms the means they chose to acquire them: their coercive behavior is simply an extension of the coercion of women inherent in state and family structures.

The juxtaposition of Cimone's superficial conversion to courtesy against the reality of his enduring bestiality ironically proves Ghismonda's very thesis: clothes do not make the man. Efigenia's pursuer thus emerges as the comic—or tragic, depending on one's point of view—antithesis to Guiscardo: "La virtù primieramente noi, che tutti nascemmo e nasciamo iguali, ne distinse; e quegli che di lei maggior parte avevano e adoperavano nobili furon detti, e il rimanente rimase non nobile. E benché contraria usanza poi abbia questa legge nascosa, ella non è ancor tolta via né guasta dalla natura né da' buon costumi; e per ciò colui che virtuosamente adopera, apertamente sé mostra gentile" (IV.1.40). The issue is indeed one of birth, not in economic terms but as birth with nobility of character.[27] Guiscardo

---

27. Michelangelo Picone argues that Ghismonda's is "una definizione della nobiltà ancorata non al fattore esterno dell'ereditarietà del sangue, ma al fattore interno del perfezionamento

was born poor but noble; Cimone, wealthy but base. Nature, in Ghismonda's scheme, may admit economic ascent or descent, but not changes in character, and such applies to Cimone as well. Indeed, what Panfilo, who views Cimone somewhat heroically, cannot bring himself to say directly about him, he does imply in the specular *novella ad incastro* of Lisimaco, equally frustrated in love and equally violent: "l'onestà diè luogo a amore" in Lisimaco's decision to kidnap Cassandrea.[28] Efigenia's helpless surrender to Cimone is a gesture of female subservience to tyranny that relegates her to the opposite pole from Ghismonda.

Thus the first story, rather than break free of the previous day's mold, replicates it. True, a genuinely tragic ending is averted, but only through a compromise at the expense of legitimate marriage contracts and any interest in female happiness. Panfilo's conclusion is revealing: "dopo alcuno essilio Cimone con Efigenia lieto si tornò in Cipri e Lisimaco similmente con Cassandrea ritornò in Rodi; e ciascun lietamente con la sua visse lungamente contento nella sua terra" (V.1.71). The grammatical insistence on the male subject, and the accompanying insistence on the happiness of the male, effectively excludes the two women as subjects of happiness: their feelings simply do not matter. In his essay on the fourth day, Roberto Fedi had located the day's origins in the tale of Alibech (III.10). This story too leads back there, inasmuch as the female model first realized in an Alibech whom Rustico "contro a' voler di lei . . . rimenò in Capsa" (III.10.32) is here not only resurrected but strangely idealized. While the men must pay the price of *alcuno essilio* for their actions, the scandal they have provoked ("In Cipri e in Rodi furono i romori e' turbamenti grandi e lungo tempo per le costoro opere," V.1.70) does not lead to a reversal of fortune for the female victims, who live out their lives with their kidnappers.

The shadow of Day IV hangs over Filostrato's story as well. He prefaces it with a reference to the previous day's drama: "Io sono stato da tante di voi tante volte morso perché io materia da crudeli ragionamenti e da farvi piagner v'imposi, che a me pare, a volere alquanto questa noia ristorare, esser tenuto di dover dire alcuna cosa per la quale io alquanto vi faccia ridere . . ." (V.4.3). He then tells the ribald tale of Caterina and the nightingale, which

interiore operato, oltre che dalla virtú, proprio dall'amore" ("Dalla lai alla novella" 331). The question in the present story is whether a love such as Cimone's, which like Ghismonda's is a *fol'amor* or "amore-passione" (332), really can lead to this perfection.

28. Marcus observes that "What Cimone does on a personal level, Lisimaco does at the level of the state as magistrate of the island of Rhodes, for he bends the laws to the exigencies of his own passions by using his office to facilitate a jail break, a double kidnapping, and wholesale slaughter" ("The Sweet New Style Reconsidered" 9). Her analysis tends to validate the story's structural complexity, since by inserting the story of Lisimaco within that of Cimone Boccaccio effectively offers in the day's first tale evidence of the duality of patriarchal terror, both personal and political.

returns to the terrain of marriage. Like the female protagonists of the Day IV stories, Caterina falls in love with a boy, Ricciardo dei Manardi, who frequents her home. Her overprotective parents strangely neglect to consider the risk the boy represents: "niuna altra guardia messer Lizio o la sua donna prendevano che fatto avrebbon d'un lor figliuolo" (V.4.6). The story thus sets up in terms nearly identical to that of Ghismonda and Guiscardo, in which Tancredi never dreamed that his daughter would develop any interest in Guiscardo because he saw him as a son.[29]

When the young couple is discovered, naked and asleep, on Caterina's balcony, her parents seek to remedy their inattention. Giacomina, the mother, leaps to accuse Ricciardo: "la donna, tenendosi forte di Ricciardo ingannata, volle gridare e dirgli villania" (V.4.37). Messer Lizio stops her, assuming the voice of reason: "Donna, guarda che per quanto tu hai caro il mio amore tu non facci motto, ché in verità, poscia che ella l'ha preso, egli sì sarà suo. Ricciardo è gentile uomo e ricco giovane; noi non possiamo aver di lui altro che buon parentado: se egli si vorrà a buon concio da me partire, e' gli converrà che primieramente la sposi, sì che egli si troverà aver messo l'usignuolo nella gabbia sua e non nell'altrui" (V.4.37–38). Lizio urges his wife to understand that there is more to consider than her sense of betrayal. In his argument he stresses a practical element that was often missing in the Day IV stories, particularly Ricciardo's class and wealth, which make him an acceptable match for Caterina. The wife's subsequent silence suggests that she is willing to compromise with her husband: "Di che la donna racconsolata, veggendo il marito non esser turbato di questo fatto e considerando che la figliuola avea avuta la buona notte e erasi ben riposata e aveva l'usignuol preso, si tacque" (V.4.39). The sentence describes her conflicting identification with husband and daughter that puts her in a position of perhaps less equality with Lizio than first appears. The story suggests that the notion that the sharing of resources in marriage, as described by Aristotle, is contingent on a hierarchy of authority, with men at the top.

In fact, while Lizio treats his wife respectfully, he still shows a capacity for menace. In his speech to his wife he warns her to be quiet and then suggests that Ricciardo will have little choice but to marry Caterina: "se egli si vorrà a buon concio da me partire." In presenting this solution to Ricciardo, he first details his indignation, then repeatedly makes a similar

---

29. Marcus draws some useful comparisons between the two tales (*An Allegory of Form* 55–59). Most noteworthy perhaps is her observation that "Tancredi opted for tragedy by plotting a revenge as dark and secret as the lovers' intrigue had been. But Lizio opts for comedy by instantaneously granting Caterina and Ricciardo the chance to enjoy such evenings on a permanent basis, thus signaling his willingness to transmit power from the old generation to the new—a process which Tancredi could not bring himself to accept" (58).

threat: "acciò che tu tolga a te la morte e a me la vergogna. . . . in questa guisa puoi e la mia pace e la tua salvezza acquistare: e ove tu non vogli così fare, raccomanda a Dio l'anima tua" (V.4.43). Ricciardo really has no option but to marry Caterina, though he also understands that by doing so he will return to the good graces of his future father-in-law, sparing him further *vergogna* and restoring his peace. Lizio makes an implicit promise that as long as Ricciardo agrees to the plan, there will be no hard feelings.

Facilitating the happy ending here is the fact that the two young people love one another: Ricciardo has fallen fiercely in love with Caterina, and she, upon noticing it, reciprocates his love. Marriage thus represents the logical conclusion to their story, satisfying her parents' desire that she marry someone of her own rank and her own desire for a love that her parents have modeled in their own marriage. Nevertheless, Filostrato in his conclusion seems principally interested in Ricciardo: "Ricciardo . . . sposò la giovane . . . e poi con lei lungamente in pace e in consolazione uccellò agli usignuoli e di dì e di notte quanto gli piacque" (V.4.49).

The story provokes universal laughter among the ladies and prompts Fiammetta to observe that "Sicuramente, se tu ieri ci affligesti, tu ci hai oggi tanto dileticate, che niuna meritamente di te si dee ramaricare" (V.5.2). Her use of the verb *affligere* necessarily recalls the *Decameron*'s opening aphorism, "Umana cosa è aver compassione degli afflitti," suggesting that Filostrato's rule had returned the ladies to the state of affliction they endured before Boccaccio came along to comfort them. The tale of Caterina begins to look like a gesture of compassion, a sign that the erstwhile king is human after all.

The notion of female agency returns to the fore in Fiammetta's introduction to her own story, the tale of Federigo degli Alberighi: "A me omai appartiene di ragionare; e io, carissime donne, da una novella simile in parte alla precedente il farò volentieri, non acciò solamente che conosciate quanto la vostra vaghezza possa ne' cuor gentili, ma perché apprendiate d'essere voi medesime, dove si conviene, donatrici de' vostri guiderdoni senza lasciarne sempre esser la fortuna guidatrice, la quale non discretamente ma, come s'aviene, smoderatamente il più delle volte dona" (V.9.3). Her introduction synthesizes Filostrato's position and the women's response to it. She acknowledges the power of women, "quanto la vostra vaghezza possa ne' cuor gentili," as Filostrato had done earlier: "sempre per la bellezza d'alcuna di voi stato sono a Amor subgetto" (III.Conc.5). While Filostrato laments that his service has gone unrecognized, "né l'essere umile né l'essere ubidente né il seguirlo in ciò che per me s'è conosciuto alla seconda in tutti i suoi costumi m'è valuto" (III.Conc.5), Fiammetta counters by asserting a woman's right to choose her lover, and her obligation to choose carefully and according to opportunity, "dove si conviene." Her remark that women should not be passive to fortune equates the power of fortune, here understood in the terms seen in Day II as an external force over which we have little control, with the men who claim the right to make decisions on behalf of the women whose lives they govern. She thus counters Filostrato's complaint with one of her own: fortune often assigns love *non discretamente*, without discernment, presumably for women's preferences, and *smoderatamente*, too abundantly. In other words, women should undertake to determine their own sexual futures before someone else does it for them, though the situation that Fiammetta describes differs from many of the others because the woman is actually in a position to make her own choices.

The story itself involves all three types of family relations, parenthood, marriage, and brotherhood. While the *novella* draws attention to Federigo, plot developments hinge significantly on Monna Giovanna's position as wife, mother, and sister. As the story begins she is both married and a mother, "ne' suoi tempi tenuta delle più belle donne e delle più leggiadre che in Firenze fossero" (V.9.6), and she remains steadfastly indifferent to Federigo's extravagant gestures and loyal to her husband. Federigo behaves as *smoderatamente* as fortune itself, making a public spectacle of his love. The husband, who dies early on, guards his wealth rather more cautiously, leaving his considerable estate to his son and only secondarily to his wife, should the son predecease her. The vertical passage of wealth suggests in the father a traditional patrilinear, hierarchical concept of parenthood that supersedes any obligation he has incurred to his wife. For her, however, the economic arrangements are secondary to her love for her son, as evidenced by her concern for his failing health and her futile attempt to secure Federigo's falcon, which the boy has identified as key to his recovery. Once the son dies, the inheritance becomes hers, and her brothers, absent up until now, enter the picture. They pressure her to remarry, because she is "ricchissima e ancora giovane" (V.8.39): she seems to pass from one state of subjugation to another, finally returning to where she had started, her birth family. Unlike so many of the women of these two days, however, Giovanna professes no interest in future love; indeed, she resists her brothers' pressure. Ultimately, she surrenders: "La quale, come che voluto non avesse, pur veggendosi infestare, ricordatasi del valore di Federigo e della sua magnificenzia ultima, cioè d'avere ucciso un così fatto falcone per onorarla, disse a' fratelli: 'Io volentieri, quando vi piacesse, mi starei; ma se a voi pur piace che io marito prenda, per certo io non ne prenderò mai alcuno altro, se io non ho Federigo degli Alberighi'" (V.9.39–40). Giovanna thus yields to her brothers' pressure while making her own choice. They call her *sciocca*, foolish, judging him beneath her because "non ha cosa del mondo" (V.9.41). She famously replies that she would rather have a man in need of wealth than wealth in need of a man.

The reply confirms Giovanna's intention to establish a second marriage according to the Aristotelian model of aristocracy. She and Federigo will pool their resources: she will contribute wealth and he manhood, that is, character. The story concludes, however, by returning its focus to Federigo. Giovanna becomes an object to be given away, along with her money: the brothers "lei con tutte le sue ricchezze gli donarono" (V.9.43). And Federigo is the grammatical subject of the happily-ever-after event: "Il quale così fatta donna e cui egli cotanto amata avea per moglie vedendosi, e oltre a ciò ricchissimo, in letizia con lei, miglior massaio fatto, terminò gli anni suoi" (V.9.43). He acquires a woman who matches him in human qualities, and whose wealth he desires to conserve.[30] Indeed, he no longer has a reason to be a spendthrift, because he has acquired the object—Giovanna—in which he had invested so heavily. In any event, the story, with its final reckoning on Federigo, describes a world in which a woman's choices remain limited. Giovanna may not elect to remain alone; her wealth in particular appears to preclude that option. Her age and prior marriage afford her some freedom, so she can opt to wed Federigo, but there is nothing in the story to suggest that she marries him for love. Clearly she admires him: "la grandezza dell'animo suo, la quale la povertà non avea potuto né potea rintuzzare, molto seco medesima commendò" (V.9.37). Nevertheless, the love that drives so many of the protagonists of these two days, including Federigo, finds no home in her. As Sergio Zatti summarizes it, "Giovanna diventa ricca e padrona della sua libertà grazie alla morte del figlio designato erede, Federigo diventa ricco e felice, sposandola, grazie alla morte del falcone mancato salvatore del ragazzo" (245). He is instrumental to her search for freedom, while he marries for love.

Certain elements mark this story as conclusive, of not only the themed material of Day V, but also that of Day IV as well. Most significant is a narrative detail whose significance is in fact hidden: Federigo's presentation of the falcon's body parts ("le penne e' piedi e 'l becco le fé in testimonianza di ciò gittare avanti," V.9.37). Federigo presumably wants to prevent Giovanna from thinking that he has lied about the whereabouts of the bird in order to keep it for himself. In showing her its disparate parts, however, he actually

---

30. Stuard makes an important point in this context: "A woman's resulting 'incapacity' [i.e., according to Gratian] before the law mandated certain 'capacities' from her husband, first among them being his obligation to preserve her dowry" ("Burdens of Matrimony" 48). In effect by marrying Giovanna Federigo obligates himself to become a *miglior massaio;* otherwise, according to Stuard, he would be answerable before both ecclesiastical and civil courts.

repeats a gesture that we find in the Provençal antecedent to IV.9. Matzke's reconstruction reads: "Et a so q'ellal crezes ben si fetz aportar la testa denan lieis" (5–6). Significantly, Boccaccio suppresses this detail in his reelaboration: the wife requires no proof from her husband beyond his claim before choosing suicide. In reintroducing it in V.9, however, he underscores the less intimate nature of the relationship between Federigo and Giovanna, his sense that he must make his case before her. Moreover, this shared element couples with another common thread, the eating of an object of desire prized, albeit in different ways, by both parties. Both the wife and Rossiglione desire Guardastagno's heart, though only the wife eats it, and both Giovanna and Federigo desire the falcon, and both eat it. Each story thus turns on a transaction involving the object of desire, reduced in both cases both to a synecdoche for the object itself in its whole, living state, and to a metaphor for the troubled relationships that culminate in the meal.[31] In the former case the eating produces further destruction, while in the latter the meal leads to an unexpected constructive outcome. The queen, in other words, rewrites the king, or perhaps better, erases him. Filostrato turns out to have been right: she better than any other lady—or rather, better than three other ladies, for three have already ruled—knew how to *racconsolar* her *compagne*.

The tale of Federigo reaches back even further, to the Introduction to Day IV. Boccaccio perhaps insists on Federigo's presentation of proof in order to introduce the word *becco,* for in choosing that body part above all others he inserts a word that is already freighted with metaphor. Filippo Balducci had warned his son to avoid women, telling him precisely that "tu non sai donde elle s'imbeccano!" after the boy had asked for a gosling, explaining that "io le darò beccare." The son expresses his sexual desire metaphorically, as nutrition, thus alluding to a fantasized scene of sex as eating.[32] Filippo's ambiguity about how women eat, "donde elle s'imbeccano," finds clarification in Giovanna and in Federigo's misunderstanding of what she wanted

---

31. My concept of the meal as a site of transaction, particularly involving affection, differs from the taxonomy offered by Sanguineti White in her study *La scena conviviale.* While hers remains a useful review both of the history of Boccaccio's use of the meal in his works and of the specific uses to which he puts the scene in the *Decameron,* it does not locate the common denominator that links all scenes of eating, namely a desire for something other than food that unites people in a meal or that the meal provokes.

32. Indeed, alimentary scenes pop up regularly in these two days, beginning with Tancredi's visit to Ghismonda "dietro mangiare" (IV.1.17), to Gabriotto's dream of the greyhound who gnaws into his chest and runs off with his heart (VI.6), to Pasquino's use of the poisoned sage leaf to clean his teeth, "d' ogni cosa che sopr'essi rimasa fosse dopo l'aver mangiato" (IV.7.12), to the wedding banquet that Cimone ruins, to the great luncheon hosted by Nastagio degli Onesti.

when she came to him. Ready to give her something to eat, he discovers that she sought a different sort of meal. Only Giovanna's final, imperfect acceptance of Federigo rescues her from the misogynistic stereotype that Filippo purveys.

The comic ending in marriage, which runs throughout the day, thus finds its logic in both the Balducci story and Filostrato's Day IV story, which focused on love relations between men and women rather than parents or siblings. Nevertheless, Fiammetta's story offers a particular type of caution to Filostrato: a man may love as passionately as Federigo and finally obtain the object of his desire, but there is no guarantee he will acquire love as well. In finally denying the equation of marriage with love, Fiammetta anticipates Day VII, in which married women will consistently seek and find love elsewhere. She also lays the groundwork for Dioneo's story, which follows hard upon hers and offers another comic variant of the themes that have been percolating throughout the day.

If the aristocratic marriage involves the pooling of resources, then one can think of few more successful marriages than that between Pietro di Vinciolo and his wife. I have argued elsewhere that this story deserves more critical attention than it has received, particularly because of its pride of place ("Sodomitic Center" 11–12).[33] While so much attention has gone to the "central" *novella* of the *Decameron,* VI.1, relatively little has gone to the other central story, V.10. Indeed, neither story is *the* central tale; rather, they surround a fold in the book, the turning point between the first and second halves. And while the tale of Madonna Oretta has rightly been seen as an important statement about the art of storytelling, which ramifies to other significant textual *loci* (Stewart, "Novella"), the Pietro di Vinciolo story does not enjoy similar status. Yet structurally it functions as a *mise en abyme,* containing a story within its story, and so reflects the *Decameron* in miniature, offering final and important words about gender relations and textuality as the book's first half concludes.

I argued earlier that this tale has to some degree been a victim of homophobia. Its suggestion of sodomy, with all the attendant discomfort the topic provokes in a historically Catholic, heterosexual critical audience, combined with a tendency to "discount" Dioneo's contributions because of their sometimes salacious nature and their elliptical relationship to the book's principal themes, have often removed this tale from the critical conversation.[34] Its status is reminiscent of Machiavelli's famous words to

---

33. My earlier essay in this *novella* appeared at the same time as Gaylard's, which makes many of the same points about the story's centrality. But her analysis goes in a different direction from mine and reaches different conclusions about the story's import.

34. As an amusing example, I offer Ferdinando Neri's essay from 1944, in which he de-

Ludovico Alamanni upon reading the *Orlando furioso:* "mi dolgo solo che, havendo ricordato tanti poeti, che m'habbi lasciato indietro come un cazzo" (383). To be sure, critics interested in Boccaccio's relationship to Apuleius have paid close attention to the *novella,* as indeed one should, for it discloses many of its secrets in comparison to the source.[35]

In order fully to understand Boccaccio's manipulation of themes of male authority in this tale, one must first see how it miniaturizes the *Decameron* as a whole. The significant element here, borrowed from Apuleius, is the apparent redoubling of the tale's action. Pietro comes home to tell a story that is actually his own, though he does not know it yet: like Tancredi, he is an unsuspecting character in his own story. While Pietro was preparing to *cenare altrove,* as the rubric puts it, he witnessed his friend Ercolano's discovery of his wife's lover, hidden in their laundry room. As he recounts this story to his own wife, Pietro does not know that she also has hidden a lover, this time under a chicken basket in a *loggetta* near their dining room. Like other characters in the *Decameron,* Pietro is a storyteller, though he never appears listed alongside Ser Ciappelletto, the book's other sodomite, or Melchisedech, or Primas, or the hapless knight who attempts to entertain Madonna Oretta, presumably because his narrative is not a fiction. This omission is indeed strange, because Pietro's account itself demonstrates the plurivalence of Boccaccio's term *storia,* one of the four words he uses to describe his 100 narratives: it is both history from Pietro's point of view

clares that "la serie delle passioni felici si chiude con la novella di Federigo degli Alberighi, che . . . assurge all'espressione più delicata di un amor cortese e profondo" (79). To be fair, Neri regularly ignores the Dioneo stories, despite his assertion later in the essay that "la figura [dell'autore] più risentita e più determinata è infatti quella che più gli somiglia, Dioneo" (82). Rosario Ferreri, on the other hand, does include the tale in his parade of obscene passages, calling it "la novella più lontana dall'ideale di vita dei novellatori e dello stesso autore. Con esso si tocca il punto più turpe della tematica erotico-oscena del *Decameron*" (172–73). Of course his reading demonstrates Boccaccio's argument that obscenity is in the eye of the beholder, because in fact the tale contains no obscene language, nor does it overtly describe any scenes of sex.

35. On this tale and its source in Apuleius, see, among Italianists, Sanguineti White and Pastore Stocchi; Bolongaro also provides a useful reading. Walters, Halperin, Freccero, Goldberg and Menon, and most recently Eisner and Schachter, all consider the novella in its relationship to Apuleius within the context of the history of sexuality. These readings are a mixed bag. Freccero appears not to have read Boccaccio's story too closely, for she explains that the narratives in Apuleius and Boccaccio concern "a husband who returns home early to discover a young man, with whom his wife has been having an affair, concealed in his house" (43). Well-informed readers of the *Decameron* know that in Boccaccio's version the wife's first meeting with her lover happens on the night that Pietro discovers him: to be sure, she has been sleeping around, but she has yet to consummate *this* affair. Goldberg and Menon, on the other hand, interrogate details of Boccaccio's narrative with highly suggestive results, as do Eisner and Schachter.

and story from the reader's. Moreover, in its insistent redoubling—Pietro's narrative is at once the retelling of what happened at Ercolano's house, a prolepsis of events in his own house, and a retelling of the story in Apuleius, itself told by an intradiegetic narrator who is also a character in the tale itself—it bears the marks of the same sort of multilayered, palimpsestic narrative that fills so many of the pages of the *Decameron*.

Structurally, then, the story recapitulates *in nuce* the principal vector of the *Decameron* itself, its movement from history to story as indicated both in the Proem, where the author claims a lived experience as motivation for writing the book, and in the Introduction to Day I, where the historical event of the plague serves as a pretext for the fictitious gathering of the ten young people. Michelangelo Picone describes the latter as moving from a "prima parte . . . storico-cronistico" to a "seconda parte . . . storico-utopistico, nel senso che dalla storia com'è si passa alla storia come dev'essere" ("Autore/narratori" 49). In philosophical terms the movement thus extends from *is* to *ought*, from empiricism to normativity. The double narratives in Pietro's tale exhibit the same movement, albeit in an ironic key. When Pietro leaves his friend's house, Ercolano's marriage lies in ruins. Pietro's own marriage then teeters on a similar brink, but the principals find a way to save it by satisfying both parties, including a wife who, in an ironic anticipation of the tale's denouement, "due mariti più tosto che uno avrebbe voluti" (V.10.7). Pietro thereby contributes in his way to the construction of the same "nuova società" that Picone identifies with the storytelling of the ten narrators.

The story takes Dioneo significantly out of bounds, and he demonstrates his awareness of this by invoking the same sort of defense he had first deployed in I.4. While acknowledging the daring of his narrative, he justifies it by explaining that "la fatica [of storytelling], la quale altra volta ho impresa e ora son per pigliare, a niuno altro fine riguarda se non a dovervi torre malinconia, e riso e allegrezza porgervi." He goes on to admit that the coming *novella* is "in parte men che onesta," but will tell it anyway because "diletto può porgere" (V.10.4). The goal of *diletto*, which informed his defense of I.4, here returns, but with a twist: Dioneo executes a sort of preemptive censorship of the *novella* itself, urging the ladies to treat it as they would the tour of a garden: "cogliete le rose e lasciate le spine stare: il che farete lasciando il cattivo uomo con la mala ventura stare con la sua disonestà, e liete riderete degli amorosi inganni della sua donna, compassione avendo all'altrui sciagure dove bisogna" (V.10.5). Of course his suggestion that they ignore the *cattivo uomo* serves only to draw attention to him, the act of suppression inviting the return of the repressed. And indeed, the critical tradition has given much greater attention to Pietro than it has to his wife.[36]

As the story begins, Pietro and his wife have a utilitarian friendship, only half of the pairing of utility and pleasure that Aristotle envisions in a marriage. The fact that they are childless is a problem as well, for as Aristotle points out "children are a good shared by both, and what is shared binds together" (1162a29; Rowe trans. 222). In the absence of a child, they need to cement their marriage by other means, and they are struggling to succeed. He in fact has married her to put to rest rumors of his homosexuality, "forse più per ingannare altrui e diminuire la generale opinion di lui avuta da tutti i perugini che per vaghezza che egli n'avesse" (V.10.6).[37] She is similarly opportunistic, envisioning marriage as a means principally to satisfy her abundant sexual urges: "era una giovane compressa, di pel rosso e accesa, la quale due mariti più tosto che uno avrebbe voluti" (V.10.7). Each seeks the other out of a concern for his or her own good, and their

---

36. Eisner and Schachter argue that Dioneo's "remarks seem to encourage his female audience to pursue a binary reading strategy, but Dioneo acknowledges the limits of this strategy in the next sentence, where he instructs readers how to respond to the three characters of the story" (827). That response includes *compassione* for the boy, with the word recalling Boccaccio's opening aphorism to the *Decameron*, as Eisner and Schachter point out: though by extension this means that the boy was *afflitto*, which would deny that his experience at Pietro's that night had been pleasureful. To their argument that "the binary image of the rose does not quite fit the story it prefaces" I would add this point, namely that while on the one hand Dioneo is dissecting the narrative and identifying what to discard and what to save, he also tells a story that will in retrospect revisit the image of the rose and ask about its referent. If *cogliere la rosa* is a metaphor for the taking of virginity, then the story invites its readers to consider whose rose has been plucked. We know the wife is not a virgin, for she has had many lovers by now. We do not have the same certainty about the boy.

37. Goldberg and Menon problematize this sentence in intriguing ways: "The narrative begins by explaining that in response to local gossip, Pietro took a wife. The nature of the gossip is not specified. Presumably, people are talking because he has not married. Does that mean that he has a 'deviant' desire in terms of object choice, as Halperin claims?" (1614). While I agree with their conclusion, that "The premise of the story then may be less a historical window on an emerging form of homosexual identity than a plotting of what happens when too much meets too little" (1614), I find that they stretch the text a bit to make that point. It seems unlikely that Pietro's resistance to marriage would be fodder for gossip if people simply thought of him as one slow to marry. That reference, coupled with the suggestion that he marries not because of any *vaghezza*, to my mind marks his desire as not normatively heterosexual, as the story will later reveal. The wife herself affirms as much when she says that he is "così vago di noi come il can delle mazze" (V.10.55), that is, averse to women—and readers of the *Decameron* know that this same phrasing is used to describe the book's other sodomite, Ser Ciappelletto. Finally, Boccaccio leaves one other hint that Pietro is a sodomite. According to the rubric, when he hears the young man's shouts "Pietro corre là" (V.10.1), and in fact the story has him running toward the sound: "e corso alla cesta e quella levata, vide il giovinetto" (V.10.50). Dante associates sodomy with running; in his famous final lines to *Inferno* XV he says of Brunetto Latini: "Poi si rivolse, e parve di coloro / che corrono a Verona il drappo verde / per la campagna; e parve di costoro / quelli che vince, non colui che perde" (121–24).

marriage might have worked, as Goldberg and Menon point out, had the advantages they sought for themselves coincided in some way (1614). They do not, however, because while he in fact solves his problems by taking a wife, she does not gain the satisfaction she craved by taking a husband. She expresses her disappointment succinctly: "Io il presi per marito e diedigli grande e buona dota sappiendo che egli era uomo e credendol vago di quello che sono e deono essere vaghi gli uomini" (V.10.10). She expects marriage to couple utility with pleasure: in return for her dowry, which in any event he seems unlikely to need, being "un ricco uomo" (V.10.4), he should tend to her needs, sexual desires included.

Not finding what she seeks in her husband, the wife undertakes to satisfy herself elsewhere. She hires an old woman—a *mezzana*—to procure young lovers for her, which the old woman accomplishes serially: "La vecchia, non passar molti dì, occultamente le mise colui, di cui ella detto l'avea, in camera, e ivi a poco tempo un altro, secondo che alla giovane donna ne venivan piacendo; la quale in cosa che far potesse intorno a ciò, sempre del marito temendo, non ne lasciava a far tratto" (V.10.25). The wife's impulse to hide her activities from Pietro suggests that she perceives him as a threat to her sexual agency, as clearly he is, in more ways than one: by marrying her but not fulfilling her needs, he has effectively closeted her sexuality but exposed his own. The *novella* in fact reminds us about closeting on two occasions, first when Ercolano's wife hides her lover in the laundry room, and later when Pietro's wife hides hers under a basket. Pietro incarnates the threat that both women face when he discovers the wife's young lover: "vide il giovinetto, al quale, oltre al dolore avuto delle dita premute dal piè dell'asino, tutto di paura tremava che Pietro alcun male non gli facesse . . . pregollo che per l'amor di Dio non gli dovesse far male" (V.10.50–51). Later, he accuses his wife of hypocrisy for having excoriated Ercolano's wife. The wife then summons the courage to answer Pietro after noticing that he has resorted only to words and not presumably to fists: "La donna, veggendo che egli nella prima giunta altro male che di parole fatto non l'avea . . ." (V.10.55). Despite Pietro's manifest shortcomings as a husband and apparent membership in the damnable class of sodomites, he still enjoys authority, and those whom he rules acknowledge his power through their actions.

The wife defends her actions by highlighting the practical *quid pro quo* of marriage and reminding Pietro of how she has respected their union:

Ché, posto che io sia da te ben vestita e ben calzata, tu sai bene come io sto d'altro e quanto tempo egli ha che tu non giacesti con meco; e io vorrei innanzi andar con gli stracci indosso e scalza e esser ben trattata da te nel letto, che aver tutte queste cose trattandomi come tu mi tratti. E intendi sanamente, Pietro, che io son femina come l'altre e ho voglia di quel che l'altre, sì che, perché io me ne procacci, non avendone da te, non è da dirmene male: almeno ti fo io cotanto d'onore, che io non mi pongo né con ragazzi né con tignosi. (V.10.57–58)

This speech conflates several themes. First, the wife acknowledges that Pietro has upheld his financial responsibilities toward her but condemns his failure to attend likewise to her sexual needs, and she makes clear that she has taken these steps in light of his inattention. Like Ghismonda, she seeks sexual solace outside of the patriarchal structures even at considerable personal risk. At the same time, however, when she points out to Pietro that she has honored him by not consorting with men of whom he would disapprove, she pursues an argument that Ghismonda could not make and that diverges significantly from the paradigm. Guiscardo, a man beneath Ghismonda's social station, attracted her because he was "per vertù e per costumi nobile" (IV.1.6). Concerns about character do not drive Pietro's wife, however, as she simply seeks sexual satisfaction. She must therefore defend herself differently, arguing that she has respected Pietro's status by not choosing men beneath his station.

The wife's argument thus brings to a close the insistence, which runs through Days IV and V, on the male duty to provide an appropriate context, marriage, in which women may find sexual gratification. Unlike so many of the heads of household who have come before him, Pietro acknowledges this responsibility and addresses it. The crisis subsides, and the marriage finally succeeds, thanks to a felicitous coincidence: the young man whom the wife plans to take as a lover had already caught Pietro's eye. Pietro recognizes him at once as "colui a cui Pietro per le sue cattività era andato lungamente dietro" (V.10.51); the wife also notices Pietro "tutto gongolare per ciò che per man tenea un così bel giovinetto" (V.10.55). The young man becomes the resource they can share, a bizarre substitute for the child who would have bound them together, as they spend the night together in activities the exact nature of which Dioneo claims to have forgotten: "Dopo la cena quello che Pietro si divisasse a sodisfacimento di tutti e tre m'è andato di mente" (V.10.63). Pietro and his wife thus ironically achieve the sort of ideal aristocratic marriage, and perfect friendship, grounded in a recognition and acceptance by each of what is good for the other. It also creates the possibility for children, which the lover might provide in Pietro's stead, and which will become Pietro's best means to "diminuire la generale opinion di lui avuta da tutti i perugini." Dioneo describes a world in which the challenge of conflicting desires can be addressed flexibly, with less attention to form than to outcome. He is sympathetic in particular to the sexual needs of women, and he grounds his own friendship with the ladies in pleasure, endearing himself to them through his wit. The reaction to his story, "meno per vergogna dalle donne risa che per poco diletto" (V.Conc.1), suggests as much. The ladies enjoyed the story in the exact terms, *diletto*, that Dioneo had outlined, but, because of its rather salacious nature, they did not want to betray too much enjoyment for fear of appearing indecorous.

In its meditation on what happens when desires do not coincide, the story also once again allegorizes Filostrato's love experience.[38] In fact, Filostrato and Pietro share an important quality: an interest in surrogacy, as demonstrated in the king's case by his appointment of Fiammetta to clean up the mess he created. In like manner Pietro sees opportunity when it knocks, locating in the boy a source of pleasure for himself and a surrogate to attend to his wife's sexual needs.

Dioneo also provides other clues that Pietro's marriage allegorizes a dispute over storytelling and pleasure. His insistence on the key words *diletto* and *piacere* in association with the reading experience, first enunciated in his introduction to I.4, finds echo in the wife's complaint to the old woman: "se io aspetterò diletto o piacer di costui, io potrò per avventura invano aspettando invecchiare," she declares (V.10.12). In other words, the wife finds in the lover that which Dioneo wants his female audience to find in his texts. The lover who supplies the pleasure is no mere lover, however, and the reason for his arrival on the scene in the book's fiftieth story now becomes all too clear. He is the perfect Galeotto, a true go-between, "non assai certo qual più stato si fosse la notte o moglie o marito, accompagnato" (V.10.63).[39] An allegory of the *Decameron* itself, he is capable of being experienced, that is, read, by both men and women with equally pleasurable results. The exclusion of men that begins in the Proem, and that Boccaccio reaffirms in the Introduction to Day IV, here suffers an about-face, as Boccaccio finds a way for men to read the book: they must acknowledge

---

38. Dioneo had already addressed this issue in the tenth story of Day IV, in which a woman takes a lover because her husband, an old surgeon, cannot or will not fulfill her sexual desires. In that story he displayed the same sort of reluctance to name the problem that Goldberg and Menon discuss in the context of Pietro di Vinciolo (1614). He resorts again to metaphor: "ella il più del tempo stava infreddata, sì come colei che nel letto era male dal maestro tenuta coperta" (IV.10.4). It bears mention as well that the problem of mismatched desire is one that Dioneo apparently holds dear, for in his introduction to IV.10 he refers openly to another tale of his, II.10, in which Riccardo di Chinzica, "più che di corporal forza dotato d'ingegno" (II.10.5—and note the use of metaphor yet again), loses his wife by kidnap to the pirate Paganino da Monaco, with whom she decides to stay because he gratifies her sexually. Nor should we forget that mismatched desire—Rustico can no longer keep up with Alibech—eventually determines the outcome of III.10.

39. So too Gaylard (44), though without evincing the implications that follow here.

and allow women their desire. Moreover, they must be prepared to read *as* women.

This argument provides a context in which to understand fully the rubric's initial presentation of Pietro: "va a cenare altrove." While the chronology outlined in the rubric suggests that the phrase refers to Pietro's interrupted dinner at Ercolano's house, it has other implications as well. The first concerns the role of the meal as a transactional moment involving the exchange of objects of desire and, by extension, of affection, which weaves its way through Days IV and V. The narrated meal gives form to desire, often unspoken, organizing it and resolving it, for better or for worse. This intersection of eating and desire explains Pietro's act of going to eat *altrove*. For the phrase is as much a statement of fact—the meal at Ercolano's—as it is a metaphor for his own sexual desire, which is located *altrove*, both spatially and emotionally other. He goes out to eat with Ercolano, who, like Pietro himself, is somehow failing his wife, since she has taken a lover. The stepping-out underscores Pietro's impossible search for gratification in his own home, a search that will present unexpected possibilities when he discovers his wife's lover. The consumed object in the other stories—the lover's roasted heart, the beloved falcon—here takes the shape of the boy himself. So carefully does Boccaccio endeavor to create a parallelism with the other two objects that the same situation prevails: just as before, when both Rossiglione's wife and Giovanna were unaware of what they were eating, here too the wife is unaware that the boy will be an object of consumption for her: "Dopo la cena"—and not before—"quello che Pietro si divisasse a sodisfacimento di tutti e tre m'è uscito di mente . . ." (V.10.63). Whereas in Filostrato's story the dinner leads to mutual destruction, and in Fiammetta's story the lunch means loss leading ultimately to gain, in this story there is no loss, and no destruction, but only mutual gain.

The precise details of that mutual gain, and the extent to which Filippo learns to appreciate the young man from the point of view of a woman, remain unstated at the story's end: "so io ben cotanto, che la mattina vegnente infino in su la Piazza fu il giovane, non assai certo qual più stato si fosse la notte o moglie o marito, accompagnato" (V.10.63). Boccaccio's use of the verb *accompagnare* here is telling, because it furnishes the etymological link—*compagnia*, from *cum pane*, the sharing of bread—between being together and eating together. While his otherwise ambiguous phrasing[40] shades the details of what transpired in the bedroom, readers should

---

40. Translators have struggled with the sentence. Walters relies on Payne's translation, revised by Singleton: "the youth was not altogether certain which he had the more been that

not shy from the possibilities, though some readings of this story have been strangely limiting. Walters, for example, marshals historical evidence to conclude that Pietro assumed the active role in his activity with the young man, more wishing it were so than knowing it.[41] If anything, the changes Boccaccio wrought upon his Apuleian source, changes that document a shifting idea of sexual identity and sex roles from classical antiquity to the Middle Ages, broadens the range of possibilities. In other words, by having Dioneo coyly declare his ignorance of what truly happened in that bedroom, by avoiding the specificity of Apuleius, he allows the reader's imagination to run in any direction it pleases.

Dioneo's ambiguity may indeed be the true source of the discomfort this tale has provoked, and the attendant opprobrium aimed at it. Boccaccio has found a way to disturb his male readers beyond anything they have previously experienced in the text. In his earlier self-representation as passive to the assaults of men, in the Introduction to Day IV, he had limited his metaphors to the field of battle, traditionally a masculine domain: "mentre io nei vostri servigi milito, sono sospinto, molestato e infino nel vivo trafitto" (IV.Intro.8). Here he launches a surprise attack in another semantic field, summoning a profound discomfort about sodomy. For even if Pietro is not sodomized that night, he likely commits sodomy, and in neither case is the act of sodomy associated with punitive rape, as it is in

---

night, wife or husband" (441). McWilliam adopts a more prosaic solution: "not exactly certain with which of the pair he had spent the greater part of the night, the wife or the husband" (478). So too Musa and Bondanella: "he found himself not quite sure about which one he had been with more that night, the husband or the wife" (376). Generally I think we read the sentence as the latter two translations do, but Boccaccio's willful convolutions are not helpful, and it is just as possible to read the sentence as indicating that the young man did not know whether he had been more wife or husband. Critics such as Walters and Halperin, who insist that Pietro assumed the active role in penetrative sex with the boy, do just that. Eisner and Schachter examine this problem at length, concluding that "critics fix the sense of the text to emphasize a meaning conducive to their argument" (826).

41. Indeed, Walters's observation that Pietro "is nowhere characterized, overtly or by implication, as being like a woman, or effeminate" (27) strikes me as flawed logic, for it partakes of the stereotype according to which "effeminate" gay men are sexually passive without adducing any evidence either that the stereotype existed in the fourteenth century or that effeminacy equates with sexual passivity. Halperin's observation that Pietro is straight-acting in no way correlates with the type of sexual activity he might prefer: "Far from displaying a supposedly 'feminine' inclination to submit himself to other men to be sexually penetrated by them, the husband in Boccaccio plays a sexually insertive role in intercourse with the wife's lover. That, after all, is the point of the story's punchline: 'On the following morning, the youth was escorted back to the public square not altogether certain which he had the more been that night, wife or husband'—meaning, obviously, *wife to Pietro* or *husband to Pietro's wife*" (40–41). I fail to see how Boccaccio's phrase excludes the possibility that the young man performed as a "husband" to Pietro.

Apuleius.[42] Boccaccio's version suggests that men can enjoy being in the position—sexual or otherwise—traditionally associated with women. Men can have pleasure as women do.

Pietro thus shares with Filostrato the fact that a woman, his wife and Fiammetta respectively, leads each to the same place: the *corpus* or text as locus of pleasure. Dioneo undertakes to teach Filostrato that the text should be a source of pleasure, not of suffering, and that in removing the pleasure principle from storytelling he only ensures that his own misery, occasioned by women's rejection of him, will endure. The final story of the fifth day thus provides a last word about Filostrato and a reaffirmation of the fundamental crossing of reading with pleasure that gives birth to the *Decameron*. It is a fitting point of arrival after so much wandering, and a fitting anticipation of the book's second half. The morality of this tale in the end has no bearing, for while Boccaccio's narrators may judge, the *Decameron* itself resolutely does not. The story affirms instead the plasticity of pleasure, the multiple forms it can assume, which makes Dioneo's analogy of reading to a walk through a garden particularly apt.[43] Filostrato's efforts to control the storytelling discourse at the expense of his companions' pleasure, which governs Day IV and infects Day V, thus finds in Pietro's bedroom its most potent antidote.

---

42. Indeed, one may argue that it is the context of rape that makes the act of sodomy palatable in Apuleius. There is no intimation of pleasure, but only a reassertion of power by a patriarchal male.

43. Emilia will echo Dioneo's garden metaphor, with its suggestion of variety and the possibility to pick and choose, when she describes the experience of storytelling at the end of Day VIII: "e veggiamo ancora non esser men belli ma molto più i giardini di varie piante fronzuti che i boschi ne' quali solamente querce veggiamo" (VIII.Conc.4).

CHAPTER IV

Dioneo and the
Politics of Marriage

THE RELATIVE paucity of critical attention devoted to the seventh day of the *Decameron* finds compensation in the richness of the single contributions. To some degree we may attribute the lack of a sustained critical gaze to Cesare Segre, whose famous essay, "Funzioni, opposizioni e simmetrie nella giornata VII del *Decameron*," had assumed the status of last word; as Andrea Battistini puts it, "Segre . . . non sembra avere lasciato molto di più di intentato" (187). As well, the day does not offer the sort of stand-out story with a memorable protagonist—a Ciappelletto, a Ghismonda, a Madonna Oretta—to draw readers to it. Outside of the stories, considerable attention has gone to developments in the frame tale, specifically the visit to the Valle delle Donne, an event integral to Day VII even if its principal action falls at the end of Day VI. Drawing on the activities in the valley, including the stories told there, Lisa Muto has argued that "come la prima metà [del *Decameron*] ha preso il suo tono dalle parole di Pampinea, simbolo dell'ordine, dell'equilibrio e della logica, così la seconda metà ricaverà il suo tono dalle parole di Dioneo, simbolo del divertimento, del piacere e della forza invincibile della natura" (148). Muto's dichotomizing relies on a characterization of Dioneo that others have seconded. In a seminal essay on Dioneo, Alessandro Duranti calls the king "un tipo di anarchico piuttosto eccentrico che pare soffrire di complessi di esclusione" (17). Referring to Dioneo's first speech, in which he obligates the ladies to keep him entertained, Duranti observes that "Dioneo pensa alla brigata non nell'ordine della decina, ma come a un composto, provvisorio e di non facile mantenimento, di nove più uno" (5–6).

Muto's and Duranti's appraisals of Dioneo appear accurate at a distance but tend to break down from close up. After all, it is at Dioneo's prodding that Pampinea enunciates the basic norm and sketches the group's constitution. Disorderly though he may be, his relation to order, and to the very order of storytelling from which he benefits by standing in contrast to it, is in fact quite tight. As Albert Ascoli puts it, in an essay that arguably eclipses even Segre's, Dioneo "is at once outside and inside the social-political order of the *brigata*, which is itself located outside the normal social-political order of Florence" (37). Indeed, nowhere is the tension between Dioneo the insider and Dioneo the outsider more marked than in his rule.

For in fact, upon assuming the laurel crown, Dioneo performs the ultimate insider's act: he chooses a theme for his day. When the crown passes to him, there has already been one day without a theme, and Emilia will later make clear that a monarch may in fact choose not to impose one. One would think that, were he really such a "conoscitore del caos,"[1] Dioneo would have chosen to impose no theme at all. His own decision to provide a topic, particularly one that he must defend, serves as a reminder that he requires order as a backdrop for his own disorderly impulses. In truth order interests him a tad more than he himself would claim. At the same time, however, his own decision to excuse himself from the seventh-day theme and to maintain his traditional tenth slot rather than occupy the ninth, normally reserved to the monarch, suggests that while he appreciates order he prefers to keep some distance from it. I would therefore first like to revisit the question of Dioneo specifically in these terms, to see whether the *Decameron* gives any hint of the source of his conflict. The answer comes, not surprisingly, in the seventh day, and in the relationship that he, as king, institutes with the women.

The crowning of Dioneo involves the same sort of to-and-fro that earlier marked Filostrato's assumption of leadership. Elissa explains to him that "Tempo è, Dioneo, che tu alquanto pruovi che carico sia l'aver donne a reggere e a guidare: sii adunque re e sì fattamente ne reggi, che del tuo reggimento nella fine ci abbiamo a lodare" (VI.Conc.2). Her etymological figure relates rule specifically with kingship, and seems to have, in its exhortation that Dioneo give his subjects reason to praise him, an unspoken subtext in Filostrato's rule. Her challenge in fact recalls Neifile's earlier remarks when crowning Filostrato, though without the metaphors of wolves and sheep. Dioneo nevertheless does reply metaphorically: "Assai volte già ne potete aver veduti, io dico delli re da scacchi, troppo più cari che io non sono; e per

---

1. I refer here to the title of Fredi Chiappelli's study on the *Gerusalemme liberata*.

certo, se voi m'ubidiste come vero re si dee ubidire, io vi farei goder di quello senza il che per certo niuna festa compiutamente è lieta" (VI.Conc.3). Dioneo first compares himself to a chess king in order to minimize his value, as chess kings are often carved from valuable stone. He then suggests that his value for the ladies may actually eclipse that of the chess king, because if they fully obey him he will give them that (the indefinite pronoun *quello*) which makes a party fully happy, likely something of a sexual nature given his circumlocution. His words make pleasure conditional on obedience: the promise of fun comes with a demand for submission.

Introducing his theme for Day VII, Dioneo unwittingly provokes a minor skirmish with the ladies. Invoking the earlier dispute between the servants Licisca and Tindaro over whether most women are virgins when they marry, he proposes storytelling in which wives "o per amore o per salvamento di loro" (VI.Conc.6) play tricks on their husbands.[2] The theme revisits the danger that men represent to women, but the ladies object to it apparently for other reasons: "Il ragionare di sì fatta materia pareva a alcuna delle donne che male a lor si convenisse, e pregavanlo che mutasse la proposta già detta" (VI.Conc.7). The key word here is the verb *convenire*, which occupies the semantic field of decorum. Fiammetta had earlier used it to object to Filostrato's theme: "Fiera materia di ragionare n'ha oggi il nostro re data, pensando che, dove per rallegrarci venuti siamo, *ci convenga* raccontare l'altrui lagrime. . . . poi che a me non *si conviene* di mutare il suo piacere . . ." (IV.1.2; italics mine). The ladies here raise the same issue, that of *convenienza* or suitability, which also carries an important subtext, thanks to its Latin etymology in *cum venire.* In both cases they suggest to their king that he recall why they have come together, and whether what he now demands of them suits that purpose. The women also appear to have learned something from Filostrato's earlier rule: not to delay their protests. Having initially accepted Filostrato's theme without objection, they then verbalized their discomfort only the next day when telling the stories. Here, however, they respond more quickly and more forthrightly, while there is still time for Dioneo to change his mind.

Like Filostrato before him, Dioneo refuses to budge; rather, he positions himself as the ladies' defender, arguing their right to discourse about this topic. He makes three points: first, that given the tenor of the times prior rules of decorum no longer apply; second, that the women have nothing to fear from addressing salacious topics as long as they behave properly, and

---

2. Barolini notes the novelty of Dioneo's move: "he is the first ruler to propose a topic suggested by someone else" (283). I would not take this to mean that he cannot come up with his own ideas—notwithstanding his own claim to that effect—but rather that he appreciates both Licisca's talent for metaphor and her willingness to confront sexual issues head-on.

third, that they owe him the courtesy of following his rule. In describing the present circumstances, he employs judicial metaphors: "Or non sapete voi che, per la perversità di questa stagione, li giudici hanno lasciati i tribunali? le leggi, così le divine come le umane, tacciono? e ampia licenzia per conservar la vita è conceduta a ciascuno?" (VI.Conc.9). He thus invokes Pampinea's earlier claim, uttered out of his earshot, that "Natural ragione è, di ciascuno che ci nasce, la sua vita quanto può aiutare e conservare e difendere" (I.Intro.53). However, his argument also involves some sleight of hand that leaves unanswered questions.[3] In stating that the judges have abandoned the courts and the laws have fallen silent, he suggests that no one can stand in judgment of the ladies if they violate standard behavioral norms. At the same time, however, he claims that everyone enjoys the right to self-preservation, and he sees storytelling as consistent with that impulse. But his use of the passive voice, "ampia licenza . . . è conceduta," leaves unspecified the agent making this concession. It may be God, but God's laws are explicitly silent; so it seems odd indeed that God, in the face of a natural disaster, would suspend his own laws. More accurately, the unnamed agent is "we": this freedom is granted to us by us. Dioneo's argument involves the same sort of circularity that natural law arguments always involve: they project authority outside of the human agent as a way of concealing the fact that humans create their own authority.

Dioneo concedes that the ladies will stretch the limits of their *onestà* by following his lead, but to the extent that they tell stories "non per dover con l'opere mai alcuna cosa sconcia seguire ma per dar diletto a voi e a altrui" (VI.Conc.10), they exempt themselves from criticism.[4] Moreover, he reminds the group, they have behaved in a manner *onestissima* up until now, so that were they to stop speaking about less decent topics one might begin to suspect them of misbehaving elsewhere. Finally, he points out that he has been "ubidente a tutti," and now that he is king he would appreciate the same: "mi fareste un bello onore," he remarks tartly, if "avendomi vostro re fatto, mi voleste la legge porre in mano, e di quello non dire che io avessi imposto" (VI.Conc.14). His tone here becomes decidedly less jocular, as his defense of women's interests slides into a veiled accusation against

---

3. Excellent on this point is Giovannuzzi, "Le parole e le cose" 472–73. For another analysis of the speech see Barolini 283–85.

4. With its distinction between saying and doing, the sentence adumbrates the opposition highlighted by Barolini in her essay "*Le parole son femmine e i fatti sono maschi:* Toward a Sexual Poetics of the *Decameron.*" Dioneo's use of the word *opere* as synonymous with *fatti* rather complicates the gender binary, however, not unlike Barolini's own observation that "*fatti* are masculine, but the word 'fatti' is a *parola,* and thus feminine" (281). Boccaccio's choice to have Dioneo use a feminine noun here may be a subtle reflection of the speaker's audience, which is entirely female, their *opere* being uniquely feminine activities.

them. Perhaps driven by the same desire to preserve that status quo that had earlier motivated their tepid response to Filostrato, or by their reflexive respect for male authority, the ladies comply: "Quando le donne ebbero udito questo, dissero che così fosse come gli piacesse" (VI.Conc.16). The king's authority is absolute.

The self-defense deserves attention for another reason as well: Dioneo is not the only male voice in the *Decameron* that must defend itself. While Filostrato simply refuses to engage the women, the authorial voice famously offers two self-defenses, first to his male critics and later to his female readers who may object to some of his stories. In the latter context he makes a particularly relevant statement: "Saranno per avventura alcune di voi che diranno che io abbia nello scriver queste novelle troppa licenzia usata, sì come in fare alcuna volta dire alle donne e molto spesso ascoltare cose non assai convenienti né a dire né a ascoltare a oneste donne. La qual cosa io non nego, per ciò che niuna sì disonesta n'è, che, con onesti vocaboli dicendola, si disdica a alcuno: il che qui mi pare assai convenevolmente bene aver fatto" (Conc.3). Boccaccio recurs to the issue of *convenienza* or decorum in remarks that seem especially evocative of the Day VII stories, and he answers the criticism in the same terms of *onestà* that Dioneo had earlier deployed. Readers of the *Decameron* who locate Boccaccio's ideological soulmate in Dioneo will find comfort here.[5]

But wait a minute. The claim that Dioneo is Boccaccio's alter ego in the *Decameron* conflicts with another, which I have sustained along with Federico Sanguineti, that associates the son of Filippo Balducci with Boccaccio. Yet both theses may be true: perhaps Filippo Balducci's son grew up to be Dioneo. The very tendencies seen in the young Balducci, what Sanguineti has called "un istintivo e naturale aprirsi all'amore" (144), appear in Dioneo as well. So too does Dioneo seem to have internalized the father's attraction to order, not as religiosity but more generally in his need to control. Like the Balducci boy and Boccaccio himself,[6] Dioneo hangs suspended between desire and order. Not only that, he appears to have learned something from Filippo's labeling of women as *papere*. Filippo's unintentional lesson about the arbitrariness of language informs the seventh day where, as Stefano Giovannuzzi puts it, "ogni gerarchia crolla, diventa astratto segno verbale. Per soprammercato, si fa strada una nozione instabile del linguaggio—prossima ai nominalisti medievali, come aveva intuito De Sanctis e capace di stimolare aperture verso la più bruciante modernità—che se pure non vuole essere il centro esplicito del *Decameron* e perciò non viene mai direttamente

---

5. On the history of Boccaccio's use of Dioneo and the identity play see Duranti 3–5.
6. Or at least the Boccaccio of his autobiographical fictions; see Sanguineti.

allo scoperto, lo assedia in modo inesorabile" ("Le parole e le cose" 500). The destabilizing mobility of signifiers is one of Filippo's most important, albeit unintentional, lessons.

Nor is it insignificant that Dioneo's young shadow, the Balducci boy, appears in the fourth day, another day ruled by a male. I have already pointed out two links between Days IV and VII, namely the ladies' reluctance to embrace the stated theme and the argument about *convenienza*. In a sense the Filippo Balducci story is a generative locus not only for the tales of the fourth day but for those of the seventh, inasmuch as both days explore the institutional obstacles to sexual fulfillment typically associated with men. Whereas in Day IV repression of the hedonistic impulse can lead to death, in Day VII hedonism finds its place within an authoritarian context: the wife survives any threat constituted by her husband and enjoys her pleasure while continuing to feign subservience. Dioneo and the Balducci boy are both avatars of hedonism, and in this way too they represent the "ideale di vita" that Cesare Segre locates in Boccaccio's text ("Funzioni" 133).

In what follows then I shall explore the ways in which Day VII looks back on Day IV. Dioneo's rule represents another example of the return of the repressed in the *Decameron*, specifically as repressed patriarchal order. The king thus brings to his job, along with the many quirks of his own personality, the capacity for a different sort of response to Filostrato. If Fiammetta offers a transparent though imperfect antidote simply by flipping the Day IV theme in the Day V stories, Dioneo introduces the possibility of a different sort of patriarchy, one that pays rhetorical lip service to Aristotle's notion of the aristocratic marriage while behaving rather more oligarchically. But in order fully to exorcize the ghost of Day IV, Filostrato and his rule cannot simply be ignored; rather, he and it must be engaged.

The Valle delle Donne

Dioneo struggles between an impulse to further women's interests, albeit in his own idiosyncratic way, and the uncomfortable sense that to do so compromises his socially constructed role as a male. He takes his authority not so much from the models already established by the women, understanding power as having been redefined to include women, as he does from his own identity as an eccentric anarchist, to use Duranti's felicitous phrasing. In this role he attempts to balance Filostrato's open hostility toward women's interests. Nevertheless, the fact that he must argue his support of women reflects the ladies' own suspicion, generated by the audacity of his proposal as well as by their previous experience with Filostrato, and a sort of reductiveness about human behaviors and interests that, while it may apply equally to both women and men, understandably troubles the women more. After all, it reminds them, unpleasantly, of their own socially constructed position, subservient to men, without allowing them to represent women's lives outside of the context of unhappy marriages or desire for male companionship. The ladies' only recourse, having acceded to Dioneo's narrative demand, is to take flight, which they do at once.

In responding to the women in this fashion, suggesting their shared interests and concerns and subtly pressuring them, Dioneo models the behavior of a husband in an aristocratic marriage, his own attitudes reflected perhaps most accurately in those of messer Lizio, Caterina's father in *Decameron* V.4. His friendship with his female companions involves both utility and pleasure, the two constituents of marriage, because his theme will presumably give useful vent to their desire while providing them with some fun. He anticipates the seventh day's theme by relocating the friendship dynamic in the nuptial arena, and the ladies, understanding how his plan benefits them and reminded of the patriarchal imperative, submit. At the same time, they undertake activities of their own that further suggest a spousal game with the men. Just as Fiammetta assumed a position of leadership of the women in the face of Filostrato's monarchy, so now does Elissa, who minutes before had surrendered her crown, come forward to propose a trip to the Valle delle Donne. To be sure, her position differs somewhat from that of Fiammetta, who spoke out when the storytelling had begun. Elissa makes her suggestion during a marginal moment, just after the crowning of the new king but before the new day, when the king would preside at storytelling. The liminal time corresponds to the liminal activity undertaken. The ladies separate themselves from the men for the first time since they left Florence; in decamping to the Valle delle Donne they reconstitute themselves as they were in Santa Maria Novella, where they deliberated before inviting the men to join them. Moreover, they undertake what is clearly a liminal ritual, bathing in the lake in a gesture of purification not unlike baptism.

The episode's center of interest falls upon the nature of the place—its seclusion, its amphitheaterlike shape, its Edenic flora and abundant water—and the use the women make of it, bathing and fishing. As Thomas Stillinger has detailed, Boccaccio describes the place and the activities there from a variety of perspectives, all of which belong to absent viewers: "the repeated evocation of the observer who is *not* there defeats its own apparent purpose. [. . .] the viewpoint is that of the absent onlooker" ("The Language of Gardens" 108–9).[7] The play of presence and absence that Stillinger describes aligns the episode with the *Decameron*'s broader exploration of eavesdropping while instituting the dynamic of the absent onlooker, present at but simultaneously excluded from the action, which the seventh day will identify with the cuckolded husband. Despite all its insistence on the valley as a *locus amoenus*, and its multiple sources in other garden narratives, including Dante, the *Roman de la Rose*, and Ovid's *Metamorphoses*, the episode is finally a political one, and the politics are entirely sexual.[8]

The political element of the episode, at least from the point of view of the members of the *brigata*, becomes explicit when Pampinea, returning with the others to the villa, laughingly tells Dioneo that "Oggi vi pure abbiamo noi ingannati" (VI.Conc.33). Her phrasing, and in particular her use of the verb *ingannare*, links the activities of the Valle to their forthcoming storytelling, as Barolini has argued ("Le parole e le cose" 284). Jumping the gun, the ladies had engaged in a *beffa* of their own in a sort of proleptic imitation of the narratives of the next day, and it falls to Pampinea, who had previously challenged Filostrato, to invest political meaning in an activity that for Elissa simply connoted pleasure: "se di venirvi vi piace, io non dubito punto che quando vi sarete non siate contentissime d'esservi state" (VI.Conc.18). In other words, they, and not the chess king, will provide the fun at the party. To be sure, her proposal comes after Dioneo, having won affirmation of his theme ("dissero che così fosse come gli piacesse," VI.Conc.16), had sent everyone off to frolic: "il re per infino a ora di cena di fare il suo piacere diede licenzia a ciascuno" (VI.Conc.16). However, to see the king's dismissal as giving license to all is to deny another reading of this sentence: that Dioneo had sent every off to have *his* fun, to do as he pleased. After all, the *festa* he had envisioned would involve both men and women, and the ladies had started the party without him. By decamping to the valley in search of their own pleasure, the women affirm that they do not need men after all.[9] Dioneo's startled response to the news, "E come? . . . comin-

---

7. Tobias Gittes argues instead that the viewers are there: "The *Valle* is an amphitheater of the erotic in which the naked women disport for both their own delectation and that of the invisible 'viewers' who look down upon them from the windows of the six villas: 'viewers' who are representative of the readers of Boccaccio's text for they enjoy the same privileged view and the same immunity" (152). Gittes locates proof for his assertion in the narrator's observation that the ladies decide to take a bath, "senza alcun sospetto d'esser vedute" (VI.Conc.29). In truth the statement strikes me as yet another of Boccaccio's impossibly ambiguous remarks, most safely interpreted as an allusion to the possibility of onlookers rather than an affirmation of same.

8. On the garden sources for this episode see Stillinger, Kern, and Gittes.

9. Along these lines, Gittes convincingly suggests that "such a display of self-sufficient sexuality ('Oggi vi pure abbiam noi ingannati') as a means of coping with sexual deprivation should be taken as a type of masturbation—the most universally available *remedium amoris*

ciate voi prima a far de' fatti che a dir delle parole?" (VI.Conc.34), suggests not simply that the women have acted beyond his expectations but also that the news does not entirely please him, as if somehow his intended order, *parole* before *fatti*, men as well as women, had been upended.[10]

Pampinea's reference to the ladies' *inganno* points as well to an earlier liminal time and space. When she first proposes to the men, in Santa Maria Novella, that they all escape to the country, Boccaccio narrates that "I giovani si credettero primieramente essere beffati" (I.Intro.88). Thus the *Decameron* itself nearly suffers an aborted takeoff thanks to suspicion about the women's intentions, one grounded in the belief that women are predisposed to play tricks on men. In his essay on the seventh day Giovannuzzi points out that the stories themselves actually break down the barrier between storytelling and action, *raccontare* and *fare*, on which Dioneo bases his defense of his choice of theme: "Pervicacemente la brigata contraddice se stessa e tesse il rapporto—la cui negazione era stata preliminare all'accettazione del tema di Dioneo—fra l'universo del racconto e quello in cui si trovano i novellatori" (479). The collapse of such an artificial distinction should come as no surprise, given that the men see the women themselves as capable of *beffe* and the women prove the men right at the end of the sixth day. The world of the stories cannot help but invade the world of the storytellers, and vice versa, for in fact the two worlds are one.

Further evidence supporting a tandem reading of these two episodes comes in the description of the *locus amoenus* to which the group repairs. Reassured that there is no trickery involved, the three men readily agree to Pampinea's plan for escape, and by the very next paragraph they have arrived at the first villa, which reads very much as the convex analogue to the Valle delle Donne: "Era il detto luogo sopra una piccolo montagnetta, da ogni parte lontano alquanto alle nostre strade . . . in sul colmo della quale era un palagio con bello e gran cortile nel mezzo, e con logge e con sale e con camere" (I.Intro.90). Striking here is the group's relation to the palace and the perspective that each entails. In the above-cited passage the travelers occupy the palace that sits atop the hill; they thus are in a position to look down upon the surrounding countryside, in effect mastering it. In the Valle delle Donne, on the other hand, the ladies occupy the low space of the countryside, looking up at the six palaces that loom above them. Their

---

and one intimately associated with the erotic text" (168).

10. Barolini too emphasizes how the politics here become sexual: "The *novelle* of Day 7— although made of words, *parole*—serve as vicarious *fatti* encouraging the *Decameron*'s ladies to progress from *parole* to real *fatti*. . . . Words can be liberating, words can lead to deeds, or, in the logic of our proverb, women can become men. For, according to our proverb, Dioneo's question can be construed: 'Are you beginning to act like men rather than like women?'" (284–85).

retreat to nature in no way denies the force of civilization; indeed, they are reminded, even in this most secluded place, of the possibility that they are being watched.

The position of the palaces with respect to the women in turn anticipates the transformation of the Valle delle Donne into the Valle della Brigata. The ladies visit the valley, enjoy its spalike comforts, then return to camp to tell the men what they have done, whereupon the men, led by Dioneo, visit it themselves: "Il re, udendo contare la bellezza del luogo, disideroso di vederlo, prestamente fece comandar la cena: la qual poi che con assai piacer di tutti fu fornita, li tre giovani con li lor famigliari, lasciate le donne, se n'andarono a questa valle" (VI.Conc.36). There is no direct espionage on the men's part; that is accomplished rather by the device of the absent onlooker. Nevertheless, the three men, accompanied by still other men, visit a place specifically identified with women; it is, after all, the Valle delle Donne. The narrative sequence relates not to garden descriptions, but rather to other narratives in which men enter women's spaces. It is, for example, reminiscent of the means by which Guiscardo gains access to Ghismonda's bedchamber. As visitors to the valley must enter "per una via assai stretta" (VI.Conc.19), so too does Guiscardo first enter the *grotta*, a natural antechamber to Ghismonda's bedroom, through "uno spiraglio fatto per forza nel monte," the mouth of which was covered "da pruni e da erbe do sopra natevi." From the cavern Guiscardo proceeds to the bedroom "per una segreta scala" (IV.1.9). Fiammetta's allusion here to female sexual anatomy finds echo in the access to the Valle, where the narrow path opens onto an erotic space that is the natural equivalent of Ghismonda's bedroom—complete with the possibility of espionage.

The bathing element of the Valle episode suggests another narrative source: Ovid's tale of Diana and Actaeon. That Boccaccio had the Ovidian episode in mind seems unquestionable; as Stillinger points out, the *Decameron*'s description of the place as "artificio della natura e non del manual" (VI.Conc.20) borrows from Ovid's "arte laboratum nulla: simulaverat artem / ingenio natura suo" (3.158–59). Moreover, as Stillinger notes, Diana's company includes seven nymphs, a number that corresponds to the *Decameron*'s seven ladies (118; though to be fair the analogy is imperfect: there are eight women in the Diana scene, including the goddess, and only seven in the *Decameron*). Further evidence that Boccaccio may have Diana and Actaeon in mind comes from the *Caccia di Diana*, which has not received much attention despite Branca's citation of it (1356):

In una valle non molto spatiosa
Di quattro montagnette circuita,

Di verde erbette e di fior copiosa,
Nel mezzo della qual così fiorita
Una fontana chiara bella e grande,
Abbondevole d'acqua, v'era sita:
E l'acqua che superflua si spande
Un rivo fa che tutte l'erbe bagna,
Poi n'esce fuor da una delle bande:
D'albori è piena ciascuna montagna,
Di frondi folti sì ch a pena il sole
Tra esse può passar nella campagna. . . . (II.1–12)

Boccaccio will make clear shortly thereafter that this is Diana's bathing place:

Quivi Diana, che 'l tiepido foco
Ne' casti petti tien, ricolse quelle
Che invitate furono al suo gioco.
Poi comandò che esse entrasser nelle
Chiarissime onde e, de' freschi liquori
Lavando sé, sé rifacesser belle. (II.22–27)

No narrative of the scene of Diana bathing can avoid the subtext of Actaeon's inadvertent invasion of her sacred space. That she can resist that intrusion, punishing Actaeon by transforming him into a stag whose own hounds will then dismember, reflects her dominion over the place. Boccaccio's women, however, allow Dioneo and the men to enter. They may feel powerless in the face of the king's authority, or they could simply want to be accommodating. Yet another possibility looms: that of a broadly conceived exhibitionistic impulse, a desire to show the men where they have frolicked in order to fuel the men's fantasies about what happened there earlier. Indeed, Boccaccio effectively rescues the episode from its Ovidian antecedent and his own prior reelaboration of it by reversing the dynamic of the absent onlooker and present object of desire. When the men arrive, they become present onlookers to the absent objects of desire. Consistent with the theme for the next day, which offloads real sexual desire onto narrative, the valley retains its frisson of sexuality, a promise unfulfilled. When the men and women are there together, they must keep their clothes on.

In other words, the return to nature that the valley offers cannot be fully Edenic. The valley cannot be a prelapsarian space where men and women gambol naked and innocent; all parties are too compromised by their knowledge of sex for that to happen. Moreover, the decision to turn the Valle delle Donne into the Valle della Brigata necessarily involves an increase in the number of signifiers of civilization. Dioneo will add new elements to the six *castelletto*-like *palagi* that already signal the press of civilization.[11] He orders that "alcun letto" be brought there, not a surprising choice considering that the bed will be the signal locus for many of the stories told under his aegis. Beyond that, the group carries "una gran salmeria" (VII.Intro.2) to supplement the natural pleasures the space already offers.[12] If the women donate natural beauty, the men contribute the tools with which to exploit it. The visit to the valley thus represents a first example of the pooling of resources that is key to the success of the aristocratic marriage. Dioneo recognizes and accommodates the contribution that the women can offer in first identifying this erotic space, and they surrender it to a purpose that will suit the group as a whole.

So the Valle delle Donne is not a place of unbridled pleasure; rather, it is one of disciplined pleasure, a place of compromise. As if to signal the sort of concord that the group realizes here, Boccaccio turns what had earlier been an exception into a rule. The *Decameron*'s narrator does not record the reaction of members of the group after every story. However, when he does, he typically limits the account to the ladies; only occasionally does he note the reaction of *tutti* or of "tutta la brigata" (VI.Conc.1), or of "ciascuna delle donne e degli uomini" (VI.2.2).[13] The inclusion of the men's reactions contrasts with the practice, consistent with a book dedicated to women, of addressing only the ladies in the introduction to each tale; the marked presence of listening men serves to remind us that they are eavesdropping on stories told to the women.[14] In Day VII the ladies continue to be

---

11. It is never clear what purpose these towers serve. As suggested already, they may provide good sightlines for voyeuristic amusement, or they may provide protection from the outside. Winfried Wehle offers the following explanation: "Le mure naturali del Paradiso, costituite dalle colline circostanti, sono coronate di *sei* edifice fortificati—prodotti dall'arte dell'uomo civilizzato. Essi—con una citazione della tradizionale iconografia cristiana che vuole il Paradiso esagonale—segnano i confini del paradiso della Valle e la proteggono dagli influssi esterni. I segnali sono inequivocabili: perché la natura possa mostrarsi dal suo lato ideale, occorre l'artificio dell'uomo" (358). While the traditional hexagonal iconography of Paradise is clearly key here, what remains less certain is how Boccaccio puts this iconography to work.

12. I would thus disagree with Kern's assertion that "if the laws of society and those of religion are silent [as Dioneo claims], the voice of Nature is to be listened to. Her laws prevail. . . . Dioneo proclaims thus the reign of Nature" (519). To the extent that the group brings its own laws along to the valley, Nature takes a back seat.

13. This last example constitutes an interesting case of hypallage, which Lanham defines as "[a]wkward or humorous changing of agreement of application of words" (56). In this case the choice of *ciascuna*, which appears to be dictated by Boccaccio's arrangement of the two complements, the feminine coming before the masculine, also has the amusing effect of underscoring how the men belong to a group of women, and not vice versa.

14. I therefore do not agree with Janssens's observation in this context that "the term

the announced audience of the stories, but the narrator regularly records the response of the entire group. After the first story he notes that "Con grandissime risa fu la novella d'Emilia ascoltata e l'orazione per buona e per santa commendata da tutti" (VII.2.2; here and below italics mine). After the fourth tale we learn that "ciascun [aveva] commendata la donna" (VII.5.2). The fifth tale brings this reply: "Meravigliosamente era piaciuta a tutti la novella della Fiammetta, affermando ciascuno ottimamente la donna aver fatto e quel che si convenia al bestiale uomo" (VII.6.2). After the sixth story Boccaccio reports that "Questo avvedimento di madonna Isabella da Pampinea raccontato fu da ciascun della brigata tenuto maraviglioso" (VII.7.2). The reaction to the seventh tale reads: "Stranamente pareva a tutti madonna Beatrice essere stata maliziosa in beffare il suo marito, e ciascuno affermava dovere essere stata la paura d'Anichino grandissima . . ." (VII.8.2). In only two cases, the second and the eighth tales, do we learn of the ladies' response; there is no recorded reaction to the ninth tale.

The phrasing here is telling. Had Boccaccio consistently divided the group into women and men, as he does elsewhere, he would have called more precise attention to the presence of the men, understood as a group separate from the women. By here writing the group as a whole, he suggests that, for this day at least, the men are fully integrated; they are not eaves-droppers on a narrative discourse intended for women. Such an arrangement is consistent with the spirit of compromise that informs the day as a whole. The ladies accept Dioneo's theme, in part because they must, but also because he convinces them that talking about sex will ironically help preserve their reputation as oneste. In return he brings the storytelling to their place, a place associated with women and their pleasures. It is a fitting place for the narratives that will ensue, as each in its own way will highlight women's pleasure, often at the expense of men.

The Day VII Stories and the Return of the Patriarchal Household

The stories told under Dioneo's rule continue the conversation about the nature of marriage, with particular attention to the modalities of friend-ship, or lack thereof, that inform marriages. Through storytelling the group establishes criteria that authorize women to explore extramarital options while still preserving their marriage. Women have clear motives for work-

---

'ladies' summarizes the whole group" (141). The specificity of the audience identified partakes, as I have already suggested, of a larger rhetorical strategy for dealing with male readers of the text.

ing out their problems while maintaining the semblance of a solid marriage, because of the dangers attendant to the exposure of their adultery. There is more at work here, though, and to understand it I believe we need to shift our attention away from the varieties of adulterous strategies pursued by the female protagonists and back onto their marriages themselves. The women of the seventh day experience some sort of disillusionment with regard to their respective marriages; the unions fall short of the standard set by the aristocratic model that combines utility and pleasure. The marriages are something of a sham, oligarchic marriages that privilege male prerogative over the interests of women, but that advertise themselves as aristocratic. It is thus an ongoing *beffa* played out before a public audience. The challenge confronting the female protagonists involves how they can preserve the appearance of a successful marriage while finding comfort outside of its confines. Their *beffe* are thus continuous with their everyday reality, which is focused on appearances. The ironic result is that the wife's adultery actually shores up the marriage, enabling it to function in ways that it had not previously.

Most of the stories are explicit about what has gone wrong; in other cases the reader may hazard reasonable inferences. The first story relates the *semplicità* of Tessa's husband, Gianni Lotteringhi, to her falling in love with Federigo di Neri Pegolotti. The second story emphasizes the couple's poverty and gives voice to Peronella's frustrations over their lack of money. In the third story, an exceptional case, it appears that the wife's own gullibility leads to her adultery. In the fourth, fifth, and eighth tales the husband's jealousy is the explicit motive for the wife's adultery. The sixth story turns on the fact that the husband, Messer Lambertuccio, does not satisfy his wife, presumably in the sexual arena. In the seventh story, another exception, the wife allows the lover's eloquent pleas to convince her to yield to him. The ninth story is less explicit about the marital problem, though it appears to involve the advanced age of Nicostrato, the husband, and the relative youth of his wife, Lidia.

Common throughout the stories is the wife's sense of danger when her husband happens upon the scene. "Oimè! Giannel mio, io son morta, ché ecco il marito mio," cries Peronella in the second story (VII.2.12). In the third tale, Madonna Agnesa exclaims, "Io son morta, ch'ecco il marito mio" (VII.3.25). When the husband returns home in the sixth story, his wife "si tenne morta" (VII.6.15). More than simple metaphors of peril, these statements reflect the real danger that women face, particularly when they violate sexual norms established by men to protect male interests. We have already seen, thanks to the Madonna Filippa story, that some cities even institutionalize the threat, punishing female adultery with death. Elsewhere the threat remains a domestic reality, as in the eighth story, where the adulterous wife escapes violence only because she has substituted her maid for herself, "pregandola che senza farsi conoscere quelle busse pazientemente ricevesse che Arriguccio le desse, per ciò che ella ne la renderebbe sì fatto merito" (VII.8.16). As feared, the husband beats the woman black and blue, despite her pleas that he stop: he is too driven by his *furore* (VII.8.20) to heed her cries. After cutting off her hair, he announces that he is off to report on her behavior to her brothers, "'appresso che essi vengan per te e facciane quello che essi credono che loro onor fia e menintene: ché per certo in questa casa non starai tu mai più'" (VII.8.21). In his outrage he decides to combine the limited punishment of the beating and shearing with the longer-term humiliation of separation from him and further punishment by her brothers.

The *beffe* themselves rely on the use of either deceptive language or a combination of deceptive language and deceptive stagecraft. Examples of the use of deceptive language include the first story, in which Gianni Lotteringhi's wife, Tessa, alerts her lover to her husband's presence by manufacturing an incantation aimed at driving away the "ghost" that is the lover: "Fantasima, fantasima che di notte vai, a coda ritta ci venisti, a coda ritta te n'andrai: va nell'orto, a piè del pesco grosso troverai unto bisunto e cento cacherelli della gallina mia: pon bocca e fiasco e vatti via, e non far mal né a me né a Gianni mio" (VII.1.27). Tessa successfully communicates that there will be no sex tonight ("a coda ritta te n'andrai") because Gianni is home with her; she also indicates to her lover where she has left their dinner. As earlier examples show, the couple's failure to eat together correlates with an interruption of the affective exchange, here expressly sexual, that the shared meal connotes. Instead, having enchanted the ghost, she returns to bed with her husband, thus suggesting that all is well in her marriage.

The tale bears other significant characteristics, not the least of which is the double ending. Emilia acknowledges to her audience a variant version of the story, according to which the wife uttered a different incantation to chase away the ghost. The specifics of this variant explain in part why Emilia has not adopted it. In this version the wife tells the *fantasima*, "la testa dell'asino non vols'io, ma altri fu, che tristo il faccia Iddio" (VII.1.32). Her remark is illogical: the wife is in no position to know that Gianni has shown up because someone turned the ass's skull, which she used to signal him. Emilia then goes on to explain that she had learned from "una mia vicina, la quale è una donna molto vecchia," that both versions are true, except that the second happened to Gianni di Nello and not Gianni Lotteringhi. The repetition suggests the extent to which women in Florence are cheating on their husbands, but it also alludes to the stories to come, each of which is in some way a variant of this tale. In that context the association of Gianni, whether Lotteringhi or di Nello, with the *fantasima* assumes new meaning. Significantly, the *fantasima* enjoys a double gender. Grammatically it is feminine, but its most salient characteristic, the *coda ritta*, genders it as male. The gender crossing suggests the double status of the ghost itself: it is a figure of both repressed female sexual desire and the man who will satisfy it. As such, it rises to the level of emblem, and its diaphanous nature ensures its easy passage from one narrative to the next. It is, moreover, a perfect emblem of deception, for it is something that both is and is not there.

In the fourth tale, Monna Ghita mixes language with stagecraft by first engineering to get her husband out of the house—exclusion signals culpability—and then explaining to her neighbors that she has locked him out because he is a drunkard. The story is noteworthy in the seventh-day sequence because, unlike in the other tales, Ghita publicly exposes the problem in her marriage. Not surprisingly, however, it is not the real problem, jealousy, but a concocted one, drunkenness, which she has created and which she denounces. Her public plea leads to efforts to coerce better behavior from Tofano, specifically from her relatives, who hear about the problems and beat Tofano up. He then must appeal to her to take him back, and as she had used intermediaries on her behalf, so does he. Not only does he promise again never to be jealous; he also gives her permission "che ogni suo piacer facesse, ma sì saviamente, che egli non se ne avvedesse" (VII.4.30). In other words, he asks her to maintain the sham of their marriage for the sake of his own reputation. The couple thus moves ironically from a state of oligarchy to one of aristocracy, because they now pool their resources—he gives up his jealousy, she pursues her affairs discreetly—in order to further the public sham that they are a happy couple.

As in the other days headed by a king, the male voices receive careful, though here decidedly asymmetrical, distribution. Filostrato tells the second tale, offering an important introduction to which I shall return, and Panfilo the ninth. Dioneo tells the tenth tale, exceptional in the structuring of the *Decameron*'s days because normally the monarch tells the ninth story, and his story does not hew to either of the models identified above. By giving the ninth position to Panfilo, Dioneo substitutes another male voice in the space normally assigned to the monarch, the significance of which I shall explore shortly.

In introducing his tale Filostrato offers a curious rationale for telling stories of women's *beffe* that supplements the one already given by

Dioneo. Undergirding his argument is the concept of retributive justice. He explains that because men constantly play tricks on their wives, the ladies should celebrate any news of similar tricks played by wives on their husbands. In other words, the revenge for male perfidy is storytelling by women. Nowhere does Filostrato endorse women's *beffe;* rather, he simply seeks to reinforce Dioneo's arguments about why such a topic is suitable to women. Furthermore, Filostrato states, the ladies should broadcast the news as widely as possible, because if men knew that women know about their tricks they might curb their behavior. He thus appears to suggest that storytelling can have a positive impact on the ways of the world, increasing marital fidelity and mutual respect. All of this leads to his own conclusion: "È adunque mia intenzion di dirvi ciò che una giovinetta, quantunque di bassa condizione fosse, quasi in un momento di tempo per salvezza di sé al marito facesse" (VII.2.6). In truth Filostrato does not need to offer his rationale, which Giovannuzzi calls a "mediocre pedagogia maritale" ("Le parole e le cose" 478), and the story itself is a non sequitur. There are no apparent revenge motives in it; indeed, if anything Peronella's apparent reasons for cheating, poverty, are at best illogical. Moreover, it is important to recall that it is Filostrato, after all, who is advancing this argument about what is in women's best interests. That fact alone should make his claim suspect, and indeed later events will call into question whether the ladies agree with him that to publicize their trickery is a good idea.

The tale itself mocks the model of the aristocratic marriage by playing on the notion of the pooling of resources. Peronella and her husband are poor laborers, he a mason, she a spinner, and there is no indication of discord in the marriage beyond the pressures of poverty, as her later speech to him makes clear. When he returns home unexpectedly one morning, she rails at him for taking time off of work, explaining that they cannot afford his vacations and insisting that she will not agree to the sale of her clothing to makes ends meet. The verbal assault recalls that of other wives who attempt to deflect their guilt by going on the offense. Peronella's "Intendi sanamente, marito mio" (VII.7.18) echoes the words of Pietro di Vinciolo's wife, "E intendi sanamente, Pietro," (VII.10.58), as she excoriates him for attacking her hypocrisy (and like Peronella's husband Pietro had come home early). Peronella cedes to the advances of her suitor, Giannello Scrignario, simply because he woos her, though the fact that he is a "giovane de' leggiadri," a handsome young man, probably helps seal the deal. So does his last name, which literally means "maker of safes," suggesting an association with security, financial and otherwise, that she doubtless finds attractive. He does appear to be well-off, because when she claims that he has offered her seven silver coins for their barrel, he makes no complaint. He is clever too, taking advantage of the husband's seclusion in the barrel to have sex with Peronella. The unnamed husband, on the other hand, distinguishes himself principally for his naïveté, never wondering why Peronella has locked the door with a man inside, and instead praising her for wisely doing so.

The trick by which Peronella avoids exposure involves her explanation, capitalizing on her husband's own statement that he has brought home a buyer for their barrel, that she too has procured a buyer. He believes her because Giannello plays along, explaining that he has inspected the object and demanding that it be cleaned before he will agree to the sale. As the husband enters the barrel, Giannello enters the wife, and the two simultaneous acts of scraping suggest that there are two sources of capital here, the barrel and Peronella. The satisfaction of her sexual desires with Giannello thus ironically strengthens Peronella's marriage, because it advances the couple's financial well-being. Just as her husband works to sell to the barrel, so too does she.[15]

Indeed, what begins as a tale of simple adultery assumes an odor of prostitution. Walter Davis has called the tale "an example of ironic harmonizing, whereby the lover becomes buyer and the husband becomes pimp" (11). Whether Peronella had intended from the beginning to profit financially from sex is unclear, though as I stated above she likely associated Giannello with money, thanks to his surname. Either way, she certainly knew that when she invented the ruse to explain his presence to her husband he would have no choice but to pay. Her cunning thus enables her to trick her husband into thinking her motives were pure while relieving her lover of his cash. But the question of whether Peronella prostitutes herself deserves closer scrutiny. In this regard it bears notice that this story follows close upon the tale of Madonna Filippa (VI.7), also told by Filostrato, in which the people of Prato unlink uxorial adultery from uxorial prostitution, presumably because the former involves a gift to men and the latter an expense. In the present case Giannello engages in sex and buys a barrel. Since he takes home something for which he pays, the barrel, technically there is no prostitution. Still, the association of sex with money in the tale arguably casts a bad light on Peronella. She starts to look like a complement

---

15. In this light Giovannuzzi's claim, that the story "comprende esattamente due storie in parallelo, interpretate dagli stessi attori: quella godereccia di Peronella e dell'amante Giannello Scrignario che vogliono recare 'ad effetto' il loro 'giovinil disiderio' e l'altra, economica, del marito, preoccupato di vendere il 'doglio'" ("Le parole e le cose" 479), seems not quite right. Filostrato insists from the beginning that both husband and wife are working to advance the family economically, and the success of the story depends on the surprising convergence of their independent efforts to accomplish that goal. The two stories cannot be parallel if they intersect.

to Madonna Filippa, apparently engaging in the type of behavior for which Prato, at least, would put her to death.

Even if Filostrato's impulse here is finally conservative, consistent with a belief that marital harmony serves everyone's best interests, the *brigata* does not embrace him. The ladies latch on to only one aspect of the story, the simile of the Parthian mares: "Giannello . . . a lei accostatosi, che tutta chiusa teneva la bocca del doglio, e in quella guisa che negli ampi campi gli sfrenati cavalli e d'amore caldi le cavalle di Partia assaliscono, a effetto recò il giovinil desiderio . . ." (VI.2.33–34). The recorded reaction suggests both embarrassment for the ladies and transgression of norms of decorum on Filostrato's part: "Non seppe sì Filostrato parlare obscuro delle cavalla partice, che l'avvedute donne non ne ridessono, sembiante faccendo di rider d'altro" (VII.3.2). Parthia, an enemy of Rome, was famous for its cavalry, so the allusion enjoys a certain historical resonance. The women find the analogy embarrassing because it signifies too overtly: it belongs to the sort of crude discourse one associates with Tindaro and Licisca, not with the *brigata*.

There is, however, more at work here than the ladies' discomfort and Filostrato's inappropriateness. In recording the women's reaction, the narrator relies on his own omniscience to mark the difference between what amuses the women and that about which they feign amusement. In other words, in reacting to Filostrato's tale his audience enacts a *beffa*, laughing about one thing while pretending to laugh about another. They appear to be caught up in the air of female duplicity that permeates the day, beginning with the trip to the Valle delle Donne. They also isolate his story. Elissa, who follows Filostrato, relates her own contribution not to his but to Emilia's first tale of the day. Fiammetta will make a similar link when introducing her story, the fifth, with explicit reference to the theme of jealousy just introduced by Lauretta, who narrates the fourth tale. The women will have no opportunity to tie their narratives to those of the other two men, because Panfilo and Dioneo will narrate the ninth and tenth stories respectively; thus control of the day's thematic dynamic finally and assertively reverts to the men.

That notwithstanding, the women do manage to leave their ideological stamp on the day, and it comes in Fiammetta's introduction to her tale. Two pieces of circumstantial evidence combine to underscore the privileged nature of her rather long remarks: first, the status accorded her as corrector of male errors, when she narrates the first story of Day IV and subsequently becomes queen of Day V; and second, the location of her tale, the fifth, at the very center of the nine thematic stories. Moreover, the fact that she casts her argument about jealousy in legalistic terms points to its importance as a commentary about relations between men and women.

Fiammetta asserts that women who take action against unjustifiably jealous men do so in self-defense: "E se ogni cosa avessero i componitori delle leggi guardata, giudico che in questo essi dovessero alle donne non altra pena aver constituta che essi constituirono a colui che alcuno offende sé difendendo" (VII.5.3). Her argument cuts neatly along gender-based lines: the lawmakers are grammatically masculine and the "crime"—retribution—that she attributes to women is the equivalent of self-defense by *colui*, again a grammatically masculine subject. Her hypothetical implies that the lawmakers were not thorough, and that a female perspective, clearly excluded from the normative process, would have resulted in a different set of laws. She then levels a series of accusations against jealous men:

> . . . i gelosi sono insidiatori della vita delle giovani donne e diligentissimi cercatori della lor morte. Esse stanno tutta la settimana rinchiuse e attendono alle bisogne familiari e domestiche, disiderando, come ciascun fa, d'aver poi il dì delle feste alcuna consolazione, alcuna quiete, e di potere alcun diporto pigliare, sì come prendono i lavoratori de' campi, gli artefici delle città e i reggitori delle corti, come fé Idio che il dì settimo da tutte le sue fatiche si riposò, e come vogliono le leggi sante e le civili, le quali, allo onor di Dio e al ben comune di ciascun riguardando, hanno i dì delle fatiche distinti da quegli del riposo. Alla qual cosa fare niente i gelosi consentono, anzi quegli dì che a tutte l'altre son lieti fanno a esse, più serrate e più rinchiuse tenendole, esser più miseri e più dolenti: il che quanto e qual consumamento sia delle cattivelle quelle sole il sanno che l'hanno provato. (VII.5.3–5)

The polemic may claim two important antecedents. First, it reads as a complement to Boccaccio's own description, in the Proem to the *Decameron*, of the misfortunes suffered by ladies in love. Both statements note the forced enclosure, and both speakers assert that only one who has experienced this degree of suffering can understand it. Second, the remark about "le leggi sante e le civili" echoes Dioneo's own reference to "le leggi, così le divine come le umane" (VI.Conc.9). Both speakers posit continuity between the two sets of laws, which essentially reduplicate one another in establishing the same norms even if the means of coercion—threat of earthly punishment or eternal damnation—differ. The two cite the laws in order to make different points, however. For Dioneo the laws no longer apply because of a natural disaster, while Fiammetta discusses the jealous men who refuse to apply them.

Fiammetta's remarks are not gratuitous. She clearly understands the purpose of law—she makes reference to the *ben comune*—and its organization. Her decision to frame the question on territory that Dioneo has already staked out, and to borrow language from Dioneo, reinforces her status as a spokeswoman for women's interests. In effect she uses her introduction and story to reclaim the day from Dioneo, reinventing the uxorial *beffa* as revenge narrative and not, as the king would have it, as motivated by love or danger. To be sure, she thanks Lauretta for inspiring her—"la precedente novella mi tira a dovere similmente ragionare d'un geloso"— and she takes care to underscore that, like Lauretta, she is talking about irrationally jealous husbands. Unlike Lauretta, however, Fiammetta finds a way to capitalize on the theme in order to give voice to women's anger about irrational jealousy, declaring "ciò che si fa loro dalla lor donna, e massimamente *quando senza cagione ingelosiscono*, esser ben fatto" (VII.5.3; italics mine). She makes that same distinction at the end of her polemic: "ciò che una donna fa a un marito *geloso a torto*, per certo non condennare ma commendare si dovrebbe" (VII.5.6). She thus takes care to draw a distinction between the more morally compromised female protagonists of the earlier stories—Tessa, Peronella, Madonna Agnesa—and her own, who like monna Ghita has much more clearly drawn motives for cheating on her husband.[16]

Finally, there is a third element to Fiammetta's speech, wholly original to her, which reinforces its polemical nature. She faults jealous men for not allowing women to rest on Sunday, *il dì settimo,* despite the ordinance of divine and human laws. Surely somewhere in the back of her mind lurks an awareness that this is the seventh day of storytelling, wherein she and her companions find themselves under male rule and laboring under protest. Her express desire that women be allowed, like men, *alcun diporto* on the *dì delle feste,* uttered in the very place of *diporto* that the women had so enjoyed the day before, suggests that she associates the current arrangement with work more than pleasure.

The story itself reinforces her points. She describes her protagonist as the beautiful victim of her husband's irrational jealousy: "avendo una bellissima donna per moglie di lei divenne oltre misura geloso; né altra cagione a questo avea, se non che, come egli molto l'amava e molto bella la teneva e conosceva che ella con tutto il suo studio s'ingegnava di piacergli, così estimava che ogn'uomo l'amasse e che ella a tutti paresse bella e ancora che ella s'ingegnasse così di piacere altrui come a lui (argomento di cattivo uomo e con poco sentimento era)" (VII.5.7). Fiammetta's description

---

16. Of the first three female protagonists of the day, Peronella and Agnesa have no explicit motive for their adultery. Tessa's motive is slender, apparently having to do with Gianni's *semplicità*.

conforms perfectly to Aristotle's definition of an aristocratic marriage gone bad: "If the man lords it over everything, his rule changes into oligarchy; for the distribution in that case takes no account of worth, or of where his superiority lies" (1160b35; Rowe trans. 220). Beyond that, one is left to wonder whether her remarks serve further to skewer another marriage, the one Dioneo has constructed figuratively with the women. Just as this wife undertakes to please her husband, so too the ladies earlier, in acquiescing, "dissero che così fosse come gli piacesse" (VI.Conc.16) And like a Dioneo who resists the women's pressure to change his topic, this husband simply tightens the screws: "E così ingelosito tanta guardia ne prendeva e sì stretta la tenea, che forse assai son di quegli che a capital pena son dannati, che non sono da' pregionieri con tanta guardia servati" (VII.5.8). This remark also correlates with her earlier observation that jealous men are "diligentissimi cercatori della . . . morte" of women. Moreover, its ominous reference to surveillance serves to remind us that the space that the group now enjoys, the Valle delle Donne, is surrounded by six hills, each topped by a castle-like *palagio:* as I suggested earlier, it is hard to determine whether these are simple palaces or watchtowers, and what purpose they serve.

Her husband's jealousy provokes the wife to seek retribution, explicitly described as such: "Per che, veggendosi a torto fare ingiuria al marito, s'avvisò a consolazion di se medesima di trovar modo, se alcuno ne potesse trovare, di far sì che a ragione le fosse fatto" (VII.5.10). Since he refuses to obey the law, she takes the law into her own hands, engendering to communicate with a certain Filippo, who lives next door and who had previously caught her eye, so that they can arrange a tryst. In order to absent her husband from the bedroom she plays her trick. She asks to go to confession for Christmas, and the husband consents but, irretrievably jealous, disguises himself as a priest in order to hear it. He thus engineers a clever form of eavesdropping, listening in on his wife's confession to someone she believes to be a third party. She of course recognizes him and "confesses" to nightly visits from a priest who casts a spell over her husband in order then to have sex with her. Outraged, the husband later posts himself at the couple's front door in order to catch the priest upon entering; upstairs meanwhile the wife entertains Filippo, who enters through the roof. When the husband tells her that he knows of her confession she explains that she was speaking in encoded language and that the priest to whom she was referring was none other than the husband himself, at that moment disguised as a priest.

The wife's incomplete account of her trick—she fails to mention the lover—has the effect of reordering the couple's marriage. The husband misreads his wife's explanation as reassurance that he has no cause for jealousy, even though she has warned him that "se voglia me ne venisse di porti le corna, se tu avessi cento occhi come tu n'hai due, mi darebbe il cuore di fare i piacer miei in guisa che tu non te ne avvedresti" (VII.5.58). Chastened, he casts aside his jealousy: "ebbe la donna per buona e per savia, e quando la gelosia gli bisognava del tutto se la spogliò, così come quando bisogno non gli era se l'aveva vestita" (VII.5.59). The wife now acquires the freedom she had been missing and discreetly pursues her affair: "Per che la savia donna, quasi licenziata a' suoi piaceri, senza far venire il suo amante su per lo tetto come vanno le gatte ma pur per l'uscio, discretamente operando poi più volte con lui buon tempo e lieta vita si diede" (VII.5.59).

This final sentence of the *novella* strikingly recalls the other happily-ever-after conclusions of those other Day V stories where emphasis fell on the happiness of the male protagonist with no similar account of the happiness of the female. Here the emphasis falls wholly to the woman, in accord with the day's focus on how sagacious women can construct their own happiness. A similar ending completes the fourth story, wherein Tofano "le diè licenzia che ogni suo piacer facesse, ma sì saviamente, che egli non se ne avvedesse" (VII.4.30), and the eighth, which likewise includes a jealous husband: "s'aperse la via a poter fare nel tempo avvenire ogni suo piacere, senza paura alcuna più aver del marito" (VII.8.50). Two other stories, the seventh and the ninth, conclude with statements about the mutual happiness of the two lovers. In all of these cases what remains unsaid in the other stories here becomes explicit: the *beffa* has the effect not only of saving the woman in a difficult situation, but also of allowing her to live her sexual life as she pleases. Justice for women thus involves not simply the transitory pleasure of single experiences, but a fundamental reordering of their lives.

In the ninth story Panfilo offers a sort of counterexample to Filostrato's tale, that of a woman who succeeds thanks not to reason but to luck. Lidia, his protagonist, emerges as a negative model: "E per ciò non consiglierei io alcuna che dietro alle pedate di colei, di cui dire intendo s'arrischiasse d'andare, per ciò che non sempre è la fortuna disposta, né sono al mondo tutti gli uomini abbagliati igualmente" (VII.9.4). Unlike the other female protagonists, she dares to embrace her lover in full sight of her husband, claiming that what he sees is the effect of enchantment. Panfilo discourages such actions because he understands the risks that Lidia, and adulterous wives like her, run when they behave secretly: by flaunting her adultery, Lidia foolishly elevates her danger.

The story enjoys marked importance, inasmuch as it occupies the space traditionally reserved to the monarch, here Dioneo, who will subsequently violate his own rule by refusing to follow the theme. Vacating the monarch's spot for his preferred one, he appoints a male vicar to give voice to the story that typically best represents the monarch's intentions when choosing the theme. In an essay that in many ways may offer the last word on this story, Albert Ascoli details how it institutes the theme of the Pyrrhic victory, specifically in terms of patriarchs who think they are in charge but whose exertion of power in fact backfires on them.[17] The theme extends throughout the day, as every cuckolded husband believes his wife to be obedient while she in fact has successfully subverted his authority. Ascoli highlights the names in the story, almost all of which come from its source, Matthew of Vendôme's *Comoedia Lydiae*. The singular exception involves the substitution of Nicostrato for Decius. Ascoli proposes that Boccaccio chose the name "Nicostrato" as part of his Greek etymologizing, in which case the name would mean "defeated by victory," thus suggesting the very idea of the Pyrrhic victory (29). Looking beyond its meaning for the story, and more broadly for the day's narration, the name Nicostrato finds other resonance in the *Decameron:* specifically, it rhymes with Filostrato. The representation of Nicostrato thus suggests a value that transcends the story itself, because it hints at Panfilo's opinion of Filostrato's rule.

In this context it is important to note that the story actually calibrates reader sympathies toward the wife and the husband. Panfilo's introduction of Nicostrato is as important for what it says as for what it does not say. Nicostrato is a *nobile uomo* who, "già vicino alla vecchiezza la fortuna concedette per moglie una gran donna non meno ardita che bella" (VII.9.5). Panfilo then goes on to detail Nicostrato's love for hunting and his particular affection for Pirro, "il quale . . . oltre a ogn'altro amava e più di lui si fidava" (VII.9.6). The age difference between Nicostrato and Lidia hints at the theme of the husband's sexual inadequacy, which Lidia will later confirm. Still, it only hints at this problem, and we do well to remember that other older men, particularly Maestro Alberto in I.10, are quick to chide women who equate old age with impotence. Panfilo's abrupt shift from

---

17. The notion of the Pyrrhic victory in fact applies retroactively to the three stories that structure Day IV. In the first, Tancredi wins the battle of wills with Ghismonda only to lose her. In the fifth, Lisabetta's brothers put an end to her affair with Lorenzo, only to see her die of a broken heart and, upon discovering Lorenzo's head, flee from Messina. Most strikingly of all, in the ninth story Rossiglione punishes his wife's affair with Guardastagno only to witness her suicide, whereupon he too flees. The wife hurls herself from a high window: "La finestra era molto alta da terra, per che, come la donna cadde, non solamente morì ma quasi tutta si disfece" (IV.9.24). The final detail serves to emphasize the window's height, clearly greater than the top of Nicostrato's pear tree. In both cases the man in the superior position, looking down from above, earns a victory that is truly a defeat. The only difference between the Day IV stories and those of Day VII is that in the former case the patriarch must recognize his defeat, whereas in the latter he remains ignorant of it. By pointing out that power can be both transitory and illusory, Panfilo thus offers comfort to women whose subjection to male authority often entails suffering.

describing the marriage to describing Nicostrato's activities and affection for Pirro, however, suggests that his heart is not really in this marriage, which may better explain Lidia's complaints about his inattentiveness.

Lidia, on the other hand, is "non meno ardita che bella"; she too loves Pirro: "s'innamorò forte, tanto che né dì né notte che in altra parte che con lui aver poteva il pensiere" (VII.9.5, 7). The intensity of her feeling for Pirro is a warning sign, as is Panfilo's remark about her daring, and the fact that he does not reciprocate, or pretends not to reciprocate, her feelings only fuels them: "di che la donna intollerabile noia portava all'animo" (VII.9.7). She appears to suffer in fact from the most extreme case of *fol'amor* to be found in the *Decameron*. Indeed, the triangular relationship that Panfilo installs here resembles the one that governed relations between Tancredi, Ghismonda, and Guiscardo, though with some variants. In the earlier tale the head of household was a father, whereas here he is a husband, and while Tancredi loved his daughter too much, Nicostrato appears to love his wife too little. In both cases the object of the female character's desire is a servant, the *valletto* Guiscardo or the *famigliare* Pirro, and both women go to extraordinary lengths to obtain the desired object.[18]

The question on which the story soon turns is whether Nicostrato's inattentiveness to his wife justifies her actions. As a way of holding her off, Pirro demands what he thinks are three impossible proofs of her devotion to him: first, that she kill her husband's sparrow hawk; second, that she give him a lock of her husband's hair; and third, that she give him one of her husband's healthy teeth.[19] Lidia first kills the hawk in full view of her husband and his friends, a deed that so shocks Nicostrato that he shouts his disbelief at her. She offers the following rationale:

Signori, mal prenderei vendetta d'un re che mi facesse dispetto se d'uno sparviere non avessi ardir di pigliarla. Voi dovete sapere che questo uccello tutto il tempo da dovere esser prestato dagli uomini al piacer delle donne lungamente m'ha tolto; per ciò che, sì come l'aurora suole apparire, così Nicostrato s'è levato e salito a cavallo col suo sparviere in mano n'è andato alle pianure aperte a vederlo volare; e io, qual voi mi vedete, sola e malcontenta nel letto mi son rimasa; per la qual cosa ho più volte avuta voglia di far ciò che io ho ora fatto, né altra cagione m'ha di ciò ritenuta se non l'aspettare di

---

18. In his reading of the novella of Tancredi and Ghismonda, Picone argues that "il fatto che qui l'iniziativa erotica sia tolta al *partner* maschile per essere consegnata a quello femminile è dovuto alla pressioni esercitate dalla memoria dell'episodio dantesco di Francesca" ("Dalla lai alla novella" 341). The same may be said of this story, further linking it to IV.1.

19. Pirro's three conditions reinvent the topos of the obstacles to be overcome that are part of the *fol'amor* tradition (Picone, "Dalla lai alla novella" 334).

farlo in presenza d'uomini che giusti giudici sieno alla mia querela, sì come io credo che voi sarete. (VII.9.34–35)

Lidia addresses her audience in a prosecutorial way, beseeching their favorable judgment of her and explicitly calling her actions a vendetta. The comparison of kings to hawks is less audacious than it might seem, because in fact Lidia is taking revenge on her husband, the king of her household, by killing the hawk. She protects herself by making a public case for their actions, and she wins the sympathy of her male listeners, who turn on Nicostrato, declaring "come la donna ha ben fatto a vendicar la sua ingiuria" (VII.9.36). Panfilo, however, inserts a significant qualifier: "credendo non altramenti esser fatta la sua affezione a Nicostrato che sonasser le parole" (VII.9.36): in other words, they believe her unconditionally.

Lidia's principal accusation against Nicostrato is that he prefers the sparrow hawk's company to her own: she is lonely. She eroticizes the bird when explaining how her husband leaves her unhappy in bed when off birding; in effect she accuses him of failing to pool carnal resources, as is his spousal duty. This remark about the bed, coupled with other references to birds in erotic contexts—the tale of Caterina and the nightingale leaps to mind, as does Federigo degli Alberighi's falcon—retroactively sexualizes the activity of birding itself. The Nicostrato who prefers to watch his bird fly in open fields rather than keep her bed warm is a Nicostrato who pursues other forms of erotic pleasure—and Boccaccio's language here allows the full range of graphic interpretations—rather than sex with his wife. Lidia thus encodes a public announcement of her discontent with her husband, explaining as well why she is seeking a lover. Pirro, the object of her desire, witnesses the scene and the speech, and presumably decodes her language to understand better her pursuit of him.

Lidia's sadism, in any event, becomes central to the *novella*, and rather than repel Pirro it confirms her ardor for him. She first kills the sparrow hawk by smashing it against a wall: "presolo per li geti al muro il percosse e ucciselo" (VII.9.32). After she laughingly tears hairs from Nicostrato's beard, she answers his protests by belittling him: "Or che avesti, che fai cotal viso per ciò che io t'ho tratti forse sei peli della barba?" (VII.9.39). She later persists in extracting his healthy tooth "quantunque egli forte per dolor gridasse" (VII.9.53). Each of these actions receives the same graphic attention. Pirro reacts favorably to her gestures; after she kills the sparrow hawk he says to himself, "Alti principi ha dati la donna a' miei felici amori: faccia Idio che ella perserveri!" (VII.9.37). He clearly does not feel any loyalty to Nicostrato, as passion overrides order. Eventually he becomes an accomplice to her betrayal, participating in the key lie about the enchanted pear tree, beneath which they will have sex while Nicostrato watches.[20]

The story ends with another vendetta, as Lidia has Pirro cut down the pear tree: "corri e va e reca una scure e a un'ora te e me vendica tagliandolo" (VII.9.77). She then pronounces herself satisfied, uttering a grandiose lie: "Poscia che io veggio abbattutto il nemico della mia onestà, la mia ira è ita via" (VII.9.79). The story concludes with a happy arrangement that recalls the Day V stories: "Così il misero marito schernito con lei insieme e col suo amante nel palagio se ne tornarono, nel quale poi molte volte Pirro di Lidia e ella di lui con più agio presero piacere e diletto" (VII.9.80). Panfilo could not be more explicit about the mutuality of the happiness, with the key nouns *piacere* and *diletto* here repeated. It is difficult however to celebrate a betrayal so rooted in cruelty and risk. If anything the story suggests the dangerous extent to which desire can drive a lover.

Important as well is the adjective, *misero*, used to describe Nicostrato. Beyond signifying cheapness, it vacillates in Trecento Italian between "infelice," unhappy, and "malvagio," wicked.[21] Its meaning here is crucial to a conclusion about Nicostrato. The former is clearly more sympathetic to him, the latter hostile, and the story, with its initial insistence on his neglect of his wife and its accounts of her cruelty toward him, allows both. It is also, I would venture, an apt adjective for Filostrato, who hovers somewhere between unhappy in his love misery and wicked in his tyrannical rule. Inasmuch as Panfilo does not choose between one or the other meaning, then he may be saying, through the figure of Nicostrato, that there is more than one way to look at Filostrato, that depending on one's point of view, atop the pear tree or beneath it, the erstwhile king looks different.

Dioneo's story concludes the day's narration, but unlike the other nine days in which he tells the last story, his tale does not stand in counterpoint to the monarch's tale that immediately precedes it; rather, it is the monarch's tale. In his introduction he refers to his unique position:

> Manifestamente cosa è che ogni giusto re primo servatore dee essere delle leggi fatte da lui, e se altro ne fa, servo degno di punizione e non re si dee giudicare: nel quale peccato e riprensione a me, che vostro re sono, quasi

---

20. The story presents a nice complementarity to Filostrato's tale of Peronella, in which Giannello mounts Peronella after her husband climbs into the barrel. In this story Pirro mounts Lidia after Nicostrato mounts the tree: "e montovvi sù" (VII.9.69). The twin gestures would appear to suggest Nicostrato's error in pursuing a sporting life at the expense of his wife: his search for pleasure will—ironically because he has climbed a pear tree—yield no fruit.

21. The 1612 first edition of the *Vocabolario degli Accademici della Crusca* offers all three definitions, citing from Boccaccio, Dante, and Petrarch. It does not cite this instance of the word.

costretto cader conviene. Egli è il vero che io ieri la legge diedi a' nostri ragionamenti fatti oggi con intenzione di non voler questo dì il mio privilegio
usare ma, soggiacendo con voi insieme a quella, di quello ragionare che voi
tutti ragionato avete. Ma egli non solamente è stato ragionato quello che io
imaginato avea di raccontare, ma sonsi sopra quello tante altre cose e molto
più belle dette, che io per me, quantunque la memoria ricerchi, ramentar
non mi posso né conoscere che io intorno a sì fatta materia dir potessi cosa
che alle dette s'appareggiasse. E per ciò, dovendo peccare nella legge da me
medesimo fatta, sì come degno di punigione infino a ora a ogni ammenda
che comandata mi fia mi proffero apparecchiato, e al mio privilegio usitato
mi tornerò. (VII.10.3–6)

Dioneo represents himself as prepared to shed the Dioneo he has always
been and to *soggiacere* to the rule just as the others had. But instead he
seizes the opportunity to be his old self, in effect blaming his companions: one of them told the story he would have told, along with so many
other wonderful ones. He announces that he is ready for punishment while
simultaneously flattering his companions, effectively ensuring that no
punishment will be forthcoming.

By excusing himself from his own rule, Dioneo turns his monarchy into
nothing other than a *beffa*, by which he tricked his companions to follow
a lead he had no intention of following himself. That he offers himself as
ready for punishment, presumably by the next monarch, the soon-to-be-
named Lauretta, aligns him with Filostrato, who had transgressed in his
own way and accepted punishment in the form of a corrective theme. But
the offer seems disingenuous at best, for as Dante's devil had pointed out
when claiming the soul of the likewise duplicitous Guido da Montefeltro,
"assolver non si può chi non si pente, / né péntere e volere insieme puossi
/ per la contradizion che nol consente" (*Inf.* XXVII.118–20).

In introducing his story Dioneo ignores Panfilo's, leaping instead back
to Elissa's tale, the third, in which Frate Rinaldo sleeps with his *comare*, the
mother of his godchild. The choice of Elissa's tale as a reference point has
the effect of repeating Panfilo's move, casting the female protagonist in a
particularly bad light. Frate Rinaldo uses false logic to persuade her to sleep
with him, and Elissa notes that she "logica non sapeva e di piccolo levatura
aveva bisogno" (VII.3.22). In other words, she was lacking in formal education—her street smarts are well-refined, as she thinks up a trick to cover
her tracks when her husband returns home unexpectedly and finds Frate
Rinaldo with her—and she was easy. It is little wonder that Lauretta follows
with a tale that gives stronger justification for the woman's transgressions.
But in preferring Elissa's story over Lauretta's Dioneo reveals the sort of

tension between himself and Lauretta that threatens to spill over into her choices for the following day. That she explicitly rejects this option suggests a desire on her part to end the retributive cycle that informs both the tales and the relations between men and women in the group.

Dioneo's story likewise involves a *comare*, Monna Mita, the wife of Ambruogio Anselmini, whose child is the godson of Tingoccio Mini. Tingoccio's best friend is Meuccio di Tura: "quasi mai non usavano se non l'un con l'altro, e per quello che paresse s'amavano molto" (VII.10.9). Indeed, despite Dioneo's insistence on the element of the *comare*, the story effectively shifts the day's thematic gears. If the other stories had examined the failed friendships of husbands and wives and the new friendships with other men that wives build, Dioneo moves to a different terrain of friendship. Focusing on the homosocial, he undertakes to study how the triangulation of best friends with a woman affects their relationship. It thus recalls Filostrato's Day IV story of the two Guglielmos, and it anticipates the story that Panfilo will tell as king of the tenth day.

The story turns on two key elements. First, the two friends have promised one another that whoever dies first will return from the dead to tell the other about the afterlife. Second, both men have fallen in love with Mita, though only Tingoccio succeeds in realizing his desires with her, and Meuccio finds out. Meuccio does not tell Tingoccio that he knows about the affair, however, because he believes his knowledge will give him a strategic advantage in the future: "sperando di dovere alcuna volta pervenire al fine del suo disiderio, acciò che Tingoccio non avesse materia né cagione di guastargli o d'impedirgli alcun suo fatto, faceva pur vista di non avvedersene" (VII.10.14). Before Meuccio can realize his advantage, however, Tingoccio dies, literally of excessive sex: "trovando Tingoccio nelle possessioni della comare il terren dolce, tanto vangò e tanto lavorò, che una infermità ne gli sopravvenne" (VII.10.15). Tingoccio's death is fortuitous, as it enables a resolution to the question of both the afterlife and Meuccio's desire for Mita. As promised, Tingoccio returns to Meuccio after three days, reporting on his experience in Purgatory. He tells of trembling with fear as he awaited punishment for sleeping with his *comare*, and of explaining his fear to another soul waiting in line with him: "E egli allora, faccendosi beffe di ciò, mi disse: 'Va, sciocco, non dubitare, ché di qua non si tiene ragione alcuna delle comari!'" (VII.10.28). The news reassures Meuccio, who at tale's end, "lasciata andar la sua ignoranza in ciò per innanzi divenne savio" (VII.10.30), presumably feeling no moral compunction about sleeping with Mita, should the opportunity arise.

While the story distances itself from the others in the day, it also includes one element that unites it with them. While it is not explicitly stated, Tingoccio returns to visit Meuccio in the form of a *fantasima*, likely one with a *coda ritta*. He did, after all, die of too much sex. Moreover, he shares with the earlier *fantasima* his identity with adulterous desire. At the same time, Dioneo's metaphor for Tingoccio's ultimately fatal excessive sex equates the wife with property. With this dismissive attitude toward women—they are objects of sexual desire whose status is questionable—the tale brings the day's narration to a close on a far different note whence it began. Dioneo's attitude toward women, as it transpires in the story, differs markedly from his more supportive tack taken when defending his choice of theme over the ladies' objections. One is left to wonder which is the real Dioneo or whether both voices are more performative than authentic. Certainly the story's tone is more consistent with Dioneo's voice as it resounds elsewhere, suggesting that his defense of his female companions' right to discourse about any topic they choose was more a disingenuous strategy aimed at consolidating his own power. If such is in fact the case, then yet another *beffa* emerges, this one played on the reader who is invited to see Dioneo as sympathetic to women's concerns and prepared to work with them according to a certain altruistic model of friendship, but who finally cares more about himself than anyone else. The sexes make no real progress here except that they succeed in maintaining a greater semblance of amity than they had under Filostrato. It remains to be seen whether Panfilo can do anything more to bridge this gap.

The Remains of the Day

Just as the shadow of Day IV hangs over Day V, so too does Day VIII revisit Day VII. To be sure, the mark is lighter, as befits a day in which the ten find an early compromise to resolve their tensions. Still, later remarks and narratives reflect back on the seventh day, enriching it with meanings that were not altogether apparent as the day unfolded. The rather more indirect look back comes in part from the way in which Lauretta juxtaposes her theme to Dioneo's, after he had acknowledged that she might need to make some repairs: "Madonna, io vi corono di voi medesima reina della nostra brigata; quello omai che crederete che piacer sia di tutti e consolazione, sì come donna comanderete" (VII.Conc.1). Dioneo's remark about *consolazione*, and his recognition that Lauretta will rule *come donna*, suggest an awareness on his part that in ruling as a man he has not necessarily offered the sort of comfort to the ladies that they desire.[22] His statement bears a

---

22. Branca glosses *donna* as "*signora*: termine usato correntemente, per il suo aristocratic

tone of concession similar to that of Filostrato, who upon crowning Fiammetta had described her as best prepared to *racconsolar* their female companions—and the etymological link between the kings' use of *consolazione* and *racconsolar* may be more than a coincidence.

While Fiammetta had seized upon Filostrato's charge to align Day V in formal opposition to Day IV, Lauretta formulates the Day VIII theme by using a strategy of avoidance. Upon receiving the laurel crown, she explicitly eschews using the theme for her day as a means of exacting revenge on Dioneo: "Dioneo volle ieri che oggi si ragionasse delle beffe che le donne fanno a' mariti; e, se non fosse che io non voglio mostrare d'essere di schiatta di can botolo che incontanente si vuol vendicare, io direi che domane si dovesse ragionare delle beffe che gli uomini fanno alle lor mogli" (VII. Conc.3). She names instead a broader topic: "quelle beffe che tutto il giorno o donna a uomo o uomo a donna o l'uno uomo all'altro si fanno" (VII. Conc.4). The simile and the use of the verb *vendicare* suggest that in any event, revenge has come to Lauretta's mind, and her phrasing leaves open the possibility.[23] In part she may be drawing on Fiammetta's response to Filostrato, but the issue of vengeance, and more specifically of revenge narrative, extends naturally from the long seventh day, in terms of both the *brigata*'s experience and the stories told. That Lauretta mentions revenge only to reject it may also have an ideological basis, for by simply flipping the Day VII theme and having the group tell stories of *beffe* played by husbands on their wives, she risks tossing everyone into a morass of misogynistic narrative. Despite her best efforts, misogyny wheedles its way into the day, although through an unexpected voice, that of Pampinea.

Lauretta's attempt to free the eighth day from the narrow confines of the seventh finds both opposition and echo in Neifile's introduction to her story, the first of Day VIII. Despite the queen's apparent discomfort with the theme of men playing tricks on women, Neifile charges right ahead with a story about same: "con ciò sia cosa che molto si sia detto delle beffe fatte dalle donne agli uomini, una fattane da uno uomo a una donna mi piace di raccontarne, non già perché io intenda in quella di biasimare ciò che l'uom fece o di dire che alla donna non fosse bene investito, anzi per commendar l'uomo e biasimar la donna e per mostrare che anche gli uomini sanno beffare chi crede loro, come essi da cui egli credono son bef-

---

valore, a indicare le regine di queste brigate cortesi" (1400). However, Boccaccio could have formulated this statement in any number of ways that would not have highlighted the fact that Lauretta is a *donna*, with the suggestion that ruling as a woman differs from ruling as a man.

23. Lauretta's use of the adverb *incontante* implies a choice between revenge now and revenge later, not between revenge and no revenge.

fati" (VIII.1.2). Neifile casts her tale precisely in terms of opposition to the previous day's theme that Lauretta had avoided. She goes on to qualify her choice as not so much *beffa* as *merito*, criticizing the wife's failure to guard her chastity: "per ciò che, con ciò sia cosa debba essere onestissima e la sua castità come la sua vita guardare né per alcuna cagione a contaminarla conducersi . . . affermo colei esser degna del fuoco la quale a ciò per prezzo si conduce" (VIII.1.3). Her insistent shift in terminology may be read as a generalized critique of the behavior of the Day VII women, and in any event it makes the point, perhaps in opposition to Lauretta, that sometimes revenge is deserved. Wrapping up her argument she makes a clear distinction: "dove chi per amor, conoscendo le sue forze grandissime, perviene, da giudice non troppo rigido merita perdono, come, pochi dì son passati, ne mostrò Filostrato essere stato in madonna Filippa osservato in Prato" (VIII.1.4).

Neifile's final clause, which consists of two dodecasyllables rhyming and assonant in *-ato* (Filostrato/stato/prato) and alliterative in *f*, draws attention to its content, specifically the mention of Madonna Filippa as a woman who compromises her chastity but nevertheless earns pardon. The comparison makes sense superficially because of Neifile's discussion of the relative merits of simple adultery versus uxorial prostitution, and by her assertion that women who prostitute themselves deserve to be burned at the stake, which was the prescribed punishment in Prato as well.[24] Madonna Filippa ends up also being a model for women, inasmuch as her adultery is rooted in *amor* and not in money. The story itself thus finds its rationale in identifying a certain type of adultery that deserves praise and not censure.

Neifile's introduction thus invites a retroactive classification of the Day VII women according to their motivations for adultery. In only four of the nine themed stories are the women explicitly described as being in love with their suitors. In the first story Tessa is *innamorata* of Federigo di Neri Pegolotti; in the sixth Madonna Isabella "s'innamorò d'un giovane il quale Leonetto era chiamato" (VII.6.5); and in the eighth, told by Neifile herself and significantly the last of the day's stories narrated by a woman, Monna Sismonda "s'innamorò d'un giovane chiamato Ruberto" (VII.8.5). Finally, in the ninth tale, Lidia *s'innamorò forte*—thus aberrantly—with Pirro. The other Day VII women, while not explicitly in love, also do not prostitute themselves, though as we have seen Peronella comes mighty close. Neifile's argument thus becomes an indirect if somewhat skewed defense of

---

24. The story itself, which features a wife who prostitutes herself, would appear to confirm the exact nature of Prato's original law, that it punished simple adultery and uxorial prostitution. However, in her introduction Neifile makes no mention of wives but simply of women who prostitute themselves, so in fact the question remains open.

the Day VII women against any future detractors: first, whatever you say about them, you cannot accuse them of prostituting themselves, and second, if they gave themselves to men not their husbands because of love, they deserve the same praise accorded to Madonna Filippa. Their behavior should not be judged criminal, by either the laws of man or the laws of God.

As I observed earlier, Filostrato's own Day VII story of Peronella referred back in its own way to the Madonna Filippa story, thanks to its combination of sex and money. That story returns as a subtext of Neifile's Day VIII tale, thanks to her invocation of Filostrato and the combination of sex and money that informs the Peronella story, suggesting prostitution. The story came with Filostrato's introduction, in which he praised exposure of women's trickery as a means to get men to behave themselves. Neifile's story involves the same issues while reversing the action. The object of affection, Madonna Ambruogia, demands not just discretion from her paramour, Gulfardo, but also payment, specifically 200 gold florins, before she will satisfy his desires. The latter demand exposes Ambruogia as unworthy of Gulfardo's love; as Mazzotta points out, her demand "violates the free exchange of love, draws it within the law of the marketplace" (191). Neifile punningly casts his feelings in the courtly love tradition—"pregandola che le dovesse piacere d'essergli del suo *amor cortese*" (VIII.1.6; italics mine)—but she quickly shows that she attaches no sentiment to love. For this she may perhaps be forgiven, because in some ways she is parroting his own ethos in responding to him. He is, after all, a *tedesco al soldo*, a mercenary soldier, so his courtly values are already questionable. In any event, he resolves to trick her: "pensò di doverla beffare" (VIII.1.8). He does so by borrowing money from her husband, which he then delivers to her as payment for her services. She complies, only to discover that the payment Gulfardo has rendered was her husband's money, so she enjoys no net gain. The *beffa* is clearly a case of *merito*, as Ambruogia's failure to reciprocate Gulfardo's love identifies her as a bad model for women.

Given the density of this story's associations with tales told by Filostrato, one might apply his principle about how to coerce good behavior to this tale. If exposure is in fact a good means of coercing good behavior from men, then exposing men's trickery should likewise be a good way of coercing good behaviors from women. Neifile in fact inscribes the concern about exposure into her story: Ambruogia demanded that her affair with Gulfardo "non dovesse mai per lui esser manifestato a alcuna persona" (VIII.1.7). Gulfardo actually respects that injunction, but the news leaks out anyway, thanks to Neifile. So adulterous women run two risks: first, that their husbands might discover their behavior, and second, that they will be exposed through narrative. Given this double danger, the message for women would appear to be not to commit adultery in the first place, to remain, in other words, *oneste*. Here then is where Neifile's invocation of Madonna Filippa really begins to matter. As Paolo Cherchi points out, the notion of *onestà* has its roots in Cicero's *honestum* or honorableness, as elucidated in the *De officiis* (*L'onestade e l'onesto raccontare* 29–36). According to Cicero, the honorable consists of those actions that are praiseworthy. Neifile may be suggesting that adulterous wives deserve pardon because in the end Madonna Filippa had done something not only useful but also honorable. The lady herself had suggested the former in her argument about sharing "quel che gli avanza," that which was left over after she had satisfied her husband, with "un gentile uomo che più che sé m'ama" (VI.7.17). As for what precisely she does that is honorable, it is double. The universal acclaim she earns from the people of Prato—"quasi a una voce tutti gridarono la donna aver ragione e dir bene" (VI.7.18)—goes both to her logic of sexual generosity, *aver ragione*, and to the eloquence of her self-defense, *dir bene*. She stands therefore as a qualified model for a wife's adultery: if wives take care to make their husbands happy, then they may share the leftovers with a *gentile uomo* whom they truly love. At the same time, Filippa gets the chance to defend herself only because her husband thinks twice before punishing her himself. An adulterous woman's safety is never guaranteed.

Indeed, the risks attendant to women who cheat on their husbands, and more broadly women who play tricks on men, become a topic in three later stories in Day VIII. Even when it falls short of murder, the specter of male retribution raises the question of whether the end of the *beffa*, pleasure, justifies its means, the trick itself. The first of this group is the famous story of Elena and the scholar, which I have already discussed previously. Here I call attention to Pampinea's introduction, which parses the dynamics of the *beffa* in practical as well as ethical terms.

Pampinea begins with a general statement about the *beffa*: "Carissime donne, spesse volte avviene che l'arte è dall'arte schernita, e per ciò è poco senno il dilettarsi di schernire altrui" (VIII.7.3). One practical joke often earns another, so one should be careful not to enjoy the *beffa* too much. She then goes on to point out that while the group has told many stories about *beffe*, none has included a *vendetta*: Lauretta's rejection of the theme of revenge appears to have held.[25] Her own case will involve a *giusta retribuzi-*

---

25. Pampinea also seems to be making an implicit distinction between a *vendetta*, which her story will recount, and Neifile's earlier *merito*, which she in turn had distinguished from a *beffa*. Curiously, though, Pampinea's notion of *giusta retribuzione*, which she associates with the *vendetta*, applies as well to the *merito* found in Neifile's story. The insistence on nomenclature is in any event yet another reflection of how Day VIII opens up beyond the confines of Day VII.

one against a Florentine woman, the widow Elena, "alla quale, la sua beffa presso che con morte, essendo beffata, ritornò sopra il capo" (VIII.7.3). Pampinea faults Elena for not being cognizant of the risk she ran in playing her trick in the first place. She thus presents her story as offering a salutary lesson for its audience: "E questo udire non sarà senza utilità di voi, per ciò che meglio di beffare altrui vi guarderete, e farete gran senno" (VIII.7.3). Her introduction thus begins and ends with an emphasis on *senno*, wisdom, an intelligence that transcends the ability to carry off a clever trick and which includes an ability to measure risk. Pampinea is concerned more with how women can keep themselves safe in the first place, and one may infer from her words that the surest means does not involve not getting caught. For as some of the Day VII stories demonstrate, the risk of exposure, here literalized as Elena's naked exposure under a hot sun, is real. Elena herself expresses that fear: "O sventurarata, che si dirà da' tuoi fratelli, da' parenti e da' vicini, e generalmente da tutti i fiorentini, quando si saprà che tu sii qui trovata ignuda? La tua onestà, stata cotanta, sarà conosciuta essere stata falsa; e se tu volessi a queste cose trovare scuse bugiarde, che pur ce ne avrebbe, il maladetto scolare, che tutti i fatti tuoi sa, non ti lascerà mentire. Ahi misera te, che a un'ora avrai perduto il male amato giovane e il tuo onore!" (VIII.7.73–74). Only when she is trapped does Elena realize the extent of the danger, which is not merely physical but social as well. By telling the story Pampinea seeks to impart in her companions the *senno* that Elena lacked.

It is perhaps not surprising to hear this argument from Pampinea. She appears to trade on her long-standing authority among the women to offer a cautionary tale, so that they will not comfort themselves with misguided notions of safety. And yet it does not appear that all the ladies share her sense of alarm. Fiammetta, who follows her, offers her tale as an explicit antidote to the previous one, almost denying the gravity of the risk that Pampinea has outlined: "Piacevoli donne, per ciò che mi pare che alquanto trafitte v'abbia la severità dell'offeso scolare, estimo che convenevole sia con alcuna cosa più dilettevole ramorbidare gl'inacerbiti spiriti; e per ciò intendo di dirvi una novelletta d'un giovane, il quale con più mansueto animo una ingiuria ricevette e quella con più moderata operazion vendicò; per la quale potrete comprendere che assai dee bastare a ciascuno se quale asino dà in parete tal riceve, senza volere, soprabondando oltre la convenev-olezza della vendetta ingiuriare, dove l'uomo si mette alla ricevuta ingiuria, vendicare" (VIII.8.3). Fiammetta's remarks almost suggest that Pampinea has violated her own edict that "ciascun generalmente . . . niuna novella altra che lieta ci rechi di fuori" (I.Intro.101), perhaps by allowing the theme of women's danger to penetrate too deeply the narrative space. The scholar's behavior may be an overreaction, as Fiammetta suggests, but he succeeds in exacting his revenge nonetheless, a point that Fiammetta misses. So she proposes instead to tell a tale that involves a more clear-cut *quid pro quo*, deploying a rhetoric of moderation in order to calm the women's *inacerbiti spiriti*. Even though there may be ample justification for the *vendetta*, she explains, it should take a form that does not *inguriare*. This message, which may be meant more for the men than for the women, has the unintended consequence of affirming the verisimilitude of Pampinea's story: if men need to learn not to overreact, then they are likely overreacting.

Which story offers the more plausible model remains unclear. The difference between the two lies in part in the different social pressures at work. Elena had offended the scholar to no small degree by exposing a defect in his intelligence—he did, after all, fall into her trap—and he avenges himself by showing that the intelligence she had mocked actually has some teeth. Fiammetta's protagonists Zeppa and Spinelloccio, on the other hand, have no intellectual pretenses. Both come from "buone famiglie popolane" and have a long-standing friendship: "così s'amavano, o più, come se stati fosser fratelli" (VIII.8.4–5). When he discovers that Spinelloccio has slept with his wife, Zeppa simply arranges to have sex with Spinelloccio's wife on top of a trunk in which Spinelloccio is locked. In the end everyone understands that Zeppa has restored the balance; Spinelloccio tells him that "noi siam pari pari" (VIII.8.34), and the friendship endures. It almost seems that the friendship matters more than the wives' fidelity, because preservation of the former drives the action. Zeppa also understands the risks attendant when events become narrative: "conoscendo che per far romore né per altro la sua ingiuria non ne diveniva minore, anzi ne crescea la vergogna" (VIII.8.9). So the vendetta aims to be constructive, not destructive as the scholar's had been.

As a counterpoint to Pampinea's story, this tale does not end up denying the possibility of the sort of retribution that the scholar wreaks upon the widow. Rather, it conjures a social situation and certain conditions in which nobody gains from doing irreparable damage. Posner's notion of sunk cost, which I discussed earlier,[26] applies here as well, and in particular to the comparative logic of the scholar and Zeppa. The latter in fact appears to consider what Posner calls sunk cost when reasoning that he cannot decrease his injury: "No matter how much harm you do to the aggressor, the harm you have suffered will not be undone" (27). The story in this sense also further exposes the defects in the scholar, because despite his lack of educa-

---

26. See chapter I.

tion Zeppa appears to be able to reason more effectively. However, there is no promise that a man will think about sunk cost when considering his response to injury, so a woman who harms a man could end up confronting either a scholar or a Zeppa.[27] Under the best of circumstances she might hope for a Rinaldo de' Pugliesi, Madonna Filippa's husband, who allows the law to exact his revenge for him. But these two stories make the point that men still consider private revenge to be a valid option, and Boccaccio's male readers perhaps even more so after reading the Madonna Filippa story, where the law did not end up protecting her husband's interests as he had expected.

In introducing the ninth story Lauretta furthers the conversation, drawing a comparison between Zeppa and the scholar: "Assai bene, amorose donne, si guadagnò Spinelloccio la beffa che fatta gli fu dal Zeppa; per la qual cosa non mi pare che agramente sia da riprendere, come Pampinea volle poco innanzi mostrare, chi fa beffa alcuna a colui che la va cercando o che la si guadagna. Spinelloccio la si guadagnò" (VIII.9.3). Her adverb *agramente* recalls Fiammetta's earlier remark about her companions' *inacerbiti spiriti*, suggesting that the story of Zeppa and Spinelloccio has succeeded in its intended restorative effect. Lauretta also achieves synthesis, showing how Fiammetta's tale proves Pampinea's point, that the *merito* of the victim matters in judging the actions of the trickster. While she is talking ostensibly of men, because she is referring to the previous story, her statement of principle extends to all those, the gender-neutral *chi*, who have engaged in *beffe* over the previous two days, inviting a rereading of the tales to determine whether the victims somehow deserved their fate. Any woman who played a trick on a meritorious man should earn less censure than a woman who plays a trick on one undeserving. Still, the fact that Lauretta invites judgment about *beffe* suggests that for her the social value of a *beffa* is not absolute. Her own choice of a story, involving characters from the Calandrino cycle, situates the practical joke in a context in which the notion of merit seems far less subject to debate. Moreover, there are no women here, and the question of retribution does not arise.

The last word on *beffe* and retribution falls, not surprisingly, to Dioneo, allowing him to complete the cycle he had initiated with his choice of a Day VII theme.[28] Having propelled this sequence, the erstwhile king now

---

27. It is important to remember that while in Fiammetta's story Zeppa exacts his vengeance from Spinelloccio, he could just as easily have visited it upon his wife. He in fact confronts her about her adultery but rather than punish her makes her an agent of his revenge against Spinelloccio.

28. In truth the cycle does not end here, as *beffa* stories appear in Day IX as well. The formal conclusion of the theme, at the end of Day VIII, is itself a trick played on the reader.

addresses the question of offense and retribution in broader terms, recasting it in a way that isolates it from the danger of the real world. Reprising Pampinea's theme about the *beffa* as *arte*, he defines the terms by which one may appreciate it: "manifesta cosa è tanto più l'arti piacere quanto più sottile artefice è per quelle artificiosamente beffato" (VIII.10.2). The pleasure lies in witnessing the skill of one-upmanship against a worthy adversary. He then goes on to explain that he will tell the story that the group will like best, since the initial trickster, here the clever Sicilian Iancofiore, "era maggior maestra di beffare altrui" (VIII.10.3) and yet wound up outsmarted. The introduction thus conflates the question of the quality of a practical joke—here a swindle—with the quality of the tale told. The storyteller shares with the trickster the fact that they both practice an *arte*, one that involves creating a fictional plot. The tale itself makes this point repeatedly, as first Iancofiore sends one of her associates, "la quale ottimamente l'arte sapeva del ruffianesimo" (VIII.10.11), to spin a number of *novelle* to Salabaetto, culminating in the claim that he had caught Iancofiore's eye. Once he realizes how she has tricked him out of his money, Salabaetto punishes her deceit by elaborating his own fictions, which she foolishly believes.

The success of Dioneo's recasting of the *beffa* as art form relies on an assumption that the ladies are greater connoisseurs of storytelling than they are undifferentiated partisans of women. The assumption is not unfounded, because Iancofiore is one of those whom many Sicilian woman "del corpo bellissime ma nemiche dell'onestà" (VIII.10.7), therefore not the type who would engender sympathy. He thus expects his audience to overlook the story's gender tension, and the defeat of the trickster Iancofiore, in favor of its artistry, because Salabaetto succeeds in outwitting a clever foe.[29] One has the sense that he is arguing here also on behalf of himself, offering a final defense of the theme of the *beffa* by inviting his audience to reify the narrative, ignore its real-life implications, and enjoy the *novella* and the *beffa* itself as works of art. To the beauty of the natural world that the ladies offer in response to his initial call, Dioneo replies by reaffirming the beauty of the world of narrative. His own libertinism finally dissolves in a paean to an aesthetic of order as realized in a good plot.

---

29. Dioneo may also hope that the women finally share a greater identity as Florentines than they do as women, for Iancofiore's final words, "Chi ha a fare con tosto, non vuole esser losco" (VIII.10.67) affirm the brilliance of Tuscan artistry when it comes to *beffe*.

CHAPTER V

The Rule of Panfilo
Fables of Reconciliation

I N HIS essay "From *controversia* to *novella*" Paolo Cherchi describes the last day of the *Decameron* as "a protracted courtly controversy where the debate revolves around *levels* of courtliness rather than around opposite systems of values or contradictory laws" (129). Cherchi's association of the tenth day with the *controversia* form turns out to be more apposite than he may have intended, for few days of the *Decameron* have provoked such widely divergent readings as this one has. On the one hand there are those who follow the lead set by Vittore Branca, for whom "lo splendido crescendo dell'ultima Giornata sembra voler fissare in una solenne atmosfera encomiastica i più alti motivi, le più grandi idee-forza che avevano regolato lo svolgersi della grandiosa ed eterna commedia umana" (14). Critics of this bent include Cherchi, Victoria Kirkham (in *The Sign of Reason*), Marga Cottino-Jones (in *Order from Chaos*), and Teodolinda Barolini ("The Wheel of the *Decameron*"). Dissenters include Robert Hollander and Courtney Cahill, who in their essay "Day Ten of the *Decameron*: The Myth of Order" undertake to dismantle the happy-ending scenario; Luciano Rossi, who entitles his reading of the day "La maschera della magnificenza amorosa"; and Stefano Giovannuzzi ("La novella di Gualtieri"), for whom the tenth day is a minefield of conflict.

In addition to disagreements about the overall thrust of the day, energetic debates have centered on specific stories, most notably the last one. Indeed, the last tale stands *sui generis* in the *Decameron* as perhaps the most enigmatic in the collection, and its relationship to the others has roiled the interpretive waters. So meticulously does Boccaccio elaborate his rhetorical crescendo that many readers, seemingly bereft after Dioneo has pushed the *Decameron* overboard, have pursued a teleological reading that makes Griselda the sum of all its parts.[1] Such a reading originates in Branca, who identifies in Griselda "espressioni altissime delle tre grandi forze," fortune, love, and ingenuity, which he sees as structuring the entire collection and more specifically as recapitulated with precise order in the tenth day. Informing this logic is a conviction that Boccaccio must have followed the path laid by Dante: for Branca, the *Decameron* is indeed "un'opera cioè architettata e svolta secondo lo schema fissato per la 'comedia' dalla più autorevole tradizione medievale: da Uguccione da Pisa e da Giovanni da Garlandia a Dante" (14). Griselda, for all intents and purposes, substitutes for the *Primo mobile:* she is the organizing principle to which the entire work tends. In other words, any anxiety of influence Boccaccio may have felt with regard to Dante has given way to a critical anxiety of influence that turns the *Decameron* into a shadow *Comedy,* as if the only way to make a statement in the Trecento is to follow Dante's trajectory.[2]

What follows, then, is informed by a conscious resistance to a deterministic fallacy according to which the *Decameron,* in imitation of the *Commedia,* reaches for its own Empyrean. If anything, the tenth day can be read as a joke played on readers who want, indeed expect, ascendancy; and indeed Dioneo's own tendency to upend themes should prepare us for that eventuality. Dioneo's intervention is ingenious because it exposes the dependence of hermeneutics on desire rather than empiricism. That said, I would not deny all continuity between the first nine stories of Day X and its famous tenth story; rather, I would locate it elsewhere than in Griselda's own bizarre magnanimity. The day finds its unity instead, I would argue, in the triumph of the homosocial. Its orderly progression begins by describing a world practically devoid of women (tales 1, 2, and 3), in which men must negotiate directly to remove conflicts that threaten amity. It then moves to a set of stories (4 through 9) in which women enter the mix but are, to borrow Gayle Rubin's term, essentially trafficked,[3] each in her turn

---

1. Richard Kuhns associates this tendency with the fact that Boccaccio provides themes for eight of the days: "Since there are ten days of storytelling, eight with specific themes and two of free-for-all, readers seek to uncover a developmental sequence: say, from unawareness to increasing awareness, from primitive morality to sophisticated moral judgments, from immaturity to social and political maturity, and so on" (17).

2. For a similar argument see Hollander and Cahill 112–13.

3. For Rubin women function as barter: "The 'exchange of women' is a seductive and powerful concept. It is attractive in that it places the oppression of women within social systems, rather than in biology. Moreover, it suggests that we look for the ultimate locus of

a *mediatrix* facilitating the realization of a social harmony between men. Griselda crystallizes this tendency by presenting the paradoxical case of a woman whose centrality signals not agency but contingency. To the extent that she synthesizes the mythic and the real, she does so to point out the negotiations that women must undertake to survive in a world run by men.

As Day X represents the triumph of the homosocial, so too does it provide a consistent means by which male friendship is realized: the gift. As Marcel Mauss points out in his classic study on this topic, the gift serves to affirm social bonds: "there is a succession of rights and duties to consume and reciprocate, corresponding to rights and duties to offer and accept. Yet this intricate mingling of symmetrical and contrary rights and duties ceases to appear contradictory if, above all, one grasps the mixture of spiritual ties between things that to some degree appertain to the soul, and individuals, and groups that to some extent treat one another as things" (14). Describing what he calls a "constant exchange of a spiritual matter," Mauss describes the variety of objects and services that may be subject to exchange: "food, women, children, property, talismans, land, labour services, priestly functions, and ranks—[are] there for passing on, and for balancing accounts" (14). The tenth day bears witness to a similar variety of exchange objects.[4] In the early stories, absent women, the gift is material (X.1), service-oriented (X.2), or personal (X.3). In the later stories women themselves can be the gift, as in the fourth, fifth, and eighth stories, or material, as in the sixth, seventh, and ninth. The tenth story too involves specific though rather more complicated gifts, which I shall discuss later. In their own study of Day X, Hollander and Cahill have illuminated the contractual aspect that subtends so many of the stories. Friendship becomes a contract in Day X, and gifts seal the deal.

---

women's oppression within the traffic in women, rather than within the traffic in merchandise. It is certainly not difficult to find ethnographic and historical examples of trafficking in women. Women are given in marriage, taken in battle, exchanged for favors, sent as tribute, traded, bought, and sold. Far from being confined to the 'primitive' world, these practices seem only to become more pronounced and commercialized in more 'civilized' societies" (175).

4. Cherchi situates the gift giving in a different context: "Semmai gioverà sottolineare che in tutte [le novelle] è presente un dono—ora materiale ora spirituale, ma sempre commisurato allo stato e alla qualità sia del donatore sia del ricevente—, secondo la norma che regola il beneficio quale era stato illustrato da Cicerone e soprattutto da Seneca: sono doni sempre gratuiti, cioè motivati da generosità spontanea e non dettati da interesse, e sono sempre indice di magnificenza senza ostentazione" (*L'onestade e l'onesto raccontare* 99).

The Sign of Paradox

From the moment of his inevitable appointment all signs point to a felicitous reign for Panfilo. In crowning him, Emilia envisions his rule as offering an opportunity to correct all the errors of the previous rulers:[5] "Signor mio, gran carico ti resta, sì come è l'avere il mio difetto e degli altri che il luogo hanno tenuto che tu tieni, essendo tu l'ultimo, a emendare" (IX. Conc.2). He replies with praise for Emilia, who had released her companions from themed storytelling, but he also reinstitutes the rule of the theme: "giudico che sia bene il ritornare alla legge usata" (IV.Conc.4).[6] He explains the theme, "chi liberalmente o vero magnificamente alcuna cosa operasse intorno a' fatti d'amore o d'altra cosa" (IX.Conc.4), as one that will enable the group to transcend death: "Queste cose e dicendo e faccendo senza alcun dubbio gli animi vostri ben disposti a valorosamente adoperare accenderà: ché la vita nostra, che altro che brieve esser non può nel mortal corpo, si perpetuerà nella laudevole fama . . ." (IX.Conc.5). Panfilo's vision here is consistent with interests expressed as far back as the tale of Ser Ciappelletto. It also has the—perhaps inadvertent—effect of relocating the group under the shadow of the plague. Anticipating a return home, Panfilo seems to understand that he and his friends will also reenter real time, a temporality marked by mortality, which necessitates a different way of thinking.

With this gesture Panfilo establishes both the type of friendship and the family model that will inform his governance. If for Filostrato friendship was grounded in utility and for Dioneo it lay in pleasure, for Panfilo the friendship model is one of goodness, of concern for a *bene* that transcends the material. The family model of his governance will likewise reference fraternity rather than paternity, Filostrato's model, or marriage, Dioneo's. Neither sexual tension nor the demands of an irascible parent structure the group's relations this time; indeed, unlike the previous two kingships, this one sounds an initial note of amity: "La tema piacque alla lieta brigata" (IX. Conc.6). And yet, as is often the case, intentions and effects differ. Readers of the tenth day have repeatedly commented on how the group gets caught up in a competition over who can narrate the greatest example of

---

5. I therefore agree with Thomas Greene, for whom "the queen's allusion to 'amendment' seems . . . something more than a formula of courtesy" (308).

6. Panfilo's judgment here comes as no surprise. Emilia had anticipated that Day X would return to a theme when announcing that Day IX would be free of one: "io estimo, avendo riguardo quanti giorni sotto certa legge ristretti ragionato abbiamo, che, sì come a bisognosi, di vagare alquanto e vagando riprender forze a rientrar sotto il giogo non solamente sia utile ma oportuno" (VIII.Conc.4).

magnificence, attaching to it a number of interpretations. Cherchi is rather nonjudgmental: "Every story teller aims at excelling over the previous one by retelling a story of magnanimity or liberality or any other courtly virtue which operates at a level slightly higher than the one attained in the previous narration" ("From *controversia* to *novella*" 129). Hollander and Cahill see it instead as a sign of a disturbing disharmony among the assembled, characterizing the competition as a rivalry that associates the tenth day with the previous four, which had marked a darkening of the *Decameron* (152). For Marcus, "Such a competitive mode subverts the very theme of magnificence, for this virtue suggests the disinterested outpouring of wealth in Dante's sense of celestial economics, where giving increases rather than decreases the donor's assets" (*An Allegory of Form* 96). The dynamic, in which the choice theme provokes tensions within the group, in fact mimics the pattern established under the other two kings, suggesting that no matter how hard a king tries to be conciliatory he cannot help but stir up trouble. The reconciliation that Thomas Greene describes as an extension of his notion of accommodation is rather more an ideal that the day projects than one it enacts.[7]

Boccaccio thus launches the tenth day under the sign of paradox. It is a fitting choice, because in the end, the author has tossed too much up in the air for it all to land neatly, and perhaps we as readers have been naïve to expect the grand synthesis we so much desired. Indeed, rather than grant readers satisfaction by representing unadulterated social harmony, Day X makes clear that harmony is selective, and that sacrifice often accompanies the resolution of conflict. In this way it recalls Day V, in which the happy endings sometimes accrued only to men. The inverted models that characterized the sojourn in the country, and that principally involved granting extraordinary agency to women, are about to be flipped back over.

The day also exposes another fundamental paradox, this one about gift giving. Many of the stories, and the very act of sharing them among the members of the *brigata*, involve an implicit rivalry between the parties of exchange that can trump altruistic intent. The gifting of stories in the tenth day bears out Mauss's claim that "We must always return more than we receive; the return is always bigger and more costly" (63). Gift giving thus synthesizes rivalry and generosity, simultaneously exposing social harmonies and social tensions; it is as if by their very choice of generosity the

---

7. Speaking of the tenth day, Greene writes: "these nine stories of magnanimity, in their juncture of a finer creativity and a higher self-denial, reach out to extend the formula of accommodation to a profounder principle of success. This firmer equilibrium, this wiser and more tender healing, deserves rather the term 'reconciliation,' because it transcends the *ad hoc* extemporization of the typical ending" (310).

members of the *brigata* are caught between serving their own interests and serving those of their companions.

As if to second Panfilo's vision of fraternal order, many stories feature the sacrifice of sexual desire, which Teodolinda Barolini characterizes as "generosity in a particularly aggravated form" ("The Wheel of the *Decameron*" 237). In the fourth story, after gaining the assent of his peers that he has every right to take possession of his beloved Catalina, Gentile de' Carisendi remains good to his word to treat her as a sister, restoring her and her newborn infant to her husband with the declaration that she is his *comare*, a relation that here implies a respect for the same sexual boundaries that had been abrogated in Dioneo's story at the end of Day VII, and that Gentile himself had crossed by fondling her in her tomb. The conversion of the beloved into a sister also marks the following story, when Ansaldo, who again by all rights may take carnal possession of his beloved Dianora, decides rather to treat her "non altramenti che se mia sorella fosse" (X.5.22). In the next story, a chastened and elderly Re Carlo renounces his desire for Ginevra, finding a husband both for her and for her sister "non come figliuole di messer Neri ma come sue" (X.6.35). These stories reflect the day's predominant conservative impulse, according to which the pursuit of erotic desire must cede to a duty to maintain order.[8] That order involves an element that heretofore has enjoyed little attention: the ability of men to get along, to preserve their relations as foundational to a functional society.

The stories themselves complicate the bliss. As they focus on the homosocial, they provide precious few models of magnanimous women, with the exception of the daunting Griselda. The tales idealize a world in which men get along, one where women, if they enter the picture at all, do so as vehicles to the perfection of male friendships. One is reminded, in this context, of Heidi Hartmann's definition of patriarchy: "relations between men, which have a material base, and which, though hierarchical, establish or create interdependence and solidarity among men that enable them to dominate women" (14). To the extent that the last day of the *Decameron* lays the groundwork for a return to Florence, it does so in part by reminding women that they will soon return to the same margins of experience, organized by men, that men have often occupied during their two-week sojourn in the country.

8. Hollander and Cahill likewise see the theme of order as informing much of the Day X narrative, and they trace it through legal issues, specifically involving contracts, that structure many of the stories. They express doubts about the nature of the order represented in these pages, however, subtitling their essay "The Myth of Order" and demonstrating ways in which Boccaccio subverts any appearance of order in the tenth day. While I will take exception to some of their claims, my own reading aligns with theirs in that we all see the theme of munificence as promising more than it delivers.

The Return of the Eavesdropper

Throughout this book I have highlighted the role played by patriarchal figures in relation to other characters, principally but not exclusively female. As I suggested in chapter I, this theme first appears in the author's Proem and gains particular resonance in the Introduction to Day I, as well as in the author's self-defense which opens Day IV. In the two days I have examined up until now, the patriarchal figures—fathers, brothers, and husbands—stand outside of the tales' significant relationships, which typically couple women with lovers to whom they are not married. What distinguishes Day IV from Day VII, as I have argued, is the degree of success with which the female character negotiates this triangle. In the triangular stories of Day IV the woman, along with her lover, falls victim to the retributive impulse of the authority figure, while in Day VII she manages to escape punishment by concealing her illicit relationship from her husband. Day X begins by reinventing the model of the outsider male, but with a new twist. Here a situation of estrangement between two male characters finds resolution thanks to espionage, either in the form of a subordinate spy or when one of the two disguises himself in order to effect his own snooping. If Day IV addressed the consequences of inadvertent discovery, and Day VII the avoidance of same, Day X features the secret agent, whose espionage leads not to disaster but to reconciliation.

The day's first three tales constitute something of a trilogy of espionage. In the first story, Messer Ruggieri, who has traveled to Spain drawn by the fame of Re Alfonso, leaves in pique after observing that the king directs his largesse at everyone but Ruggieri himself. The king orders one of his servants to spy for him: "Appresso questo, commise il re a un suo discreto famigliare che, per quella maniera che miglior gli paresse, s'ingegnasse di cavalcare con messer Ruggieri in guisa che egli non paresse dal re mandato e ogni cosa che egli dicesse di lui raccogliesse sì che ridire gliele sapesse; e l'altra mattina appresso gli comandasse che egli indietro al re tornasse" (X.1.8). The second and third stories feature a creative variant of this procedure, in which disguise enables the protagonist to carry out his own espionage. In the second story the reprobate Ghino di Tacco plays host to the infirm Cluny abbot, establishing a direct relationship with the abbot while claiming to be one of Ghino's servants in order to reinvent himself outside of his reputation. In the third story, a young Mitridanes, frustrated in his efforts to gain fame as the most generous man in the world, resolves to murder his archrival in generosity, Natan. Arriving at Natan's castle he encounters his enemy, who identifies himself as one of Natan's servants and offers Mitridanes instructions on how to kill him.

In all three cases the espionage leads to a resolution of the conflict, which in turn involves gift giving. Re Alfonso, learning of the cause of Ruggieri's upset, demonstrates that fortune, not the king, had failed him, then stands up to fortune by bestowing his jewels on Ruggieri. In the second story, Ghino di Tacco gives the gift of his medical skill to cure the Cluny abbot of his stomach upset, then reveals himself to the abbot, explaining that his nefarious nature extends not from "malvagità d'animo" but from being a "gentile uomo e cacciato di casa sua e povero e avere molti e possenti nimici" (X.2.21). The combination of his careful treatment of the abbot and the restitution of all of the abbot's possessions serves to prove his point. In the third tale, Mitridanes discovers that Natan's generosity extends to offering up his very life to the young man, and so shamed he abandons his plan. In addition to resolving the immediate crisis, these generous acts also serve to seal a friendship. Ruggieri returns happily to Tuscany with the evidence of his own worth that he had sought. The Cluny abbot befriends Ghino and demonstrates his friendship by effecting the reconciliation of Ghino and his archenemy, Boniface VIII. Mitridanes calls Natan his *carissimo padre* (X.3.28), with Natan calling him *Figliuol mio* and assuring him that "niuno altro uom vive il quale te quant'io ami" (X.3.30–31).[9]

These stories share another common element: the almost complete absence of women. With the exception of the anonymous *feminella* who visits Mitridanes in the third story and points out that Natan had shown her greater generosity, these tales describe a world devoid of women. Instead we have men of great power—Re Alfonso, the pope, the Cluny abbot—or great wealth—the aforementioned three, plus Ruggieri, Natan, and Mitridanes—many of whom seem lonely, and who seek to overcome that loneliness not with women but by the company and affirmation of other men. Ruggieri's quest for recognition, while consistent with chivalric values, also involves solitary travel to a faraway land, and his disappointment after receiving no gifts from the king has nothing to do with his need for wealth, because he is already *ricco* upon departing for Spain. Ghino di Tacco seems similarly isolated, exiled from Siena and living in Radicofani, rejected by nearby powerful men, including the pope, because of his habit of violence and thievery.[10] His estrangement seems particularly painful

---

9. Hollander and Cahill point out the Christological evocations in these forms of address, suggesting this subtext as the reason for the *brigata*'s subsequent return to amorous themes: "It is as though none of the members of the *brigata* desired to contribute another intrinsic challenge to Christ's unsurpassed munificence" (125). For their argument that the story actually parodies the theme of munificence, and the old lady's role in exposing that parody, see 127–28.

10. For valuable details about the historical Ghino di Tacco , see Chiappelli's essay.

because he knows he has something socially valuable to offer, his medical talent, but no opportunity to show it. The pope recognizes his role in curing the sick abbot, who has described Ghino as *mio medico* (X.2.28), by making him a knight of the Order of the Hospitallers. The third story records no friends for Mitridanes, who appears to seek fame for his liberality as a substitute for love. He finds true happiness only upon receiving the selfless love of a Natan whose generous nature includes a willingness to die that Mitridanes might be happy.

The first three stories thus forthrightly establish that the tenth day is about men; they all seem to radiate in one way or another from Melisso's predicament of friendlessness and King Solomon's enigmatic instruction to him, "Ama," in Emilia's Day IX story. Panfilo has carefully constructed his theme in order to allow women into the picture—"chi liberalmente o vero magnificamente alcuna cosa operasse intorno a' fatti d'amore o d'altra cosa" (IX.Conc.4)—but women enter the narrative stream in earnest only in the fourth story. Not surprisingly, it is Filostrato who tells the third story, which includes a female character whose presence serves only to underline just how marginalized women have become: she arrives almost spectrally to make a point and then disappears so quickly that the story records no redress of her complaint. Perhaps awakened by this, Lauretta opens the fourth story by announcing that it is high time to introduce an amorous element: "Giovani donne, magnifice cose e belle sono state le raccontate, né mi pare che alcuna cosa restata sia a noi che abbiamo a dire, per la qual novellando vagar possiamo, sì son tutte dall'altezza delle magnificenzie raccontate occupate, se noi ne' fatti d'amore già non mettessimo mano, li quali a ogni materia prestano abondantissima copia di ragionare" (X.4.3). In essence, Lauretta points out that the narrative line pursued up till now has reached a dead end: nothing can surpass what has already been said. So the time has come to change course, specifically by adding the element of love to the mix. Strikingly, however, this new element does not cancel out the already prevalent feature of male friendship. Love enters the picture, but the homosocial does not leave, and women, rather than assume center stage, become pawns in negotiations between men.

The Amorous Sequence: Male Friendship and the Status of Women

The amorous sequence presents four stories that link male friendship to the status of women, either because the negotiation over a woman's status leads to friendship (stories 4 and 5) or because the friendship is central to the outcome of a question involving a woman (stories 8 and 9). The seed of this development lies in the second tale, which records that Ghino di Tacco became "amico e servidore di santa Chiesa e dello abate di Clignì" (X.2.31). In the other two tales the protagonists make a magnanimous gesture, but there is no suggestion that friendship results. Ruggieri returns to Tuscany from Spain with the king's gifts, and we have no idea whether the two ever meet again. Mitridanes and Natan likewise take leave of one another after a companionable interlude, with Mitridanes learning only that he could never surpass Natan in liberality. The failure of such generous acts to cement a friendship suggests that friendship requires more than simple generosity in order to blossom. Certainly it demands proximity or, to borrow again from Mauss, membership in a local social network; one has the sense that the relationships between Ruggieri and the king, and Natan and Mitridanes, wither in part due to separation. Ghino di Tacco, while out of direct contact with both the pope and the Cluny abbot, nevertheless remains a friend of both because their respective orbits overlap, thanks to Ghino's new service with the Hospitallers.

The tales involving women clarify the question. Men find a way to be friends when they successfully relegate women to a position where they no longer threaten to disorder male society.[11] If in the fourth day women tried to seize the initiative for their erotic lives and suffered a bad outcome, and if in the seventh they succeeded, in the tenth day men remain singularly in charge. It should come as no surprise then that all four of these stories, in one way or another, involve a claim regarding a woman and the resolution of same. In the new mercantile society that Boccaccio highlights, nothing avoids commodification.

The first two stories in this sequence reelaborate tales told as part of the *quistioni d'amore* episode in Boccaccio's early romance, the *Filocolo*. Understanding the significance of Boccaccio's choice of these tales for reelaboration in the *Decameron* requires a brief excursus about the *Filocolo*'s *quistioni* themselves. These constitute a debate about love, led by Fiammetta and carried out by an assembled group of thirteen travelers in a Neapolitan garden. As Victoria Kirkham points out in *Fabulous Vernacular*, her study of the *Filocolo*, the group is arranged symmetrically in a circle, with Fiammetta and her lover, Caleon, sitting opposite one another. When

---

11. This is Gayle Rubin's key point in her essay: "If it is women who are being transacted, then it is the men who give and take them who are linked, the woman being a conduit of a relationship rather than a partner to it. . . . If women are the gifts, then it is men who are the exchange partners. And it is the partners, not the presents, upon whom reciprocal exchange confers its quasi-mystical power of social linkage. The relations of such a system are such that women are in no position to realize the benefits of their own circulation" (174).

Caleon, the central narrator of the thirteen, takes his turn, rather than tell a tale he asks Fiammetta what becomes the central question of the discussion: "Graziosa reina, io disidero di sapere se a ciascuno uomo, a bene essere di se medesimo, si dee innamorare o no. E questo a dimandare mi muovono diverse cose vedute e udite e tenute dalla varie oppinioni degli uomini" (*Fil.* IV.43). In her response Fiammetta recapitulates Aristotelian friendship theory in a Christian idiom, here applying it to erotic circumstances: "amore è di tre maniere, per le quali tre, tutte le cose sono amate; alcuna per la virtù dell'uno, alcuna per la potenza dell'altro, secondo che la cosa amata è, e similmente l'amante" (*Fil.* IV.44). The three types are *amore onesto*, *amore per diletto*, and *amore per utilità*, corresponding to Aristotle's friendship based on the good and on pleasure and utility. Fiammetta lauds the first type as "buono e diritto e il leale amore, il quale da tutti abitualmente dee esser preso" (*Fil.* IV.44): in other words, yes, all men should love, for their own good, but they should fall into the correct kind of love, the ennobling kind. Fiammetta condemns the other two types, even against Caleon's defense of erotic love, and in so doing she appears to direct lovers toward one of the other two options, presumably that of *amore onesto*.

That the two tales Boccaccio extracts from the *quistioni* come from a philosophical context rooted in the comparison of *amore onesto* to *amore per diletto* and *amore per utilità* is not without significance, because both tales record the transcending of an initial *amore per diletto* of the basest type, unvarnished sexual desire, in a friendship that permanently reorders the relation between the three parties involved, lover, wife, and husband. That reordering removes the woman as an object of contention, allowing the two men to form a social compact that is a social good because it removes a disordering rivalry that could lead to graver conflicts.

Boccaccio significantly rewrites both tales in their transfer from the *Filocolo* to the *Decameron*, the changes suggesting new thematic emphases that are consistent with the overall messages of the tenth day.[12] In the *Filocolo* version of X.4, the dramatic scene in which Gentile de' Carisendi asks Niccoluccio Caccianimico to respond to his hypothetical question about servants and property, in order to establish that Niccoluccio's wife now belongs to Gentile, is wholly absent. In X.5 Boccaccio eliminates much of the earlier narrative devoted to developing the relationship between the putative lover Tarolfo and Tebano, the magus who delivers the May garden in January. He also sharpens the development of the friendship between the putative lover, now named Ansaldo, and Gilberto, Madonna Dianora's husband. In both cases the changes shift the focus onto the way in which a

---

12. Padoan offers a valuable analysis of Boccaccio's changes: "Mondo aristocratico" 21–24.

question about a woman's status leads to friendship between the two men who contend for her, suggesting that friendship is possible only once the rivalry over a woman has been removed. In both cases too, the means to eliminating the rivalry involves the offer of the woman as a gift.

The fourth story finds Gentile de' Carisendi, in the midst of an act of necrophilia, discovering that his beloved Catalina has not in fact died, then restoring her to health and eventually to her husband and earning enduring friendship with the latter. The process of restitution involves a scene in which Gentile asks the woman's husband, Niccoluccio, to reflect on the circumstances by which Catalina fell into his, Gentile's, hands, and to deliberate over the question of who may now claim title to her. Women are commonly property of their husbands in the *Decameron*, though they are not always loved; and *Decameron* women are often loved by men who cannot commodify them through marriage. Gentile's situation is unique: he loves a woman who is not his wife, yet for a time she becomes his property.

In the story's central scene Gentile reintroduces Niccoluccio to his wife at a dinner-party ritual construed under the banner of friendship. While there is no record that their friendship predates the dinner, Gentile is something of a public man, having served as *podestà* in Modena, so the staging is not wholly implausible. He invites Niccoluccio and other *gentili uomini* of Bologna to his banquet, then announces to the assembled group his intention to honor a Persian custom by which one may "sommamente onorare il suo amico": "egli lo invita a casa sua e quivi gli mostra quella cosa, o moglie o amica o figliuola o che che si sia, la quale egli ha più cara, affermando che, se egli potesse, così come questo gli mostra, molto più volentieri gli mosterria il cuor suo" (X.4.24). The additional element of the banquet, which is not part of the original ritual as Gentile concocts it, treads the well-worn path of *Decameron* meals, which generally involve an element of affective exchange.[13] In the present case the story turns not on the restitution of Catalina to her husband, but rather on how that restitution binds Gentile and Niccoluccio in friendship.

By Gentile's account of the Persian tradition, the most prized possession is usually a female member of the household, though he leaves open the possibility of the exchange of something else, something inanimate, thus suggesting that the value we attach to objects may combine sentiment and economic appraisal. By specifying the element of a prized wife or female friend or daughter he prepares his guests for what they are about

---

13. As a rule, the meal or banquet setting involves the exchange of an object that somehow stirs up the feelings of the two participants. Federigo's falcon seals the deal with Giovanna; serving her lover's heart at dinner destroys the relationship between Rossiglione and his wife; Pietro di Vinciolo and his wife share dinner with her guest, then a bed with him.

to see, which only affirms the notion of women as transferable property. Whatever he trots out, according to Gentile, has both intrinsic value—its owner loves it best—and symbolic value in representing the owner's affection for his guest. The latter value transcends the former, as the custom seeks not simply to show off what the host loves the most but to cement the friendship. If one accepts this premise, then bringing out Catalina will allow Gentile to accomplish two goals: first, he will show his audience what he loves best, and second, he will demonstrate his affection for his guests, particularly Niccoluccio. This latter gesture can only be a sham, as Gentile appears to have organized this party in part to embarrass Niccoluccio before his peers, before returning Catalina to him.

Before introducing Catalina, Gentile asks his assembled guests the critical question on which the whole story turns: "Egli è alcuna persona la quale ha in casa un suo buono e fedelissimo servidore, il quale inferma gravemente; questo cotale, senza attendere il fine del servo infermo, il fa portare nel mezzo della strada né più ha cura di lui; viene uno strano e mosso a compassione dello 'nfermo e' sel reca a casa e con gran sollicitudine e con ispesa il torna nella prima sanità. Vorrei io ora sapere se, tenendolsi e usando i suoi servigi, il suo signore si può a buona equità dolere o ramaricare del secondo, se egli raddomandandolo rendere non volesse" (X.4.26–27). The inquiry, absent in the *Filocolo*, goes to the heart of determining a woman's status, legal or otherwise. The key element complicating the question of ownership appears to be that of *ispesa*, expense, specifically understood as an investment that entitles one to some sort of return. That Gentile understands the financial question to raise thorny legal issues becomes clear in the language of his question, when he wonders whether the first *signore* can demand restitution of the servant *a buona equità*, justly or fairly.

My translation does not grasp the legal complexity of the question Gentile raises, for Boccaccio's invocation of *equità* returns us to the matter, previously explored in the case of Madonna Filippa, of *epieikeia*, or reasonableness. While elsewhere in the *Summa* Aquinas borrows the Greek term from Aristotle, he does at one point provide a Latin translation for it: "apud nos dicitur æquitas" (*ST* 2a2æ. 120, 1). In addressing the question of whether equity is a part of justice, Aquinas describes it as "a part of justice taken in the widest sense. . . . epieikeia is a norm over and above legal justice. Epieikeia thus stands as a kind of higher rule for human actions" (*ST* 2a2æ. 120, 2). The formulation of that higher rule comes in locating the space between legislative intent and legislative language, particularly when following the latter as opposed to the former harms the public good, the *commune bonum*. In the present case Gentile appears to be asking whether Niccoluccio may reasonably ask for restitution of his wife, even if she now

legally belongs to someone else: in other words, whether a broadly conceived notion of intent, linked to the common good, trumps the narrow
confines of the law. Tumbling into Gentile's trap, Niccoluccio answers no,
denying that a *buona equità* predicate justifies restitution. While on the
one hand this is the response that Gentile had hoped for, on the other it is
also a response with which he does not agree.

Gentile's guests appear to think that their host is playing a game, not
asking a question with serious implications. They entrust their reply to
Niccoluccio "per ciò che bello e ornato favellatore era" (X.4.28): for them
the situation requires verbal dexterity rather than reasoned legal thinking.
Niccoluccio proves his own limitations when affirming that the servant
would remain the property of the person who had picked him up off the
street. He offers an important rationale: since the first owner had in effect
thrown the servant away, "niuna noia, niuna forza, niuna ingiuria [il sec-
ondo] faceva al primiero" (X.4.29). In other words, one cannot suffer a loss
when one has willingly disposed of something. The reply betrays the sort
of economic rationalism that has infected Niccoluccio's thinking: he reasons
that the servant becomes the property of his new owner by default, "per li
benifici del secondo usati." This sort of analysis stands in direct contrast to
the language Lauretta employs to describe Gentile and the values he comes
to embody. She consistently refers to him as a *cavaliere*, and the language
of his question, focusing on a "buono e fedelissimo servidore," which he
echoes later in referring to the wife as a "leale e fedel servo" (X.4.38), suggests subscription to a courtly ethos that predates the sort of pragmatic
profit-based thinking of Niccoluccio.

Indeed, Gentile's progress from necrophiliac to steward of courtly values is so complete by the end of this scene that he frames Catalina's restitution as the gesture of gift giving that he had originally invoked. His
scorn for Niccoluccio and his way of thinking is patent: "io non ti rendo tua
mogliere, la quale i tuoi e suoi parenti gittarono via, ma io ti voglio donare
questa donna mia comare con questo suo figlioletto" (X.4.42).[14] The importance of Gentile's question regarding status now becomes clear, as he can
offer Catalina as a gift only if everyone agrees that she belongs to him.[15] In

---

14. This curious detail, absent in the *Filocolo* version where the wife reportedly dies in
childbirth, may owe itself to a desire on Boccaccio's part to create a moral space within which
Gentile may return Catalina to her husband. The hypothetical in fact elides this detail, suggesting that Niccoluccio was directly responsible for the disposal of Catalina; the fact that he
was not makes him a less vile person than if he had presided at the entombment of his still-
living wife.

15. One may fairly argue, however, that in asking whether Niccoluccio may reasonably
ask for his wife back, Gentile actually cedes the point that by all measures she has remained
his wife. His own words throughout the story suggest as much: he refers to Niccoluccio as

asking for nothing in return, Gentile makes a gesture at once magnanimous and humiliating, because he gives up something of great value while denying its recipient the right of reciprocation: he may not be quite as *gentile* as his name suggests.[16] Still, the gesture suggests that he has transcended his initial *amore per diletto* in favor of *amore onesto*, and Lauretta's language echoes the shift. She has Gentile affirm to Niccoluccio that Catalina "mai o col padre o colla madre o con teco più onestamente non visse" (X.4.43), and in her peroration she affirms that Gentile "giovane e ardente, e giusto titolo parendogli avere in ciò che la tracutaggine altrui aveva gittato via e egli per la sua buona fortuna aveva ricolto, non solo temperò onestamente il suo fuoco, ma liberalmente quello che egli soleva con tutto il pensier disiderare e cercare di rubare, avendolo, restituì" (X.4.48). Gentile's *onestà* extends, as a public man, to his recomposition of a sundered family, which arguably contributes to the common good, inasmuch as it repairs the disorder created when Catalina was erroneously buried.[17]

Gentile's gesture secures for him both public praise and an enduring relationship with Niccoluccio, the only form of reciprocation available to him. Lauretta records both in the story's penultimate paragraph: Gentile's guests "il commendaron molto, e commendato fu da chiunque l'udì," and Gentile "sempre amico visse di Niccoluccio e de' suoi parenti e di quei della donna" (X.4.45–46). To some degree the latter is mandated by Gentile's self-declaration as *compare* to Catalina: he undertakes to create an acceptable permanent relationship with her. While reviling Catalina and Niccoluccio's relatives for their role in her premature burial, he ends up metaphorically marrying into the whole family, becoming *amico* of the entire clan—except of course for Catalina, who appears to fall into another category. Lauretta offers these gestures as signs of good character, establishing Gentile as the type of person whom Niccoluccio would want as a friend. She further argues that his gift surpasses that of the other protagonists of the earlier tales. The king of Spain, she states, merely gave away his scepter and crown, and the Cluny abbot at no personal cost reconciled Ghino and the pope, while Natan offered his neck to his enemy: presumably he represents less of a gift than Catalina because, as Lauretta puts it, he is *un*

---

vostro marito, though in handing her over to Niccoluccio he describes her as "non . . . tua mogliere . . . ma . . . questa donna mia comare con questo suo figlioletto" (X.4.42).

16. In the *Filocolo* version of this tale (IV.67) the protagonist has no name. Boccaccio's decision to name him Gentile is clearly not without thematic implications.

17. Given Gentile's status as a public man, I believe his *onestà* constitutes a form of Ciceronian *honestum* as featured in the *De officiis* and commonly translated in English as honorableness. Cherchi, who argues that Boccaccian *onestà* involves a far more complex semiosis (*L'onestade e l'onesto raccontare del* Decameron), summarizes the *honestum* as "non . . . una virtù particolare, ma l'insieme delle virtù o la virtù stessa" (26).

vecchio, and she is a desirable young woman. Whether the constellation of relationships that the tale records at the end has a solid basis on which to endure is a question that the tale does not answer.

Two final points do emerge, however. First, Lauretta's invocation of *fatti d'amore* as an appropriate topic for storytelling at this point comes to enjoy an expansive definition through the tale, as she sets out to demonstrate how erotic love can be subsumed under a greater social purpose. What is key here is not the one or the other—*amore per diletto* versus *amore onesto,* leaving aside the question of *amore per utilità*—but rather how the two interact to create an order in which two men with potentially conflicting interests over a woman can find accommodation rather than resort to disruptive violence. In this way the tale revisits others, such as IV.9, reinventing a solution to the triangular conflicts that courtly love engenders in order to privilege homosocial amity. Second, and perhaps more important for the overall direction of the *Decameron,* the tale reinvents the *Galeotto* as woman. It is after all Catalina who, albeit passively, unites Gentile and Niccoluccio in friendship. While nothing so crude as pander or pimp, she functions nonetheless as a go-between, and in this sense reinvents womanhood as a means by which men solidify their relation to one another. That function will play itself out in the stories that follow.

While the fifth story conjures a more altruistic picture of friendship, it also delineates more sharply the status of the woman. In a tale that is all about exchange value, Madonna Dianora emerges as the ultimate commodity, and the two male protagonists cement their friendship by removing her as an object of barter. The story presents a similar love triangle, except that in this case the object of affection, Dianora, is alive and well. She understands herself in terms of exchange value and first introduces this element, offering herself in trade to Messer Ansaldo, who is courting her, if he can produce a May garden in January. The nature of her request marks the first significant difference between the tale's earlier iteration in the *Filocolo* and Boccaccio's revision of it for the *Decameron.* In the former the wife's character is somewhat shadier; we learn only that she is a *donna nobile* and *bellissima.* The putative lover, Tebano, pesters her, "seguendo d'Ovidio gli ammaestramenti, il quale dice l'uomo non lasciare per durezza della donna di non perseverare, però che per continuanza la molle acqua fora la dura pietra" (*Fil.* IV.31). She worries that her husband may hear about his efforts and think that she is somehow implicated in them, so she conceives *una sottile malizia* to unburden herself. Boccaccio's use of the word *malizia* connotes fraud: the wife is striking a bargain she has no intention of honoring. When the wife, now named Dianora, reappears in the *Decameron,* she is again "una bella e nobile donna" who now "meritò . . . per lo suo valore d'essere amata sommamente da un nobile e gran barone" (X.5.4), Her *valore* corresponds to her lover's status as "uomo d'alto affare" (X.5.4), nudging both of them into the mercantile sector despite their noble lineage. The lover, now named Ansaldo, no longer takes a page from Ovid's book but rather pursues her doggedly and fruitlessly. Dianora's request of the May garden rouses less ethical suspicion, thanks to Boccaccio's suppression of the word *malizia;* he describes her instead as frustrated: "essendo alla donna gravi le sollicitazioni del cavaliere" (X.5.5). Mostly she wants to be rid of him, and appropriately she has no real interest in the garden, typical locus of love: "con una nuova e al suo giudicio impossibil domanda si pensò di volerlosi torre di dosso" (X.5.5).

Dianora's request unleashes a series of maneuvers that lead to crisis. Ansaldo negotiates a high price in order to accommodate her request, "per grandissima quantità di moneta convenutosi" (X.5.10), to a necromancer in exchange for the required garden. News of the necromancer's involvement alerts Gilberto to potential danger, prompting him to encourage his wife to keep her promise: "inducendomi ancora la paura del nigromante, al qual forse messer Ansaldo, se tu il beffassi, far ci farebbe dolente" (X.5.15). While recognizing that her motives were good, he also upbraids her for marketing her chastity: "egli non è atto di savia né d'onesta donna d'ascoltare alcuna ambasciata delle così fatte, né di pattovire sotto alcuna condizione con alcuno la sua castità" (X.5.14). She must correct her dishonorable behavior by either fulfilling the promise or by finding some other way to be exonerated from it: "Voglio io che tu a lui vada e, se per modo alcun puoi, t'ingegni di far che, servata la tua onestà, tu sii da questa promessa disciolta: dove altramenti non si potesse, per questa volta il corpo ma non l'animo gli concede" (X.5.16). Gilberto requires, in other words, that she come up with a solution, even at the expense of her own chastity: if necessary, she must make a gift of herself.

While Branca finds in Gilberto's words an allusion to Livy's story of Lucretia, for whom "It was the mind . . . that sinned, not the body; without intention there could never be guilt" (I.59), one cannot help but recall as well the words of the devil who carries off Guido da Montefeltro: "né pentére e volere insieme puossi / per la contradizion che nol consente" (*Inf.* XXVII.119–20). Gilberto's advice casts him among the fraudulent counselors, for he suggests that it is possible to commit the act of sex with Ansaldo without willing it, precisely the sort of reasoning that Lucretia had sought to obviate with her suicide. At the same time, he is not wholly at fault, for it was Dianora herself who initially interpreted Ansaldo's love in an erotic key: "E se io potessi esser certa che egli cotanto m'amasse quanto tu di', senza fallo io mi recherei a amar lui e a far quello che egli volesse" (X.5.6).

She promises servitude in exchange for Ansaldo's service; she does not appear to understand at this point that there are many ways to love.

By the time she meets with Ansaldo, however, she appears to have gained a greater understanding of love: "Messere, né amor che io vi porti né promessa fede mi menan qui ma il comandamento del mio marito, il quale, avuto più rispetto alle fatiche del vostro disordinato amore che al suo e mio onore, mi ci ha fatta venire; e per comandamento di lui disposta sono per questa volta a ogni vostro piacere" (X.5.20). She accurately describes the situation: she has not come out of love or to keep a promise. Rather, because her husband understands that Ansaldo's efforts, specifically inasmuch as they involve a dangerous necromancer, outweigh any concern for her or Gilberto's honor, he has decided to make a gift of her to Ansaldo. She also captures the essence of the situation in characterizing Ansaldo's feelings as *disordinato amore*, a love that seeks fulfillment in sex rather than in higher forms of expression. In identifying Ansaldo's condition in this way she shows herself to have the same *intelletto d'amore* as the women who, in the *Vita nuova*, point out to Dante his own *disordinato amore*, inasmuch as he claims that his blessedness lies in words of praise of Beatrice though he fails to praise her. The speech has the effect of changing Ansaldo's mind, but not because he recognizes his love as disordered. Rather, looking right past her, he finds that her husband's generosity moves him: "dalla liberalità di Gilberto commosso il suo fervore in compassione cominciò a cambiare" (X.5.21). He explains that he does not want to be "guastatore dello onore di chi ha compassione al mio onore" (X.5.22), in other words Gilberto, and he asks that she thank her husband "di tanta cortesia" (X.5.22). With her speech Dianora thus accomplishes two goals, one intended and the other not. She fulfills Gilberto's instruction that she get out of her commitment while conserving her *onestà*, and she mediates the creation of a bond between the two men, rooted in their mutual appreciation of *onore*. Indeed, news of Ansaldo's generosity "strettissima e leale amistà lui e messer Ansaldo congiunse" (X.5.23).

The solution to her crisis also has the side effect of neutralizing the most serious threat, that of the necromancer. Impressed by Gilberto's generosity in honor and Ansaldo's in love, the necromancer decides to be generous in his recompense, absolving Ansaldo of his payment for the garden, which ran to a "grandissima quantità di moneta" (X.5.10). If the necromancer's decision to write off his costs strikes readers as inverisimilar, they are likely reading accurately, as this is but one in a series of suggestions that the day is shedding its mimetic skin. A series of relations that improperly derive from Dianora's dangerous ethics thus finds a new ethical order founded on a *liberalità* that ablates fundamental economic principles of exchange. In her conclusion too, Emilia insists on Ansaldo's generosity, apparently seeing his as the greater sacrifice. All three men give something up: Gilberto his wife's chastity, Ansaldo his sexual fulfillment, and the necromancer his payment. That Emilia would define Ansaldo's as the greater sacrifice rescues her from the degraded economic values that give texture to the story while simultaneously suggesting that Ansaldo, because of his investment, had earned his return.

Nevertheless, the story requires mutual sacrifice in order that the two principals may seal their friendship. In his final speech to Dianora Ansaldo expresses concern not for her, but for her husband: he does not want to ruin the honor of "chi ha compassione al mio amore" (X.5.22), namely Gilberto, and he proposes to keep her as his sister in exchange for her relaying his thanks to Gilberto for *tanta cortesia*. His feelings toward Dianora change: "spento del cuore il concupiscibile amore, verso la donna acceso d'onesta carità si rimase" (X.5.25): no longer a slave to *amore per diletto*, he now feels *amore onesto*. The elevation of his love suggests that he has discovered a means of expression that transcends erotic desire, not just because of Dianora's qualities but also because he esteems Gilberto and recognizes the importance of maintaining a social order rooted in friendship.

The Final Trio: Women, Friendship, and Justice

As Day X nears its end, it suffers particular harm because of the charisma of Griselda. So wholly does she dominate the day that the tenth story seems to supplant the ninth, even though the ninth story, here narrated by Panfilo, ideally realizes the monarch's intentions in assigning the theme. Moreover, Griselda's attraction has led readers to overlook the unity of the last three stories, a unity that mirrors the trinity of the first three tales of the *Decameron*. Whereas the first trio addressed questions of transcendence, here the issues addressed are immanent and introduce a new theme to the women/friendship dynamic that courses through the day. That element is justice, by no means new to the day—one need think only of the first story and Alfonso's righting of the wrong done to Ruggieri—but which here assumes new dimensions thanks to the association of the *mediatrix* with allegory. In what follows, then, rather than read Griselda as a case apart, I shall read her as the culmination of a carefully prepared process that begins with the eighth story and which revisits the topos of the apotheosis of woman in order to demonstrate how it, and women's status and safety in general, is wholly contingent on men.

With the eighth story, featuring the friendship of Tito and Gisippo, the question of a woman's status begins its ascent, thanks to a number of allegories that assign transcendent value to womanhood. Whereas in the earlier stories a friendship results from a woman's mediation, here the friendship predates the entry of the woman, Sofronia, onto the scene: the Roman Tito has come to Athens to study philosophy, whereupon he befriends Gisippo and then falls in love with Sofronia, promised in marriage to his friend. Upon learning of Tito's feelings, Gisippo gives Sofronia to him, and later, when their maneuver is discovered, they defend themselves and their friendship against members of her family who claim Gisippo had no right to consign her to Tito. A later series of peregrinations leads all three to Rome, where they reunite under Tito's roof after Gisippo marries Tito's sister, Fulvia. The tale thus concludes with two intersecting triangles of desire, both involving Gisippo and Tito and each mediated by a different woman, Gisippo's *sposa* turned Tito's wife, and Tito's sister turned Gisippo's *sposa*. There thus emerges a complicated international kinship involving a Greek and a Roman man and a Greek and a Roman woman.

From the onset of the action, Tito and Gisippo remain inseparable, so much so that one wonders how there could be room for a third party in a relationship that already mimics marriage.[18] Filomena describes their friendship as "una fratellanza e una amicizia sì grande . . . che mai poi da altro caso che da morte non fu separato: niun di loro aveva né ben né riposo se non tanto quanto erano insieme" (X.8.7). Tito, moreover, clearly understands his desire for Sofronia as conflicting with his love for Gisippo: "tu il dovresti fuggire, se quello riguardassi che la vera amistà richiede e che tu dei" (X.8.15). He sees his desire as violating the rules of friendship: "or non conosci tu, sì per li ricevuti onori da Cremete e dalla sua famiglia e sì per la intera amicizia la quale è tra te e Gisippo, di cui costei è sposa, questa giovane convenirsi avere in quella reverenza che sorella?" (X.8.13). His impulse to convert his erotic desire for Sofronia into a sibling affection is of a piece with his sense that the desire is somehow incestuous: "Quante volte ha già il padre la figliuola amata, il fratello la sorella, la matrigna il figliastro?" (X.8.16). There is of course no real incest here; rather, the sentence accurately reflects Tito's scrambled psychology: he senses that his love for Sofronia somehow violates an established order, the order of his

---

18. In her essay on this story (*The Sign of Reason* 237–48), Kirkham argues that Boccaccio intends this pair of friends to enter a pantheon of classical friendships that includes Damon and Pythias, Theseus and Pirithous, Nisus and Euryalus. Kirkham locates the principles of friendship and the moral issues at work in this tale in Cicero's *De amicitia* and *De officiis*. Reaching different conclusions, Mazzotta also relies on Ciceronian texts in his reading of the tale (*The World at Play* 254–60), which undertakes to reconstruct the thought of the Greek philosopher Aristippus, whose name Boccaccio borrows for this tale.

relationship with Gisippo. He is correct, but not for the reasons he thinks. When he reveals the truth to Gisippo, the latter upbraids him not for loving Sofronia but for hiding his feelings from his friend: "Tito, se tu non fossi di conforto bisognoso come tu se', io di te a te medesimo mi dorrei, sì come d'uomo il quale hai la nostra amicizia violata, tenendomi sì lungamente la tua gravissima passione nascosa" (X.8.25). More clear-headed than Tito, he reaffirms the order of their friendship by privileging his friend's interests over his own: "senza indugio diliberò la vita dello amico più che Sofronia dovergli esser cara" (X.8.24). In his reflexive subordination of his own conjugal desires to Tito's, Gisippo also mimics the subordinate political status of Athens vis-à-vis Rome, a relation that will be made explicit later on.

At the core of Tito's confusion over his desire for Sofronia is her status as Gisippo's *sposa*. By *sposa* Tito of course means *promessa sposa*, but the elision of the semantic—and legal—distinction suggests that simply by entering into this contract Sofronia's parents have transferred authority over her to Gisippo. Gisippo appears to understand the situation similarly, because when Tito confesses his love for Sofronia, he refers to her as "a me sposata" (X.8.26). He continues: "Egli è il vero che Sofronia è mia sposa e che io l'amava molto e con gran festa le sue nozze aspettava; ma per ciò che tu, sì come molto più intendente di me, con più fervor disideri così cara cosa come ella è, vivi sicuro che non mia ma tua moglie verrà nella mia camera" (X.8.30). The sentence divides the marriage ritual into three events: first, betrothal (*sposa*), then the wedding ceremony itself (*nozze*), and finally consummation of the marriage (*moglie . . . nella mia camera*). The question of Sofronia's status, that is, to whom she is in fact married, hangs on the issue of when her marriage to Gisippo becomes official.

This issue is by no means settled in the Middle Ages. Yalom describes betrothal as "almost as binding as marriage" (51), citing the English case of Christina of Markyate, who delayed her marriage for several years and eventually won the freedom to enter the religious life. Before her case was adjudicated, however, her family had a priest pressure her to complete the marriage, arguing that betrothal was the equivalent of marriage. The institution of public banns, on the other hand, suggests that betrothal did not equal marriage, because one or another party could annul the betrothal should evidence surface during the three weeks of the banns that would invalidate the contract. Possible causes, according to Yalom, included a prior marriage of one or the other party, a prior engagement of one or the other party, or prohibited degrees of consanguinity (53). Nor did a public marriage ceremony suffice to affirm the marriage, as consummation came to be a key feature of the ceremonies surrounding marriage, even to the extent that it required a witness in order to ensure that the marriage was binding.

Gisippo's actions suggest that he believes that while he has legal control over Sofronia's fate, he is also not legally married to her and can thus consign her to Tito. At the same time, he and Tito both appear to sense that they are on weak legal footing, because they do not publicize the new arrangement, keeping it even from Sofronia. The wedding itself is murky at best. Tito marries Sofronia in Gisippo's bedroom, "ogni lume avendo spento" (X.8.47), and with no witnesses. She fully expects to receive Gisippo, and without revealing his identity to her Tito asks her whether she will marry him; she agrees. He pretends to be kidding around with her, "quasi come sollazzando chetamente la domandò se sua moglie esser voleva" (X.8.48), so that she will think the question is a lead-up to the consummation of her marriage. She plays along, agreeing to marry him, and he places a ring upon her finger, announcing, "E io voglio esser tuo marito" (X.8.49); they then have sex without her ever learning that he is Tito. Sofronia is thus tricked into marrying a man to whom she was not promised; the two young men apparently have no intention ever of revealing the truth to Sofronia, but must when Tito's father dies and he has to return to Rome.

When the private matter, known exclusively to Tito and Gisippo, becomes public, the question of Sofronia's status also comes out in the open. Upon learning the truth of her marriage Sofronia first responds by looking at the two "un poco sdegnosetta," then bursts into tears and runs home to her parents, where she tells them of "lo 'nganno il quale ella e eglino da Gisippo ricevuto avevano, affermando sé esser moglie di Tito e non di Gisippo come essi credevano" (X.8.52). She too believes that events have made her Tito's wife. The news provokes a scandal, and Gisippo finds himself caught in the middle, shunned by his own family and hers as well. In a show of loyalty Tito steps forward to defend Gisippo and the marriage. Capitalizing on the craven nature of the Greeks—Filomena explains that their bark is worse than their bite—he summons his "animo romano e senno ateniese" (X.8.55) to argue for the legitimacy of the union. His claim rests on two foundations, both of which skirt the question of when a marriage becomes final. He first asserts that the marriage itself is proof of divine will: "mia moglie Sofronia è divenuta dove lei a Gisippo avavate dato, non riguardando che *ab eterno* disposto fosse che ella non di Gisippo divenisse ma mia, sì come per effetto si conosce al presente" (X.8.58). This clever rhetorical ploy effectively divests both Gisippo and Tito of any responsibility for their conspiracy: they were merely pawns of the gods with no free will of their own.

Tito's second argument appears already in the first one, when he says that "lei a Gisippo avavate dato." He will soon elaborate on this point, explaining that her family criticizes Gisippo "per ciò che colei m'ha data per moglie col suo consiglio, che voi a lui col vostro avavate data" (X.8.61). The parents, having assigned Sofronia to Gisippo, in Tito's mind have made her Gisippo's property, marriage ceremony or no. According to Tito Gisippo has behaved wisely, respecting "le santi leggi della amicizia," and he notes that "il legame dell'amistà troppo più strige che quel del sangue o del parentado" (X.8.62). One is reminded here of Guiscardo's reply to Tancredi, once the father has discovered his affair with Ghismonda: "Amor può *troppo più che* né voi né io possiamo" (IV.1.23; italics mine). The use of this construction, again in a marked statement, exposes the nature of what is at stake here, as a theory of friendship between men comes to substitute for a theory of love between a man and a woman.

Tito's arguments convince, though not only for their logic. He also includes some saber rattling of his own, reminding his audience that he is after all a Roman, and a Roman of high birth, and that if they choose to pursue the matter further they will have to answer to the power of Rome. With his statement about friendship Tito effectively enunciates the law that rules his and Gisippo's actions, and with his threat about Roman power he identifies the means by which he will enforce that law. After he leaves his interlocutors consult and concur: "Quegli che là entro rimasono, in parte dalle ragioni di Tito al parentado e alla sua amistà indotti e in parte spaventati dall'ultime sue parole, di pari concordia diliberarono essere il migliore d'aver Tito per parente, poi che Gisippo non aveva esser voluto, che aver Gisippo per parente perduto e Tito per nemico acquistato" (X.8.88). Some combination of Tito's arguments convinces his audience, and they make a practical decision that recalls other decisions made under coercion, such as the Traversari girl's accession to marry Nastagio degli Onesti, another eighth-day story narrated by Filomena. Indeed, Sofronia's redirection of her love for Gisippo sounds very much like the Traversari girl's sudden reversal on the question of Nastagio: "sì come savia, fatta della necessità virtù, l'amore il quale aveva a Gisippo prestamente rivolse a Tito" (X.8.89). Like all things, love is a commodity, and a woman should invest it prudently.[19]

In its bare bones the story has significant allegorical dimensions. The name Sofronia's means "wise," so the Roman Tito's coming to Athens to

---

19. Bartolomea, the wife of Riccardo di Chinzica, makes this point succinctly when explaining why she would never return to him, after she has found fulfillment with her kidnapper Paganino: "io non intendo per ciò di mai tornare a voi, di cui, tutto premendovi, non si farebbe uno scodellino di salsa, per ciò che con mio grandissimo danno e interesse vi stetti una volta" (II.10.40). The culinary metaphor, which hilariously reduces Riccardo to the status of a dry tomato, and the economic language make clear that Bartolomea is thinking about her value in the household.

study philosophy and falling in love with a wise woman figures nothing more than the boy's liking his major. More to the point of the story, however, Sofronia's actions suggest that a wise woman knows better than to stand in the way of men's friendship. Her accommodation of that friendship and her family's acceptance of her marriage to Tito represent singular affirmations of a woman's place, subordinate to the wishes of men.

In the lengthy paean to friendship with which Filomena concludes, she introduces a new and surprising dimension that further exalts women. She identifies friendship as praiseworthy "sì come discretissima madre di magnificenzia e d'onestà, sorella di gratitudine e di carità, e d'odio e d'avarizia nemica" (X.8.111). The statement effectively recapitulates the day, identifying the relationship—friendship—that motivates the acts of *magnificenzia* narrated therein, acts that often counterbalance hatred or avarice. She reiterates these personifications when, in the series of rhetorical questions that follow, she identifies friendship as *costei*, the agent of all the good that happened in the story. One may say, with apologies to Machiavelli, that friendship is a woman, and a woman with agency. In other words, it is something female that creates the bonds of affection between men that are foundational to society. Thus do all the women who figure in the development of male friendship in this story and the earlier ones, thanks to Filomena's troping, assume their rightful dimension as allegories of friendship itself, and specifically of friendship between men. That these female characters have no apparent agency should no longer disturb us for, as it turns out, they are agency itself, put to the service of male comity. They should well rejoice in their instrumental roles, for they are furthering a cause that transcends their own interests, the cause of friendship that, as Aristotle reminds us, is foundational to society. At the same time, in their reconfiguration as allegories they assume an evanescent quality. In the moment at which they bring men together, they vanish.

The ironic apotheosis of womanhood realized in this tale not only anticipates its almost absurd extension in Griselda but also suggests a different type of transcendence for women than we see in Dante (the divine woman), as well as a resistance to the sort of demystification of women that one sees in Petrarch. Here woman transcends herself in another way, as an allegory of the social compact between men that, as Aristotle points out, begins on the personal level but leads to the construction of entire societies. Boccaccio's point here is moreover entirely consistent with the initial thrust of the book, specifically his own recitation of how another woman, the object of his unrequited passion, strengthened the bonds of friendship in his own life: "Nella qual noia tanto rifrigerio già mi porsero i piacevoli ragionamenti d'alcuno amico e le sue laudevoli consolazioni, che io porto fermissima opinione per quelle essere avenuto che io non sia morto" (Proem.4). That he then turns his back on these very friends and dedicates the book instead to women is not the act of an ingrate, but rather the start of a long process of exploration of the meaning of womanhood that culminates here, where women find their proper place in a world of men.

It may appear at first glance that such an important argument comes at a strangely unmarked place in the *Decameron*. After all, Boccaccio appears to privilege other *loci* in his book, such as the first and tenth tale, or the ninth, normally told by a monarch, or the fifth, the central tale of a day. And yet, as Victoria Kirkham points out (*The Sign of Reason* 159), the Middle Ages subscribed to the Pythagorean association of the number eight with Justice, which is of course a central aim of law. Boccaccio's association of women with justice here assumes an ironic dimension, the understanding of which is essential as the *Decameron* moves toward its conclusion. Justice here is revealed not as the enforcement of law, assuming that Gisippo had no legal right to transfer Sofronia to Tito, but as the result of a series of negotiations between men, the determining factor of which is the superior power of one man, here the Roman, over the other, the Greek. One cannot separate Tito's final accommodation of Gisippo from the fact that Tito ends up with what he wants, Sofronia, and it is impossible to know whether he would have extended similar generosity had he been the loser in their conflict over the woman. Gisippo arguably emerges as the better friend because of his willingness to make great sacrifices in order to preserve the friendship. Boccaccio's warning here about the subordination of justice to power, while adumbrating the action of the two remaining stories, also stands as a sobering reminder to those who would hope for an earthly justice in imitation of the moral axis that defines divine justice.

Questions of justice hang over the ninth story as well, here applied to international relations. Indeed, the allusions to international law issues found in the eighth story—Tito's threat of Roman war against Greece—become explicit in the ninth, where the action develops against the background of the Third Crusade. By invoking war Boccaccio simply amplifies the legal questions already present in the *Decameron,* moving them across borders. Kelsen compares war to the sanction in domestic law, as response to a delict: "International law exhibits the same character as the law of individual states. Like the latter, it is a coercive system. And in the reconstructed legal norm of international law, as in the reconstructed legal norm of the state legal system, a material fact (regarded as harmful to the community) is linked with a coercive act, as condition with consequence. In international law, the specific consequences of an unlawful act are reprisal and war" (*Introduction* 108). In the case of the ninth story, Panfilo, the narrator, describes a specific condition of injury that has led to war: "al tempo dello 'mperador Federigo primo a racquistar la Terra Santa si fece per li cristiani un general passaggio" (X.9.5). The verb *racquistar* here suggests the injury, the loss of territory claimed by Christians. For all of its religious overtones, the Crusade is here reduced to a territorial dispute in which the Christian party, believing it has suffered harm, undertakes a reprisal on the party that it contends illegally exercises sovereignty, expressed as the application of domestic law, over territory it has not ceded to the Saracens. While the reasons for the international contact at a personal level thus differ—in the eighth story it is philosophical education that sends Tito to Athens, while in the ninth it is espionage about the Christian preparations for war that sends Saladin to Pavia as a spy—both stories dramatize a test of a friendship whose international and ideological stresses ultimately challenge it. While the eighth story presents a rather cynical example of the endurance of friendship, the ninth reaches for a more altruistic model, facilitated in no small part by a woman: Torello's wife Adalieta.

The reader gets a first whiff of Adalieta even before she steps out onto the story's main stage. Torello sends her advance warning that he plans to bring guests home—the message is almost so trite today as to bring laughter at the very thought—and she organizes a banquet for them, "non con feminile animo ma con reale" (X.9.20). Already she transcends her own womanhood, a sign that she has some ulterior value, one associated with neither her class—her husband is *un gentile uomo* and not royalty—nor her gender. She first appears to Saladin in a highly artificial, almost ceremonial way. Summoned by her husband, she comes to meet his guests: ". . . essendo bellissima e grande della persona e di ricchi vestimenti ornata, in mezzo di due suoi figlioletti, che parevan due agnoli, se ne venne davanti a costoro e piacevolmente gli salutò" (X.9.28). Each element of the description rings with allegorical tones. We already know of her *animo reale*, which implies authority. Superficially her imposing size and beauty further suggest authority, while her beautiful clothing associates her with rhetoric, and the angelic nature of her two sons suggests the relationship between human and divine.

On a deeper level, the arrangement of the group, with the mother appearing between her two young sons, bears a striking resemblance to medieval iconography of justice. Boccaccio would have been well familiar with this iconography, seeing it, for example, in the Lorenzetti Allegory of Good Government in the Palazzo Pubblico in Siena, where Justice, as a woman, holds a scale, in which an angel kneels, in each hand. Giotto's grisaille fresco of Justice in Padua's Scrovegni Chapel likewise shows justice,

again female, holding two small dishes containing angels.[20] Given the association of justice with angels the detail of Boccaccio's description, according to which Adalieta's sons "parevan due agnoli," becomes anything but
casual. Torello does not simply present his wife to Saladin, he presents
Christian justice, figured as a capacity to reward and punish. Adalieta's
presence is thus cautionary, a reminder to Saladin that while in Pavia he is
subject to Christian law. The men welcome her: "Essi vedendola si levarono
in piè e con reverenzia la ricevettero, e fattala seder tra loro gran festa fecero
de' due belli suoi figlioletti" (X.9.28). By receiving her so warmly, Saladin
and his companions effectively agree to live by the terms of Christian law
while in a Christian land, secure in the implicit guarantee that despite its
local authority Christian law will not ignore their interests.

The allegory does not end there. Adalieta also confers gifts upon her
guests, a gesture that by her own account is her idea: "Allora la donna con
lieto viso disse: "'Adunque veggo io che il mio feminile aviso sarà utile, e
per ciò vi priego che di spezial grazia mi facciate di non rifiutare né avere a
vile quel piccioletto dono il quale io vi farò venire, ma considerando che le
donne secondo il lor picciol cuore piccole cose danno, più al buono animo di
chi dà riguardando che alla quantità del don, riguardiate'" (X.9.30).

The speech is eloquently disingenuous, because for all her rhetorical
gestures of self-diminution, encapsulated in the repetition of the adjective
picciolo, Adalieta essentially acts in her husband's stead during his absence:
she rules *de facto*, conferring symbolic gifts. She even goes so far as to suggest that she surpasses her husband in wisdom, for she represents the very
idea of the gift as the product of an albeit "inferior" *feminile aviso*, and she
describes it as reflecting the "buono animo di chi dà," in other words, her
buono animo, not her husband's. She then shows the gifts, "due paia di robe,
l'un foderato di drappo e l'altro di vaio, non miga cittadine né da mercatanti
ma da signore, e tre giubbe di zendado e pannilini" (X.9.31). Ostensibly
wifely gifts, offered because "voi siate alle vostre donne lontani," there can
be little doubt that they also convey symbolic value. This is particularly
true for the two *robe*, as they are each lined, suggesting an inner value
that their external appearance conceals. Their respective linings, as Branca
suggests, make them suitable for summer (*drappo*) and winter (*vaio*). With
their similar outward appearance and different linings, the two cloaks also
serve as a reminder that whatever specificities, ethnic, religious, and so
forth, may distinguish their wearers, we are all generally the same. The
tre giubbe work a similarly homogenizing effect, here specifically as Chris-

---

20. My warm thanks to my colleague Cathleen Fleck for leading me to these images.

tianizing the foreigner. As Adalieta puts it, "io ho delle robe il mio signore vestito con voi" (X.9.31): in other words, they are the same clothes that her husband wears. The logic of her gesture now becomes transparent: after first appearing as a sign of justice, she makes a first claim about the essential sameness of men only finally to complete a symbolic act of conversion of her presumably non-Christian guests, essentially performing the Crusade at home. Her guests accept the gifts, suspecting that Torello has intuited that they are something more than merchants, thus misunderstanding slightly the import of her gesture. Still they acknowledge the gravity of the exchange: "Queste son, madonna, grandissime cose e da non dover di leggier pigliare, se i vostri prieghi a ciò non ci stringnessero, alli quali dir di non non si puote" (X.9.32). Whatever they think they are getting, in accepting it they embrace it.

Adalieta's role as giver of gifts does not end there, for she bestows another important gift that will play a similar role in the story. Upon Torello's departure she gives him a ring of hers, explaining: "Se egli avviene che io muoia prima che io vi rivega, ricordivi di me quando il vedrete" (X.9.47). Now, we know from the story of Saladin and Melchisedech, which lurks beneath the surface of this one, that a ring is a symbol of law; in bestowing this ring upon her husband as he leaves the Christian world, Adalieta reminds him that even though she may be far away, even dead, he is still subject to the Christian law that in some way emanates from her. Her gesture mandates his return to Pavia, not simply because he loves his wife, but because no friendship can undermine his duty to submit to her. When in Alessandria, in fact, he is known as "il cristiano di Saladino" (X.9.51), and even before Saladin facilitates his repatriation he repeatedly tries to escape.

Adalieta's choices, born of her *feminile aviso*, turn out to be crucial in bringing the tale to its happy ending. When in Alessandria and working as Saladin's falconer, the sultan recognizes Torello thanks to his unique smile. The clothing Adalieta had given the sultan furnishes material proof of Torello's identity, and Saladin reveals his own, making recourse to a pun: "Voi siete messer Torel di Stra e io son l'uno de' tre mercatanti a' quali la donna vostra donò queste robe; e ora è venuto il tempo di far certa la vostra credenza qual sia la mia mercatanzia, come nel partirmi da voi dissi che potrebbe avvenire" (X.9.57). The mercantile pun, which picks up on the exchange between Torello and Saladin when the two parted ways outside Pavia, associates friendship with the notion of exchange, eliding the distinction between the exchange of an Aristotelian good, *bene,* and the exchange of goods, *beni.* Indeed, Saladin then bestows his own gift upon Torello: "di reali vestimenti il fé vestire" (X.9.59), clothing of a quality similar to that which Adalieta had earlier given him. This gesture, which again points to the centrality of Adalieta's role in the story, also has the effect of bestowing Saracen identity upon Torello. Each friend now enjoys dual identity: his own and that of his friend. Indeed, Saladin tells Torello, "pensate che non io oramai, ma voi qui siate il signore" (X.9.58): in essence, the Christian merchant has become the sultan.

These rituals make a point about international law. Each set of clothing serves to remind its wearer, symbolically, that while he lives in a foreign land he is also subject to a law not his own. In accepting the clothing, each protagonist affirms the territorial sovereignty of the state in which he finds himself when the gift is offered. Such recognition of borders effectively obviates the need for war. By accepting Saladin's jurisdiction over a land claimed by Christians, Torello denies the claim. Just as Saladin had ceded Melchisedech's point about the equality of the three religions back in I.3, so too here does a Christian make a similar concession. This recognition further squares with the supernatural signs that undermine the Christian invasion. Upon arriving at Acri Torello and the Christian army find themselves beset by "una grandissima infermeria e mortalità" (X.9.49), not unlike the plague that drives the *brigata* into the countryside, "per operazion de' corpi superiori o per le nostre inique opera da giusta ira di Dio a nostra correzione mandata sopra i mortali" (I.Intro.8). According to this predicate one may apply a similar argument to the epidemic that strikes Acri, suggesting that God was not on the side of the Christian army that day, not necessarily because God had become an enemy of the Christians, but because He wanted the religions to coexist peacefully.

It should come as little surprise, then, that the other object that serves to prove identity, beyond the clothing Adalieta had given Saladin, turns out to be the ring she gives her husband when he leaves Pavia. Beyond reminding us of the tale of the three rings, it also functions within the story as a symbol of Adalieta herself. As she tells him, "Se egli avviene che io muoia prima che io vi rivega, ricordivi di me quando il vedrete" (X.9.47). She is asking him to be faithful to her memory, and in doing so she associates faith with justice. Returning to Pavia with the ring, Torello reaffirms his loyalty not just to his wife but to the justice she represents. What remains unclear is whether, after the changes he has undergone, she is prepared to recognize him. In his absence she has come under pressure from her family to remarry, and she has resisted for the year, month, and day that Torello had requested of her.[21] Wondering about her enduring loyalty to him, Torello

---

21. A year, a month, and a day total 396 days, a number divisible not only by 3, thus reinforcing the Trinitarian allusions in the story (Saladin travels with two companions and three servants; Adalieta appears with two of her sons; she gives the men three *giubbe*), but also by 9, appropriate since this is the ninth story of the day.

subjects her to a test. He arrives at her wedding banquet wearing the Saracen clothes in which he had returned to Pavia and claiming to be sent by
Saladin as an ambassador to the King of France. He concocts a native custom as bogus as the one used earlier by Gentile de' Carisendi, according
to which an outsider attending a wedding banquet shares a cup of wine
with the bride. Adalieta's agreement to the ritual implies that under certain
circumstances foreign law may be applied where it enjoys no sovereignty.

When Adalieta recognizes the ring she and her husband are reunited in
a scene that is among the most vividly described of the entire *Decameron*:
"preso [the ring] e fiso guardato colui il qual forestier credeva e già cono-
scendolo, quasi furiosa divenuta fosse gittata in terra la tavola che davanti
aveva, gridò: 'Questi è il mio signore, questi veramente è messer Torello!' E
corsa alla tavola alla quale esso sedeva, senza avere riguardo a' suoi drappi o
a cosa che sopra la tavola fosse, gittatasi oltre quanto poté, l'abracciò stret-
tamente, né mai dal suo collo fu potuto, per detto o per fatto d'alcuno che
quivi fosse, levare infino a tanto che per messer Torello non le fu detto
che alquanto sopra sé stesse, per ciò che tempo da abracciarlo le sarebbe
ancora prestato assai" (X.9.107–8). This scene too resonates with allegory.
In recognizing Torello Adalieta figures the capacity of justice to discern the
truth. The clothing, Saracen clothing, functions as a blindfold; nevertheless,
she sees, for in the end clothing does not alter identity, despite the story's
repeated suggestion that it does. Her other actions appear to have another
source: the reaction of Moses to his discovery of the Golden Calf in Exodus
32. Angry that the Israelites are worshiping a false god, an angry Moses
smashes the tablets of the law just as Adalieta, *quasi furiosa*, upends her
table, identifying her true lord. The table at which she sits represents her
submission to a new lord, her new husband; by upending it she denies his
authority over her, reaffirming Torello's.

If Torello is her lord, the source of her law, then Adalieta emerges definitively as an allegory of justice. She embodies justice because she begins
the cycle of reciprocity that characterizes the story, fulfilling Aquinas's
definition of justice as the application of the Golden Rule.[22] The story's per-
ambulations, in which gifts bestowed establish patterns of reciprocity, facilitate a return in the end to the status quo, arguably a desired outcome of
acts of justice. That status quo includes not merely the reunification of the
spouses but the territorial claims that had led to the initial contact between
Christian and Saracen. Adalieta has facilitated not merely a friendship but
an international accord as well. The story does not simply demonstrate that

---

22. See *ST* 2a2æ. 58, where Aquinas explicitly defines justice as the application of the
Golden Rule.

the two peoples can get along, thus obviating the need for warfare; it also suggests that while the two cultures may mix each finally has a legitimate claim to its own territory under international law.

As is the case with most of the day's stories, this one comes with an explicit link to its predecessor, here furnished by Panfilo in his introduction. He begins by affirming Filomena's claim that friendship enjoys scant respect nowadays, then continues by explicitly denying any practical purpose to the group's storytelling: "E se noi qui per dover correggere i difetti mondani o pur per riprendergli fossimo, io seguiterei con diffuso sermone le sue parole; ma per ciò che altro è il nostro fine, a me è caduto nell'animo di dimostrarvi . . . una delle magnificenzie del Saladino . . ." (X.9.4). This remarkable statement about the purpose of storytelling, coming as it does from the king at the end of the day's themed stories, deserves attention. It alludes to what Paolo Cherchi has identified as the principle of *onesto raccontare* that informs the *brigata*'s storytelling: "raccontare per il raccontare, senza altro utile" (89). The notion of storytelling without utility, of which Cherchi finds the tenth day to be particularly representative, also helps explain the increasing inverisimilitude of the day's stories, beginning with the King Alfonso's gift of his treasures to Ruggieri and recurring in such narrative details as the necromancer's cancellation of Ansaldo's debt in the fifth story, the Roman murderer's confession in the eighth, Torello's magic carpet ride, and finally Griselda herself. Only a storytelling that is explicitly detached from a will to correct by example can accommodate such startling and distracting details.

Panfilo's remark also allows us to measure the distance he has traveled from the first day, when he attempted to lead by imitating the preacher, to now, when he leads by crystallizing, in negative terms, what the group's purpose has been all along.[23] He now recognizes the limits on human perfection: "acciò che per le cose che nella mia novella udirete, se pienamente l'amicizia d'alcuno non si può per li nostri vizii acquistare, almeno diletto prendiamo del servire, sperando che quando che sia di ciò merito ci debba servire" (X.9.4). In other words, because we can never hope to enjoy the perfect friendship depicted in the story, rooted in the Aristotelian good, we

---

23. On this point Cherchi and I differ. He takes Panfilo's renunciation of the *sermone* as of a piece with the "campo dell'onesto" (97) in which the stories situate themselves, as opposed to that of the *exemplum* or sermon: "il ruolo di predicare o di sermoneggiare e di educare spetta ai predicatori e ai maestri, cioè a persone che hanno finalità pratiche e utilitaristiche" (100). Cherchi's largely synthetic reading of the *Decameron* leads him to overlook exceptions to his rule, even though he concedes, following Giorgio Padoan's lead (in "Mondo aristocratico e mondo comunale"), that the Ciappelletto story is exceptional. I should add that he misidentifies Panfilo here as the "*narratrice* che prende la parola per narrare la nona novella" (100; italics mine).

can at least enjoy the *servire* that it exemplifies, hoping that our own service may some day find similar reward: in other words, justice by Aquinas's definition. Panfilo is making a distinction here between the affection that informs perfect friendship and the behaviors that demonstrate it, arguing that we can perform friendship even if we do not fully experience it spiritually. At tale's end he returns to these themes, sounding a note of disillusionment in the face of what he has just narrated: "Cotale adunque fu il fine delle noie di messer Torello e di quelle della sua cara donna e il guiderdone delle lor liete e preste cortesie; le quali molti si sforzan di fare che, benché abbian di che, sì mal far le vagliono, che fatte l'abbiano: per che, se loro merito non ne segue, né essi né altri maravigliar se ne dee" (X.9.113). In other words, it is wrong to demand return for services rendered, for true justice, as Aquinas points out echoing the Aristotle of the *Ethics,* is voluntary. Altruism is not about contractual exchange, and those who lament the lack of *merito* have no one but themselves to blame.

The themes of fraternity and altruism that unite the tenth day find their ironic recasting in the last story. In his introduction Dioneo goes out of his way to deny continuity: "Mansuete mie donne, per quel che mi paia, questo dì d'oggi è stato dato a re e a soldani e a così fatta gente: e per ciò, acciò che io troppo da voi non mi scosti, vo' ragionare d'un marchese, non cosa magnifica ma una matta bestialità, come che ben ne gli seguisse alla fine; la quale io non consiglio alcun che segua, per ciò che gran peccato fu che a costui ben n'avenisse" (X.10.3). Dioneo plays on similarities and differences: like the others, his story will focus on the powerful, but unlike the others, he will recount a *matta bestialità:* Boccaccio borrows here from Dante's terminology to associate Gualtieri's behavior with violence.[24] This initial focus on Gualtieri has not deterred critics from studying Griselda, a far more appealing and intriguing figure. Gualtieri is so unappealingly vile—he bears none of the perverse charm of the great sinners of the *Inferno*—that readers understandably gravitate toward her. Even Dioneo himself appears to experience this effect, introducing the tale as about Gualtieri but concluding it with words about Griselda. The very earliest readers follow his lead; Petrarch entitles his Latin translation *De insigni*

---

24. The phrase is first used in *Inferno* XI as Virgil describes the structure of hell: "Non ti rimembra di quelle parole / con le quai la tua Etica petratta / le tre disposizion che 'l ciel non vole, / incontinenza, malizia e la matta / bestialitade?" (79–82). In the *Esposizioni sopra la Comedia* Boccaccio glosses the phrase as follows: "Questo adiettivo 'matta' pose qui l'autore più in servigio della rima che per bisogno che n'avesse la bestialità, per ciò che bestialità e matteza si posson dire essere una medesima cosa. È adunque questa bestialiità similmente vizio dell'anima opposto, secondo che piace ad Aristotile nel VII dell'*Etica,* alla divina sapienza . . ." (551). For a fine reading of Boccaccio's use of Dante's terminology and its relationship to Aquinas see Mazzotta 126–29.

obedientia ed fide uxoria, shifting the attention entirely onto her.[25] Even critics who try to focus on Gualtieri do not always succeed; Giovannuzzi, who entitles his compelling essay "La novella di Gualtieri," in the end has relatively little to say about the marquis and shifts his attention elsewhere. To the extent that the evolution of the critical tradition follows Dioneo's lead, we should first observe that with this story Boccaccio has succeeded in instilling in virtually all readers of the *Decameron* a sympathy for women who are victimized by tyrannical men. The story thus comes as a final reply to his male critics, whom Boccaccio first records as objecting that he likes them too much. It exposes the hypocrisy of this critique by showing that everyone can find a woman to like.

The question of Griselda's transcendence lies at the heart of the critical tradition, and by extension of a reading of the *Decameron* that has it transcending itself. The story itself abounds with signs of her transcendence, duly recorded by critics. Such a reading, however, risks removing Griselda from the story's immediate context, in a sense accounting for her behavior as a sign of her own sense of detachment from earthly matters rather than as a reaction to the torturous situation in which she unexpectedly finds herself. If we accept that Griselda floats above the story, then Dioneo's lesson for his female audience is that they abjure earthly things and understand their own future suffering as part of a process that will bring them reward later.

My own reading, which I now offer, resists the allegorization of Griselda, for a simple reason. It seems to me the key to any allegorical reading lies in Dioneo's own suggestion that Griselda transcends her humanity: "Che si potrà dir qui? Se non che anche nelle povere case piovono dal cielo de' divini spiriti, come nelle reali di quegli che sarien più degni di guardar porci che d'avere sopra uomini signoria. Chi avrebbe, altri che Griselda, potuto col viso non solamente asciutto ma lieto sofferir le rigide e mai più non udite pruove da Gualtier fatte?" (X.10.68). The rhetorical question should clue us in to the fact that something is amiss: even Dioneo is not sure what to make of his story. He recovers quickly, offering two contradictory possibilities. Everything here is up for grabs and wholly dependent on Dioneo's inflection.[26] He could be asking his first question with a sincere

---

25. Segre argues ("Perché Gualtier di Saluzzo odiava le donne?" 289) that Petrarch's reading "ha fatto scuola," generating hundreds of transcriptions and translations into a number of European languages, effectively supplanting Boccaccio's original. On Petrarch's translation see also Marcus, *An Allegory of Form* 99–100.

26. To my knowledge few readers have considered this possibility. Rossi notes the *tono scanzonato* of Dioneo's comment ("Ironia e parodia nel *Decameron*" 404), while Segre remarks on the "enfasi volutamente affettata" of Dioneo's second question ("Perché Gualtieri di Saluzzo odiava le donne?" 288).

tone or an exasperated one; he could deliver his first reply with a serious or an ironic voice; and he could ask his second question, arguably the most crucial one, similarly in either of two ways. Critics who exalt Griselda do so because they accept Dioneo's words as sincere. According to such a reading Griselda's face would be *lieto* because she enters the story having already transcended her humanity and seeing the course of her life as serving a divine purpose. The counterargument is that Griselda's happy face denotes the sort of joy in suffering that in a religious context denotes sanctity, but that in a secular one denotes masochism. I would advance a third path that restores Griselda to her relationship with Gualtieri, namely that she enters the marquis's life aware that she is a construct, and that she accepts his treatment of her because she understands that it is the only way to preserve her figuration, which has become more important to her than any sense of self that predated her marriage. She willingly puts herself at the service of a cause, the institution and preservation of harmony between Gualtieri and his subjects, and in so doing serves to indicate to Boccaccio's female readers that their own survival is wholly contingent on their willingness to subordinate their own desire to the demands of male comity.

The homosocial here finds its expression in the relationship between Gualtieri and his vassals.[27] At the outset that relationship is tense, as the two parties have different visions of friendship. His subjects express a utilitarian view, urging Gualtieri to marry, while the marquis prefers to pursue pleasure: "in niuna altra cosa il suo tempo spendeva che in uccellare e in cacciare, né di prender moglie né d'aver figliuoli alcun pensier avea; di che egli era da reputar molto savio. La qual cosa a' suoi uomini non piaccendo, più volte il pregaron che moglie prendesse, acciò che egli senza erede né essi senza signor rimanessero, offerendosi di trovargliel tale e di sì fatto padre e madre discesa, che buona speranza se ne potrebbe avere e esso contentarsene molto" (X.10.4–5). His subjects urge marriage not because they see it as a good thing for Gualtieri, but because they see it as a good thing for themselves. They correctly understand that the marquis, by virtue of his public role, transcends himself, and in urging him to marry they imply as much. As monarch not only does he embody the law; he must also ensure its preservation by producing offspring who will embody it after his death. Dioneo's exposition also includes an important comment about Gualtieri's reluctance to marry and father children: "da che egli era da reputar molto savio." What is not clear here is what precisely makes Gualtieri *savio*, perhaps his (misogynistic) recalcitrance to marriage, or his recognition, of

---

27. Baratto (Realtà e stile 342–45) insists on the importance of the feudal setting for a full understanding of the *novella*.

which Dioneo has prior knowledge, that he is not cut out for family life, in which case he demonstrates wise self-knowledge. Either way, as Dioneo endorses Gualtieri's initial position he also exposes flaws in Gualtieri that threaten order in Saluzzo.

In response to the pressure exerted by his subjects, Gualtieri pushes back, and the tension over who will determine his future threatens to overwhelm the story. In agreeing finally to marry, he points out that they are pressuring him, "voi mi strignete a quello che io del tutto aveva disposto di non far mai" (X.10.6): something is clearly amiss, the hierarchy of power inverted. In attaching terms to his acquiescence Gualtieri seeks to restore order by exerting control over his marital situation: "Ma poi che pure in queste catene vi piace d'annodarmi, e io voglio esser contento; e acciò che io non abbia da dolermi d'altrui che di me, se mal venisse fatto, io stesso ne voglio essere il trovatore, affermandovi che, cui che io mi tolga, se da voi non fia come donna onorata, voi proverete con gran vostro danno quanto grave mi sia l'aver contra mia voglia presa mogliere a' vostri prieghi" (X.10.8). Suddenly he embodies a Petrarchan oxymoron, hoping to arrange a happy enchainment. Moreover, in announcing his decision to take a wife, Gualtieri elevates her to a symbol of his power, threatening his subjects with dire consequences if they fail to honor her as he demands, particularly since they have put him in this place to begin with. He makes clear that she will be his invention, both as discovery and as creation. He claims the right to be her *trovatore*, the troubadour, he who both seeks the woman and sings her praises, turning her into a poetic fiction.[28] He renews his emphasis on honor when announcing that he has found a bride: "pensate come la festa delle nozze sia bella e come voi onorevolmente ricever la possiate" (X.10.12), and they agree: "I buoni uomini lieti tutti risposero ciò piacer loro e che, fosse chi volesse, essi l'avrebber per donna e onorebbonla in tutte cose sì come donna" (X.10.13). The subjects' universal happiness, *lieti tutti*, reflects their affirmation that Gualtieri has fulfilled his social contract with them; as part of the terms they accede to his demand ("come *donna* onorata") to honor Griselda as *donna*, not merely as a woman but as his female counterpart. The agreement replicates not just the feudal model of service but the courtly love ethos as well. It also makes explicit that whatever transcendent power Griselda represents descends from Gualtieri and nowhere else.

The scene in which Gualtieri publicly dresses Griselda bears further

---

28. Cavallini's exclusion of this possibility—"Qui il *nomen agentis* (formato col suffisso—*tore*) letteralmente significa: colui che trova" (177n.14)—frankly baffles me. The use of *trovatore* to mean troubadour is attested already in the thirteenth century, appearing, for example in story 21 of the *Novellino*: "A lui [emperor Federigo] venieno sonatori, trovatori e belli favellatori. . . ."

signs that he is the source of her power: "in presenza di tutta la sua compagnia e d'ogn'altra persona la fece spogliare ignuda: e fattisi quegli vestimenti che fatti aveva fare, prestamente la fece vestire e calzare e sopra i suoi capelli, così scarmigliati come erano, le fece mettere una corona . . ." (X.10.19).[29] Not only does her groom dress her; he also covers the most disordered part of her, her *capelli scarmigliati,* with a symbol of his order, the crown. Indeed, as Dioneo records, her new clothes suggest a more profound transformation: "La giovane sposa parve che co' vestimenti insieme l'animo e' costumi mutasse. Ella era, come già dicemmo, di persona e di viso bella: e così come bella era, divenne tanto avvenevole, tanto piacevole e tanto costumata, che non figliuola di Giannucole e guardiana di pecore pareva stata ma d'alcun nobile signore . . ." (X.10.24). Dioneo describes the metamorphosis as one of class: she no longer looks like the daughter of a shepherd but rather like the daughter of a nobleman. By giving her new clothes, Gualtieri thus finesses the exogamy of his marriage with a patina of endogamy: Griselda needs to appear noble in order to project the authority Gualtieri has invested in her. At the same time, however, Dioneo carefully underscores that this is all a game of appearances, for in fact Griselda remains what she always was, the shepherd's daughter. She acquires a sort of rhetorical gloss because she is Gualtieri's construct.

The redressing ceremony thus symbolically enacts his reply to the social disorder, embodied in his subjects' effrontery, that Gualtieri's refusal to marry has provoked. Indeed, just before leading his men to Griselda, he makes a speech whose theme is reciprocity. He reminds them that he is marrying "più per compiacere a voi che per disiderio che io di moglie avessi" and that in return they had promised "d'esser contenti e d'onorar come donna qualunque quella fosse che io togliessi," and he describes the

---

29. The issue of dressing and redressing has earned considerable critical attention about this tale. For Cottino-Jones ("Fabula vs. Figura" 46) "the undressing corresponds to the ritual or renunciation of her previous condition of existence and the dressing represents her outfitting for the new life to come." Lanza sees in it a particularly resonant example of Gualtieri's sadism (26). For Mazzotta "in formal terms the language of clothing and nakedness, traditionally charged with allegorical resonances, heightens the allegorical thrust of the events narrated" (123). In his essay "Ironia e parodia nel *Decameron,*" which offers a probing analysis of Boccaccio's parody of Dante, Luciano Rossi explains the scene in metaliterary terms: "qui Boccaccio *mette a nudo* il procedimento di tanti racconti 'comici,' in cui gli 'ingannatori' (Ciappelletto, Frate Alberto, Alatiel, ecc.) ricorrevano al travestimento e alla maschera per disorientare gli antagonisti. I 'travestimenti' di Griselda non alterano, invece, la natura dell'eroina, che resterà in ogni senso Donna" (402). For a general review of clothing in the *Decameron* see Weaver, who discusses Griselda on pages 705–6. It is noteworthy, finally, that for her final redressing Griselda and her ladies in waiting repair to her room, out of view of the public. This is the only action of the tale that takes place in a private setting, a recognition that her naked body is no longer fit for public viewing.

marriage as the fulfillment of their contract: "venuto è il tempo che io sono per servare a voi la promessa e che io voglio che voi a me la serviate." He instructs them to consider how they can receive her honorably, "acciò che io mi possa della vostra promession chiamar contento come voi della mia vi potrete chiamare" (X.10.10–12). Griselda's status in all of this could not be clearer: she is the *mediatrix* needed to ensure the harmonious friendship between Gualtieri and his subjects.

In other words, Griselda assumes the dimensions of a gift. Just as Gualtieri had received Griselda from her father, so too does he then bestow her on his people, and in each case the exchange entails obligation.[30] It is little wonder then that, once he chases her from the house, his subjects, whose objections to his behavior he had successfully repressed, return as a sort of snarky Greek chorus. They implore him to clothe her in exchange for her service: "Quanti dintorno v'erano il pregavano che egli una roba le *donasse*, ché non fosse veduta colei che sua moglie tredici anni o più era stata di casa sua così poveramente e così vituperosamente uscire, come era uscirne in camiscia . . ." (X.10.47; italics mine). The subjects rightly understand these relationships to be about exchange, and they are concerned that their marquis not behave dishonorably by failing to recognize the exchange value in Griselda's thirteen years of service. Her departure moreover equates with a return of the disorder that had threatened Saluzzo years before, when Gualtieri was too busy hunting to think about marriage. Having disposed of his children—for all anyone knows, they are dead—he has apparently terminated the succession.

Griselda accepts the requirements of her role set forth by Gualtieri: "era tanto obediente al marito e tanto servente, che egli si teneva il più contento e il più appagato uomo del mondo" (X.10.24). The adjective *contento* here recalls Gualtieri's desire to *esser contento* in marital chains: she is a dream come true. Discovering her extraordinary nature, his subjects likewise revise their opinion about him: "dove dir soleano Gualtieri aver fatto come poco savio d'averla per moglie presa, che egli era il più savio e il più avveduto uomo che al mondo fosse, per ciò che niuno altro che egli avrebbe mai potuto conoscere l'alta vertù di costei nascosa sotto i poveri panni e sotto l'abito vilesco" (X.10.25). The clothes, in other words, now fit the lady. As she serves her husband she also becomes instrumental in his rehabilita-

---

30. Dioneo does not disclose the terms of the agreement with Giannucole, limiting himself to saying that Gualtieri, "con lui, che poverissimo era, si convenne di torla per moglie" (X.10.9). Given the reference to Gualtieri's poverty one may infer that the contract involved some exchange of money to compensate him for the loss of her labor. When Gualtieri arrives to marry her, he finds her "che con acqua tornava dalla fonte" (X.10.16): clearly, she helps her father around the house.

tion: each rises and falls on the back of the other. Once Dioneo has set this pattern, he offers no indication that it breaks off. She needs him as much as he needs her, which suggests that her behavior, which has led critics to see in her a *figura Cristi* (Cottino-Jones, "Fabula vs. Figura"), or the personification of humility (Kirkham, *The Sign of Reason*), or of Job (Smarr 191–92; Mazzotta 123–24; Bessi), or of Stoic *apatia* (Baratto 343; Cherchi, *L'onestade e l'onesto raccontare* 101), does not so much signal an otherworldly virtue as it does partake of a perverse but mutually efficacious compact that Griselda signed early on with her words of acquiescence, "Signor mio, sì" (X.10.21). As Lanza details (25–26), her masochism perfectly complements his sadism; together they play a public game the end of which is to show their audience the raw truth of absolutism.

Indeed, Griselda's restoration after enduring years of Gualtieri's breath-taking cruelty makes precisely the point that all agency in the end depends on the grace of the absolute monarch. It is here that the double value of her identifying noun, *donna* as both woman and *domina*, the female lord, reaches fruition. In fact she models obedience rather ineffectually. His subjects recoil at Gualtieri's behavior and repeatedly denounce him: "credendo che egli uccidere avesse fatti i figliuoli, il biasimavan forte e reputavanlo crudele uomo e alla donna avevan grandissima compassione" (X.10.39); when he announces his intention to remarry "da assai buoni uomini fu molto ripreso" (X.10.40); and so forth. Even her former ladies-in-waiting, while accepting their new *donna*, Griselda's daughter, implore Gualtieri to restore some of his former wife's dignity by clothing her properly for the occasion of his new marriage; they simply cannot wholeheartedly accept that he has done the right thing. These complaints come despite Griselda's earlier public avowals of loyalty to him. Her speech to Gualtieri upon her divorce is a masterpiece of submission: "io conobbi sempre la mia bassa condizione alla vostra nobilità in alcun modo non convenirsi, e quello che io stata son con voi da Dio e da voi il riconoscea. . . ." She describes her rise in status as a loan, not a gift, and describes herself as happy—"a me dee piacere e piace di renderlovi"—to return her ring to him. She even predicates her request for a simple shift in exchange for her virginity on his judgment of whether her body is *onesto* or not (X.10.44–45). Later, when asked to return to help prepare for Gualtieri's "wedding," she replies, "Signor mio, io son presta e apparecchiata" (X.10.51), a reelaboration of her earlier "Signor mio, sì." Her recognition of Gualtieri's power identifies her as expertly attuned not only to her husband but to her situation, something Gualtieri's subjects never understand or fully recognize. In objecting to his treatment of her, they in fact violate their agreement to honor her, because by acquiescing to him she is telegraphing that the correct way to honor her is to accept that she knows what she is doing.

To summarize what we have so far: Griselda emerges as Gualtieri's willing object of manipulation, and she rightly understands that her figuration as *donna* depends entirely on him. When she returns home Dioneo comments that she went back to work with her father, "con forte animo sostenendo il fiero assalto della nemica fortuna" (X.10.48), which may refer to Gualtieri's cruelty, but it may just as well reference the loss of status that she rather enjoyed. When he announces his intentions to remarry, Dioneo narrates her deep hurt because she had not been able to shed the love she felt for him, an astonishing fact, as he himself will suggest in his comments at the end. When Gualtieri asks her opinion of his new bride, she replies: "A me ne par molto bene; e se così è savia come ella è bella, che 'l credo, io non dubito punto che voi non dobbiate con lei vivere il più consolato signor del mondo; ma quanto posso vi priego che quelle puncture, le quali all'altra, che vostra fu, già deste, non diate a questa, ché appena che io creda che ella le potesse sostenere, sì perché più giovane è e sì ancora perché in dilicatezze è allevata, ove colei in continue fatiche da picciolina era stata" (X.10.59). By referring to herself in the third person she suggests that the woman she was as Gualtieri's wife was somehow other, alienated from herself. The *puncture* are as much a metaphor for the pain she suffered as his wife as they are an allusion to the stitching together of her new clothes, and by extension the new her. While Griselda may indeed fear that her replacement could not sustain the role, there is another way to read her plea: that she not be replaced, that no one supplant her as the model of obedience that Gualtieri had made of her. The danger of substitution is not new, as Boccaccio knows full well. One only need think of the accusation Beatrice hurls at Dante in the earthly paradise—"Sí tosto come in su la soglia fui / di mia seconda etade e mutai vita, / questi si tolse a me, e diessi altrui" (*Pur.* XXX.124–26)—or, somewhat anachronistically, of Petrarch's effort to replace Laura with the Virgin at the end of the *Rime sparse*, to understand where this is leading. With an almost Pirandellian awareness of her own fictitiousness, Griselda struggles to preserve her status: she wants to be Gualtieri's unique object of punishment, because it is her only means to survive.

Dioneo thus uses this tale, appropriately the last story in the *Decameron*, to expose the mechanisms that lead to the creation of poetic fictions. He reduces that work to a discourse on power, specifically the power of the word, the deployment of which relies wholly on the will of the author. When it comes to women, he appears to argue, transcendence is an artifact:

to the extent that the figure of woman points beyond herself, it is not to God but to the man who constructed her. It is Dante who brings the dead Beatrice back to life, conferring on her a literary immortality to which he alludes at the end of the *Vita nuova* but which he had somewhat delayed and could very well have cancelled. Petrarch does as much by allowing Laura to remain dead; if anything by this act he demonstrates, much more cynically than Dante, the power that poets hold over the women they claim to love. Small wonder, then, that he liked this *novella* of the *Decameron* best of all, for it conforms wholly to a writerly ethos by which exploitation masquerades as exaltation. That Griselda achieves her longed-for immortality in no way cancels her contingency: it is but for the power of her creative agent, Gualtieri, that she survives.

The dynamic that Griselda and Gualtieri play out on the stage of the *Decameron* does finally transcend itself, but only to the extent that Gualtieri transcends himself, as indeed he does. The significance of his being a *marchese*, a monarch, intersects with the discourse of power that has run through many of the hundred tales. Monarchs lay rhetorical claim to their authority as coming from God, with the earthly kingdom replicating its divine model. Gualtieri's creative impulse, expressed in his decision to marry outside of his circle and transform his bride into a *marchesana*, essentially replicates that same impulse in God the Father; as Mazzotta puts it, he "arrogates to himself literally what is God's unique lordship over human events" (125). So too as God is a source of divine law, Gualtieri is the source of human law. His treatment of Griselda, which amounts to the imposition of a set of arbitrary rules that require her obedience, serves to make two points. First, because the monarch enjoys absolute power, he is free to impose any laws he wishes, whether they conform to natural law or not: in effect by imposing them, he dictates their conformity. Second, the survival of those who are subject to absolute law, in this case women, depends entirely on their conformity to the rules as set. Griselda's greatest strength is her willingness to play along; had she been unwilling, her story would have ended much sooner.

Finally, Gualtieri's expression of power tells us something about justice, a topic that had already been percolating in the two prior stories. With his tale Dioneo effectively denies that women can embody justice, because justice lies wholly in the hands of men who deploy power. Justice turns out to rely on a play between the moral category, what Kelsen calls justice as social happiness, "a social ordering that is absolutely right, that fully achieves its objective by satisfying everyone," and the purely functional alternative, conformity to positive law (*Introduction to the Problems of Legal Theory* 16). The end of the story would appear to validate the former definition, for after all everyone is happy, not just Gualtieri and Griselda but the people of Saluzzo who had been so worried about succession and who celebrate Griselda's restoration, presumably because their concerns about succession are once again allayed. That notion of justice comes, however, only by means of the second definition, for Gualtieri's sense of justice is wholly and solipsistically rooted in his demand that others obey him. If anything Dioneo, particularly with his final remarks, exposes the irony of any claims that equate justice with morality, for Gualtieri's path to justice makes a hash of moral notions.

Dioneo thus brings the storytelling of the *Decameron* to a close by answering an epistemological question with which it began, way back in the Ciappelletto story: how can one be certain of anything beyond the senses? The startlingly banal answer—one cannot—makes recourse to yet another form of the *donna-angelo* that had so transfixed an earlier generation of Italian poets. And yet the tale's insistence on how her observers, beginning with Gualtieri, perceive Griselda, of how they all participate in constructing her, makes rather a different point than does the earlier ethos of the *donna-angelo.* Dioneo does not simply affirm Griselda's divinity; rather, he posits her divinity as a product of the human imagination. In this way he confirms what the *Decameron* has long suggested about natural law: it is a human invention, not a divine one. Dioneo installs a sort of metatrope; he tropes the earlier troping of women and in so doing exposes the troping for what it is. He also reminds his audience of *mansuete donne*—and the adjective associates them with Griselda—that while they will be the objects of male exaltation they will also be subject, like Griselda, to male control, and specifically to an order that puts women at the service of relations between men. In this way he manages finally to transcend his own pleasure-based attitude toward women, demonstrating his true friendship for them, rooted in a concern for their well-being.

Any reading of the tenth day that follows Panfilo's lead, focusing exclusively on the question of magnanimity, thus subjects it to a flattening that denies its integrity with the rest of the text. The problems posed by the tenth day in no way exist in a vacuum; instead, they capitalize on and continue a dynamic that has haunted much of the *Decameron.* In offering a final meditation on the nature of friendship and the status of women, a word that manages to interweave the two themes, the day also manages to bring to a conclusion the *Decameron*'s lengthy consideration of the function of law in human relations. That all of this happens under the guidance of Panfilo, "all love," suggests that the day runs on an altruistic impulse in its treatment of the seven ladies. And yet the message communicated under the rubric of altruism, a message that at once exalts women and effaces them, suggests that women will never enjoy the sort of true friendship that the male characters of Day X realize; the notion of a reconciliation of the sexes remains a dream unfulfilled. Women are simply too overdetermined, their meaning too contingent on men, to enjoy the simple loyalty and affection that men can feel for one another. Perhaps such opportunities lie in a world outside of men, but for now such a dream cannot be realized. The seven ladies themselves affirmed as much when they invited the men to join them, thus setting up the initial tension between the sexes that endures to the end of Day X. This is perhaps the most sobering message of the last day, its final enactment of male retribution against the marginalizing female. For in the tenth day it is the men who occupy the center and the women who stand at the margins. They may be powerful women, capable of embodying and accomplishing great things on behalf of men, but their power is forever contingent, because it is subject to the limits imposed by men.

WORKS CITED

Primary Sources

Alighieri, Dante. *Convivio*. Ed. Piero Cudini. Milan: Garzanti, 2008.

———. *La Divina commedia*. 3 vols. Ed. Natalino Sapegno. Florence: La Nuova Italia, 1976.

———. *Monarchia*. Ed. Maurizio Pizzica. Milan: Rizzoli, 2001.

———. *Monarchy*. Trans. and ed. Prue Shaw. Cambridge: Cambridge University Press, 1996.

———. *Vita nuova—Rime*. Ed. Fredi Chiappelli. Milan: Mursia, 1987.

Apuleius. *The Golden Ass*. Trans. E. J. Kenney. London: Penguin, 2004.

Aquinas, Thomas. *Commentary on the* Nicomachean Ethics. Trans. C. I. Litzinger, O.P. Chicago: Henry Regnery, 1964.

———. *In decem libros Ethicorum aristotelis ad Nicomachum Expositio*. Ed. Raimondo M. Spiazzi. Turin: Marietti, 1949.

———. *On Law, Morality, and Politics*. Trans. Richard J. Regan. Indianapolis, IN: Hackett, 2002.

———. *Summa Theologiæ*. Latin text and English translation, Introductions, Notes, Appendices and Glossaries. 30 vols. London: Blackfriars, 1972.

Aristotle. *Nichomachean Ethics*. Trans. Christopher Rowe. Philosophical Introduction and Commentary by Sarah Broadie. Oxford: Oxford University Press, 2002.

———. *Nichomachean Ethics*. Trans. Terence Irwin. Indianapolis, IN: Hackett, 1999.

———. *The Politics*. Trans. T. A. Sinclair. London: Penguin, 1992.

Augustine. *On Christian Doctrine*. Trans. J. F. Shaw. Mineola, NY: Dover, 2009.

Boccaccio, Giovanni. *La caccia di Diana e le Rime*. Ed. Aldo Francesco Massèra. Turin: UTET, 1914.

———. *The Decameron*. Trans. G. H. McWilliam. Harmondsworth, UK: Penguin, 1984.

———. *The Decameron*. Trans. Mark Musa and Peter Bondanella. New York: Mentor, 1982.

———. *The Decameron*. Trans. John Payne, rev. Charles Singleton. Berkeley: University of California Press, 1982.

———. *Decameron*. Ed. Vittore Branca. Milan: Mondadori, 1976.

———. *Esposizioni sopra la* Comedia *di Dante*. Ed. Giorgio Padoan. Milan: Mondadori, 1994 [1965].

————. *Filocolo.* Ed. Mario Marti. Milan: Rizzoli, 1969.

————. *Genealogie deorum gentilium.* Ed. Vittorio Zaccaria and Manlio Pastore Stocchi. Milan: Mondadori, 1998.

Cappellanus, Andreas. *The Art of Courtly Love.* Trans. John Jay Parry. New York: Norton, 1969.

[Cicero.] *Ad C. Herennium de ratione dicendi (Rhetorica ad Herennium).* Trans. Henry Caplan. Loeb Classical Library I. Cambridge, MA: Harvard University Press, 1989.

————. *Cato Maior de Senectute—Laelius de Amicitia—De Divinatione.* Trans. W. A. Falconer. Loeb Classical Library XX. Cambridge, MA: Harvard University Press, 1923.

————. *De inventione—De optimo genere oratum—Topica.* Trans. H. M. Hubbell. Loeb Classical Library II. Cambridge, MA: Harvard University Press, 1993.

The Five Books of Moses. A Translation with Commentary. Trans. Robert Alter. New York: Norton, 2004.

The Holy Scriptures According to the Masoretic Text. Philadelphia: Jewish Publication Society of America, 1955.

Livy. *The Early History of Rome.* Trans. Aubrey de Sélincourt. Harmondsworth, UK: Penguin, 1985.

Machiavelli, Niccolò. *Le grandi opere politiche. Volume primo. Il principe. Dell'arte della guerra.* Ed. Gian Mario Anselmi and Carlo Varotti. Turin: Bollati Boringhieri, 1992.

————. *Lettere.* Milan: Feltrinelli, 1961.

Marsilius of Padua. *Defensor pacis.* Trans. Alan Gewirth. New York: Columbia University Press, 2001.

The Marx-Engels Reader. Ed. Robert C. Tucker. New York: Norton, 1972.

The New Testament of the Jerusalem Bible. Ed. Alexander Jones. Garden City, NY: Doubleday & Company, 1967.

Il Novellino (Le ciento novelle anitke). Ed. Giorgio Manganelli. Milan: Rizzoli, 1975.

Ovid. *Metamorphoses.* With an English trans. by Frank Justus Miller. 2 vols. Loeb Classical Library XLII–XLIII. Cambridge, MA: Harvard University Press, 1977–94.

Passavanti, Jacopo. *Lo specchio della vera penitenza.* 2 vols. Milan: Società tipografica dei classici italiani, 1808.

Petrarca, Francesco. *Canzoniere.* Ed. Gianfranco Contini. Turin: Einaudi, 1964.

————. *De sui ipsius et multorum ignorantia.* Ed. Enrico Fenzi. Milan: Mursia, 1999.

Prosatori del Duecento. Trattati morali e allegorici, Novelle. Ed. Cesare Segre. Turin: Einaudi, 1976.

Vocabolario degli Accademici della Crusca. Venice, 1612. http://vocabolario.signum.sns.it.

Secondary Sources

Alchourrón, Carlos E., and Eugenio Bulygin. "The Expressive Conception of Norms." *Normativity and Norms.* 383–410.

Almansi, Guido. *L'estetica dell'osceno.* Turin: Einaudi, 1974.

————. *The Writer as Liar: Narrative Technique in the* Decameron. London: Routledge & Kegan Paul, 1975.

Ascoli, Albert Russell. "Boccaccio's Auerbach: Holding the Mirror Up to Mimesis." *Studi sul Boccaccio* 20 (1991): 377–97.

———. "Pyrrhus' Rules: Playing with Power from Boccaccio to Machiavelli." *Modern Language Notes* 114 (1999): 14–57.

Auerbach, Erich. *Mimesis: The Representation of Reality in Western Literature.* Trans. Willard R. Trask. Princeton, NJ: Princeton University Press, 1974.

Autori e lettori di Boccaccio. Atti del Convegno internazionale di Certaldo (20–22 settembre 2001). Ed. Michelangelo Picone. Florence: Franco Cesati, 2002.

Auzzas, Ginetta. "I codici autografi. Elenco e bibliografia." *Studi sul Boccaccio* 7 (1973): 1–20.

Barański, Zygmunt G. "*Alquanto tenea della oppinone degli epicuri:* The *auctoritas* of Boccaccio's Cavalcanti (and Dante)." *Mittelalterliche Novellistik im europäischen Kontext; kultuwissenschaftliche Perspectiven.* Berlin: Erich Schmidt Verlag, 2006. 280–325.

Baratto, Mario. *Realtà e stile nel* Decameron. Vicenza: Neri Pozza, 1970.

———. "Struttura narrativa e messaggio ideologico." *Il testo molteplicato.* 29–47.

Barolini, Teodolinda. *Dante and the Origins of Italian Literary Culture.* New York: Fordham University Press, 2006.

———. "Notes toward a Gendered History of Italian Literature, with a Discussion of Dante's *Beatrix Loquax.*" *Dante and the Origins of Italian Literary Culture.* 360–78.

———. "*Le parole son femmine e i fatti sono maschi:* Toward a Sexual Poetics of the *Decameron (Decameron* II 10)." *Dante and the Origins of Italian Literary Culture.* 281–303.

———. "The Wheel of the *Decameron.*" *Dante and the Origins of Italian Literary Culture.* 224–44.

Battistini, Andrea. "Il 'triangolo amoroso' della settima giornata." *Introduzione al* Decameron. Ed. Michelangelo Picone and Margherita Mesirca. Florence: Franco Cesati, 2004. 187–201.

Bausi, Francesco. "Gli spiriti magni. Filigrane aristoteliche e tomistiche nella decima giornata del *Decameron.*" *Studi sul Boccaccio* 27 (1999): 203–53.

Bessi, Rossella. "La Griselda del Petrarca." *La novella italiana.* 711–26.

Best, Myra. "*La peste e le papere:* Textual Repression in Day Four of the *Decameron.*" *Boccaccio and Feminist Criticism.* 157–68.

Bianchi, Luca. "'Aristotele fu un uomo e poté errare': Sulle origini medievali della critica al 'principio di autorità.'" *Filosofia e teologia nel Trecento. Studi in ricordo di Eugenio Randi.* Ed. Luca Bianchi. Louvain-La-Neuve: Fédération Internationale des Instituts d'Études Médiévales, 1994. 509–33.

Blythe, James M. "Family, Government, and the Medieval Aristotelians." *History of Political Thought* 10 (1989): 1–16.

Boccaccio and Feminist Criticism. Ed. Thomas Stillinger and F. Regina Psaki. Chapel Hill, NC: Annali d'Italianistica, 2006.

Bolongaro, Eugenio. "Positions and Presuppositions in the Tenth Tale of the Fifth Day of Boccaccio's *The Decameron.*" *Studies in Short Fiction* 27 (1990): 399–404.

Booth, Wayne C. *The Rhetoric of Fiction.* Chicago: University of Chicago Press, 1973.

Branca, Vittore. *Boccaccio medievale.* Florence: Sansoni, 1956.

Brundage, James A. "Adultery and Fornication: A Study in Legal Theology." *Sexual Practices & The Medieval Church.* 129–34.

———. "Sex and Canon Law." *Handbook of Medieval Sexuality.* 33–50.

Bruni, Francesco. "Comunicazione." *Lessico critico decameroniano.* 73–92.

Bynum, Caroline Walker. *Holy Feast and Holy Fast: The Religious Significance of Food to Medieval Women.* Berkeley: University of California Press, 1988.

Cavallini, Giorgio. *La decima giornata del* Decameron. Rome: Bulzoni, 1980.

Cesari, Anna Maria. "L'Etica di Aristotele del Codice Ambrosiano A 204 inf.: un autografo del Boccaccio." *Archivio storico lombardo* 93–94 (1968): 69–100.

Chatman, Seymour. *Story and Discourse: Narrative Structure in Fiction and Film.* Ithaca, NY: Cornell University Press, 1980.

Cherchi, Paolo. "From *controversia* to *novella.*" *L'alambicco in biblioteca: Distillati rari.* Ed. Francesco Guardiani and Emilio Speciale. Ravenna: Longo, 2000. 119–32.

———. *L'onestade e l'onesto raccontare del* Decameron. Fiesole: Edizioni Cadmo, 2004.

———. "Sulle 'quistioni d'amore' nel *Filocolo.*" *Andrea Cappellano i trovatori e altri temi romanzi.* Rome: Bulzoni, 1979. 210–17.

Chiappelli, Fredi. *Il conoscitore del caos: Una "vis abdita" nel linguaggio tassesco.* Rome: Bulzoni, 1981.

———. "Discorso o progetto per uno studio sul *Decameron.*" *Studi di italianistica in onore di Giovanni Cecchetti.* Ed. Paolo Cherchi and Michelangelo Picone. Ravenna: Longo, 1988. 105–11.

Chiecchi, Giuseppe, and Luciano Troisio. *Il* Decameron *sequestrato: Le tre edizioni censurate nel Cinquecento.* Milan: Edizioni Unicopli, 1984.

Clubb, Louise George. "Boccaccio and the Boundaries of Love." *Italica* 37 (1960): 188–96.

Compagni, Dino. *Cronica delle cose occorrenti ne' tempi suoi.* Ed. Guido Bezzola. Milan: Rizzoli, 2002.

Corti, Maria. *Principi della comunicazione letteraria. Introduzione alla semiotica della letteratura.* Milan: Bompiani, 1980.

Cottino-Jones, Marga. "Fabula vs. Figura: Another Interpretation of the Griselda Story." *Italica* 50 (1973): 38–52.

———. *Order from Chaos: Social and Aesthetic Harmonies in Boccaccio's* Decameron. Washington, DC: University Press of America, 1982.

———. "The Tale of Abraham the Jew (*Decameron* I.2)." *The* Decameron *First Day in Perspective.* 77–88.

D'Andrea, Antonio. "Esemplarietà, ironia, retorica nella novella interrotta del *Decameron.*" *Formation, codification, et rayonnement d'un genre médiéval: la Nouvelle. Actes du Colloque International de Montréal, 14–16 October, 1982.* Montreal: Plato, 1982. 123–30.

Davis, Walter R. "Boccaccio's *Decameron:* The Implications of Binary Form." *Modern Language Quarterly* 42 (1981): 3–20.

The Decameron *First Day in Perspective.* Ed. Elissa B. Weaver. Toronto: University of Toronto Press, 2004.

Delcorno, Carlo. *Exemplum e letteratura: Tra Medioevo e Rinascimento.* Bologna: Il Mulino, 1989.

———. "Modelli agiografici e modelli narrativi. Tra Cavalca e Boccaccio." *La novella italiana.* 337–63.

Deligiorgis, Stavros. *Narrative Intellection in the* Decameron. Iowa City: University of Iowa Press, 1975.

De Rougement, Denis. *Love in the Western World.* Trans. Montgomery Belgion. Princeton, NJ: Princeton University Press, 1983.

Dionisotti, Carlo. "Appunti su antichi testi." *Italia medioevale e umanistica* 7 (1964): 77–131.

Duranti, Alessandro. "Le novelle di Dioneo." *Studi di Filologia e critica offerti dagli allievi a Lanfranco Caretti.* Rome: Salerno, 1985. 1–38.

Durling, Robert M. "Boccaccio on Interpretation: Guido's Escape (*Decameron* VI.9)." *Dante, Petrarch, Boccaccio: Studies in the Italian Trecento in Honor of Charles S. Singleton.* Ed. Aldo S. Bernardo and Anthony L. Pellegrini. Binghamton, NY: Medieval & Renaissance Texts & Studies, 1983. 273–304.

———. "A Long Day in the Sun: *Decameron* 8.7." *Shakespeare's "Rough Magic": Renaissance Essays in Honor of C. L. Barber.* Ed. Peter Erickson and Coppélia Kahn. Newark: University of Delaware Press, 1985. 269–75.

Eisner, Martin G., and Marc D. Schachter. "*Libido Sciendi:* Apuleius, Boccaccio, and the Study of the History of Sexuality." *PMLA* 124 (2009): 817–37.

Fedi, Roberto. *Francesco Petrarca.* Florence: La Nuova Italia, 1975.

———. "Il 'regno' di Flostrato. Natura e struttura della Giornata IV del *Decameron*." *Modern Language Notes* 102 (1987): 39–54.

Ferreri, Rosario. "Il motive erotico-osceno nella cornice del *Decameron*." *Studi sul Boccaccio* 26 (1998): 165–78.

Fido, Franco. *Il regime delle simmetrie imperfette. Studi sul* Decameron. Milan: Franco Angeli, 1988.

———. "The Tale of Ser Ciappelletto (I.1). *The* Decameron *First Day in Perspective.* 59–76.

Fleming, Ray. "Happy Endings? Resisting Women and the Economy of Love in Day Five of Boccaccio's *Decameron*." *Italica* 70 (1993): 30–45.

Forni, Pier Massimo. *Adventures in Speech: Rhetoric and Narration in Boccaccio's* Decameron. Philadelphia: University of Pennsylvania Press, 1996.

———. "Boccaccio's Answer to Dante." *Thought* 65 (1990): 71–82.

———. *Forme complesse nel* Decameron. Florence: Leo S. Olschki, 1992.

———. "Therapy and Prophylaxis in Boccaccio's *Decameron*." *Romance Quarterly* 52 (2005): 159–61.

Freccero, Carla. *Queer/Early/Modern.* Durham, NC: Duke University Press, 2006.

Gaylard, Susan. "The Crisis of Word and Deed in *Decameron* V, 10." *The Italian Novella.* 33–48.

Getto, Giovanni. *Vita di forme e forme di vita nel* Decameron. Turin: G. B. Petrini, 1972.

Gibaldi, Joseph. "The *Decameron* Cornice and the Responses to the Disintegration of Civilization." *Kentucky Romance Quarterly* 24 (1977): 349–57.

Ginzburg, Carlo. "Dante's *Epistle to Cangrande* and Its Two Authors." *Proceedings of the British Academy* 139 (2006): 195–216.

Giovannuzzi, Stefano. "La novella di Gualtieri (*Decameron*, X 10)." *Filologia e critica* 21 (1996): 44–76.

———. "Le parole e le cose. La Settima giornata del *Decameron*." *Lingua e stile* 32 (1997): 471–503.

Girard, René. *Deceit, Desire and the Novel: Self and Other in Literary Structure.* Trans. Yvonne Freccero. Baltimore: Johns Hopkins University Press, 1976.

Gittes, Tobias Foster. "Boccaccio's 'Valley of Women': Fetishised Foreplay in *Decameron* VI." *Italica* 76 (1999): 147–74.

Goldberg, Jonathan, and Madhavi Menon. "Queering History." *PMLA* 120 (2005): 1608–17.

Greene, Thomas M. "Forms of Accommodation in the *Decameron.*" *Italica* 45 (1968): 297–313.

Guerra Medici, Maria Teresa. *L'aria di città: Donne e diritti nel comune medievale.* Naples: Edizioni Scientifiche Italiane, 1996.

Guglielmi, Guido. "Una novella non esemplare del *Decameron.*" *Forum Italicum* 14 (1980): 32–55.

Halperin, David. *How to Do the History of Homosexuality.* Chicago: University of Chicago Press, 2002.

Handbook of Medieval Sexuality. Ed. Vern L. Bullough and James A. Brundage. New York: Garland, 1996.

Hartmann, Heidi. "The Unhappy Marriage of Marxism and Feminism: Towards a More Progressive Union." *Women and Revolution: A Discussion of the Unhappy Marriage of Marxism and Feminism.* Ed. Lydia Sargent. Boston: South End Press, 1981. 1–41.

Haug, Walter. "La problematica dei generi nelle novella di Boccaccio: La prospettiva di un medievista." *Autori e lettori di Boccaccio.* 127–40.

Herlihy, David. *Medieval Households.* Cambridge, MA: Harvard University Press, 1985.

Hollander, Robert. *Boccaccio's Dante and the Shaping Force of Satire.* Ann Arbor: University of Michigan Press, 1997.

———— and Courtney Cahill. "Day Ten of the *Decameron:* The Myth of Order." *Boccaccio's Dante and the Shaping Force of Satire.* 109–68.

————. "The *Decameron* Proem." *The* Decameron *First Day in Perspective.* 12–28.

Introduzione al Decameron. Ed. Michelangelo Picone and Margherita Mesirca. Florence: Franco Cesati Editore, 2004.

Iser, Wolfgang. *The Act of Reading: A Theory of Aesthetic Response.* Baltimore: Johns Hopkins University Press, 1978.

The Italian Novella: A Book of Essays. Ed. Gloria Allaire. New York: Routledge, 2003.

Janssens, Marcel. "The Internal Reception of the Stories within the *Decameron.*" *Boccaccio in Europe: Proceedings of the Boccaccio Conference, Louvain, December 1975.* Ed. Gilbert Tournoy. Leuven: Leuven University Press, 1977. 135–48.

Javitch, Daniel. "Cantus Interruptus in the *Orlando furioso.*" *Modern Language Notes* 95 (1980): 66–80.

Jordan, Tracey. "'We are all one flesh': Structural Symmetry in Boccaccio's Tale of the Prince and Princess of Salerno." *Studies in Short Fiction* 24 (1987): 103–10.

Karras, Ruth Mazo. "Prostitution in Medieval Europe." *Handbook of Medieval Sexuality.* 243–60.

Kelsen, Hans. "Aristotle's Doctrine of Justice." *What Is Justice?* 110–36.

————. *General Theory of Law and State.* Trans. Anders Wedberg. New York: Russell and Russell, 1973.

————. *Introduction to the Problems of Legal Theory.* Trans. Bonnie Litschewski Paulson and Stanley L. Paulson. Oxford: Clarendon Press, 1992.

————. "The Law as a Specific Social Technique." *What Is Justice?* 231–56.

————. "The Natural-Law Doctrine before the Tribunal of Science." *What Is Justice?* 137–73.

————. *Pure Theory of Law.* Trans. Max Knight. Berkeley, CA: University of California Press, 1978.

————. *La teoria dello stato in Dante.* Trans. Wilfrido Sangiorgi. Bologna: Massimiliano Boni, 1974.

————. *What Is Justice? Justice, Law, and Politics in the Mirror of Science.* Berkeley:

University of California Press, 1957.

Kern, Edith G. "The Gardens in the *Decameron* Cornice." *PMLA* 66 (1951): 505–23.

Kirkham, Victoria. *Fabulous Vernacular: Boccaccio's* Filocolo *and the Art of Medieval Fiction.* Ann Arbor: University of Michigan Press, 2001.

———. *The Sign of Reason in Boccaccio's Fiction.* Florence: Olschki, 1993.

Kuhns, Richard. Decameron *and the Philosophy of Storytelling: Author as Midwife and Pimp.* New York: Columbia University Press, 2005.

Lanham, Richard A. *A Handlist of Rhetorical Terms: A Guide for Students of English Literature.* Berkeley: University of California Press, 1969.

Lanza, Maria Teresa. "Della povera Griselda e di un certo teatrino della crudeltà." *Problemi* 66 (1983): 22–47.

Leone, M. "Tra autobiografismo reale e ideale in *Decameron* VIII, 7." *Italica* 50 (1973): 242–65.

Lessico critico decameroniano. Ed. Renzo Bragantini and Pier Massimo Forni. Bologna: Bollati Boringhieri, 1995.

Lotman, Juri M. "Il metalinguaggio delle descrizioni tipologiche della cultura." *Tipologia della cultura,* ed. Juri M. Lotman and Boris A. Uspenskij. Milan: Bompiani, 1975. 145–81.

Marchesi, Simone. *Stratigrafie Decameroniane.* Florence: Olschki, 2004.

Marcozzi, Luca. "'Passio' e 'ratio' tra Andrew Cappellano e Boccaccio: La novella dello scolare e della vedova (*Decameron* VIII, 7) e i castighi del *De Amore.*" *Italianistica* 30 (2001): 9–32.

Marcus, Millicent. *An Allegory of Form: Literary Self-Consciousness in the* Decameron. Stanford French and Italian Studies XVIII. Saratoga, CA: Anma Libri, 1979.

———. "An Allegory of Two Gardens: The Tale of Madonna Dianora (*Decameron* X, 5). *Forum Italicum* 14 (1980): 162–73.

———. "Misogyny as Misreading: A Gloss on *Decameron* VIII, 7." *Stanford Italian Review* 4 (1984): 23–40.

———. "The Sweet New Style Reconsidered: A Gloss on the Tale of Cimone (*Decameron* V, 1)." *Italian Quarterly* 81 (1980): 5–16.

Matzke, John E. "The Legend of the Eaten Heart." *Modern Language Notes* 26 (1911): 1–8.

Mauss, Marcel. *The Gift: The Form and Reason for Exchange in Archaic Societies.* Trans. W. D. Halls. New York: Norton, 2000.

Mazzotta, Giuseppe. *The World at Play in Boccaccio's* Decameron. Princeton, NJ: Princeton University Press, 1986.

Migiel, Marilyn. *A Rhetoric of the* Decameron. Toronto: University of Toronto Press, 2003.

Moe, Nelson. "Not a Love Story: Sexual Aggression, Law and Order in *Decameron* X 4." *The Romanic Review* 86 (1995): 623–38.

Moravia, Alberto. "Boccaccio." *L'uomo come fine e altri saggi.* Milan: Bompiani, 1964. 135–58.

Murphy, James J. *Rhetoric in the Middle Ages: A History of Rhetorical Theory from Saint Augustine to the Renaissance.* Berkeley: University of California Press, 1974.

Muto, Lisa M. "La novella portante del *Decameron:* La parabola del piacere." *La nouvelle: Formation, codification et rayonnement d'un genre médiéval. Actes du Colloque International de Montréal (McGill University, 14–16 octobre 1982).* Ed. Michelangelo Picone, Giuseppe Di Stefano, and Pamela D. Stewart. Montréal:

Plato Academic Press, 1983. 145–51.

Neri, Ferdinando. "Il disegno ideale del *Decameron*." *Storia e poesia*. Turin: Chiantore, 1944. 73–82.

Nichols, Stephen G. "An Intellectual Anthropology of Marriage in the Middle Ages." *The New Medievalism*. Ed. Marina S. Brownlee, Kevin Brownlee, and Stephen G. Nichols. Baltimore: Johns Hopkins University Press, 1991. 70–95.

Normativity and Norms: Critical Perspectives on Kelsenian Themes. Ed. Stanley L. Paulson and Bonnie Litschewski Paulson. Oxford: Clarendon Press, 1998.

La novella italiana. Atti del Convegno di Caprarola 19–24 1988. Rome: Salerno, 1989.

Lotman, Juri M. "Il metalinguaggio delle descrizioni tipologiche della cultura." *Tipologia della cultura*, ed. Juri M. Lotman and Boris A. Uspenskij. Milan: Bompiani, 1975. 145–81.

Orlando, Francesco. *Per una teoria freudiana della letteratura*. Turin: Einaudi, 1973.

Padoan, Giorgio. *Il Boccaccio, le muse, il Parnaso e l'Arno*. Florence: Olschki, 1978.

———. "Mondo aristocratico e mondo comunale nell'ideologia e nell'arte di Giovanni Boccaccio." *Il Boccaccio le muse il Parnaso e l'Arno*. 1–92.

———. "Sulla genesi e la pubblicazione del *Decameron*." *Il Boccaccio le muse il Parnaso e l'Arno*. 93–122.

Paris, Gaston. "La legende des trios anneaux." *La poésie du moyen age: Leçons et lectures. Deuxième série*. Paris: Librairie Hachette, 1903. 131–63.

Pastore Stocchi, Manlio. "Un antecedente latino-medievale di Pietro di Vinciolo (*Decameron* V 10)." *Studi sul Boccaccio* 1 (1963): 349–62.

Pelikan, Jaroslav. *Mary through the Centuries: Her Place in the History of Culture*. New Haven, CT: Yale University Press, 1996.

Picone, Michelangelo. "L''amoroso sangue': La quarta giornata." *Introduzione al Decameron*. 115–39.

———. "L'arte della beffa: L'ottava giornata." *Introduzione al Decameron*. 203–25.

———. "Autore/narratori." *Lessico critico decameroniano*. 34–59.

———. "Dal lai alla novella: Il caso di Ghismonda (*Decameron, IV 1*)." *Filologia e critica* 16 (1991): 325–43.

———. "Leggiadri motti e pronte risposte: La sesta giornata." *Introduzione al Decameron*. 163–86.

———. "Il macrotesto." *Introduzione al Decameron*. 9–31.

———. "The Tale of Bergamino (I.7)." *The Decameron First Day in Perspective*. Ed. Elissa B. Weaver. Toronto: University of Toronto Press, 2004. 160–78.

Poole, Gordon. "Boccaccio's *Decameron* IV, 5." *Explicator* 47 (1989): 3–4.

Posner, Richard. *Law and Literature: A Misunderstood Relation*. Cambridge, MA: Harvard University Press, 1998.

Potter, Joy Hambuechen. *Five Frames for the* Decameron: *Communication and Social Systems in the* Cornice. Princeton, NJ: Princeton University Press, 1982.

Power, Eileen. *Medieval Women*. Cambridge: Cambridge University Press, 1997.

Psaki, Regina. "Boccaccio and Female Sexuality: Gendered and Eroticized Landscapes." *The Flight of Ulysses: Studies in Memory of Emmanuel Hatzantonis*, ed. Augustus A. Mastri. Chapel Hill, NC: Annali d' Italianistica, 1977. 125–34.

Ramat, Raffaello. "L'introduzione alla quarta giornata." AA.VV. *Scritti su Giovanni Boccaccio*. Florence: Olschki, 1964. 92–107.

Raz, Joseph. "Kelsen's Theory of the Basic Norm." *Normativity and Norms*. 47–67.

Rinaldi, Evelina. "La donna negli statuti del comune di Forlì: Sec. XIV." *Studi storici* 18 (1910): 185–99.

Ross, Alf. "Validity and the Conflict between Legal Positivism and Natural Law." *Normativity and Norms.* 147–63.

Rossi, Luciano. "Ironia e parodia nel *Decameron:* Da Ciappelletto a Griselda." *La novella italiana.* 365–405.

———. "La maschera della magnificenza amorosa: La decima giornata." *Introduzione al* Decameron. 267–89.

———. "Il paratesto." *Introduzione al* Decameron. 35–55.

Rubin, Gayle. "The Traffic in Women: Notes on the 'Political Economy' of Sex." *Toward an Anthropology of Women.* Ed. Rayna R. Reiter. New York: Monthly Review Press, 1975. 157–210.

Sanguineti, Federico. "La Novelletta delle papere nel *Decameron.*" *Belfagor* 37 (1982): 137–46.

Sanguineti White, Laura. *Boccaccio e Apuleio: Caratteri differenziali nella struttura narrativa del* Decameron. Bologna: Edizioni italiane moderne, 1977.

———. *La scena conviviale e la sua funzione nel mondo del Boccaccio.* Florence: Olschki, 1983.

Scaglione, Aldo. *Nature and Love in the Late Middle Ages.* Berkeley: University of California Press, 1963.

Schlink, Bernhard. "Best Lawyer; Pure Law." *New York Times Magazine,* 18 April 1999.

Segre, Cesare. "Funzioni, opposizioni e simmetrie nella giornata VII del *Decameron.*" *Le strutture e il tempo: Narrazione, poesia, modelli.* Turin: Einaudi, 1974. 117–43.

———. "Perché Gualtieri di Saluzzo odiava le donne?" *Dai metodi ai testi: Varianti, personaggi, narrazioni.* Turin: Nino Aragno, 2008. 287–94.

———. "Semiotia e filologia." *Semiotica filologica: Testo e modelli culturali.* Turin: Einaudi, 1979. 5–21.

Serpieri, Alessandro. "L'approccio psicoanalitico: alcuni fondamenti e la scommessa di una lettura." *Il testo molteplicato.* 49–73.

Sexual Practices & The Medieval Church. Ed. Vern L. Bullough and James Brundage. Buffalo, NY: Prometheus Books, 1982.

Sherberg, Michael. "The Patriarch's Pleasure and the Frametale Crisis: *Decameron* IV–V." *Romance Quarterly* 38 (1991): 227–38.

———. "The Sodomitic Center of the *Decameron.*" *Essays in Honor of Marga Cottino-Jones.* Ed. Laura Sanguineti White, Andrea Baldi, and Kristin Phillips. Fiesole (Florence): Edizioni Cadmo, 2003.

Smarr, Janet Levarie. *Boccaccio and Fiammetta: The Narrator as Lover.* Urbana: University of Illinois Press, 1986.

———. "Ovid and Boccaccio: A Note on Self-Defense." *Mediaevalia* 13 (1987): 247–55.

Stewart, Pamela D. "Boccaccio e la tradizione retorica: Le definizione della novella come genere letterario." *Stanford Italian Review* 1 (1974): 67–74.

———. "La novella di Madonna Oretta e le due parti del *Decameron.*" *Yearbook of Italian Studies* (1977): 27–40.

———. "The Tale of the Three Rings (I.3)." *The* Decameron *First Day in Perspective.* 89–112.

Stillinger, Thomas C. "The Language of Gardens: Boccaccio's 'Valle delle Donne.'" *Boccaccio and Feminist Criticism.* 105–27.

———. "The Place of the Title (*Decameron,* Day One, Introduction)." *The* Decameron *First Day in Perspective.* 29–56.

Stone, Gregory B. *The Ethics of Nature in the Middle Ages: On Boccaccio's Poetaphysics*. New York: St. Martins Press, 1998.

Stuard, Susan Mosher. "Burdens of Matrimony: Husbanding and Gender in Medieval Italy." *Medieval Masculinities: Regarding Men in the Middle Ages*. Ed. Clare A. Lees. Minneapolis: University of Minnesota Press, 1994. 47–59.

Il testo molteplicato. Lettura di una novella del Decameron. Ed. Mario Lavagetto. Parma: Pratiche Editrice, 1982.

Tronci, Francesco. *La novella tra letteratura, ideologia e metaletteratura. Studi sul* Decameron. Cagliari: Cooperativa Universitaria Editrice Cagliaritana, 2001.

Usher, Jonathan. "Pieces of Dante among Cipolla's Relics." *Lectura Dantis* 13 (1993): 22–31.

Virgulti, Ernesto. "Lies My Father Told Me: Boccaccio's *Novelletta* of Filippo Balducci and His Son." *The Italian Novella*. 15–32.

Walters, Jonathan. "'No More than a Boy': The Shifting Construction of Masculinity from Ancient Greece to the Middle Ages." *Gender and History* 5 (1993): 20–33.

Warner, Marina. *Alone of All Her Sex: The Myth and the Cult of the Virgin Mary*. New York: Wallaby, 1978.

Weaver, Elissa. "Dietro il vestito: La semiotica del vestire nel *Decameron*." *La novella italiana*. 701–10.

Wehle, Winfried. "Sull'antropologia iconografica del *Decameron*." *Autori e lettori del Boccaccio*. 343–61.

Wilkins, Ernest Hatch. *The Making of the* Canzoniere *and Other Petrarchan Studies*. Rome: Edizioni di Storia e letteratura, 1951.

Yalom, Marilyn. *A History of the Wife*. New York: Perennial, 2002.

Zatti, Sergio. "Federigo e la metamorfosi del desiderio." *Strumenti critici* 36–37 (1978): 236–52.

INDEX